Tokyo Underworld

THE FAST TIMES AND HARD LIFE
OF AN AMERICAN
GANGSTER IN JAPAN

Robert Whiting

PANTHEON BOOKS   NEW YORK

Library of Congress Cataloging-in-Publication Data

Whiting, Robert.
Tokyo underworld : the fast times and hard life of an American
gangster in Japan / Robert Whiting.
p.   cm.
Includes bibliographical references and index.
ISBN 0-679-41976-4
1. Zappetti, Nicola.   2. Gangsters—Japan—Tokyo—Biography.
3. Americans—Japan—Tokyo—Biography.   4. Crime—Japan—Tokyo—
History—20th century.   5. Black market—Japan—Tokyo—
History—20th century.   I. Title.
HV6248.Z36W55   1998
364.1'092—dc21
[B]   98-20685   CIP

364.1
092
whit

Random House Web Address: www.randomhouse.com
Book design by Misha Beletsky
Printed in the United States of America
First Edition
9 8 7 6 5 4 3 2 1

Author's Note: The translations of articles presented here are mine. I alone bear
responsibility for any errors.

IN MEMORY OF THE LATE, GREAT KITTY

CONTENTS

TOKYO UNDERWORLD

PROLOGUE

America's relationship with Japan began in 1853, when Commodore William Perry and his squadron of Black Ships forcibly ended centuries of self-imposed isolation and opened up the nation to the rest of the world. For years afterward, however, the number of expatriate Americans who actually lived in that country at any one time was measured in the low hundreds. Those silk traders, oil merchants, teachers, missionaries, military attachés, and so forth, were almost totally segregated, socially and geographically, from the general population.

The war in the Pacific helped change all that. When it was over, Japan suddenly found itself playing unwilling host to over half a million occupying soldiers and civilians. Historians called it the biggest meeting between two cultures since Rome took Carthage.

The libraries are filled with historical tomes, doctoral theses, and personal memoirs recording the vast changes that resulted: the creation by starry-eyed New Deal "Japan experts" of a new constitution; the semi-successful attempt to introduce democracy; Japan's slow, painful metamorphosis from shattered nation to global economic power. The alliance also produced a considerable number of institutes, foundations, goodwill associations, academic departments, think tanks, libraries, endowments, trade agreements, treaties, sister cities, and thousands of reassurances of the two parties' essentially friendly and cooperative pursuit of peace, prosperity, and human happiness.

But there is another side to the U.S.–Japan equation that is far less known if inextricably bound up in the whole. It is an alternate, separate layer of reality, a shadowy universe of characters—gangsters, corrupt entrepreneurs, courtesans, seedy sports promoters, streetwise opportunists, intelligence agents, political fixers, and financial manipulators—who perhaps have done as much in their own right to influence U.S.–Japan affairs as their more refined and respected peers. Significantly, it has not always been easy to distinguish the latter from the former.

Japanese authors have written much about what they call variously the Underground Economy, the Invisible Empire, the Shadow Government, and the *Yami Shakai* (Dark Society), among other things—and have dealt at length with American's participation in it. However, the history of this chaotic orb and the efforts of Americans and Japanese to exploit, use, and abuse each other within it has largely remained untold in the West.

Among the more notable by-products of this dynamic sub-culture, for example, has been a postwar black market perhaps unprecedented in character; a secret Wall Street cabal that sub-verted official U.S. policy in Japan: an extraordinary, jingoistic professional wrestling boom enthusiastically promoted by a tan-dem of political leaders and underworld bosses and led by a na-tional sporting icon with a hidden past; a ruthless Korean gang lord vying for control of the city involved in a secret connection with the U.S. government and the CIA; a professional wrestler and Tokyo jewel thief named "Gorgeous Mac"; nightclub host-esses trained in the art of international industrial espionage; Lockheed, the granddaddy of all aircraft scandals; financial gangsters; an underworld stock market manipulator who nearly made it to the portals of the White House; assorted con artists, gold smugglers, and an American "Mafia Boss of Tokyo" from New York who founded one of the world's great nightspots— where many of these characters congregated.

This book tells the story of that bizarre demimonde. It is a parable of greed, arrogance, duplicity, and revenge that spans fifty years and bares many hidden layers in the U.S.–Japan rela-tionship. The tale it tells parallels the great shift of wealth from America to Japan and more recent shifts back the other way. It reveals as much about the baser emotions that have united Japa-nese and Americans in the fashioning of the postwar era as it does the vast cultural differences that habitually separate them.

1. THE FIRST

BLACK MARKET

Urgent notice to enterprises, factories and those manufacturers in the process of shifting from wartime production to peacetime production. Your product will be bought in large quantities at a suitable price. Those who wish to sell should come with samples and estimates of production cost to the following address:

Shinjuku Market, 1-8-54, Tsunohazu, Yodobashiku, Shinjuku Tokyo.

Kanto Ozu Gumi
August 18, 1945

It was surely some kind of record for speed. Three days after the end of the war—and a full ten before the first American soldier set foot in Japan—the above newspaper advertisement appeared for what would be the nation's first postwar black market. One of the very few paid announcements in print at the time, it was a call to commerce hardly anyone expected so quickly, given the wretched, bomb-ravaged condition of Tokyo.

Once a teeming castle town of wood and paper houses, Japan's capital was now mostly cinder, the ground one massive flat layer of residue from the terrible B-29 Superfortress incendiary attacks. The heavily populated lowlands to the east by Tokyo Bay where the merchant and artisan classes had lived and worked had all but been obliterated, as had vast sections of the neighboring industrial city of Kawasaki and the port of Yokohama, further to the south. Drivers of what few cars there were frequently got lost because it was so difficult to distinguish the road from the rubble of shattered roof tiles and burned-out homes. All that was left standing were several marble and stone buildings in the commercial business centers of the capital, Marunouchi, Ginza, and Nihonbashi, which the Occupation authorities were planning to use for themselves.

For most of Tokyo's inhabitants existence was a living hell. Homeless, numbering in the millions, lived in jerry-built huts of chicken wire, rocks, and cardboard, occupied subway stations and air raid shelters, or camped out in large bomb craters in the street. There was so little available food that people would travel hours to the countryside to trade expensive heirlooms for a tiny share of a farmer's crop. Yet, by August 20, only five days after Japan had officially conceded defeat, the Ozu open-air market was ready to roll. Located at the main entrance of the western commuter hub Shinjuku Station—or what was left of it—it boasted a startling array of goods. Displayed on wooden crates were pots, pans, kettles, plates, silverware, cooking oil, tea, rice, leather, electrical goods and *geta* (wooden clogs), along with vast quantities of military equipment and clothing. Most of the wares for the market, which bore the romantic-sounding name *Hikari Wa Shinjuku Yori* (The Light Shines forth from Shinjuku), had been stolen from a secret supply of provisions for a ghost army of 4 million men that was to have been mobilized in the event of an American invasion of the mainland.

The Potsdam Declaration had decreed that the Japanese government would have to surrender all such materials. However, with Japan in a weird post-surrender netherworld where no one was really in charge, looters appropriated an estimated 70 percent of all supplies held in military depots throughout the country, providing the Ozu market with its windfall inventory.

The Kanto Ozu gumi (Kanto Ozu gang) was the largest crime syndicate in Western Tokyo at the time. They were *tekiya* (itinerant peddlers, racketeers), a type of gangster in Japan that for centuries had monopolized the festival vending stalls at temples and shrines. They contrasted with the *bakuto* (gamblers), who also dated back to feudal times, and with the latter-day stevedores, rickshaw drivers, and day laborers under control of the slum labor bosses, who had also formed underworld gangs.

Despite involvement in protection, narcotics, strong-arm debt collecting, strikebreaking, and blackmail, among other nefarious activities, all of them professed to be a cut above mobsters in other lands. They claimed to live by a strict code of chivalry, based on the samurai warrior's *bushido* ethic, which emphasized humility, duty, and loyalty to one's lord. They placed great value on the stoic endurance of pain, hunger, and imprisonment and saw honor in dying a violent death. (An old gangster credo went: "Strong men don't die on the tatami.")

Over the years, they aligned themselves with right-wing causes, developing a reputation as patriots in times of foreign conflict, as well as defenders of oppressed people in times of civil strife. Legend tells of the Edo-era outlaw Chuji Kunisada wielding his sword on behalf of farmers and peasants who were being treated cruelly by feudal lords; he became famous for the line, "I would like to die so that people can mourn my death." A *tekiya* chieftain was one of the heroes of the 1905 war with Russia. At the same time, however, the gang bosses and the Japanese civil authorities had also cultivated a mutually beneficial relationship in which certain mob activities were tolerated without interference from the law as long as they were accompanied by campaign donations.

During World War II, gangster-owned construction firms under government contract built and repaired airfields, dug tunnels, and constructed subterranean factories, earning a nice profit while kicking back a healthy percentage to their contractors. As the strain of a losing war intensified, gangsters helped run the POW camps and supervised imported Korean slave labor in domestic coal mines. The Tokyo Assembly even allowed *tekiya* bosses to take over as municipal tax agents, granting them legal authority to control pricing and distribution as well as the power to punish disobedience. The Metropolitan Police Board, getting into the spirit of the times, forced all stall keepers to join a tradesmen's union that was run by the mob.

At war's end, millions of demobilized soldiers, war widows, and other displaced persons began to make their way back into the cities and, as virtually all moral and government restraints subsequently collapsed, the mob strengthened its grip on the municipal economy. Open-air marts sprang into operation at every commuter line train station almost before the arriving Americans had a chance to unpack their duffel bags. The largest were at the major hubs on the Yamate Line that circled the city— Ueno, Tokyo, Shimbashi, Shibuya and Shinjuku. Within weeks, there would be an astonishing 45,000 stalls in the city, most of them under the control of the leathery-faced *Ozu-gumi* boss Kinosuke Ozu, and they provided jobs for half a million people.

The outdoor black markets were, incidentally, Japan's first experiment in democracy. Japanese society had for hundreds of years been divided into castes, socially and legally. The nobility and landed aristocracy were at the top; below them, the samurai warriors, farmers, townsmen, and *eta* (outcasts), in descending order. Status was rigidly fixed and every Japanese knew his proper rank and position in the community at large.

Centuries of feudal serfdom and national isolation under the Tokugawa Shogunate were followed by the domineering rule of military, bureaucratic, and financial cliques, starting in 1868 with the Meiji Revolution, which restored the emperor to the throne. In all, it had served to create a highly restrictive society where the arrogance of superiors was as ingrained as their subordinates' fawning obeisance.

In the Ozu and other markets, however, social rank no longer mattered. No questions were asked of applicants about their status, family origin, educational background, or nationality. Everyone was welcome, from high-ranking military officers to lowly privates, landed nobles to tenant farmers, college professors to unemployed gamblers. They all started out equally, spreading a mat on the street or setting up shop on top of a box to sell their goods. They all wore the same ragged clothes, lived in similar jury-rigged barracks of corrugated tin, and bathed out of the same oil drums. As historian Kenji Ino later wrote, "For a feudal country like Japan which had a long history of class and ethnic discrimination, this was indeed an unprecedented event."

The American Occupation officially began on September 2 with the signing of surrender documents aboard the U.S.S. *Missouri* in Yokohama Harbor. Its General Headquarters (GHQ) was located in the fortresslike Dai-Ichi building facing the Imperial Palace grounds and operated under the authority of the Supreme Commander of Allied Powers (SCAP), run by the dictatorial General Douglas MacArthur, who hardly ever consulted the Allies on anything he did. Although the occupiers were ostensibly in control (behind a shadow government of veteran Japanese bureaucrats), the black market bosses continued to operate as before. The Tokyo municipal authorities quietly continued to let them function as official tax collectors, allowing them to keep half the proceeds as payment. In addition, the mob ran the fire departments, the street-cleaning services, and all public transportation on behalf of the metropolitan government. Since the gangs also controlled the construction crews, the stevedore unions, and the operators of the newly emerging bars and noodle shops being slapped together with two-by-fours, they were, in effect, running the city.

GHQ had been assigned the massive and difficult task of democratizing a militaristic Japan—to write a new war-renouncing constitution, to abolish the Imperial Military Head-quarters, to arrest war criminals, and to lift restrictions on political, religious, and civil freedoms. However, it was in other areas where the Americans would have a more immediate impact—like the underground economy.

MacArthur had made it clear he would tolerate no cruelty, no barbarism, no individual acts of revenge, thus the 600,000 Americans in the initial Occupation force were made up by design not of combat-hardened soldiers who had fought in the jungles of the Pacific and were therefore burning with hatred for the Japanese but of mostly fresh-faced teenagers who had seen little battlefield action and who viewed occupying Japan as their first big adventure in life. These youthful occupiers proved to be prodigious suppliers of heavily rationed commodities like cigarettes, sugar, salt, chocolate, soap, rubber, and beer, not to mention the more easily obtained C-rations and powdered milk. According to one informal survey, some 90 percent of the residents at the "Nomura Hotel," a former office building in Shimbashi housing several hundred GIs in "rooms" partitioned by blankets, were out daily in their off-duty hours dealing liquor and other items from the hotel military exchange. The statistic was considered typical of the Occupation as a whole.

The primary distribution system for American plenty to make

its way to the black market gangs was comprised of thousands of young ladies who had been readied by a Japanese governmental group called the Recreation and Amusement Association to sleep with the Americans. The RAA had been established immediately after the cessation of fighting to sate the much anticipated and much dreaded Yankee libido while sparing the virginal flower of young Japanese femalehood (most of whose ranks had, in any event, been dispatched into hiding).

The association had called upon operators of bombed-out clubs, bars, geisha and quasi-geisha establishments, as well as outright houses of prostitution to mobilize all their available female talent in the cause of patriotism. And mobilize they did, with remarkable speed and efficiency.

An advance party of fifty men from the Marine Air Group 44, dispatched from Okinawa in early September to help secure the local air base at Omura in North Kyushu, was welcomed by a delegation of kimonoed women who invited them to move into an off-base "geisha house." The men spent the next few weeks there drinking beer, eating hibachi-grilled fish, and cavorting with the young ladies in residence—obligingly reimbursing their hostesses from a footlocker full of confiscated yen. (When a naval patrol happened by in late September to find some of the men lying about in the sun on a nearby beach, bearded and wearing cut-off fatigues, the officer in charge initially thought he had stumbled on a prisoner-of-war camp.) The first U.S. Army ground reconnaissance patrol to enter Tokyo, on September 2, was intercepted by an RAA truck filled with prostitutes, bedecked in their best finery; a spokesman explained that the women were "volunteers" to satisfy the lust of the Occupation forces. By October, the RAA had opened what may have been the largest brothel of its type in the world: a long open-bay barracks divided into cubicles by sheets hanging from the ceiling and with futons on the floor serving as beds. Nicknamed the International Palace and located in Funabashi in Eastern Tokyo, it processed hundreds of priapic GIs a day. It was an assembly-line operation so smooth that a soldier would leave his shoes at one end when he came in and pick them up, cleaned and shined, at the other end when he left.

There was also a half-mile strip of real estate stretching west from the Imperial Palace moat abutting the GHQ building to the Nomura Hotel, which quickly became known as Hooker Alley, in tribute to the several hundred young damsels patrolling the area. For a pack of Old Golds, the ladies would willingly cater to patrons in jeeps, in building stairwells, or in the cheerless Quonset hut complex nearby where lower-ranking men stayed—not really caring who watched. The moat around the Imperial Palace was so clogged with used condoms it had to be cleaned out once a week with a big wire scoop.

As winter set in, there were many deaths from exposure and starvation. Groups of people huddled around bonfires, covering themselves with burlap rags, shivering through the night, much too cold to sleep. Gangs of vagrants roamed through the back alleys of buildings where Americans stayed, rummaging through the trash and garbage for food. Yet thousands of well-coiffed "comfort girls" could be found at special rec centers ready to play billiards and cards with servicemen and otherwise entertain them. Several cabarets, including one six stories high, had opened up in the Ginza. In February 1946, the Mimatsu Cabaret started business next to the Ginza Mitsukoshi Department Store. All of these enterprises featured floor shows and Japanese dance bands that played Western music.

As conqueror and conqueree got to know each other better, illicit commerce grew in scope and dimension. A band of enlisted men at the Yokosuka naval base began making midnight speedboat runs across Tokyo Bay carrying loads of PX contraband to gangs on the far shore of Chiba. An NCO club manager in Sugamo took to selling sugar in hundred-pound lots to the Ozu market. A civilian American trader with the Tokyo Metals Association was stunned when an Army lieutenant came to see him, first soliciting advice on how to sell several tons of manganese he had acquired and then asking, "Do you know where I can find a buyer for a shipment of mattresses? That's the next item on my list."

By mid-1946, members of the armed forces had remitted back to America approximately $8 million a month, a sum exceeding the entire military monthly payroll. Army finance officers attributed this phenomenon directly to profit from black marketeering, and although SCAP subsequently declared it illegal to reconvert yen to dollars, the dealing continued unabated anyway, as did other forms of corruption.

By 1947, the New York *Herald Tribune* and *New York Times* were publishing accounts of American officials misusing their positions to grow rich—for example, by extorting stock and real estate from Japanese businessmen in exchange for their "cooperation." The International News Service was describing illicit links between the 8th Army Procurement Office (which controlled reconstruction expenditures) and a triumvirate of Japanese politicians, subcontractors, and gangs, while the Associated Press, for its part, was reporting on an urbane prewar *bakuto* boss named Akira Ando who had won several lucrative GHQ transportation contracts for his fleet of taxis, trucks, and private cars by bribing GHQ officials. Ando, who had grown rich during the war doing construction for the Tojo government, openly bragged that one high-ranking general was his protector. He had a black book that reportedly contained the names of hundreds of Occupation officers he had befriended whom he could frequently be seen entertaining at one of the several Ginza nightclubs and Asakusa bordellos he owned. To AP correspondent Mark Gayn, Ando's activities were part of a well-organized and well-financed campaign to corrupt the U.S. Army. But, as many cynical observers liked to point out, it was not a very difficult campaign to wage successfully.

In later years, Japanese gangsters liked to boast that *they* were the ones who, with their postwar markets, had saved Japan from starvation. However, while it may be true that the open-air stalls did help get the economy going again to some degree and feed some of the hungry masses (government rationing being so inadequate that a Tokyo District Court judge who refused to eat anything purchased illegally died of malnutrition), the men who ran them were anything but altruistic. They charged criminally high prices for their wares—the equivalent of a day's wages, say, for a stale bun or a handful of surplus cornmeal originally donated by the U.S. State Department—and also demanded outrageous fees from those who participated in their wondrous democratic experiment. To operate in the Ozu market, for instance, a seller had to pay a tribute of half of his daily profits, among other charges. Ozu himself personally ripped down the stalls of anyone who objected to such extortion, which may be why an Occupation authority would later term him the "worst criminal in Japan."

It was perhaps understandable that a self-descriptive word that *bakuto* used for a losing hand at cards, *ya-ku-za* (8-9-3), a term occasionally used to refer to Japanese mobsters in general—alluding to what some believed to be the uselessness of gang members to proper society—would gain currency as the years passed. (So would *gokudo,* meaning "scoundrel, villain, rogue.")

Attempts by honest officials in the GHQ to control crime and corruption during the Occupation were not overly successful. A four-year campaign to crack down on lawbreakers was launched in late 1947 when Colonel Charles Kades, chief of the GHQ Government Section, formally declared war on what he called Japan's "Underground Government." In a much heralded press conference, he announced that the real rulers of Japan were not the duly elected representatives of the people, as the GHQ had intended, but the "bosses, hoodlums, and racketeers who were in league with the political fixers, the ex-militarists and the industrialists, as well as the legal authorities from the judges and police chiefs on down." This, of course, was something most Japanese already knew.

Several police raids ensued, in which fully half of the known 50,000 underworld figures in the country were arrested. However, only 2 percent of them ever wound up doing any time. The rest were released, benefiting from the unwillingness of witnesses to testify, missing evidence, and pressure on the courts from corrupt politicians, including several dozen Diet members who would later admit to having taken illegal donations during the first Occupation-sponsored parliamentary elections in 1946. Black market godfather Ozu was among those tried and convicted, but the police, the public prosecutor, and other judicial officials involved in his case certified that he was too sick to be jailed. Attesting to his "high moral character," they recommended release instead, and much to the chagrin of Kades' crime fighters, Ozu walked out of jail a free man. That the intelligence wing of the GHQ was hiring Japanese gangsters at the very same time to fight Communist insurgents and break labor strikes did not further the overall effort to serve justice.

One rather unexpected result of the crackdown was the resignation of the prime minister and his entire cabinet, and the indictment of sixty-four individuals, when it became known that executives of Showa Denko, a big fertilizer producer, had been bribing Japanese government officials for low-interest loans from a reconstruction financing agency. When the GHQ campaign against crime had run its course, however, the annual total of embezzlements, forgeries, and fraudulent conversions had actually increased, as had the number of known underworld gangsters, as counted by the Japanese government's Crime Prevention Bureau.

The problem was not just the chaotic times or the possible incompetence of Americans directing the prosecution, whose unfamiliarity with local language and custom no doubt put them at a disadvantage. The problem was also that the culture of corruption was too deeply rooted in Japan to be cleaned up overnight. Despite laws long on the books that banned bribery and Confucian ethics that deemed it immoral, handouts had existed as long as there had been village politics and village bosses to dispense patronage. In the Tokugawa Shogunate era, public servants had regularly supplemented their monthly stipends with "gifts," the custom becoming so ingrained that the line between proper etiquette and downright bribery was often impossible to distinguish. The blurring of this distinction gave rise to cozy alliances of convenience among public leaders and private interests, which evolved further in the mid-nineteenth century when the parliamentarian system of government was adopted. Political parties, which controlled the lower house of Parliament and hence the national budget, grew so dependent on funds from the big financial combines for elections (as well as money and other help from the underworld) that corruption was all but inevitable.

Thus, periodic public scandals have been the rule, not the exception. In 1914, a massive bribery scandal involving Navy officials, the great trading house Mitsui Bussan, and two foreign companies—the German electronics giant Siemens and the British weapons manufacturer Vickers—brought down the government. Attempts by the authorities to suppress evidence (which included the use of hired thugs to threaten witnesses) in regard to "gratuities" paid under the table to a vice-admiral in charge of naval stores to secure a contract to build a new cruiser, were undermined when an ex-Siemens employee, on trial in Germany for an unrelated matter, revealed his knowledge of the bribes in open court testimony. Following that were scandals involving Yawata Steel (1918), Teijin (1934), and the Showa Denko firm (1948), which set the stage for even more dramatic eruptions to come, including the Lockheed Aircraft payoffs of 1976 and the stock brokerage-related graft of the 1990s.

The GHQ's ill-fated assault on the underground government was accompanied by a crackdown on crime committed by its own personnel that was only slightly more fruitful. It produced a number of dishonorable discharges, including that of an Army colonel court-martialed for selling nine dollars' worth of cigarettes. But those responsible for the disappearance of some 800,000 karats' worth of diamonds—which had been transferred to the custody of the GHQ from the Bank of Japan—were never found; nor were those who had made off with the entire armory of the disarmed Tokyo police force sometime between 1945, when the GHQ disarmed the Metropolitan Police Department and placed the weapons in securely locked storage crates in a military warehouse in Yokohama, and 1951, when the crates were opened and the contents were discovered to be missing. Throughout it all, an assortment of small-time smugglers continued their operations from a downtown office building right next to the Provost Marshal's office.

By the time the exercise was over, it had become increasingly clear that the new era of democracy and bilateral friendship being forged had a powerful, resilient underside. A pattern of illicit collusion had been established through an extraordinary mix of desperation and opportunism, and it was not about to go away.

BANK OF TEXAS

Of the many black market ventures during the Occupation involving Japanese and Americans, perhaps none was quite as successful as a company known as Lansco, a bizarre Ginza-based "general store" that was engaged in everything from illegal banking to gumball sales. Its founder was an ex-Marine sergeant from New York named Nick Zappetti, a thickset, swaggering Italian who, it might be argued, was as representative of his era as the kindhearted, chocolate-giving, children-loving GI of popular lore. Lansco was one of a series of memorable Zappetti ventures, of both the legal and illegal variety, that would highlight a long and quixotic career in the Far East.

Like many others in the Occupation netherworld, Zappetti came from a Depression-era background of poverty—in his case, the northern Manhattan Italian ghetto of East Harlem. He belonged to a family of eleven children who grew up in a cramped cold water tenement. Their father, an immigrant rough carpenter from Calebresia, made barely enough to feed everyone and pay the rent.

Zappetti was no stranger to crime, thanks to the Mafioso who controlled his neighborhood. Gaetano Luchese, better known as "Three Finger Brown," was a second cousin. Family acquaintances included Joe Rao, who was the "Boss of Booze," "Trigger" Mike Coppola, aka "King of the Artichokes," and Joe Stretch, a mobster who had his own chain of restaurants. The doctor across the street sold bootleg whiskey, and the next-door neighbor was a professional hit man—as young Nick discovered one afternoon in 1935 at age fourteen when he attended the man's funeral. The corpse had been laid out in an open casket in the adjoining flat and its face was burned a deep red.

"What happened?" he had asked his father. "Did he lie out in the sun too long?"

"No," came the reply. "He died at Sing Sing last night in the electric chair. He was executed for murder."

That was the kind of environment Zappetti had come from, a place where it was the cops who were regarded as the enemy and the robbers the role models in life. He believed that World War II was the best thing that ever happened, given the somewhat limited opportunities for advancement at home, for it got him into the military and all the way to Japan, where the choices for someone with brains and a larcenous heart were far more numerous.

Zappetti had arrived in Northern Kyushu in late August 1945 as a twenty-two-year-old first sergeant in charge of the aforementioned MAG-44 party assigned to commandeer the Omura Air Field near Nagasaki, where he had made the decision to occupy the geisha house instead of the abandoned base while awaiting reinforcements. In February 1946, when his Marine Corps hitch ended, he took a local discharge and assumed one of the 6,000 U.S. government jobs available in the GHQ—which, ironically enough, was a post as an investigator for the Civil Property Custodian Section, a department created to oversee the return of property looted by Japan in other Asian countries to its rightful owners. In early 1947 he made a trip back to the United States and returned with a Ford convertible, inside of which he had concealed several sacks of lighter flints, a highly prized commodity in Japan. There were 20,000 flints in each sack, and he sold them on the Ginza black market for more money than the car had cost.

In August of the same year, he took time out to marry a Japa-

nese woman. The event was such a rarity that film footage of
him and his bride, an English-speaking dentist, was shown on
the Pathé movie news—the announcer pointedly noting the existence of something called the Oriental Exclusion Act, which
prevented Americans from taking such war brides home. By
March 1948, however, he was back in full swing running an extremely lucrative black market beer operation in partnership
with a predacious lieutenant colonel in charge of ration tickets
in the Occupation Finance Office and a fellow investigator in the
CPC, a nisei who spoke fluent Japanese and could communicate
directly with the city's gang bosses. Once or twice a week they
would take the ration coupons out to an Occupation-approved
brewery, a rusting metal structure on the Sumida River in the
eastern part of Tokyo where, for a fee paid under the table, a
compliant Japanese clerk would quietly fill the order, in violation of GHQ rationing laws prohibiting individuals from making such large purchases. They would fill up a large military
truck with hundreds of cases of beer and sell their goods to buyers at secluded warehouses and bombed-out factories around
town for a profit of 40 cents a bottle. The next day, their beer
would be displayed in the open-air markets.

Profits from such activities made it possible for him to buy a
plot of land in the suburb of Fujisawa and build a large American-style house, where he ensconced his wife and two infant children. He had also acquired a fancy new car, a wardrobe of new
clothes, and several mistresses, whom he would entertain at the
Dai-Ichi Hotel, a Western-style establishment in Shimbashi
built for the canceled 1940 Tokyo Olympics. One of his young
lady friends was a law student, destined to become a successful
attorney, who paid her law school tuition by providing Zappetti
and his friends with oral sex on demand. There are those who
vividly remember the sight of Zappetti being driven around

downtown Tokyo in the backseat of an open convertible in broad daylight, drinking Champagne, and enjoying the X-rated ministrations of a semi-clothed female companion.

In early 1950, the beer operation was infiltrated by a zealous undercover detective from the MPD, which resulted in Zappetti's arrest by the MPs and deportation. But it didn't take long for the enterprising young New Yorker to make it back to Japan. Although his passport had been seized on his arrival in the United States and he had been subsequently booted out of his local congressman's office when he had gone to ask for it back, he simply went to pay his respects to the local Mafia Office on 116th Street, between 1st and 2nd avenues. The bosses who ran the neighborhood were more than willing to help one of their own.

"Don't worry," said one of the men, a distant relative of the family. "We can take care of the situation."

And they did. Shortly thereafter, the relative told him to fill out an application for a new U.S. passport as well as one for a commercial entrant visa for Japan and to deliver the documents to a certain someone in the mayor's office downtown. A few weeks later, Zappetti's passport came in the mail, with a visa stamped inside.

Also helpful was a "business associate" in the GHQ, a cryptographer from Brooklyn named Bob, with whom Zappetti had made preparatory inquiries before leaving.

"You see the way it's happening now," Bob had said at the time. "They got something called a Form 26. That's a list of all commercial entrant visa holders who want to enter Japan. If there are any traitors or criminals on it, which means people like you, then the GHQ puts a check mark by it, meaning entry not allowed."

"Shit," Zappetti had said. "I'll never get approved."

"Fortunately," Bob continued, "the list goes through my

hands. If your name is checked off, all I have to do is switch it with someone else's. That way you get in and some other poor slob gets his application rejected. Just call me when you get ready to come back and we'll work something out."

Zappetti placed his call and in June 1950 boarded a Northwest Airlines flight in New York City. Sixty hours later he landed at Tokyo's Haneda Airport and passed through immigration without incident. After a brief unproductive visit with his wife, who had wearied of his philandering and his criminal ways, he moved into a small house in the southwestern part of Tokyo. Then he began cobbling together the venture that would take its own unique place in Tokyo underworld history.

By bribing someone in the 8th Army, Zappetti obtained a permit that allowed him to sell goods legally to authorized military personnel. He established a company and, in late 1950, set up shop in a two-story ferro-concrete building located on a broad West Ginza avenue that was perpetually jammed with military personnel, street vendors, and smoke-belching oil drum fires.

The new company's name, Lansco, was a play on the first names of Zappetti and his new partners, a Russian Communist with a taste for booze and expensive cars, named Leo Yuskoff, whom Nick had met during his CPC days, and an entrepreneurial U.S. Army lieutenant named Al, who was transferred back to the States shortly after the company began operations. Yuskoff was a stateless White Russian in his early forties who had been born in Kobe, Japan, where his parents had settled after fleeing the Russian Revolution. One of an estimated 500 White Russians living in Japan after the war, Yuskoff could read and write Japanese better than most natives. He was simultaneously a devout Marxist and a shrewd, dedicated businessman, capable of calculating complex profit margins at the drop of a hat.

Displayed on the ground floor of the Lansco building was a wide variety of merchandise: canned and dry goods, including silk, wool, and imported London tweeds. There was assorted hardware and appliances, like Gibson refrigerators and Servo stoves, along with luxury items such as Capehart phonographs— all procured from the PX by legitimate or other means. Although the store would turn a huge profit, it had originally been intended for show—to deceive the MPs and disguise the important part of the operation, which was conducted upstairs and which was the business of illegal checks.

Among Lansco's first clients was a major American shipping company with an office in Tokyo that was looking for bigger earnings on its cash reserves than the banks were paying—at the time, 5 percent. The company deposited $2 million in Lansco's account at the Tokyo branch of the Bank of America, and Lansco sold dollar checks on that account to black market buyers for yen. The official bank rate had been fixed at 360 yen to the dollar in 1949 as part of a tight new SCAP policy following a period of wild inflation that had seen the currency balloon all the way from 15 yen. (The dollar would stay at the 360 level until 1973, when U.S. President Richard Nixon took it off the gold standard and allowed it to float on the international market.) On the street, however, with demand high due to stiff currency exchange laws and restrictions, a dollar would fetch anywhere from 480 to 520 yen, which meant considerable profits for those with greenbacks to sell. Other Lansco clients included American and Canadian construction companies under U.S. military contract who wanted a better exchange rate on their government-issued dollar checks than the banks were paying when they converted them to Japanese currency. Lansco would buy their checks at the rate of 420 yen to the dollar, then sell them on the street at 480–520 yen. Since the checks in question were seldom under $100,000 a piece, the company realized a substantial return on each transaction.

Lansco's most notable accomplishment was creating a bank

out of thin air. The Bank of Texas, as it was called, was an entirely fictitious bank with no assets, no liabilities, and no legal standing whatsoever. It was brought into being solely by printing up some official-looking but fake documents, a letterhead that displayed an imaginary address in a nonexistent Texas town, and a set of checkbooks. For sheer audacity, nothing else in the city could quite match it. Whenever Lansco needed a quick fix of capital, Zappetti would prepare a bearer's check for a certain amount—$30,000 was usually the minimum required to ensure a respectable profit—sign it at the bottom with Harry S. Truman or Franklin Delano Roosevelt, and sell it to someone in the underworld for 10 percent of its face value. The underworld buyer would in turn sell the check to someone else at a "discount," explaining that it was stolen. The buyer usually didn't care because he was planning to turn around and sell it to someone else—perhaps a Japanese entrepreneur, desperate for hard-to-get dollars. Whoever tried to cash the check at the end of the chain would realize it was worthless, but given all the go-betweens, it was almost impossible to trace the draft back to its original source.

The primary traffickers of the Lansco checks were members of the two gangs vying for control of the Ginza, the Sumiyoshi-Ikka (Sumiyoshi Family), a prewar gambling group that had traditionally run the area, and the Tosei-kai (Eastern Voice Society), a vicious gang of young Korean street toughs that had sprung up on the ashes of Japan's defeat. The Sumiyoshi and the Tosei-kai were at constant odds with each other over turf, which included the right to buy checks from the Americans, to "escort" GIs on leave from Korea, where war had erupted in June 1950, and to run protection and franchise rackets among the myriad of nightclubs, cabarets, dance halls, amusement parlors, and gambling dens springing up all over the Ginza.

Gangsters from both sides would from time to time take sudden potshots at the large clock tower atop the seven-storied Hattori Building at the Ginza 4-chome crossing, just to show who was in charge. Both gangs, in fact, earned the sobriquet "*Ginza Keisatsu*" (Ginza Police), because they were better armed than the men of the Metropolitan Police Department, who, having been relieved of their weapons by the GHQ, had been reduced to carrying wooden staves.

For the most part, the foreigners and indigent mobsters on the Ginza lived in parallel worlds that did not intersect socially; the *gaijin* ("outside people," as Japanese referred to the Westerners in their midst) kept to the cozy, if gaudy military clubs, like the Rocker 4, on one corner of the Ginza 4-chome intersection, a new multifloored pleasure palace with 2,000 hostesses ferried to work from all around the rubble-strewn city by Army shuttle buses. The gangsters hung out in their own rickety bars—typically dark establishments with bare unpainted wooden floors, vinyl-covered bar stools and booths, and smelly "outdoor" unisex toilets. The two sides only came together when business demands dictated—fake check sales, money laundering, or, as in one other memorable venture, gumball sales.

Lansco had somehow come into the possession of a thousand pounds of stolen gumballs, which the company was unable to sell. Lansco representatives went to stores, kiosks, and open-air stalls all over the Ginza, explaining that gumballs were the latest rage back in the States, but found there was absolutely no interest. The Japanese merchants they spoke with had never seen gumballs before and after one viewing said, quite candidly, that they did not care to see them again. There were all sorts of objections: The gumballs didn't suit Japanese tastes, a refrain foreign businessmen would hear quite often over the next half-century in association with any number of products; they weren't sweet enough, the artificial coloring didn't look right, they stained the hands, and so on and so forth. That Lansco had no gumball machines with which to dispense the gumballs did not help matters.

Faced with such obstinacy, Lansco turned to the Tosei-kai, employing a band of young Korean thugs from the gang to revisit all the shop owners and describe what would happen to them if they did not revise their inventory plans. This new sales strategy proved remarkably more effective than the previous one. Soon, the downtown area was inundated with gumballs. Lansco phones were ringing left and right with calls from shop owners begging for more. When Lansco raised gumball prices, the phones rang even harder.

Usually, however, such forceful tactics were not necessary. The demand for their first-floor goods among the local populace, though they were forbidden by law to buy them, proved to be far higher than anyone had expected, especially as the Occupation neared its end and a mini-boom from Korean War procurement orders began injecting the first signs of life into the economy. Lansco moved Zippo lighters by the box, nylon stockings by the carton, and the heavily rationed commodity of sugar by the sackful. They brought in their wares by the truckload and, when the coast was clear of watchful MPs and Japanese police, set them down on the sidewalk in front of the store for sale to passersby, who hauled them off in three-wheeled carts. In one insane afternoon, the company sold 4,000 pounds of stolen spaghetti. It was a time when people did not need to be strong-armed into accepting American products—with the exception perhaps of gumballs.

Another foray was into the field of slot machines. The opportunity arose to rent several slot machines and install them in the 52-room Hotel New York across the Sumida River in Eastern

Tokyo, among other spots. The hotel was a popular place for GIs on leave from the Korean War because of its bountiful supply of "onlies"—girls who would contract to spend an entire week of R&R exclusively with one soldier. Upon acquiring the slot machines, Zappetti, who was preternaturally skilled in such matters, rearranged their inner workings so that hitting the jackpot became virtually impossible. The GIs played the machines, almost never won, and never seemed to catch on. But then again, they weren't around long enough to grow suspicious. Zappetti increased slot machine revenue by purchasing bags of as yet unstamped 10-yen coins pilfered from a government printing office in Sugamo, which were usable as slot machine tokens, and he sold them to the R&R GIs.

The amount of money Lansco made was extraordinary. At any given time there was several hundred thousand dollars in cash in the company's coffers—U.S. dollars, military payment certificates, Japanese yen, even some Korean won. Membership in the company also grew. The first addition was Ray Dunston, a big, raw-boned, ruddy-faced Australian, around fifty years old, who was welcomed into the company because he possessed a valid license to sell sugar (still among the most tightly rationed commodities) and because he was willing to contribute $250,000 of his own money in operating capital. Dunston had also started an English "academy" in Tokyo, something his partners found curious since he had never graduated from high school and could barely string together two correct and complete sentences. Another addition was an American businessman formerly connected to the GHQ who was fluent in Japanese and who went on to work for the U.S. Department of Commerce in Washington, D.C. Still another was a Canadian drifter who possessed uncommon skills in the recondite art of falsifying bank documents. Also joining up were two more White Russian Communist capitalists, who would end each business day with Yuskoff in a smoke-filled yakitori shop across the street, getting drunk and singing Russian Eskimo songs. When it came time to go to bed, Leo would stagger back to the office, open up a fresh jug of sake, and curl up with it on the vinyl-covered sofa on the second floor. In the morning, the bottle would be empty. He was the only person Zappetti ever met who drank while he was asleep.

Oddly enough, the Soviet Embassy, involved in a bitter cold war with the United States and its allies, quietly encouraged Lansco's activities, offering tips and suggestions for possible business deals, in the belief that black marketeering would result in the overthrow of capitalism. As Leo put it to Zappetti somewhat absurdly late one drunken night, "Nick, I'm in this business because I want to get rich and destroy the capitalist economic system."

For a time, Lansco joined forces with a West Coast gangster named Huff, a big, mean-tempered man who ran the Evergreen general store on the eastern end of the Ginza, which was itself a front for black market goods—as a shopper discovered one day when strolled in and asked for some flour and Huff replied, "How many carloads do you need?"

Huff became famous in the Ginza underground for the time he hijacked 3,000 baskets of imported bananas from the U.S. military and sold them on the street. His connection to Lansco ended when he was shotgunned to death in a gangland killing, sometime later on a trip to Arizona. Rumor had it he was done in by California-based Asian mobsters, resentful of his success in the Far East.

Eventually, more than one of the Lansco partners would see the inside of a Japanese jail, but that would come later—much, much later, and only after the GHQ had packed up and gone home.

OCCUPATION LEGACY

The Occupation lasted six years, eight months, and fourteen days, and the amount of theft, graft, illicit sales, fraudulent conversions, and other funny business that took place during that time is impossible to calculate—although many have tried. A Japanese magazine once estimated that 10 percent of all supplies shipped from the United States during the Occupation wound up on the black markets. Another study guessed the amount of American currency brought in by streetwalkers alone from the occupiers to be a staggering total of $200 million yearly. Still other reports dealt with a secret billion-dollar slush fund created by the Japanese government from the black market sale of goods and materials *donated* by the United States. The fund, equivalent to nearly 10 percent of Japan's 1950 GNP, was reportedly used to finance the production of basic industries. (In addition, the Japanese government also sold great stockpiles of gold, silver and copper bullion, pig and scrap iron, steel, aluminum, and rubber, which they had concealed in early 1945 in anticipation of Japan's defeat.) Yet, these figures are only educated guesses and no one knows for certain the exact extent of the ill-gotten lucre. Suffice it to say that as an exercise in the cross-cultural exchange of illegal goods and services, it was suitably impressive.

Of course, the Americans liked to view their occupation of Japan as more than just one giant backstreet Wal-Mart. They preferred to focus on the concrete social and political reforms that they had seen instituted, which were designed to give the common man a break: the redistribution of land, the fostering of labor unions, the establishment of equal rights for women, and the elimination of the tyrannical *ie* (family) system—that aspect of the legal code which gave the male head of the household control over marriage, divorce, and adoption. (Japan's prewar Civil Code had stated, "Women are to be regarded as incompetent," denying them a voice in matters of law, property, and suffrage.) Indeed, it was commonly agreed that SCAP was infinitely more generous to the Japanese than the wartime Imperial Army had ever been to its Asian subjects. SCAP's behavior, most notably its decision not to indict the still-revered Sun God Emperor Hirohito for war crimes but to leave him on the throne downgraded to a figurehead, offered quite a contrast to the tales of wholesale rape and murder related by tearful Japanese refugees from Soviet-occupied Manchuria. (As the months and years passed, the failure of the Soviet authorities to account for some half-a-million Japanese prisoners of war seemed to further justify people's fears that such tales were true.) Given the reality that in the blink of an eye several hundred thousand young Caucasian soldiers had been plopped down into a country where there had never been more than a handful of Westerners at a time in any one spot (missionaries, traders, and teachers), it was remarkable that things managed to go as smoothly as they did.

Yet, far too often, the contradictory and unpleasant side of the American character manifested itself and undid much of the good that was being accomplished. Take the sudden restrictions instituted by the second wave of Occupation authorities, who, alarmed at what they perceived to be a breakdown in discipline, sharply limited fraternization between Japanese and Americans for a period of two years, from 1947 to 1949. In one fell swoop, all Japanese movie houses, subways, banks, beaches, rivers, hotels, hospitals, nightclubs, bars, and private houses were declared off-limits to Occupation troops, and Japanese citizens were banished from all military clubs and bachelor quarters, where they had hitherto been welcome. It was hardly a lesson in democracy, and, in fact, the specter of MPs bursting into Japanese-patronized establishments and even private homes to thunder "Any Americans here?!" proved an uncomfortable reminder of the wartime *Kempeitai*, or secret police, who had intruded into every aspect of Japanese life. Moreover, there were several thousand Japanese workers in the GHQ busily censoring newspapers, periodicals, and radio broadcasts critical of the GHQ, even opening personal letters and wiretapping telephone conversations, in a search for dissenters. This was all in direct contravention of the Potsdam Declaration, which had called for the establishment in Japan of freedom of speech, religion, and thought.

Thomas Blakemore, a young SCAP legal expert who had studied at the prewar Imperial University and who would later pass the bar exam in Japanese, the only American in fifty years following the war to accomplish such a feat, was one who believed the Occupation was a colossal waste of time and money. Blakemore, an official liaison to Japanese courts and constitutional scholars, whose knowledge of the language and culture was perhaps unsurpassed by any of his GHQ colleagues, was of the opinion that the Americans' high-handed, hypocritical ways had only earned them the secret enmity of the majority of their hosts—as if their bitter feelings over defeat in war were not already enough reason. (Those postwar surveys which consistently showed America to be the "favorite foreign country" of the Japanese, he liked to point out, also consistently indicated that roughly two-thirds of the population wanted nothing to do with the foreigners in their midst.)

To Blakemore, the leading offender was MacArthur, who professed to understand "the Asian mind" but probably saw less of the country in his stay than anyone else in the Occupation, limiting his vista of Japan to a daily shuttle between his office and the U.S. Embassy, where he lived. During a brief stint with the U.S. State Department in Tokyo, the Oklahoma native, who had also been an OSS agent on the Subcontinent during the war, had filed a report on a bordello in Yokohama with 100 hostesses that was illegally servicing a neighboring U.S. military base—a place where soldiers with disciplinary problems and criminal records were confined as they awaited transfer to the States. He described in his account how payoffs were routinely made to the MPs to buy their cooperation so the inmates could leave the base to visit the establishment across the street, as well as how the girls were recruited, what the VD rate was, and how it was treated. The experience reinforced Blakemore's personal belief that the Occupation was intrinsically corrupt. When ordered by his supervisor to bury the report because it would reflect badly on MacArthur, who had been boasting grandly of a "spiritual revolution" taking place in Japan (albeit one that evidently required censorship and segregation), he resigned in protest.

What troubled Blakemore more than anything else, however, was meeting the bordello's Japanese madam, whom he interviewed for three hours in the course of his research. The madam, it was plain to him, was a product of the upper classes. She was a middle-aged woman with a dignified, cultured manner who spoke very elegant, beautiful, and polite Japanese—what Blakemore, one of the few American GHQ staffers to speak the language of the people they were supposed to be governing, described as a "joy to listen to." In fact, she had been the daughter of a wealthy family that had lost everything in the war, and now, penniless, she had to resort to prostitution to survive and support her children. When she spoke in English, however, her refined ladylike image disappeared. What came out of her mouth was a horribly foul concoction of obscenities she had learned from talking to GIs. "Ottasmadda you," she asked Blakemore at one point, "You no likee fuckee? You cherry boy?" If that was an example of MacArthur's new Japan, Blakemore wanted no part of it.

Ultimately even official U.S. policy was driven, in good part, not by ideology but by financial interest and the profit motive, although that particular facet of Occupation history was not commonly known at the time. Consider the political U-turn SCAP took in 1947, along with its social one. After a year of fevered reform during which SCAP purged some 200,000 people who had held responsible positions during the war—military officers, politicians, government officials, and businessmen—while encouraging labor unions to form, Occupation policy was dramatically altered in what was known as the Reverse Course. The purged were unpurged, union activity restricted, and many other changes repealed.

The Reverse Course was ostensibly prompted by national security concerns—the rise of communism in China, the onset of the cold war with the Soviet Union, and subsequent fear of a Communist Japan (a prospect that, however, did not necessarily instill fear in all Japanese). Almost overnight, the new goal of the Occupation became one of making Japan a "bulwark against communism," as opposed to the previous one of creating a "showcase of democracy."

What most people did not know until much later was the role men from Wall Street played in it all, orchestrating, behind the scenes, a major lobbying campaign to revive the former prewar economic structure. Known as the Japan Lobby in some quarters, it was run by a semisecret group of American individuals affiliated with the Rockefellers, the Morgans, and other large U.S. multinationals that had substantial prewar business interests in Japan, long-standing close ties to leaders of the *zaibatsu* (financial combines), and, it went without saying, powerful connections in Washington. Its members included Secretary of Defense James V. Forrestal, who was also president of the large investment house Dillon, Read, William H. Draper, undersecretary of the army and future vice president of Dillon, Read; and presidential advisor John J. McCloy, the Rockefeller dynasty's main lawyer and "foreign affairs minister." These men argued that American interests lay in maintaining a highly concentrated economy in Japan under an industrial elite capable of managing it, who would make Japan a country fully capable of supporting itself, sharing some expenses with Uncle Sam in protecting Asia from the Reds, and also a country that would be attractive to American capital investment.

An early highlight of the Japan Lobby's campaign was a December 1, 1947, *Newsweek* cover story, "Far to the Left of Anything Now Tolerated in America," which helped bring great pressure on leaders in Washington to change SCAP policy. On the cover was California Senator William Knowland, a highly vocal defender of free enterprise, who had been critical of a radical *zaibatsu* deconcentration plan before the Diet known as FEC-230, in which hundreds of large companies would be broken up and awarded to the unions. (It was a plan supported by MacArthur, who held the industrial conglomerates partly responsible for the war and who had already ordered the fragmentation of Mitsui Bussan and Mitsubishi Shoji, Japan's two largest trading firms.)

"If some of the doctrines set forth in FEC-230 had been proposed by the government of the USSR or even by the Labor Government of Great Britain," Knowland remarked, "I could have understood it. It was unbelievable to me that such a document could be put forward representing the government of which I am a part."

The magazine had relied on reports compiled by a longtime Tokyo lawyer to the U.S. multinationals named James Lee Kauffman, who had taught at Tokyo's Imperial University before the war and whose clients included Standard Oil, which had been selling its wares in Japan since the late 1800s, and General Electric, which had had deep ties to the Mitsui *zaibatsu* since the nineteenth century and had helped electrify Japan. (American companies had held three-quarters of all direct foreign investment in Japan, led by GE's holdings in the Mitsui-affiliated Tokyo Shibaura Electric, better known as Toshiba.)

Kauffman, in documents first circulated to allies in the Departments of State and Defense, who then funneled them to the news media in Washington, painted a bleak picture of a socialized economy under FEC-230, one in which so many experienced executives would be purged from their jobs that the only people left to run the banks and other corporations would be "lowly clerks":

> If you have ever seen an American Indian spending his money shortly after oil has been discovered on his property you will have some idea of how Japanese workers are (already) using (new) labor laws. . . .
>
> You can imagine what would happen in a family of children of ten years or less if they were suddenly told that they could run the house and their own lives as they pleased. . . . Were economic conditions otherwise, I am convinced Japan would be a most attractive prospect for American capital.

The lobby was formally established as the American Council on Japan in 1949, and it brought to bear enough pressure to ensure that its goals were readily achieved. Only nine of the 1200 concerns targeted for possible dissolution under FEC-230 were ever the subject of SCAP action, the old wartime ruling class was effectively restored, and the *zaibatsu* industrial combines allowed to regroup. At the same time, some 20,000 leftists or Communists—the very people the GHQ had been wooing at the start of the Occupation—were put out of commission by the G-2 intelligence wing with the help of several hundred once-purged members of Japan's infamous *Tokko-tai,* or Thought Police, who had been allowed to return to action, so to speak.

By 1952, all prewar investments in Japan by U.S. companies had been fully recouped, all prewar Japanese bonds held by ACJ-affiliated companies had been repaid with interest, and all property lost or damaged from 1941 until 1945 had been compensated for—meaning that many U.S. corporations ended up making a tidy sum on the war.

The above foreign investors went on to stake out strong positions in the form of joint ventures in key Japanese industries, including petroleum refining, aluminum, electrical machinery, chemicals, and glass. They were led by the Rockefeller group, which over the fifty years following the war would be involved in more combined enterprises with Japanese companies than any other multinational. The Tokyo branches of the Chase Manhattan Bank and Bank of America were tapped to become major business financiers in Japan, allowed to extend credit in amounts equaling the Japanese national budget.

All in all, for some parties on both the highest and lowest rungs of the social ladder, the Occupation turned out to be a very profitable exercise. And the entangled web of veiled, mutually beneficial cooperation that underlay the whole process, sometimes bringing together the unlikeliest of bedfellows, was now in place. It would reveal itself often throughout the rest of the century.

2. OCCUPATION HANGOVER

The special relationship between the United States and Japan begun during the Occupation entered a new phase with the signing of the Mutual Security Treaty on April 28, 1952, which formally terminated SCAP rule. Officially hailed in Tokyo as "fair and generous," it gave Japan her freedom and stipulated that America provide Japan's defense. Yet ordinary Japanese, perhaps, found little reason to cheer. Under the terms of the treaty, Japan had been forced to commit herself, reluctantly, to America's hard anti-Communist stance vis-à-vis the Soviet Union and China and allow the stationing of 120,000 U.S. troops on 150 bases dotting the Japanese isles. The country, in effect, remained occupied, and over the next several years a string of unpleasant occurrences served to remind the people of that fact. In November 1953, a Tokyo pimp drowned after three American soldiers threw him into a central city canal. In a similar incident the following month a Japanese salaryman lost his life. Then, in 1954, it was the *Lucky Dragon* affair, in which a Japanese fishing boat was irradiated accidentally by a U.S. atomic bomb test in the Marshall Islands, causing the eventual demise of the ship's captain. These outrages were followed by successive episodes in 1957 and 1958, when bored military sentries discharged their weapons and accidentally killed off-base Japanese.

Equally annoying may have been the bombardment of propaganda delivered in Japanese and English by the Voice of America and the activities of the various U.S. intelligence agencies, who maintained a close surveillance over the people they were supposed to be protecting. The VOA had initially reported, for example, that the captain of the ill-fated *Lucky Dragon* died from a "liver ailment" (not atomic radiation as was later confirmed). It also issued other nuggets of disinformation such as the following:

Today, let's report on war brides. In the past ten years, over 5,000 war brides have gone to the United States. They have all gotten used to a new land and a new environment. They have nice, kind loving husbands and cute children and are spending each day happily.

Sometimes we are asked about racial prejudice against negroes in the U.S. Well, America is a free and democratic country and there is no such thing as discrimination. There's no difference between black and white. Both lead abundant lives.

Letters of protest sent to the VOA regarding the inaccuracies of broadcasted reports were passed on to CIA offices in the U.S. Embassy, where they were placed in a special file for potential troublemakers, who were then "interviewed" by American intelligence. Other forms of thought control included the U.S. State Department ban on export to Japan of films like John Ford's *Grapes of Wrath* and *Tobacco Road,* as well as others that dealt with social injustice in America. On the other hand, proceeds from those films the United States did allow to be shown, such as *Roman Holiday, The Greatest Show on Earth,* and *Shane,* were funneled to anti-Communist groups in Japan to circumvent yen–dollar conversion restrictions. (Revenue from petroleum sales was used in the same way, as was that from sales of the Japanese-language edition of *Reader's Digest.*)

That aside, it was business as usual. Most sectors of Japanese industry, back in the hands of prewar owners, were busy churning out, at first, armaments, munitions, equipment, supplies, and other military-related products to support the conflict in Korea. Then they moved on to other types of industrial manufacturing, thanks to a well-educated workforce willing to toil twelve to fifteen hours a day and to careful government direction of investment.

As early as 1956, Japan would pass Britain to become the world's leading shipbuilding nation. Led by Mitsubishi Heavy Industries and Ishikawaharujima, a company called Sony would already be making portable transistor radios, and the textile, steel, and mining industries would be competing internationally.

Although Tokyo was still a dusty, rubble-strewn city where homeless ex-soldiers vied with street urchins for handouts and graduates of Japan's esteemed Tokyo University drove cabs (Renault cabs because there were no domestic autos), the economic recovery was especially noticeable during the year-end holiday season, when Japanese business corporations held thank-you banquets for suppliers, clients, and workers to reward them for their devotion. Faced with a rare opulent buffet and all the alcohol he could consume for free, the impoverished, malnourished employee (whose average waist size was estimated to be about twenty-four inches) would gorge himself and inevitably wind up getting sick on the way home—which inspired a popular haiku of the time:

Christmas,
Stars in the heaven
Vomit in the street

In 1952, 1953, and 1954, the list of all income earners, Japanese or foreign, as reported by the National Tax Office, was topped by the aforementioned Blakemore, a self-confessed Japan addict who, after translating the Japanese Civil Code into English, had set up a private commercial law practice on the Ginza, taking on many of the clients of the ACJ's James Lee Kauffman, who willingly provided the introductions. He represented General Electric, RCA, International Nickel, and Dow Chemical in joint ventures with big Japanese firms. Blakemore hobnobbed with the likes of John Foster Dulles, John D. Rockefeller III (one of the five brothers indirectly controlling the Standard Oil and Chase Manhattan Bank empire and the largest single foreign investor in Japan), Shigeru Yoshida, who was prime minister of Japan from 1948 to 1954, and the Crown Prince.

To some Japanese, the tall rangy Oklahoman embodied the ideal image of the American, the one they saw in the popular

TV series *Father Knows Best.* He lived with his wife, a graphic designer with the State Department named Frances Baker, in a newly built American-style house that stood on land in central Tokyo purchased at bargain basement prices. There was a big, modern, American-style kitchen and a huge refrigerator stocked full of food. Blakemore's dogs, a pair of blooded Irish setters, ate better than most Japanese.

Tokyo was a city brimming with opportunity of all sorts where there were also thousands of other *gaijin*—ex-Occupationnaires, carpetbaggers, drifters on the make—whose presence caused many Japanese observers to bemoan the transformation of Tokyo as a "miserable colonial city."

One of them was American Ted Lewin, a thickset, flashily dressed man in his fifties, of Asian extraction it was rumored, who traversed the ruined city in a black Cadillac limousine, one of the few deluxe cars in a sea of Army jeeps and three-wheeled trucks. Lewin, a mobster formerly associated with Al Capone, introduced casino gambling to the Japanese.

Gambling was illegal in Japan and had been for centuries (the old shoguns had believed that such a ban was necessary to maintain order among the populace, even though they themselves occasionally invited the *bakuto* into the castle for a private gaming session). Indeed, the only type of public wagering allowed was on thoroughbred racing under the aegis of the Ministry of Agriculture and on municipally sponsored bicycle and motorboat races established after the war specifically to raise needed revenue for local government. In fact, the Japanese authorities took the antigambling laws so seriously they once blocked a raffle at the American Club.

But Lewin, who had been in and out of Asia since the 1930s— he had managed the Riviera Club in Manila and had reportedly maintained a business relationship with the Japanese Imperial

Army there during the early stages of the war—had a fairly good idea of how things worked in Japan. He had paid a $25,000 bribe to a certain Japanese politician, one of the first recorded post-Occupation bribes, and that was enough for the concerned authorities to look the other way while he opened up an operation on the Ginza, the Club Mandarin.

The Mandarin looked like something out of a Warner Brothers movie. On the first floor was a nightclub restaurant with a Filipino band managed by Lewin's Taiwanese associates. On the second, down a narrow back corridor near the restrooms, was the casino. There was a peephole, several levels of guards, and double-layered walls enclosed by iron shutters. In the inner sanctum stood a big Las Vegas–quality roulette wheel, as well as craps, blackjack, and baccarat tables. Thanks to the patronage of the diplomatic crowd, Japanese politicians, and assorted black market gang bosses, several hundred thousands of dollars changed hands at the Mandarin every night.

Lewin also opened another club, the Latin Quarter, in Akasaka, noted for its red curtains and risqué entertainment. As one Japanese journalist wrote, describing live sex shows and rampant drug use, "It was a real 100% American style club, meaning that the mood was one of freedom and that it operated outside the law." Lewin's Latin Quarter partner, Yoshio Kodama, was a former operative in the Japanese military who had taken part in the rape of China. His floor manager was an ex-CIA agent named Al Shattuck, a tall, rugged, bespectacled man in his thirties who, as shall be seen, was about to become famous in Japan—but in a way that he perhaps never imagined. Shattuck's Japanese assistant was a veteran of naval intelligence. Lewin's chauffeur and interpreter was a Korean-American from Hawaii with ties to the Tokyo-based ethnic Korean gang Tosei-kai.

Lewin's political contributions in high places served him well.

Although police closed down the Mandarin twice in widely publicized raids, each time, after a short interval, Lewin was back in business in a new location in the same general vicinity—still operating under the same name. He was later reported to be involved in gunrunning, drug smuggling, and prostitution as well. It was only after a phony stock scheme in which Lewin swindled Japanese and Chinese investors out of hundreds of millions of yen was uncovered that he wore out his welcome.

That other notorious foreign operation of note, Lansco, remained in business, continuing to generate profits by going into the pachinko business, a craze that swept Japan at the time. Pachinko was a form of early American pinball, introduced to Japan in the 1920s as a crude candy store game, which produced various prizes. Due to the space limitations Japan faced, the machine had evolved into a compact, upright, glass-fronted apparatus using tiny silver steel balls The player sat in front of the device and by manipulating a lever propelled a rapid succession of balls up to the top of a board covered with a maze of steel pegs, the idea being to maneuver them into special payoff slots producing bonus balls redeemable not for free games but for prizes. In the postwar era, the prizes became daily necessities like coffee, canned fruit, sugar, soap, and domestic cigarettes like Golden Bat. Since it cost so little to play and was the essence of simplicity itself, the popularity of pachinko skyrocketed. By 1953, there were over a million machines housed in some 50,000 pachinko parlors, all filled to capacity, day and night. Critics complained the pachinko boom was creating a nation of idiots and that it also increased the crime rate. Indeed, people were so eager to try it, they would literally steal for the money to play.

Under Japanese law, pachinko was technically not gambling

because the prizes were goods, not currency. But this being Japan, where there was always a dichotomy between surface appearance and reality, the winners could sell their bounty for cash at nearby back-alley exchange stores.

Lansco made money by supplying prizes (goods obtained from friends at Army post exchanges) to a chain of pachinko shops in the Ginza area owned by a Korean yakuza and even supplied ball bearings, purchased at a discount from a military supplier. However, a bizarre series of events put Lansco out of business. A frail, stateless White Russian youth named Vladimir Boborov had joined the firm as executive assistant to Zappetti along with his fiancée, a young Russian woman named Nina, who became the Lansco bookkeeper. It was Vladimir and Nina's plan to emigrate to the Soviet Union to join the Communist Party and have babies so they could donate them to the state. When Vladimir found himself unable to get a passport, however, he decided to sneak into the motherland and lay the groundwork.

Boborov and a friend drove a 1953 red Dodge all the way from Tokyo up to the port of Wakkanai, the northernmost tip of Japan on the island of Hokkaido, not far from the Russian mainland. There they procured a rowboat and headed out across the Straits of Sakhalin. The currents, however, would not cooperate. They became lost in a thick fog, and when it cleared, they discovered they were back on the Hokkaido coastline. On reaching shore they were arrested by the Japanese police and interrogated by the U.S. CIA on suspicion of being Communist infiltrators. The authorities had found the red Dodge and demanded to know who their accomplices were. Soon they were questioning Zappetti and the others on suspicion of being Communist sympathizers.

It wasn't long after that episode that "The Raid" occurred. It happened one afternoon when Zappetti and the others were at their second-floor desks in the Lansco Building, toting up quarterly profits. They had pulled out three big green metal containers—one full of Japanese yen, one for military payment certificates (MPC), and one for U.S. dollars—which they kept in a desk drawer and had counted out what amounted to over a million dollars in currency. Zappetti had just removed 3 million yen for pocket money and closed and locked the containers when in strode an American flashing an Army CID (Criminal Investigation Division) badge accompanied by several uniformed Japanese policeman.

"This is a raid," said the CID man. "Don't move. Don't touch anything. And keep your mouths shut."

A Japanese policeman reached for the three metal containers, still on the desk, only to be stopped by the man from the CID.

"Don't touch those boxes," he barked.

The policeman was momentarily stunned. Years of obeying GHQ orders had perhaps made him and his colleagues temporarily forget that the Occupation was over and the Americans were no longer in charge—ostensibly, at least. The CID man picked up all three containers and declaring he was "confiscating" them as "evidence," took them away. The Japanese police stayed around to arrest the Australian for illegal possession of MPC.

It never did become clear why Lansco was raided or what happened to the million dollars the CID had taken that day. Zappetti figured he had just been robbed by American Intelligence. At any rate, Lansco was now effectively out of business. One by one, the partners split up and disappeared. Vladimir was arrested again, this time for operating yet another incarnation of Lewin's Mandarin casino—another bizarre detour on the road to his Marxist paradise—and he was kicked out of the country after the Soviet Union agreed to take him and the Japanese government decided to issue a passport. Leo Yuskoff, Vladimir's associate at the Mandarin for a time, also emigrated to Moscow, where after being arrested by the KGB on suspicion of being an American spy he was allowed to join the party. Ray Dunston then started his English school in Tokyo, perhaps or perhaps not the only quasi-literate high school dropout to do so. And Zappetti, not knowing who to bribe in the new order and reduced to running slot machines and the "onlies" at the Hotel New York (the seedy bordello for GIs on R&R from Korea, where trade had also fallen off with the end of the Korean War), found himself drawn into the murky world of professional wrestling—yet another dubious area of U.S.–Japan commercial intercourse—and then, in turn, into armed robbery.

GORGEOUS MAC

It is difficult to exaggerate the degree to which professional wrestling captured the imagination of the post-Occupation Japanese public. Suffice it to say that the sport, one of the very, very few where Americans routinely went down to defeat at the hands of smaller Japanese, electrified the nation as nothing else had in the postwar history of Japan. Not only did it single-handedly resuscitate the wounded Japanese national psyche, still smarting from defeat in war and stung by the ongoing unofficial occupation of their country by the Americans, but it also jump-started Japan's fledgling television industry. Almost overnight, the phenomenon spawned dozens of books by serious historians and sociologists and clearly demonstrated for the first time since the war just how strongly the Japanese clung to their ideas of being Japanese.

The *puro-resu bumu*, as it was called, officially began on the night of February 19, 1954, with an unprecedented and highly dramatic tag team match held in Tokyo, pitting two professional wrestlers from San Francisco—the Sharpe Brothers, Ben and Mike, against a twenty-nine-year-old retired sumo wrestler of some repute named Rikidozan and his partner, ten-time national amateur judo champion Masahiko Kimura.

It wasn't the first professional wrestling match held in Japan; there had been a handful of exhibitions before the war. But most Japanese had preferred their own ancient sport of sumo to the sort of gouge and bite practiced by the Westerners. Sumo was a sport that dated back to the fourth century in which wrestlers wearing topknots and clad only in loincloth-like garb tried to force their opponents out of a small dirt ring. Size, weight, and strength were key factors (wrestlers were routinely expected to eat themselves into obesity), and the matches were filled with pomp and ritual tied to Shinto, Japan's native religion of nature and ancestor worship. The combatants purified themselves in sacred pre-bout rites, which included tossing salt.

This time, however, it was different. The Sharpe Brothers were the reigning world tag team champions. Ben at 6′6″, 240 pounds, and Mike at 6′6″, 250 pounds, had defended their joint title successfully for five years running and both, still in their twenties, were in their prime. They were bona fide world stars, and the fact that athletes of their magnitude had been persuaded to come to an impoverished country like Japan was considered a major coup—in those days, Japan ranked so low on the list of places to tour internationally that a visit by, say, the Belgian foreign vice minister made headlines in Tokyo. In the weeks leading up to the Sharpes' arrival, newspapers were filled with stories about them. Tickets were sold out well in advance, and so were the rights to televise the bouts on Japan's two fledgling TV networks—the quasi-national NHK and NTV, Japan's first commercial station.

Rikidozan was half a foot taller and some fifty pounds heavier than Kimura at 5′8″, 170 pounds, but when the capacity crowd of 12,000 people at Kokugikan sumo arena in Eastern Tokyo saw the four combatants together in the ring for the first time, they emitted a collective groan.

"Those Americans are huge," said the ring announcer. "How can they possibly lose?"

The symbolism was all too painfully clear, as one Japanese journalist wrote later of the event. "The difference in physical size, especially in Kimura's case, triggered painful memories among the spectators of Japan's devastating loss in the Pacific War. It was a reminder of the very deep complex Japanese felt toward the Americans."

But then the match began and something very surprising happened. Rikidozan flew into the ring and began pummeling Mike Sharpe with powerful karate chops. As the American gradually retreated under the furious onslaught and eventually gave way to his brother, the crowd erupted into an astonished cheer. When Ben Sharpe entered the ring, Rikidozan continued the frenzied attack and sent him reeling from corner to corner too, until he finally collapsed in a daze. Rikidozan pounced on him for the count of three and the fans shot to their feet in mass hysteria, tossing seat cushions, hats, and other objects into the air.

The pandemonium in the arena, however, was as nothing compared to what was going on outside. At outdoor television sets installed around Japan as promotional devices, gigantic crowds had gathered to view the proceedings, among them the 20,000 onlookers who had crammed into the tiny West Exit Square of Shimbashi Station, staring up at a twenty-seven-inch dais-mounted "General" and cheering wildly as Riki beat the Americans senseless. The mob was so large that it overflowed onto the main thoroughfare in front of the station, blocking traffic. Unable to move, taxi drivers simply parked their cabs in the middle of the street and joined the raucous throng.

In Tokyo's Ueno Park, what was described as a "black mountain" of wrestling, enthusiasts had assembled on an incline in front of a truck-mounted TV set. Many had climbed trees, rocks, and lampposts to get a better view, and several were so overcome with excitement at Rikidozan's performance that they fell off their perches, incurring serious injury and causing ambulances to shuttle back and forth from the park to the nearest hospital for much of the evening.

At other squares in Tokyo and across the archipelago, the story was the same: vast seas of delirious people weeping with joy at the extraordinary spectacle. It was estimated that between 10 million and 14 million people watched the match that night, and although it had actually ended in a one-all draw, the effect was that of a World Cup victory for the home team. It was the lead story in all the morning newspapers. Public enrapturement with the wrestler was summed up in the words of media magnate and NTV owner Matsutaro Shoriki: "Rikidozan, by his pro wrestling in which he sent the big white men flying, has restored pride to the Japanese and given them new courage."

It was a critical moment for Japan. Japan's best boxer was a bantamweight, and their baseball players, to quote one sportswriter, "looked like pygmies when up against the touring U.S. major leaguers." But Rikidozan had stood on equal ground with the foreigner. It was as if the Pacific War had just been refought—and, this time, won. Overnight, Japan had a new national hero. The next evening, interest was even higher. Coffee shops and restaurants with TV sets sold overpriced admission tickets, while entire neighborhoods squeezed into the homes of those fortunate enough to own one of the new magic boxes. When the telecast of the match began, taxis virtually vanished from the city. It was estimated that there were 24 million viewers nationwide that night—more than *one-third* of the entire population. Prior to the opening gong, an NTV announcer took time to make this unusual announcement to the nation: "A word to those people watching on street corners and in front of train stations and department stores. Please don't push. And will those people who have climbed up trees, telephone poles, and other high places, please come down before you hurt yourself?"

The main event this time was a non-title sixty-one-minute exhibition between Rikidozan and Ben Sharpe, which proved to be even more pleasing. Riki bravely endured a quarter-hour's worth of illegal blows and heinous fouls, then finally exploded in a raging flurry of karate chops to send his foe to the canvas, down for the count of three and the first fall. When the final gong sounded, Rikidozan had emerged victorious, two falls to one. For people who had had precious little else to cheer about, the ecstasy was almost unbearable.

By March 1, when the Sharpes' nationwide tour was over and Rikidozan had racked up several more victories, a full-blown national craze was under way, the economic and social consequences of which would be enormous. There was a mad rush to buy TV sets to watch Rikidozan starring in the hastily assembled program, *Mitsubishi Faitoman Awa* (Mitsubishi Fightman Hour), Japan's version of the Friday night fights, and the rate of cuts, bruises, and broken bones among primary-school children jumped dramatically as young boys around the country took to imitating Rikidozan wrestling. There were reports of viewers watching at home becoming so distraught when a foreign wrestler committed a foul they smashed their own sets in anger. A number of viewers even died of heart attacks induced by the shock of watching the ferocious images. But in the span of less than two weeks, a decade of public sycophancy of the Americans had officially come to an end.

If anyone noticed that the matches had been somewhat choreographed (which, in fact, they were) he or she was not saying, which was just fine with the promoters. The matches were in fact scripted, rehearsed, and staged with the full cooperation of the Americans, who were extremely well compensated for their trouble. If the neophyte Japanese public as yet lacked a full recognition of that fact, then so be it. It was better to focus on the therapeutic benefits of a Japanese victory. For that was where the money lay.

Competitive professional wrestling groups began springing up all over the place, along with pro wrestling magazines. Suddenly there was a great demand for *gaijin* foils. Not everyone could afford to bring over a high-profile performer like Primo Carnera, "The Walking Italian Alp," or the "Mexican Giant" Jesse Ortega. Thus, Japanese promoters looked to the most cost-effective available source, the 30,000 Westerners living in the city. There they picked up the 5'9", 220-pound Nicola Zappetti with an offer of $500 a match—more than a year's salary for a Japanese company worker (despite the fact that he knew all of four wrestling holds, which he had learned in the Marines)— and another ex-marine, John MacFarland III. MacFarland was a 6'4", 250-pound war hero from Omaha, Nebraska, who had done stints in Tokyo with the Occupation forces and later as an employee of an American construction firm at Johnson Air Force Base. Unable to forget the good life in Japan, he had returned to Tokyo in September 1955 to seek his future and found it in pro wrestling, even though he knew next to nothing about it, either.

The promoter handed Zappetti and MacFarland each a pair of trunks and a packet full of $100 bills and gave them a list of three basic rules to follow.

1. Try to stay in the ring for 30–40 minutes.
2. Don't think of what you're doing as a sport. Think of yourself as an actor.
3. Don't ever try to win.

The Americans performed in what amounted to modern-day morality plays, playing a role the Japanese called *inchiki gaijin resura* (literally, cheating foreign wrestler). From the outset of each match, they would commit foul after foul using knuckle-dusters against their smaller, lighter Japanese opponents, who, of course, did not know the meaning of the word treachery. Finally, however, enough would be enough. In a climactic burst of righteous anger, Japanese fighting spirit would prevail and the morally inferior American heel would be vanquished.

It was the pattern established for all pro wrestling matches in Japan involving Americans, and sociologists were quick to see analogies to other forms of entertainment. Wrote one Japanese university professor:

> To the viewing public, Japanese matches with the barbaric Americans resembled nothing so much as a battle between the cowboys and the Indians, battles which they had seen so much of in American westerns (like *Stagecoach*, immensely popular in Japan.)
>
> The Indians in Hollywood movies were invariably the bad guys while the cowboys—the white man—by contrast, were morally in the right, free of malice and ultimately emerged victorious. That was the appeal of such films to American moviegoers. It reinforced their perception of themselves as superior beings. And in reverse form, that was the appeal of professional wrestling to the Japanese.

The Rikidozan disease affected every segment of society, men and women, young and old, rich and poor, educated and illiterate. The comments of Machiko Kondo, a United Nations officer, born and raised in Tokyo, about the "Riki effect" on her father, were typical:

My father was an engineer. He was highly intelligent and liked intellectual TV shows: professorial debates on NHK, lectures on science and so forth. He liked to discuss German philosophy: Goethe, Hegel, and others. He was very serious minded and looked down on things that weren't intellectual.

But he became another person when professional wrestling came on, especially Japanese versus American. Something came over him. He would shoot his fist in the air, yell, jump up and down, get all excited. It was really strange. I could never understand why an intelligent person like him could watch Rikidozan so much.

To him, I guess Riki was like Robin Hood.

It soon became evident that what the public wanted to see was big, Godzilla-sized Americans cut down to size, the bigger and badder, the better. And thus economics dictated that Zappetti's career sputter to a halt. MacFarland's, on the other hand, went in the other direction. Adopting the moniker "Gorgeous Mac," and billed also by his promoter as "The Wild Bull of Nebraska," MacFarland was a great hit in defeat. He performed before large crowds on TV, appeared in magazine interviews, and quickly became well known. In early January 1956, he called a press conference to announce that he was forming his own wrestling group to capitalize on his success and also to announce his engagement to the daughter of a major *zaibatsu* family, an ardent pro wrestling fan. This was not as unusual as it might sound, given the Alice-in-Wonderland existence *gaijin* in Japan led at the time.

Although surveys consistently showed that two-thirds of the Japanese populace wanted nothing to do with foreigners, that still left a third who did, and they weren't especially picky, given the relatively limited supply and the growing postwar need for Japan to become more familiar with the rest of the world. There were thousands of semiliterate Westerners making a living teaching English in language schools and universities, homely military wives able to parlay blonde hair and big breasts into careers as models and movie actresses in Tokyo and countless other examples of career success exceeding qualifications. Demand exceeded supply. And thus MacFarland, a man with no ring experience who had become well known in Japan simply because he was American, big, and conveniently available to wrestle— and lose—on TV, was on the verge of marrying into one of the wealthiest families in the entire country. Western foreigners could do things like that in those days because the Japanese simply didn't know any better.

Unbeknownst to anyone, however, MacFarland had serious problems. He was in Japan illegally, having entered on a sixty-day tourist visa that had run out weeks earlier. His U.S. passport had also expired. And he was broke, despite his substantial earnings. He had not paid his hotel bill in weeks—it stood at well over a million yen—and he had accumulated other debts as well. He also suffered from bouts of manic depression and for six months in 1948 had been confined to Long Beach Veterans Mental Hospital, during which time he had received shock insulin treatment to cure his sudden fits of violent rage. Gorgeous Mac naturally kept that part of his curriculum vitae confidential— as he did other aspects of his personal life, like his exotic sexual preferences. He liked young Japanese men as well as women and he used the Hotel New York, which Zappetti still ran, for secret afternoon trysts.

Aware of Zappetti's criminal background, MacFarland asked for advice in making some quick cash. He needed a lot of money fast, he said one afternoon in a hushed voice, and he did not care how he got it. Zappetti replied he would be willing to help out—even participate if MacFarland was in the market for a partner—because he was in a bit of a cash crisis himself.

"Where you staying?" asked Nick.

"Imperial," came the reply.

"What's the most valuable thing they got there?"

"Diamonds," he said, after some thought, "in the arcade."

"Good. Then let's steal them."

And thus was hatched a plan for a robbery so bizarre that Tokyoites still talk about it.

THE IMPERIAL HOTEL DIAMOND ROBBERY

The Imperial Hotel was the crown jewel of Tokyo. Designed by the famous architect Frank Lloyd Wright, it had opened in 1923, the year of the great Kanto earthquake, a calamity it had survived intact when every building around it collapsed into rubble. Hailed as a miracle of architecture, it was a wide, low-slung, red brick and oya stone edifice that "floated" on pilings and boasted a lotus pond in front of the main entrance. From the outside, it looked more like an Aztec temple than a Japanese hotel (in fact, Wright had originally intended the design for a Latin American site). During the GHQ years, high-ranking military officers had stayed there, and by the mid-1950s it was generally acknowledged as the Greatest Hotel in Asia. Anybody who was anyone stayed there, from U.S. senators to Hollywood movie stars. Its musty, mausoleum-like lobby was the most popular meeting place in town.

The Diamond Shop in the hotel arcade sometimes made private showings of gems in the guest rooms—something the budding jewel thieves were banking on. Zappetti had devised a scheme whereby MacFarland would call a representative from the diamond arcade to his room for a private exhibition. He would flash open a suitcase full of cash—real money on top, newspaper clippings underneath—to "prove" he was able to pay. Then MacFarland would serve drinks to celebrate the purchase—a glass of orange juice apiece, both of which would be laced with knockout drops. Within minutes after downing the concoction, both MacFarland and the salesman would be unconscious on the floor, whereupon Zappetti, hiding in an adjoining room, would emerge to make off with the diamonds *and* the suitcase. MacFarland would be sure to wake up last and—for added effect—accuse the salesman of engineering the theft.

Zappetti thought it was a brilliant plan.

But then MacFarland decided he wanted a gun.

"What the hell do you need a gun for?" Zappetti asked, stupefied. "You're as big as Godzilla. If there's trouble, you just bash the guy's head in. We're going to knock him out with pills anyway. You don't need no gun. That's crazy."

MacFarland was adamant. "I gotta have a gun," he kept saying.

The combination of MacFarland and a pistol was frightening to contemplate, because while Zappetti thought MacFarland intelligent and rational enough most of the time, he had already caught a disturbing glimpse of MacFarland's psychologically challenged side. Zappetti had been driving the big wrestler across the Sumida River from the Hotel New York into the city center one afternoon when the Wild Bull from Nebraska suddenly snapped. He began slamming the door repeatedly with his elbow, punching the dashboard with his fists as hard as he could—bam! bam! bam!—yelling and screaming like a madman. Then, just as suddenly, like a freight train that had passed, the attack was over. MacFarland had sat back, massaged his bloodied knuckles and brooded in silence for the rest of the trip.

That was when Zappetti realized his new friend was not always playing with a full deck. It was only later he found out about Mac's extended stay at the Long Beach Mental Hospital.

"Well, if you gotta have a gun," Zappetti finally said, "then I gotta get out. That's just asking for trouble."

MacFarland professed displeasure at this defection but relented on condition that Zappetti get him the firearm. So Zappetti contacted an Army friend, who came up with a .38 caliber revolver, a holster, and several bullets. He threw away the bullets as a precautionary measure and delivered the gun and holster, as requested, to one of MacFarland's young paramours, an eighteen-year-old Korean high school dropout named "M" who was given to wearing black rhinestone-studded Latin clothes and big pompadours—fashion inspired by a mambo craze that had swept Japan. "M" had been brought into the caper after Zappetti's withdrawal along with two more accomplices from Tokyo's foreign underworld, one of them a friend of the son of the vice manager of the Imperial, who would provide MacFarland with a personal introduction to the diamond concessionaire.

On D-Day, January 15, 1956, at 10:20 AM, Imperial Hotel arcade jeweler Shichiro Masabuchi carried a briefcase filled with a number of expensive diamonds, emeralds, sapphires, and rubies to MacFarland's room. Within a half-hour, bruised and bloody, he found himself bound and dumped into the hotel bathtub, the gems on the way out the door and in possession of the robbers.

A rational criminal would have probably taken the back way out, especially if he was 6′4″ tall with a red duckbill haircut, in a land of small people who all had black hair, and more especially if it was a face that was recognizable to millions of Japanese television watchers.

But MacFarland had his own demented modus operandi.

After leaving the hotel room with "M" he took the elevator to the main lobby, where he agreeably stopped to sign autographs. Then he stood in line for a taxi in front of the hotel and met his cohorts at a Ginza coffee shop, where he handed over the gun and twelve of the sixteen diamonds in his possession to another accomplice with orders to hide them. Keeping the remaining four, he headed for the Latin Quarter, the deluxe nightclub in Akasaka in Southwest Tokyo co-owned by Lewin, where, he later testified, he sold them to the club's manager, the ex-CIA operative Shattuck, who then left for Manila.

By this time, an Imperial Hotel maid had discovered the jeweler where he had been jettisoned in the bathtub and the police had launched a citywide manhunt for the perpetrators. At 6:30 that evening, a detachment of plainclothesmen had arrived at the Latin Quarter, its chief detective holding an evening newspaper just off the presses with a photograph of MacFarland on its front page.

Because of the huge size difference between MacFarland and the detectives, none of whom stood over 5'5" or weighed more than 130 pounds, a plan of attack had been devised at police headquarters. It called for a team of seven plainclothesmen to bring him in using physical force if necessary. Each officer had been assigned to grab a body part—one for each leg, one for each arm, one man to grab the torso, another for the neck, and a detective to snap the handcuffs on.

To everyone's amazement, however, when the police approached, MacFarland meekly extended his hands and let himself be cuffed without protest.

A quick search revealed there were no diamonds on his person.

The story of MacFarland's arrest was headline news in all the Japanese dailies the following morning; featured prominently was a photo of the stern-faced chief detective, leading his man, handcuffed hands covered by a raincoat, up the steps of the MPD.

It didn't take long for the demented truth to dribble out once Masabuchi had fingered young "M", who was arrested in short order along with the others and Zappetti, who, according to "The Mambo Kid," as the press had nicknamed "M" for his Latin-esque style of dress, had supplied the gun and planned the whole thing. Police could not remember such an odd assortment of foreigners, or so many, for that matter, in a Tokyo jail at one time.

Tokyo was transfixed by the bizarre melodrama, and by week's end the odious influence of aliens in the Japanese midst was *the* major theme in the media. Featured prominently in the same week were accounts of two taxicab robberies committed by Americans and the story of three U.S. airmen who had gone "duck hunting" at a sacred swan preserve north of Tokyo, shooting rifles from a helicopter hovering overhead. However, what happened next was more memorable and not just for the theater it provided but for the peculiar lessons it offered about the Japanese criminal justice system and the Americans caught in it.

TOKYO JAIL

It was not often that Westerners saw the inside of a Japanese jail, and those who did were not anxious to return. Although the basic premise of criminal law under the new postwar constitution of Japan was the same as in U.S. constitutional law, that a man was innocent until he was proven guilty, the reality was different. As Raymond Bushell, the American lawyer who defended MacFarland, put it, "We mean it and they don't. They still have their old prewar thinking that if the police arrest you, then you are guilty until proven innocent. Otherwise why would they arrest you in the first place?"

Whereas in the United States prosecutors had to file formal charges immediately on an arrested suspect, the police in Japan were allowed to hold a man for up to twenty-three days before a formal indictment had to be issued. Moreover, whereas prisoners in America were allowed twenty-four-hour access to their lawyers, jailhouse guests in Japan were limited to a maximum of no more than one hour per day. Japanese law enforcement authorities believed that if they pushed hard enough during interrogation in the time allotted, the prisoner was bound to crack and admit his guilt. They reasoned from this fundamental truth that exercising a little unfriendly persuasion in the pursuit of justice was permissible. And if certain methods they were forced to employ to accomplish this were technically illegal, well, then, so be it. Thus were prisoners kept in bare, isolated concrete cells and forced to sit cross-legged on the floor in silence all their waking hours. And thus did they often return from the interrogation room bruised and bleeding. It was one big reason why the Japanese criminal justice system boasted a 99 percent conviction rate and would continue to do so for the rest of the century—much to the dismay of Amnesty International.

It didn't take long for MacFarland to crack. He was taken to Kosuge Detention Center, a musty gray structure in northeastern Tokyo, where he was strip-searched and thrown into a tiny windowless cell (about six by nine feet), empty except for a rotting futon, a rusted sink, a foul-smelling Western-style toilet, and a bare sixty-watt bulb that remained on twenty-four hours a day. He was forbidden to lie down (or even stand up) except between the hours of 10 P.M. and 6 A.M.

During his first two weeks in incarceration, during which he was interrogated intensively, MacFarland attempted suicide three times. The first attempt took place in his detention center cell when he smashed his jailhouse rice bowl and used the shards to slash his wrists. Upon being treated at the prison infirmary, he ripped a cleaning bucket apart, barehanded, and, with a jagged edge of metal, cut his wrists again, also carving a long angry gash on his face from his temple to his chin in the process. Then, surviving that attempt, but now flat on his back in his cell and securely handcuffed, he began a fast to the death. Soon, he was being fed intravenously.

Finally, MacFarland confessed. His confession, however, was quickly followed by the announcement that he was paralyzed from the waist down and needed medical and psychiatric treatment, which he said he was not getting in jail. This may or may not have been an attempt to use Article 39 of the Criminal Code, which stipulated that penalties "may be reduced for an act done by a weak-minded person."

"I'm going crazy," he told International News Service correspondent Leonard Saffir from a room at the International Catholic Hospital, where he had been moved under police guard. "I'm going bats. I can put a burning cigarette on my leg and not feel it. But nobody knows what's wrong."

For his first court appearance, he was carried before the judge on a stretcher by eight policemen and two prison attendants. Covered by a sheet, his left wrist bound with a bandage and another bandage covering the long scar running from his temple to his chin, he looked, to Japanese reporters covering the case, "just like an Egyptian mummy."

The judge, unmoved, sentenced him to eight years. Shortly thereafter his paralysis would disappear.

Zappetti proved a harder case to crack. Arrested in his office at the Hotel New York on a Friday afternoon, he was hauled off to the Marunouchi jail in the city center without even being allowed to put on his coat. So he huddled in his cell, over that weekend, awaiting interrogation, in sweater and slacks, minus his belt to preclude any MacFarland-like suicide attempts, under a moth-bitten blanket, turning blue from the cold.

On the following Monday his interrogation began. Every morning at precisely 9:00, he was taken to a drab, gray room with high windows, a table and two chairs, to begin eight hours of intensive questioning and pressure to confess.

Through it all, Zappetti steadfastly denied all the charges. The police sergeant conducting Zappetti's interrogation, a man named Nagata who was thin to the point of malnourishment, stopped short of striking his foreign captive, but throughout the course of the day he repeatedly slammed the table, yelled at the top of his voice, and blew cigarette smoke in his prisoner's face. Zappetti, who did not smoke, would sit there insouciantly, inhaling the blue haze, as if he enjoyed it, repeating an insult in Japanese that a gangster in the adjoining cell had taught him during a furtive late-night conversation.

Zappetti was playing for time. If the prosecutor's office could not come up with formal indictments within the allotted twenty-three days, they had to release him. And, as it turned out, it was his word against that of the "Mambo Kid" because MacFarland, who willingly fingered everyone else, had, for some reason, refused to implicate him.

Finally one day Nagata tried another ploy. If Zappetti could demonstrate that he had money, the sergeant said, the police might be inclined to believe his claims of innocence. If he didn't need any funds, Nagata reasoned, there would be no point in his being involved in a robbery in the first place, now would there?

When Zappetti was arrested he had but 100 yen in his pocket and no bank account—only a shoebox full of illegal military scrip and Japanese yen squirreled away. There was no possibility of getting any help from his wife, who wanted nothing more to do with him. But there were his parents, to whom Zappetti had been sending money regularly since his military days.

"I got plenty of money in America," he said. "I don't have to steal. When I need money I get it from there. There's no problem."

"Prove it," said his interlocutor.

He had the police send a telegram to his father in New York. "Wire $500," it read simply. "I've been arrested."

The $500, which was more than a police sergeant's annual salary, reached American Express in downtown Tokyo in two days and his captors took him there to pick it up. They handcuffed him and chained his legs and then, pulling him by a rope tied around his waist, paraded him down the street, along the Imperial Palace moat, to the American Express office, amid the midday traffic of Army jeeps and ramshackle taxis belching noxious fumes. His mobility was further hampered by the fact he had lost some thirty pounds from his jail diet and his beltless slacks were so big on him he had to hold them up by hand. The police could have driven him to the Amex office in a van, which they normally did when transporting prisoners, and they could have also gotten him some fresh clothes, especially since his sweater was sporting several new holes. But the police were purposely trying to shame him in front of the midday crowd of pedestrians, who had doubtless never seen an American in shackles and chains before, not to mention one who looked like a street bum and couldn't keep his pants up. Japan was a country that put a premium on face, and public humiliation was regarded as a particularly effective method of making a suspect admit to guilt.

At American Express, the police refused to remove the handcuffs. Zappetti had to raise both of his manacled hands to collect his $500 and sign the receipt, while somehow keeping his pants from falling down. He was then paraded back to jail the same way he had come and the money taken from him for safekeeping.

Sergeant Nagata stared hard at him in the interrogation room and said, "All right. So you got $500. But can you do it again?"

So Zappetti sent another telegram. And they all went through the same routine once more. When the money arrived, he was shackled and roped and again marched through the midday downtown crowds in his rotting, foul-smelling clothes. It was only after he had received a third cash wire, accumulating a total of $1500, that Nagata conceded enough was enough and that maybe they were not going to get anywhere by going down that road. That was good because the clerk at the Amex counter had told the American prisoner on his last visit that he would have to take his business elsewhere; he was embarrassing everyone with his distasteful presence.

On the twenty-third day of his imprisonment a deal was offered by the prosecutor. If Zappetti would admit to procuring the gun, the robbery charges would be dropped. He would be released on bail, he would be fined $800 and sentenced to eight months in prison, which would be suspended for three years. And he would not be deported, which was a major, major concession on their part. But he *had* to admit to something, he was told by his Japanese lawyer. It was a matter of face because they had already arrested him.

Thus did Zappetti agree and secure his release.

MacFarland's young accomplices received suspended sentences, but the Latin Quarter manager Shattuck was brought back from Manila to stand trial. He also refused to confess, adamantly denying he had ever taken the missing diamonds, but was tried and convicted purely on MacFarland's say-so. Shattuck claimed that MacFarland had framed him, that MacFarland had hidden the jewels somewhere but had implicated Shattuck because of a personal dispute the two had had over an unpaid debt. However, the judge chose to believe MacFarland.

Shattuck continued to protest his innocence from his prison cell, and it was left to his wife to provide the final wacky twist in the whole affair. Her name was Doris Lee, and she was a buxom blonde nightclub singer with a vague resemblance to Marilyn Monroe. She had wangled an audience with a noted Tokyo judge, a man destined for a spot on Japan's Supreme Court. The judge listened to the details of the case and advised the curvaceous foreign lady what to do: Put on her best low-cut dress, buy a bouquet of roses, and pay a visit to the management of the hotel arcade to make a personal appeal for mercy.

"Tell them you bought the diamonds from MacFarland and sold them," said the judge. "Even if you didn't do that. Tell them you didn't know they were stolen and that otherwise you never would have become involved. Then offer to make restitution. Most Japanese never have a chance to talk to a girl like you in their entire lives. When they see this big, beautiful American blonde girl coming at them with flowers and bowing in contrition . . . there's no way they'll refuse to drop the charges."

Mrs. Shattuck took the judge's advice and did as he suggested. And indeed, just as predicted, the charges were dropped and Mr. Shattuck was released, proving yet again that where foreign blondes were concerned, the normal rules did not always apply.

MacFarland spent six years behind the high grim walls of Fuchu Prison on the plains west of Tokyo. And no one ever saw the missing stones again.

The Imperial Hotel Diamond Incident, as it came to be known in the Japanese press, sent a message to the general public about American civilians in the post-Occupation era—that despite their big houses, cars, and suave image conveyed by screen stars like Gregory Peck they could be just as uncouth and stupid as anyone else and that even guests at a hotel as vaunted as the Imperial were not to be trusted. The incident helped popularize a phrase, *furyo gaijin* (delinquent foreigner), and gave the Japanese media an opportunity to criticize the authorities for their lax attitude toward foreigners.

Sociologists wrote of a decline in public and private morals because of the *gaijin*, citing the odious influence of Western-style music such as that of Perez Prado, whose smash hits "Patricia" and "Mambo Jambo" were causing young Japanese men to parade shamelessly about in gaudy black pants and the women in short parachute skirts. It was no coincidence, opinion makers noted, that the teenaged youth involved in the Imperial Hotel robbery was wearing a "mambo suit" when arrested.

The *Sunday Mainichi* called for more sweeps and roundups of "suspicious aliens" and added a dark warning, one heard often over the next forty years: "Japanese in general are foolish with regard to foreigners. But this trend has become stronger since the war. If this sort of behavior continues, then more incidents like the Imperial Hotel caper will occur. And you know what will happen to Tokyo then."

The intellectual Japanese magazine *Jinbutsu Orai* ran the following biting unequivocal editorial, entitled *"Tokyo Sokai"* (Tokyo Colony):

"Tokyo Sokai."
What a terrible expression.
The smell of bloody crime is everywhere, wafting through the air.
The incident at the Imperial Hotel makes you realize it.
It was like something out of a gang movie.
The underground world of the *gaijin* fostered the crime and who knows what roots it is laying for other dark crimes in the future.
According to the Metropolitan Police Department, there

are about 30,000 Westerners in Tokyo. About 10 percent of them are "hoodlum foreigners."

These foreigners come from various countries. Some of them have police records. Some are connected to the underworld. Some are GIs who cannot forget the easy, lenient, spoiled treatment they received during the Occupation.

Tokyo is a miserable colonial city where these hoodlum *gaijin* exist and the closer you go to the center, the more rotten it is. Black market dollars, gambling, illegal drug trafficking, and what not.

Underground Tokyo is a swamp of hell.

Gaijin crime has been increasing since the days of the Occupation. Just look at last year, 1955, alone. 170 cases of theft, 76 cases of robbery, 10 murder incidents, 20 cases of rape, 415 cases of assault, and 53 cases of narcotics sales. And these, these cases reported, represent only the tip of the iceberg. In reality, one can estimate that the figure is several times higher.

Tokyo presents a sad figure. It is taken for either a colonial city or an occupied city. As such, it cannot help but become a breeding ground for crimes by foreigners.

The newest incident of all, the robbery of the Imperial Hotel diamonds, was so stupid, and so willful, that what are we to make of it? What does it tell us when the method used was so simple and the motive so ridiculous?

Missing from the media diatribe, justifiable as it may have been, was any mention of the 300,000 thefts, robberies, kidnappings, assaults, and other mayhem that the people who invented the tea ceremony perpetrated on each other every year in Tokyo alone.

Nor was there much discussion of the major shipbuilding

scandal a year before, in which Japanese companies were bribing the government for contracts and subsidies and in which two
future prime ministers in the Yoshida cabinet were implicated
but escaped indictment.

It was a scenario that would continue to be repeated in various forms, tainting a dozen prime ministers in the process, and
cause many observers to call Japanese politics the most corrupt
in the world. A special term, *kozo oshoku* (structural corruption),
would even be coined to describe the system.

The fact of the matter was that the "Orai" and the others had
it wrong. The city was already quite sufficiently corrupt without
any outside help. The smell of the swamp, of crime, shady dealing, and corruption, *was* everywhere. It was precisely this that
had attracted the "delinquent" foreigners in the first place.

But all this was a reality Tokyoites preferred not to dwell on.
For them, the Rikidozan myth, with all its stirring reassurances,
exerted a much greater appeal.

3. SUCCESS STORY

There were 400 registered foreign firms in Japan in the mid-1950s, trying to get a foothold in a market that was open to them only in joint venture form. About one-fourth were multinationals like Du Pont, Cargill, and Merck. The rest were trading companies or small special interest businesses like Western Ammunition and Colt, which rearmed the Japanese police with Colt revolvers. Most of them operated at a loss in anticipation of big returns down the road when the Japanese government began easing the barriers and restrictions it had erected to protect the country's nascent industries. There were also the 30,000-some-odd individual Americans, British, Canadians, and others, many of whom were trying with limited success to make it on their own.

Not many would have predicted that former jailbird and deportee Nicola Zappetti would end up striking it rich and in the process create a famous landmark. But then he had help from some highly unconventional sources.

Zappetti had emerged from jail in February 1956 to find himself evicted from the Hotel New York and all his belongings missing. To conserve his remaining funds, he had been forced to take up temporary residence in an abandoned Turkish bath where the electricity and water had been cut off. It was clear he needed some other immediate means of making a living besides crime, and opening a restaurant was one idea that had come to him in jail. Unable to stomach the constant prison diet of fish, rice, and misoshiru soup, he would sit there and hungrily fantasize about his favorite foods: spaghetti with clam sauce, veal parmigiana, lasagna, and pizza—a dish it was impossible to get anywhere in Tokyo.

There were very few Western-style eateries in the city. Among them were two good German restaurants on the Ginza, Lohmeyers and Ketel's, which were run by longtime Tokyo residents from the Fatherland, Irene's in nearby Kanda, which served Russian food, a steakhouse in the Ginza run by an expatriate American, and the main dining room in the Imperial Hotel, which specialized in French cuisine. But there were enough Westerners in the city unable to gain access to the clubs and PX cafeterias on the U.S. military bases—and enough curious Japanese—to make a new restaurant work, or so Zappetti believed.

The fact that he knew absolutely nothing about the restaurant business did not deter him in the least from plunging in headfirst. He knew what good Italian food tasted like, he told himself. There was no guarantee of success, but he could not think of anything else to do that was legal. Thus, with no power in the abandoned bathhouse, he began reading books on Italian cooking during the evening, squinting in the candlelight like some medieval abbot, while in the daytime he tried to raise operating capital. He calculated that he needed 800,000 yen and offered 15 percent a year interest, guaranteed, to anyone who was interested—although he had no idea if or when he would ever really be able to repay the money,

He made the rounds of the legitimate American business community trying to lure investors, starting with the American Club and the American Chamber of Commerce. By Zappetti's own estimate, nine of every ten doors he knocked on were shut in his face.

"Why don't you get out of the country," said one man. "You're giving Americans a bad reputation."

"We don't deal with criminals and diamond robbers," said another.

"You're an embarrassment to us all," said a third.

He could not remember all the insults, he heard so many.

Eventually, however, Zappetti picked up the money. He found ten different financiers—foreign entrepreneurs living in Tokyo who, for one reason or another, decided to help him. One of them said that he was so starved for a good pizza that it was worth the risk of loaning money to open a restaurant that served one. Another thought it exotic to go into business with a famous jewel thief. Still another came up with the final 100,000 after Nick, tired of begging, threatened to introduce one of his Mafia relatives.

Then he went looking for a site.

73

Roppongi was an old residential quarter in Minato-ward in the southwestern part of the city—marked by a half-mile-long stretch of road extending from the Nogi shrine and U.S. Army Hardy Barracks at its northern end to the Russian Embassy and the American Club on its southern tip. The strip was lined with low, glass-fronted stores—*sobaya* (noodle shops), *kissaten* (tea rooms), and a florist—behind which hid rows of dark brown, tile-roofed, Western-style houses, occupied mostly by foreign businessmen and diplomats and their families. The tallest building in sight was only three stories high, and there was little indication of the teeming internationally renowned nocturnal playground the area would eventually become. Roppongi Crossing, destined to be one of the busiest intersections in the world, was then occupied only by a police box, a small bookstore, and two vacant lots. At night, the surrounding side streets were so deserted that residents spoke of seeing ghosts.

Most of the activity in Roppongi took place in the neighborhood of Hardy Barracks, a gated compound of gray, flat-topped buildings that was once a center for Japanese Imperial Army infantry regiments but now served as headquarters to the U.S. 1st Cavalry and the military daily newspaper *Pacific Stars and Stripes*. Approximately 150 streetwalkers patrolled the thoroughfare in front of the barracks' main east gate, working the constant flow of uniformed GIs entering and exiting the compound. Army jeeps and trolleys chugged to and fro past a sign that said, "Let's Prevent Noise by Ourselves."

In the immediate vicinity were the usual establishments catering to the then comparatively cash-rich GI—tailor shops, antique stores (selling centuries-old Muromachi paintings, expensive family heirlooms, and other valuable collectibles at bargain basement prices), and a rich assortment of cheaply constructed bars with names like "The Silk Hat," "The Green

Spot," and "The Cherry." The bars, identified by signboards that further expanded the scope of the English language (e.g., "We have nice girl for your enjoy") were rowdy, dark vestiges of the Occupation where GI brawls were a nightly event, often involving Russians from the embassy down the street, who would come around preaching communism to the bar girls.

From behind Hardy Barracks to the west, it was only a short hike down the hill to the notorious Akasaka nightclub Latin Quarter, the nearby Sanno Hotel, a watering hole for U.S. Army officers, and a number of unobtrusive high-walled back street geisha houses where silk-kimonoed young women strummed *shamisen* and poured sake for the city's elite Japanese clientele. However, the entire area remained devoid of any place that served accessible and edible Western cuisine, unless one counted the Hamburger Inn, a greasy spoon diner of aluminum stools and formica tables located on a corner near the American Club. Roppongi, with its heavy international population, seemed the ideal place for a restaurant, and it was there that Zappetti decided to set up shop.

He found a site on a busy corner at the southern end of the strip, a block from the Russian Embassy. It was a two-story wooden building occupied by the Wu tailor shop whose proprietor, Sam Wu, a refugee from Shanghai, also owned the building. The fledgling restaurateur made the Chinese tailor a proposition. If Mr. Wu would move all his business upstairs to allow a restaurant to open downstairs, Zappetti promised to double Wu's business.

"I notice you ain't got no American clientele," he said. "What I'll do is bring all the Americans in Tokyo to my restaurant and introduce them to you. They can have a pizza, and when they're finished, they can walk upstairs and have a suit made. Pizza and suits. Don't you think that's a great idea?"

Wu was not exactly convinced, but nevertheless, he entered into an agreement whereby Zappetti would move in and, if everything went as promised, could eventually buy the whole building at the price of 40,000 yen per *tsubo*—a *tsubo* being a unit of real estate in Japan equivalent to thirty-six square feet. Wu would then relocate elsewhere.

Zappetti set about redecorating. He painted the interior completely black so the cracks in the cheaply constructed wall would not show. He squeezed in eight booths with tables covered by red-and-white checkered cloths and lit only by Chianti bottles with burning candles stuck in them. He set up a bar on one side and on the other a Wurlitzer jukebox loaded with all the latest hits, like "Too Young," "Written on the Wind," and "Heartbreak Hotel." It was the quintessential East Village grotto.

He hired a young Japanese lady from a Tokyo business school to be his cashier, recruited a Japanese waiter from a coffee shop on the Ginza, and ensconced himself in the tiny kitchen to do the cooking, turning out pizzas, lasagna, spaghetti, and big thick steaks served with glasses of wine and large drafts of beer. He also did the dishwashing, the accounting, and the shopping. After closing, he would clean up and move two tables together for a makeshift bed. In the morning, he would go to the nearby public bath for 13 yen, enduring the stares of fellow Japanese bathers who hardly ever saw a naked white foreigner.

In the beginning, he was forced to pay his rent each day in advance before the Chinese tailor would give him the key to the front door. But he grossed 75,000 yen his first month and doubled that the next. Nicola's, as he called his restaurant, quickly became a second home for *Stars and Stripes* personnel, after a famous *Stripes* entertainment columnist named Al Ricketts announced in print it served the best meal in town, and it also became a favorite gathering spot of the diplomatic crowd.

In short order, it was time to expand. Using his restaurant

as collateral, Zappetti secured a bank loan to buy the building from Wu. But when Zappetti tried to give him the money, Wu promptly increased his price from the original 40,000 yen a *tsubo* to 80,000 yen.

"You promise pizza and suits, remember?" said the tailor. "You going to double my business, remember? Well, not one American customer came up to second floor."

"Really?" replied Zappetti, feigning surprise. "Well, I can't help it if Americans prefer to shop in the PX."

"You liar," said Wu. "Big liar. I want 80,000 yen for one *tsubo*."

Zappetti had to pony up the extra money, but soon he owned the building and had doubled *his* business.

By the end of the decade, Nicola's was, improbably, the talk of the town. Japan's economy was gathering a full head of steam, and with more and more Tokyoites eating out, the strange new Italian restaurant in Roppongi was where they often chose to go, attracted by its bizarre ambience and culinary peculiarities. Few Japanese had ever eaten dinner in such a dimly lit place or drunk draft beer with a meal, and the American-style pizza Nicola's served was such a totally new experience that some customers could be seen wrapping slices in paper napkins to take home. The sight of some stiffly conventional corporate department head depositing a wedge of pizza in his briefcase was strange enough to merit the restaurant mention in the press, and as the word spread, a line of illegally parked automobiles began to form outside, eventually curling around the block.

Moreover, every Japanese who entered was given the singularly unusual treat of being welcomed personally at the first-floor bar by the dark-haired Italian proprietor who, now having assigned cooking duties to someone else, appeared nightly, wearing expensive silk suits and a trim new mustache. (A Tokyo reporter, in writing an article about the popular restaurant, described the owner as a "smooth-talking American mobster" and declared a visit to Nicola's in general, with its eclectic mix of people, as an "exotic adventure . . . like going to a game park.")

Before anyone realized what had happened, Nicola's had become the Toot's Shor of the Far East, attracting a remarkably diverse cross-section of well known people, domestic and foreign, whom one did not ordinarily see out in public, much less in each other's company. Visiting Hollywood movie stars, for example, quickly discovered Nicola's was the only bistro in the entire city that served real American pizza. Thus Elizabeth Taylor, Mike Todd, and David Niven, in town promoting *Around the World in 80 Days*, came for dinner more than once, as did John Wayne, in Japan filming *The Barbarian and the Geisha* (and downing twenty-four straight whiskeys in one memorable sitting), and Connie Francis, who had come to plug her hit song, "Kawaii Baybee," a Japanese rendition of her chart-topping "Pretty Baby." The list of pizza-munching celebrities seen on the premises at different times included Harry Belafonte, Frank Sinatra, Sammy Kaye, William Holden, Xavier Cugat, and Rick Jason—a matinee idol in Tokyo by virtue of his popular TV series *Combat.*

Another famous diner was Crown Prince Akihito, the future emperor of Japan, who came with his popular bride-to-be, an attractive commoner named Michiko Shoda from a wealthy industrial family. Akihito, somewhat more urbane than his father Hirohito, who had been demoted from Shinto Sun God to mere mortal and had traded in his military regalia and favorite white horse for a three-piece suit and a botanist's microscope. Akihito was a seasoned world traveler. He spoke several foreign languages. He was something of a wine connoisseur and more important, at least as far as the future of Nick Zappetti was concerned, had developed a taste for Italian-American food. He had met his fiancée on a tennis court in the posh summer resort town of Karuizawa, and he launched a modern, Western-style courtship that was highlighted by the frequent pizza-eating excursions to Tokyo's trendy new trattoria.

The Crown Prince and his betrothed arrived for periodic afternoon visits that required extraordinary security measures; a cadre of plainclothes bodyguards would systematically occupy every table and empty the restaurant of all other diners before the imperial party entered for the honorable mixed pizza and beer. When word got around that such an exalted personage had given Nicola's his stamp of approval, the failed jewel thief had it made, and the autos parked outside grew so numerous they began to block the normal flow of traffic.

Still another famous guest was one Rikidozan, the wrestling champion and national hero and unquestionably the foremost cultural icon of his time. As already seen, his wrestling show, *Mitsubishi Faitoman Awa* (The Mitsubishi Fightman Hour), was so popular it had single-handedly launched the TV era in Japan; sales of TV sets had skyrocketed from the 1954 plateau of 17,000 to more than 4,500,000 by 1959. One of his matches—a draw with NWA champion Lou Thesz before 27,000 fans at Tokyo's outdoor Korakuen Stadium in 1956—had attracted the largest crowd ever to watch a wrestling event in Japan and had earned a Japanese Nielsen rating of 87 percent, a domestic record that would be surpassed only by the carriage-drawn wedding procession of the Crown Prince and Princess through the heart of Tokyo. The master of a vast business empire that included a seven-story wrestling arena, one of Japan's first bowling alleys, a large Western-style apartment complex ("Riki Apartments" in Akasaka, located behind Hardy Barracks), and a nearby nightclub where the top jazz musicians in the country played, Rikidozan came with a wide range of acquaintances. These ranged from government bigwigs who served on the board of the Japan Professional Wrestling Association to famous novelists like the young Shintaro Ishihara (a future parliamentarian who, perhaps inspired by Rikidozan, would later become Japan's leading American basher, verbally body slamming the United States in a best-selling 1990 book called *The Japan That Can Say No*) and exotic wrestlers like the bearded 600-pound Haystack Calhoun, who needed a flatbed truck to transport him around Tokyo. An avatar of Japanese virtue before the kleig lights, Rikidozan was far less restrained in private. He would stand at the bar downing double shots of bourbon and practicing out loud the insults he had picked up from American friends in his heavily accented English: *kokusakka, sonnabeechi, kommi basutado,* and so forth. He liked to grab well-wishers by the genitalia, convulsing in merriment at the ensuing yelps of pain. On occasion, he would be so overcome by his own exuberance that he would start doing a sumo wrestler's thrusting drill, slamming the pillars that supported the second-floor dining area so violently with his hands that the entire restaurant shook, causing plaster to fall from the ceiling.

Also on the scene and especially hard to miss among the free diners was a notorious Tokyo gang boss named Hisayuki Machii, a mean-looking, 6'2", 200 pounder, who was always in the company of his bodyguard—a mere 110-pound *taekwando* expert (one of the few bodyguards in town half the size of his employer) who conducted his own preliminary security check, one as thorough as that ever done by the Crown Prince's Palace Guard, before allowing the boss to enter. Outside a dozen armed men would stand watch.

Machii's gang, the Tosei-kai, a 1500-member postwar band of mostly Korean thugs, had just won a ruthless war with the pureblooded Sumiyoshi-kai, a prewar gambling gang that dated back to the Meiji era, for control of the booming West Ginza and its dense thicket of bars, cabarets, and pachinko shops. They ran protection rackets and loan collection services and even "leased" operating rights to a Korean pickpocket group. As it turned out, the Tosei-kai also promoted many of Rikidozan's matches.

Although Machii was generally the picture of propriety—he invariably handed out 10,000-yen tips, the equivalent of a month's wages, to waiters—his men were not. Any rival gangster who walked through the West Ginza without paying his respects was literally taking his life in his hands. A Tosei-kai foot soldier once slashed the face of a gang boss from Shibuya from ear to chin merely for refusing to bow his head as he passed by.

The Tosei-kai was symbolic of what had happened to the Tokyo organized crime scene. The old *tekiya* had fallen by the wayside as the street stalls gradually disappeared, and a new type of gangster had assumed control, drawn from the vast pool of jobless and homeless young men who filled the streets in the aftermath of the war. Numbering in the tens of thousands, they had formed new groups and moved heavily into the methamphetamine trade and prostitution (both of which had become illegal after the war). They carved out their own protection and gambling rings (taking several millions of dollars a day in bets on professional baseball games alone) and invented new money-making schemes like corporate extortion in the form of gang-sponsored magazines. "Reporters" for the mob-run magazine *Ginza Nippo*, for example, dug up embarrassing information on the private lives of company presidents, then solicited money for "advertising space" from their subjects *not* to publish it in their journal.

They kept offices, open twenty-four hours a day, in which they conducted their more legitimate activities, like debt collecting, wore gang badges openly on their lapels, and carried name cards showing titles or ranks such as "captain" or "elder brother" or "young associate." They also drove big American cars and aped the dress and manner of characters in American gangster movies. Instead of samurai long swords, they used guns obtained from American GIs.

Not surprisingly, the retired bosses of the postwar outdoor markets looked disapprovingly on the new generation, referring to them by the contemptuous term *gurentai* (a loose equivalent of "juvenile delinquents"). When the first American-style "hit," or shooting for hire, took place in Japan—the attack in 1958 on an infamous greenmailer (financial corporate takeover artist) named Hideki Yokoi as he sat in his downtown office—they, and the public at large, were overwhelmingly critical of the method employed.

"Wearing American gangster clothes is one thing," fumed one aging mobster in the *Shukan Tokyo* (Weekly Tokyo) magazine, in an article entitled "The Fire-Spitting Colt," "but adopting the American custom of using professional hit men? How low can the Japanese gangster fall?" (The honorable way to settle a dispute, as everyone knew, was to grab a sword, purify it by spitting sake on it, and face the enemy man to man, not sneak up on him with a gun from some dingy back stairwell.)

Such criticisms did absolutely no good, however. The New Breed was there to stay and arcane distinctions such as *tekiya* and *bakuto* were fading away; the word "yakuza" was being applied to all gangsters, and the term *boryokudan*, which literally means "violence group," was used for the gangs themselves.

A Tosei-kai captain named Matsubara was perhaps the quintessential Tokyo yakuza. A thickset, powerfully built man with a face that looked as though it had been hit by a truck, he invariably made his entrance wearing dark sunglasses, a fedora pulled down over his eyes, and a trench coat—one or more gun handles protruding from the pockets.

One night as the well-equipped TSK captain was ordering a

drink at the bar, Zappetti asked, "Matsubara, how many guns you actually got on you?"

Matsubara pulled out four revolvers—two .32s and two .38s—and laid them on the counter one by one, as if it were the most natural thing in the world.

These then were but a few of the diverse people who met nightly at the crossroads of East and West that was Nicola's—people who would write some of the more colorful, and dramatic and darker, chapters of the city's history.

UNDERGROUND EMPIRE

The underground economy denounced by Kades in 1947 was alive and growing, and many of its key players could be found at Nicola's. Foremost among them was a squat, bristle-headed, humorless man named Yoshio Kodama, often escorted by Machii or Rikidozan in his capacity as the president of the JPWA. Kodama was a powerful wealthy ultranationalist and behind-the-scenes fixer (who was also the point of entry for America's participation in this sphere).

Described by one historian as a master at channeling "unregistered" funds from big business *and* the underworld to politicians, Kodama was one of the many larger-than-life right-wingers who appeared on the scene in Japan after the restoration of the Emperor to the throne—a devotee of the Black Dragon Society, a secret rightist organization that cut a wide assassination swath through Asia in support of Japanese military and industrial expansionism.

Dubbed "Little Napoleon" by his enemies, Kodama originally made his mark in the 1930s as a government procurement agent in China, pillaging the countryside with a regiment of soldiers that included yakuza bosses he had personally recruited from

Tokyo. (A favorite Kodama modus operandi in China, postwar testimony revealed, was to enter a village and have the mayor immediately shot to ensure everyone's full cooperation in donating supplies.) Kodama's success in providing the Japanese Army and Navy with the minerals, weapons, and other materials they needed eventually earned him a post in the wartime Tojo cabinet.

Kodama also made a considerable personal profit from the sale of opium in China. By war's end, he had amassed a personal fortune of precious jewels, gold, silver, platinum, and radium, which he secretly had smuggled back to Japan. One plane he had commissioned in Shanghai was so heavily laden with plunder that the wheels collapsed on the airport runway.

Upon his return to Tokyo, Kodama was arrested by the Allies on suspicion of committing atrocities. He spent three years in a Sugamo prison as a class A war criminal suspect but was released in 1949, along with Nobusuke Kishi, Tojo's industrial minister and architect of Japan's wartime economy, on the day that Tojo and six others convicted were hanged. Occupation authorities claimed there was not enough evidence to try him, but there was widespread belief that Kodama had bought his freedom with a portion of his secret treasure and that he had supplied information about wartime government figures wanted by the GHQ, convincing the Americans in the process of his potential future value to them. In fact, despite bitter complaints in private about life under the "rule of the white man," he soon went to work for G-2, where officials found his old network of agents, ex-military friends, and underworld associates indeed useful in countering the growing leftist movement in Japan. While infiltrating domestic Communist groups, Kodama found time to become Ted Lewin's partner in the infamous Latin Quarter and used his vast fortune to foster close relationships with postwar political leaders. He provided the funds that started the conservative Liberal

Party and donated even more in 1955, when it merged with the Democratic Party to form the American-backed *Jiyu-Minshu-To*, the party of the *zaibatsu*, which went on to rule Japan for the next thirty-eight years and over which Kodama exerted great influence.

In 1958, Kodama went to work for the CIA, maintaining a professional relationship of considerable intensity that included helping to funnel agency money clandestinely to associates in the LDP and anti-Communist groups. One of Kodama's assignments was to cozy up to Indonesian President Sukarno and assess for the agency the potential for the popular nationalist leader of turning Communist. (While Kodama was doing this, his business associates in a firm called Tonichi Trading Company were laying plans for business ventures in Djakarta, in part by supplying female companionship to the Indonesian president, a known womanizer, on his trips to Tokyo, continuing a tradition begun by previous Japanese business partners of Sukarno. Tonichi would eventually be rewarded with lucrative equipment and construction contacts.)

While working for G-2 intelligence, Kodama had come in contact with another operative, the aforementioned Machii. The son of a Korean factory owner from Seoul and a Japanese mother, Machii had first made his name in the postwar black market running a band of young thugs. Nicknamed "Fanso" (Violent Bull) as a youth, he had won several barroom brawls versus larger American GIs, including one encounter with a U.S. Marine colonel, a karate black belt, whom Machii knocked out cold with one punch. He was famous for once having snapped a set of handcuffs in a fury over being arrested. After emerging victorious in several turf scuffles with pro-North Korean groups in Tokyo as the Korean peninsula headed toward civil war, he began to call his gang, euphemistically, "an armed force for the self-defense of South Koreans."

His exploits won him the attention of the Occupation's G-2 intelligence wing, who put him on their payroll as an anti-Communist fighter and strikebreaker, and he went on to take part in several street battles against leftist protesters, often fighting side by side with pistol-toting members of the CIA.

As unlikely as it may have seemed, the combination of Machii's G-2 contacts and his knowledge of the Korean underworld on both sides of the Japan Sea (he had spent much of his youth in Seoul) earned him a spot with Kodama on an inspection tour of the Korean DMZ led by John Foster Dulles's party in June 1950, shortly before the outbreak of the Korean War.

By the mid-1950s his curriculum vitae included two arrests for manslaughter with his bare hands and several others for extortion and assault. Yet Machii never went to prison, thanks to his American connections in high places. He was either released on bail, acquitted, or placed on probation. The Tokyo chief prosecutor, who was known for his constant pursuit of the gang chieftain, was once quoted as saying, "Every time we tried to get him, we were always pulled back. We'd bring him in, but each time there was pressure from above and he'd wind up being released."

The older Kodama took him under his wing and became an "adviser" to the Tosei-kai, helping Machii to become a naturalized Japanese citizen. Kodama and Machii joined forces in many enterprises, among them the professional wrestling promotion business, investing heavily in Rikidozan, whom Kodama saw as a symbol of a rejuvenated Japan and poster boy for the conservative right. While the TSK men helped stage many matches in the Tokyo area, handled the concessions and provided security, Kodama bought and ran the evening daily *Tokyo Sports,* which he turned into the bible of pro wrestling, devoting the bulk of the coverage to Rikidozan and creating an emotion-filled vehicle for unifying emerging Japanese nationalism, which of course was necessary to the effort to fight communism.

The matches continued to follow the same highly successful pattern, one in which pure-hearted Japanese heroics defeated American villainy, thereby pumping up the national psyche. Among the willing and well-paid participants in the charade were wrestlers like the "bloodsucking demon" Freddie Blassie, who helped inaugurate the color TV era by slashing Riki with a hidden fingernail file and biting him in the forehead—a display of bloodletting that caused five elderly men and three elderly women watching at home around the country to die from the shock. At the same time, however, as it was later revealed, a large percentage of the profits from pro wrestling and related businesses were secretly donated to the conservative pro-American LDP, an irony that appeared to bother none of the parties involved. Another irony that bothered absolutely no one was that in order to circumvent tight currency exchange laws, foreign wrestlers had to be paid in black market dollars.

The governing body of professional wrestling was the Japan Professional Wrestling Association, and its organizational chart was a revealing microcosm of the power structure in Japan, above and below the surface. Kodama was the president. The commissioner of the JPWA was the vice-premier of the LDP, Bamboku Ono, who called his appointment to the post an "honor impossible to refuse." Several JPWA commission members were high-ranking Parliament members, including a future prime minister, Yasuhiro Nakasone, who even maintained an office in one of Rikidozan's Tokyo buildings, free of charge. Others included the CEO of Matsushita, one of the richest men in Japan, who bought television airtime for the matches, the head of NTV, which broadcast them, and the head of Daiei Film Studios, which made movies about them, while a retired police detective sat on the board of the advertising wing. The auditor of the JPWA was "Ginza Machii" who was also a "bodyguard" to Bamboku Ono and had secretly inducted Rikidozan into his gang in a ceremony at the Club Riki, thereby completing the unholy circle.

The confluence of legitimate and illegitimate forces described here reached a zenith of sorts in 1960, when Kodama helped his old prisonmate Nobosuke Kishi, who had gone on to achieve the premiership in 1958 and ram through an extension of the unpopular Mutual Security Treaty with the United States in 1960, deal with wide opposition and massive street demonstrations. These came from students, leftists, and ordinary citizens who did not believe that Japan was really benefiting from the treaty or that the United States could possibly save Japan from nuclear attack. They were especially upset that the man behind the treaty was a former class A war criminal suspect whose career had been resuscitated with the support of the Americans.

After the night of May 19–20, 1960, when the treaty extension was endorsed by Parliament, and police, called in by the LDP, had physically removed protesting Socialist Party members squatting inside in front of the Lower House Speaker's chamber, literally grabbing them by the collar and pulling them back, protests increased in size and intensity—to the point that several hundred thousand angry people snake-danced through the streets daily. U.S. president Dwight Eisenhower had been scheduled to visit Japan to commemorate the treaty's renewal—the plan called for him to ride in an open-car motorcade with the Emperor from Haneda Airport into the city—but the Japanese government seriously began to reconsider this idea in light of the severity of the disturbances and the fact that the maximum deployable policemen numbered only 15,000.

Kodama helped the LDP organize a "security force" of approximately 30,000 gangsters and right-wingers, among them the members of the Tosei-kai and the Yokohama-Yokosuka-based Inagawa-kai. The mobilization orders for this incredible army called for them to be armed with meter-long wooden staves and, after gathering at Tokyo's Meiji Shinto shrine to pray for heavenly assistance in "fighting the degenerates," to be deployed at various spots between the airport and the center of the city, ready to assist the police at the first hint of trouble. Banners, placards, leaflets, loudspeakers, badges, and armbands were prepared, along with a fleet of trucks, ambulances, six helicopters and eight Cessna airplanes. The LDP appropriated nearly $2 million to pay for it all.

An honorary delegation of five elder *tekiya oyabun*, or gang bosses, was dispatched to visit the U.S. Embassy to make a courtesy call on U.S. Ambassador Douglas MacArthur II, nephew of the former SCAP chief. The group included the aging Shinjuku boss Kinosuke Ozu, a man once branded by the Occupation as the most dangerous criminal in the city. History does not record whether the *sakazuki*, a ritual exchange of sake cups to connote brotherhood among yakuza, was performed during the meeting, but MacArthur did cable the State Department that a force of 30,000 young men of various "athletic organizations" was ready, if needed, to help the police out.

The "I Like Ike" yakuza army was never used, as the demonstrations grew increasingly violent and the Eisenhower trip was canceled, but the idea was roughly, perhaps, the equivalent of the Chicago mob joining the Cook County police to keep order during the 1968 Democratic Convention. Unthinkable in the United States, of course, but completely in character with the self-image of the yakuza foot soldier.

"We're not like the Mafia," went their mantra. "Mafia are criminals who commit crimes for money, who sell their services to the highest bidder. But not yakuza. We have a tradition of helping society."

As gang boss Machii put it when it was all over, "Even in dirty swamps, lotus blossoms bloom."

Still another Machii–Kodama project involving U.S. interests was laying the groundwork for a normalization peace treaty between the Republic of Korea and Japan, in the face of bitter feelings among the Korean people toward the Japanese because of Japan's brutal wartime occupation of the peninsula. The U.S. government naturally wanted closer ties; they had several hundred thousand soldiers stationed in Japan and the ROK to counter the Communist threat. Kodama and friends had in mind somehow using reparations money that would be paid and taking full advantage of the investment opportunities that would subsequently open up.

It certainly helped that Machii's close friend was the head of the Korean Central Intelligence Agency, a man who, with the support of the U.S. CIA, helped engineer the downfall of the staunchly anti-Japanese Syngman Rhee in 1960 in favor of the more cooperative military dictator Park Chung Hee, thereby guaranteeing the United States would have its NATO-style military alliance in the Pacific. Rikidozan's new Tokyo penthouse was the site of many secret meetings involving ROK and LDP officials, Kodama and Machii, and the head of the KCIA—which were later concluded over pizza in Roppongi. That Tokyo underworld figures were helping to effect U.S. policy in Asia in such a way was, of course, amazing to contemplate, but not particularly disturbing to the U.S. government if the letters of commendation praising Machii's role in helping normalize relations between Japan and the ROK that later adorned his office walls were any indication. (The peace treaty was signed in 1965, and when the $800 billion in reparations became available, Kodama and Machii helped spend it on the Korean peninsula, opening up casinos, hotels, cabarets, and other ventures in Seoul.)

Nicola Zappetti was given an unprecedented glimpse inside this profligate world when he was invited to a private card game organized one night by Rikidozan; he was, he was told, the first American to be so honored. It was a rare look inside a world that Japanese knew existed, but seldom saw—and a reminder that in Japanese society, there was always more going on than meets the eye.

This particular event took place at a residence in the suburbs of Tokyo surrounded by a high wall and shuttered tightly despite intense nighttime summer heat. Inside, seated on both sides of a long, rectangular table in the living room and cooled by several large fans, were about twenty men, all dressed in expensive business suits. Zappetti recognized many of them from the newspapers and television and from their visits to his own restaurant. There were movie celebrities, business tycoons, LDP politicians, Tokyo gang bosses, and a highly placed member of the Tokyo Metropolitan Police Department. It was as if Frank Sinatra, Henry Ford, Jack Kennedy, and Sam Giancana had all sat down to play a game of poker.

Each player had, Zappetti estimated, 20 million to 30 million yen on the table, in stacks of freshly minted 10,000-yen notes. Behind each player stood a bodyguard—coat opened and holstered handgun exposed. There were .45s, .38s, and .357s. At the door stood two nasty-looking wrestlers—Rikidozan apprentices—holding shotguns. Outside, lurking in the bushes, were more armed guards, Doberman pinschers and German shepherds at their sides.

It was necessary, given the strict laws against firearms and gambling in Japan, for protection from cops, as well as robbers. In fact, if the police had raided the house, there would almost certainly have been a shoot-out. The players were far too important to let themselves be caught.

The game, *kabu*, was a sort of Japanese baccarat, played with a traditional deck of forty-eight illustrated Japanese *hanafuda*, or flower cards, each representing a numerical value from 6 to 1. A white cloth was spread over the table and along its middle ran a thin line. The dealer, Rikidozan, sat at the head of the table and dealt out six cards facedown, three on either side of the line, then called for bets to be placed. The players either bet on which side would have the lowest total or which side would have the highest. The minimum bet was 100,000 yen. After the bets were placed, Rikidozan's attendants counted the money on each side. Both had to be equal in order to complete a hand, and Riki was the "balancer." If one side had 30 million and the other only 12 million, Riki would bet 18 million yen to balance it out. The house would take a 5 percent cut of each pot, an arrangement, Zappetti did not fail to notice, that was unlikely to threaten Rikidozan's acknowledged standing as one of the richest men in the land.

Zappetti had laid down 100,000 yen, nearly six months' salary for one of his waiters, but by far the lowest bet on the table. The cards were turned over and he lost. He put ten more 10,000-yen bills on the table, the cards were dealt, and he lost again. He laid down another 100,000 yen on the table and lost a third time. Around him money was being shifted back and forth in stacks of 1 million yen. Players were cursing to themselves, furiously scribbling in notebooks, jotting down x's and o's, making red and blue marks, and doing calculations on tiny *soroban* (abacuses). The air was blue with cigarette smoke. Young wrestling trainees served drinks, lit cigarettes, and offered up hot towels—like male geisha. Others counted the house take, stacking it into neat piles.

Zappetti kept losing. He lost the next hand and the next one and the next after that. He lost ten times in a row. While he had gone through his million yen, Zappetti estimated that Rikidozan had bet a total of 100 million yen. Riki had a huge stack of money in front of him and Zappetti had absolutely nothing. What's more, he had no more money to bet. All the cash he had brought with him had fit in an envelope, which he had casually stuffed inside his suit coat. Everyone else had carried theirs in bulging briefcases and satchels.

It would have been bad manners, Zappetti thought, to get up and leave, so he borrowed a million yen from the house. Thirty minutes later, he had lost that, too. Then he borrowed and lost a second million, and a third. Zappetti considered himself a wealthy enough man, but he decided he didn't want to play in this game anymore. Almost all the other players were losing in the house cut alone what he had been betting per hand. Thus when Rikidozan proffered yet another stack of yen in his direction, Nick shook his head.

"Fuck no," he had said. "I don't know what the hell I'm doing. Call off the dogs and let me go home."

All in all it had been quite a lesson. In what, Zappetti wasn't sure. But later that night, Zappetti stopped thinking of Japan as a "poor" country.

THE MAFIA BOSS OF TOKYO

No American ever utilized the Tokyo underground to further his own interests quite like the proprietor of Roppongi's hot new restaurant. Consider, for example, a dispute that arose between Zappetti and Club 88, one of many nightclubs that had opened in the neighborhood in the wake of Nicola's success. A shadowy den of dark curtains, begowned hostesses, and live entertainment, the 88 had begun serving pizza and advertising it on the menu as "Nicola's Pizza," without permission. When Zappetti complained to the manager—an Englishman in his forties named Leo Prescott—the man refused to change his menu, arguing that no one could claim a copyright on such a "common name." Zappetti mentioned the problem one night to Rikidozan in passing, wondering out loud what to do, and the wrestler offered to solve it for his favorite restaurateur as a personal favor.

"We'll just go make a typhoon," Riki had said.

A few nights later, Riki, a burly friend he had recruited, and Nick paid a visit to the 88. While Nick watched, Riki and his companion staged a mock fight. The two men began throwing wild punches at each other, missing intentionally and hitting waiters instead. They threw tables and chairs across the room, shattering a large mirror on one wall and smashing all the liquor bottles displayed behind the bar. Then they demolished a grand piano sitting in one corner. The manager stood by horrified, trying in vain to get them to stop. When the two men had finally finished, the place was a complete shambles.

That was the end of the pizza problem. After that Riki saw fit to create yet two more such typhoons against businesses in the area who had somehow offended Zappetti. The three typhooned establishments eventually moved out of Roppongi.

And then there had been the matter that arose in 1959 with the opening of a branch restaurant of Nicola's in front of Yokota Air Force Base in the western suburbs of Tokyo. Yokota Nicola's was a big, white, brightly decorated concrete building with a large parking lot, a neon sign, and a sea of red-and-white checkered cloths inside that, from the start, was always brimming with pizza-hungry servicemen and their girlfriends (not to mention bored military wives and their off-base Japanese lovers). It had started out as a joint venture. Zappetti had bought the land and put up the building while a Japanese partner handled the day-to-day operations. Things went smoothly for a while until there was a dispute over money the partner had spent from the company's checking account. When Zappetti went out to Yokota for a confrontation with his partner about it, he found a local gangster waiting for him instead—a tall, reedy figure dressed completely in white—white summer suit, white shirt, white tie, white hat, and white shoes. He looked like a character out of the *Untouchables*, then playing on TV—dubbed into Japanese. The Japanese Frank Nitti, without so much as uttering hello, informed Nick that his organization, the Tanashi gang of Yokota, was taking over the restaurant.

Nick discussed the matter with Rikidozan, who in turn discussed the matter with Machii, who then arranged for a meeting with the Tanashi gang leader the next day. At ten the following morning, the Tosei-kai chieftain and a dozen short, hollow-cheeked, pasty-faced men in dark, baggy suits entered Yokota Nicola's, all of them bearing guns or knives of one sort or another and very nasty scowls.

They sat down at a large table, facing their opposite number, and talked, if that was the word for it. There was a great deal of guttural underworld slang punctuated by a lot of finger pointing and posturing. Zappetti had no idea what they were talking about. Finally, the Tosei-kai boss put forth an offer in which Mr. Nicola would buy out his partner at a fair price and gave everyone a night to think about it. The next morning, the two sides reached an agreement. The Japanese partner would sell, the Tanashi gang would vacate the premises, and Nick would pay a sum of money to the Tosei-kai that would be used as a solatium to the mother of the nineteen-year-old Tanashi gang member who had had his intestines sliced out with a butcher knife the previous evening in a Yokota city snack bar during a confrontation with a foot soldier belonging to the Machii family.

For a country like Japan, where business decisions are made only after weeks, sometimes months, of meetings and consensus achieving to foster the desired *wa*, or harmony, this was warp speed.

The events of Yokota were a reflection of the gang turmoil that was increasingly afflicting Tokyo. According to the National Police Agency, which attempted to keep track of such things, the number of badge-carrying gangsters in the nation as a whole had swollen alarmingly. From a prewar total of several thousand, the total had risen to 56,000 by 1951 and then from there nearly quadrupled by the end of the decade. It was the largest concentration of organized crime members in history, several times the number of Mafiosi in the United States, and was attributed in part to Japan's precipitous economic growth, which had spawned thousands of new bars and nightclubs ripe for shaking down— as well as to the maturation of Japan's baby boomers, which created new legions of juvenile delinquents.

In the subsequent battle for territory, there had been a wave of violent confrontations in which the old yakuza motto, "Wash Blood with Blood," was taken quite literally: a lieutenant in the Shibuya Ando-gumi instantly disemboweled with a butcher knife for accidentally stepping on a pack of cigarettes dropped by a rival gang member; a Shinjuku foot soldier tied to the railroad tracks for a grisly early morning meeting with the first commuter train in reprisal; an Asakusa gang boss shot dead in a midnight cemetery shoot-out—his opposite number slain in a predawn machine-gun battle in front of Ueno Station.

Extortion, assault, and theft rates skyrocketed. Although Tokyo would later develop a reputation as one of the world's safest cities, in that era, the burgeoning entertainment hubs were being described in the press as "hotbeds of crime" and the surrounding streets unsafe for anyone after midnight. The radio carried public service announcements urging people to hide their kitchen knives so that intruders could not use them as weapons.

The rivalry between the Sumiyoshi and the Tosei-kai, which

had begun in the ashes of postwar Tokyo, had intensified. The older Sumiyoshi had grown to some 8,000 members in twelve loosely allied subgroups in the greater metropolitan area and parts north had gained control of the Tokyo docks, among other things. (The 7,000-member Inagawa-kai ran the Yokohama and Yokosuka ports to the south.) Although the Tosei-kai had solidified at 1500 members after taking over the West Ginza, the two gangs were also competing fiercely for territory in the growing Roppongi–Akasaka area—as the center of the city began moving westward—vying for the right to "protect" the scores of tiny bars popping up in the region's new multistoried concrete buildings.

Nicola's continued to be caught in the unrest. Twelve young Sumiyoshi thugs had refused to pay for a large meal at the restaurant one night in 1961. They told the American owner that Roppongi was *their* territory and that free meals were the price he had to pay for their protection. The cement-necked Zappetti, an ex-marine boxer who had learned to fight on the streets of New York, had coolly invited them to a parking lot across the street to fight—either one by one or all at once—and in the end, they had backed down. It was a story that had instantly spread in Roppongi because the youths were "trainees" attached to a notorious Tokyo wing of the Sumiyoshi yakuza syndicate known as the Kobayashi-kai. The next day their leader, Kusuo Kobayashi, had paid him a visit to apologize and settle the bill, but that incident had been followed by more trouble, highlighted by a sword battle a block away, outside a club run by a captain in the Machii family, involving some twenty participants of the Sumiyoshi and Tosei-kai. In that scuffle, a Tosei-kai soldier named Kaneko had had his left hand sliced off. The hand was lying nearby on the pavement, wristwatch still attached and ticking, when the police arrived.

It was not what one would call a stable business environment.

KILLER IKEDA

As Machii's Tosei-kai carved out its territory in Roppongi, Nicola's became the gang's informal headquarters, tables occupied every night by pizza-munching yakuza, in apparent emulation of their boss. Sales of alcoholic beverages rose in proportion. Given the yakuza's somewhat menacing presence and the volatile personality of the proprietor, conflict was perhaps inevitable. And it came in the form of a famous encounter between the American owner and a well-known, renegade mobster affiliated with the Tosei-kai, "Killer" Ikeda.

Ikeda was a wiry, hollow-cheeked, sinister-looking desperado with a nasty temper, a missing little finger, and a leather case he constantly carried around containing six handleless ice picks sharpened on both ends. He reminded people of Richard Widmark's psychopathic killer in *Kiss of Death*, which had been popular in Tokyo. The word around Roppongi was stay out of his way because he was the meanest gangster in town.

He had walked into Nicola's one night in the summer of 1963 with five other gangsters and a touring professional wrestler from the States who, coincidentally, went by the name Killer Austin and demanded the proprietor join his party for a drink. Zappetti had been sitting at the bar in his restaurant, drinking with a visiting stand-up comic from Los Angeles named Kenny Pearce, who was appearing in a Roppongi-area club. It was past midnight, he was well on his way to getting drunk, and he refused. The reply was a curt, "I don't sit with gangsters," which was not exactly true because the fact of the matter was he *always* sat with Machii and his friends whenever they came in. But Zappetti simply did not like the churlish Ikeda and he didn't care who knew it. Besides, he thought that Ikeda was just trying to impress everyone at his expense.

Killer Ikeda naturally took offense. He rose to challenge Zappetti and Zappetti blasted him in the mouth, sending him sprawling to the carpeted floor. Then the unstrung American flattened a second, then a third member of the group. Then he straightened his tie, and, nimbly stepping over bodies, made his way out the door and into the Roppongi night.

Ikeda and his companions regrouped and set out in pursuit. They scoured the Akasaka and Roppongi area for the next three hours with no success, until finally at 3:30 in the morning, they arrived at Tom's, a seedy, all-night watering hole on the northern end of the Roppongi strip. Tom's was a simple, narrow, glass-front saloon, enveloped in a constant haze of blue smoke. It consisted of a counter, several bar stools and booths, a lower level, and a video jukebox imported from Europe that played such tunes as "The Ballad of the Alamo" in French and "Itsy-Bitsy Teeny-Weeny Yellow Polka Dot Bikini" in Italian. A sign on the wall, in English and Japanese read, "Out of money, out of Tom's." Tom's was patronized by gangsters, hookers, people from the entertainment industry, *Stars and Stripes* personnel, Russian embassy workers and *gaijin* expatriate drifters who were all attracted to its film noir ambience and general sleaze.

Nearly four hours after his humiliating encounter at Nicola's, Ikeda was passing the time on the first-floor level, irritably throwing his ice picks into the wall, when in staggered the *gaijin* enfant terrible himself, Pearce at his side, to take a seat at the counter.

"Howzzit goin' Ikeda," he said thickly, ordering a beer.

Ikeda glared in his direction and then suddenly wheeled to fire an ice pick into the wall—the steel tip of the pick burying itself deeply in the wood.

"You think you can do that?" he sneered.

Zappetti wiggled down off his stool, removed his jacket, retrieved the ice picks and proceeded to hurl all of them, one by one, sideways at the wall, intentionally caroming them off the wooden panels onto the linoleum floor. Then he climbed back on his seat and nonchalantly took a sip of his beer.

Ikeda drew a gun out of his pocket, walked over, and pressed the barrel to Zappetti's left temple.

Accounts vary as to what happened next, but the commonly accepted version has Pearce slipping a switchblade into Zappetti's hand and Zappetti snapping it open and placing the blade at Ikeda's throat.

"Let's do this together," he said, beginning to draw blood. "You pull the trigger and I'll slit your fucking throat. On the count of three. Let's go."

Then, he started counting.

"One . . ."

By the time he got to three, Ikeda had put the gun on the counter and walked out with his men.

The incident further elevated the esteem in which Zappetti had been held by the denizens of the Tokyo underworld. Not only had he not backed down, but he had followed the universal gangland code of conduct by keeping his mouth shut later when the police came around asking questions, ensuring that no arrests were made. He had even magnanimously picked up the tab for Ikeda's departed party. Thus, those who only a short while earlier had thought to kill him were forced, by convention and by Machii's subsequent order, to abandon their plans for reprisal.

A visiting American newspaper columnist from the New York *Daily Mirror* named Lee Mortimer got wind of the story, which went on to take its place in Roppongi folklore, and wrote an article about it for his paper. In it he introduced Nick Zappetti, noted restaurateur from East Harlem, New York, as the Mafia boss of the city.

The title stuck.

And Zappetti did nothing to persuade anyone to the contrary.

KIM SIN RAK

Of all the characters in the tangled web of the underground economy, perhaps no one had more to hide than Rikidozan. In one of the great ironies of history, Rikidozan, the pure-hearted symbol of national virility, was, unbeknownst to anyone except a small handful of people (Machii and Kodama among them) actually a Korean, born with the honest name of Kim Sin Rak to a poor working-class family in what is now North Korea. It was a fact that if made public would, by his own calculation, have cost him 50 percent of his fan base due to anti-Korean prejudices long held among the Japanese.

Although racially Japan belonged to the Mongoloid group of people that also gave rise to the Hong Kong Chinese and Koreans and, in fact, much of what Japan prized as its own culture— Zen Buddhism, written characters, kimono, stylized painting —was first assimilated from China or Korea. (Koreans, for example, claimed that the Imperial Court hat was derived from the Korean *tabi*, a two-toed sock that Japanese had not initially realized was footwear). The idea of Japanese specialness was one that Japanese leaders had long promoted—to insulate the country from foreign influence and foster a national identity.

When Japan opened herself to the outside world with the advent of Meiji reform, her leaders simultaneously advocated modernizing while promoting the cult of the Emperor as a direct descendant of the Sun Goddess and the guardian of Japan's *kokutai*, or national essence. The twentieth-century militants also appropriated the idea as they rose to power and extended their hegemony across the Japan Sea. Even in postwar newly democratized Japan where everyone was purportedly equal, non-Japanese were regarded as inherently less equal than others.

Near the very bottom of the Japan social totem pole was anyone of Korean descent. The Japanese had annexed Korea in 1910, and since that time there had been a general view of Koreans, among the sons of Nippon, as uneducated and primitive and Korean culture as not worthy of study. In fact, during the latter part of the Japanese occupation, the founders of the so-called Greater Asian Co-Prosperity Sphere would not even allow Koreans to speak their own language—in so little regard did the rulers hold the people they had subjugated—and forced over a million and a half of them to come to Japan as slave labor. (After the war, 600,000 chose to stay on, assuming Japanese names and hiding their identities, rather than face the political turmoil that divided the Korean peninsula back home. Gang boss Machii, by contrast, openly boasted of his dual heritage.)

Rikidozan had first come to Japan in 1939 as a strapping teenager, brought by a touring sumo wrestling scout from Nagasaki who signed him on with the Tokyo Nishinoseki stable, one of several licensed stables in the country. There, as per custom, he was given a ring name, Rikidozan, and began his training.

Although records in the Sumo Hall of Fame and Museum correctly listed his name and birthplace, the feeling among those in the Nishinoseki stable was that the public would not accept a Korean in what was known as the sport of the Emperor and was seen as the epitome of the national ethos. It was thus heretical to claim that a Korean, or anyone of any other nationality for that matter, could defeat a Japanese sumoist. As a result, the public fiction was concocted that young Kim had been born Mitsuhiro Momota, the pure-blooded son of Minosuke Momota of Omura, Kyushu—the scout who had discovered him. Later hagiographies would even describe, in amazing detail, free of the slightest trace of irony, a fabricated childhood and a fictional athletic career at Omura High School.

By virtue of his brawn and aggressiveness, Rikidozan quickly made his mark on the sumo circuit, proving himself through competition in periodic fifteen-day championship tournaments held around the country. He rose fast through sumo's strictly graded system of divisions, passing several hundred other competing wrestlers, until he reached the top division of the best forty combatants—the major leagues of sumo, so to speak. Through it all, he endured the brutal dawn-to-dusk regime of a sumo trainee, which included the practice-ring beatings with a bamboo cane to correct bad form and the unpleasant requirement of ministering to the needs of the senior wrestlers in the group bath and toilet. He also bore the occasional whispered taunts of "Garlic Breath," a patronizing reference to the Korean preference for hot, spicy food, from superiors who knew of his background.

Rikidozan was within striking distance of the top three ranks in all of sumo—*sekiwake* (junior champion), *ozeki* (champion), and *yokozuna* (grand champion)—ranks which were awarded by the Japan Sumo Association, the supreme governing body of the sport. But then Japan surrendered and the sport of the Emperor went into a tailspin. The sacred, historic hall of sumo, the *Kokugikan*, where all the Tokyo tournaments were held, had not only been damaged during the bombing raids but was also expropriated by the invading Americans, who repaired it, renamed it Memorial Hall, and began holding pro wrestling matches there. Thus, people who had believed in the divine wind, the Sun God, and the indomitability of the Imperial Japanese Army were forced into a serious reexamination of their pantheon.

In 1949, when some semblance of order had been restored, the San Francisco Seals, a minor-league baseball team, visited Tokyo and played to standing-room-only crowds; a sumo tourney, held at the same time elsewhere in the city, drew only 75 percent of the arena's capacity. Throughout the land, there were vast numbers of young boys sporting baseball caps, but only a few wearing the sumo loincloth.

As he started to feel the financial strain from his sport not turning a profit, Riki quit sumo and took a job in construction. His new employer was a tattooed yakuza gambler from the Sumiyoshi gang and sumo fan named Shinsasku Niita, who had special connections inside the GHQ. Under Niita, Riki supervised construction projects at U.S. military camps, studied English in his spare time, and spent his evenings carousing on the Ginza, where one night he participated in a losing cabaret brawl that dramatically changed his life. His victorious opponent was a visiting Japanese-American Olympic wrestling medalist and All-Hawaiian Body Building champion named Harold Sakata, who would later gain fame playing the steel-top-hat-flinging villain Oddjob in the James Bond movie *Goldfinger.*

In the wake of the altercation, the two men became friends and Sakata introduced Riki to a group of American professional wrestlers who were in Japan putting on a charity exhibition for the Occupation forces, seeking to promote growth of their "sport" in Japan. One thing led to another, and soon Rikidozan was training and wrestling in the States, where he proved to be more successful than anyone anticipated. Too unsophisticated to do anything but fight all out, he combined a spirited karate chop attack with sumo thrusting techniques to compile a 295–5 record in a year's worth of competition. *Boxing Magazine* ranked him in its annual list of the top ten pro wrestlers in the world.

Before departing for the United States in February 1952, Rikidozan had acquired Japanese citizenship and legally changed his name to Mitsuhiro Momota. The government family register now listed the Momotas of Nagasaki as his lawful parents and Omura his officially recognized birthplace. The move was necessary, in part, because his real country of birth was now known as the Communist People's Republic of North Korea and was an avowed enemy of the United States. The only way he could get a visa to the United States was to have a Japanese passport. The only way he could get either one was to bury any trace of his true identity. But, as he also discovered while wrestling in Honolulu, his first stop, there were other reasons to keep up the charade.

Billed as the "Japanese Tiger," he found his every move cheered by an audience of almost exclusively Japanese-Americans, waving Rising Sun flags and lustily yelling *banzai*. As one Japanese correspondent explained, describing the phenomenon in a dispatch back home, "These were the people who had been put in detention camps during the war and had been insulted after the war with words like 'Jap'! When they saw Riki's glorious victories, they felt their pride had been restored to them." For the man known as "Garlic Breath," that must have been indeed hard to swallow. As were the taunts about Pearl Harbor when he wrestled on the mainland, where the matches were racially charged in reverse. There, he found himself appearing alongside assorted Asians passing themselves off as Japanese with names like "Tojo" or "Mr. Moto," wearing goatees and mustaches and exotic "Oriental" garb of red silk robes with high *getas*. They burned incense, flung salt, and used every dirty trick they could think of—falling to their knees, begging for mercy, then when the opponent had turned triumphantly away, launching a ferocious blow to the back of the head, a "sneak attack," as it were. Demeaning as it may have been, the fans loved it and the economic lessons were obvious.

Thus, at the end of his U.S. hegira, Rikidozan returned to Japan and solicited support from Niita and others, including the ubiquitous Kodama, and launched his storybook career. It only worked, as Rikidozan well knew, because everyone viewed him as "Japanese." He, Kodama, Machii, and the others believed that if the Japanese ever discovered the truth, he would lose billions and billions of yen in ticket and advertising revenue and Mitsubishi might even cancel his contract. Riki's predicament was such that he felt comfortable confiding his secret to Nick Zappetti but kept it from people on his own staff.

"I can tell you Neeku," he said, "because you're American and you don't care. But Japanese. Never."

Zappetti understood fully because there was a man on his staff who was Korean but was hiding the fact from his children, lest they be discriminated against when choosing a school or applying for a job.

The great Rikidozan deception reached its apogee in January 1963, when Rikidozan was sent to South Korea on a goodwill tour at the request of Kodama and the LDP to help break the ice that still existed between the ROK and Japan and thereby pave the way for the normalization treaty that so many interested parties wanted.

Despite intense anti-Japanese feelings in the ROK, where bitter memories of the long, brutal Japanese occupation and wartime atrocities remained, Rikidozan was a huge hero there. In fact, many Koreans had naturally assumed he was one of them because the Chinese ideographs for Rikidozan, although pronounced differently, represented the name of a mountain in Korea—a fact most people in Japan remained blissfully unaware of. (The name was a subtle way by which Rikidozan could hang onto his identity.)

In Seoul, Riki was given an imperial welcome. He rode in an open-car parade from the airport, and Korean newspapers blared his name in the headlines: "A Visit To His Homeland after 20 Years," "He's Become Japanese, but His Blood Hasn't Changed."

Back in Japan, however, all lips were remarkably sealed. Only one paper made mention of Riki's origins, the relatively obscure *Tokyo Shimbun*, which ran a translation of an AP article which quoted Riki as saying at a Kimpo Airport press conference, "I am extremely happy to be back in my own country after twenty years." When the men of the JPWA saw that, the paper went on the organization's permanent personal blacklist. It was almost as if the press did not want the public to know. Then again, perhaps it was the public that did not want to know.

The facts about his birthplace were not all that Rikidozan was hiding. Another secret was that he had a daughter whom he had fathered during a 1943 sumo tour of Korea. She lived in Pyonyang, she was active in the Communist Party, and she was a member of the North Korean national women's basketball squad. Riki had met her for the first time later in 1963, when she had made a clandestine visit to Niigata Harbor on the Sea of Japan, when a ship on which she was traveling with her teammates made a brief stop there. At that time, he had promised to bear the expenses for the entire North Korean Olympic squad so it could take part in the 1964 Tokyo Olympics. Then there was the letter Rikidozan had received later that year from an elder brother in Pyonyang who informed him that Kim Il Sung, the president of the Democratic People's Republic of North Korea, was a huge fan of his, that the Supreme Leader had films of all of Rikidozan's matches, and that he absolutely loved seeing a native North Korean beating the blue-eyed, white-skinned capitalist warmongers senseless. Rikidozan was so moved by this development that he had decided to become a Communist and return to live in North Korea after the Olympics—or at least he was according to an article published in a North Korean monthly magazine in 1983, which quoted Rikidozan's brother at length. Of course, the latter, if true, was something the Americans would not be likely to welcome, given who Rikidozan was—and the fact that he had been privy to the secret peace treaty negotiations with the ROK government.

Also alarming to many people was Rikidozan's increasing in-

ability to control himself in public. Granted, Rikidozan's behavior had always been somewhat erratic, and twenty-four hours
with him could certainly shatter any preconceptions one might
have about Japan as a soft, nonviolent place. There had been the
night, for instance, that Rikidozan put on a karate chopping
demonstration for his evening's companion, Zappetti, at the
opening of a new restaurant in Shimbashi, owned by a movie actress Riki knew only casually. Riki had ordered the staff to bring
out all the dishes from the kitchen. He lined them all up into
stacks of varying height and then shattered them with a succession of karate chops. The actress, shocked beyond words, burst
into tears, but Riki just cackled with glee and threw down a wad
of 10,000-yen notes on the table, enough to purchase several
restaurants' worth of dishware.

Moreover, there were times he seemed to take the American-
bashing role he had perfected in the ring far too seriously. He
once lacerated the face of a noisy American diner in Irene's
restaurant in Tokyo with a broken beer bottle. On another occasion, he threw an argumentative Swedish pilot out of the window of a second-story hotel bar in Osaka, mistaking him for an
argumentative American.

Ex-*Stars and Stripes* reporter Corky Alexander was present the
night Rikidozan sat in the Hamburger Inn, the all-night greasy
spoon at the southern foot of the Roppongi strip favored by
Americans. "Riki was there with three women at a back table,"
Alexander recalled. "He was drunk. He unzipped his fly and
started masturbating. That was Rikidozan's way of saying 'Fuck
you' to the foreigner."

But now addiction to drugs and alcohol was making him even
worse, as difficult to imagine as that may have been. He was taking stimulants to gear himself up for matches, tranquilizers to
bring himself down afterward, and sleeping pills at bedtime,

preceded by copious quantities of liquor. Appearing in 200 matches a year, this made for a lot of wear and tear on the body—chemical and otherwise. In the mornings, Riki would awake in a stupor, but in the afternoon, at the practice gym as the drugs wore off, he would fly into uncontrollable rages, to the great misfortune of those around him. There had been a midnight drinking session with Zappetti in which he had exploded in anger at a young woman who had apparently chosen to spend the night with the American instead of him. After nearly breaking her jaw with a karate chop, he had picked her up and thrown her completely over the roof of a parked car.

Thus, when Rikidozan was mortally wounded in a knife attack at an Akasaka nightclub on December 8, 1963, and died two weeks later, it came as no surprise to many people. The story of what happened on that fateful night is as well known in Japan as the facts about the gunfight at the OK Corral are in the United States and bear some retelling here. The knifing had taken place at the New Latin Quarter, which had been built after the old Latin Quarter had burned down—or, as some cynical reporters put it, had *been* burned down, given the vast sum of insurance money that was later paid out. It was located in the basement of the recently opened Hotel New Japan, one of the many showpiece hotels popping up around Tokyo in preparation for the upcoming 1964 Olympics. The NLQ was, everyone agreed, far more luxurious than its predecessor. It had a hundred of the city's most beautiful hostesses, eighty dimly lit tables, spectacular floor shows from the States, and a staff of forty men and women. It also boasted deluxe marble-floored American-style rest rooms, with attendants inside, a first for Tokyo—as was the tipping basket in each facility. It was a favorite hangout of the international intelligence community, agents from the KGB, CIA, and MI6 often vying with each other for the same hostess.

Rikidozan had come in that night with his coterie of attendants in a seriously florid state. Now, seated at a table near the NLQ stage, Riki started throwing coasters at the band—a group on tour from the United States—shouting drunkenly at its black members, "*Neeguro go homu. Sonnabeech.*"

He danced with a hostess for a few numbers, and when the music stopped playing he walked with her arm in arm to the rest room area. At about the same time, a twenty-four-year-old member of the Sumiyoshi-kai named Katsushi Murata got up to visit the men's room, too. The young gangster belonged to the Ginza wing of the Sumiyoshi, a company called Dai-Nippon Kogyo, which supplied bandsmen, musicians, and singers to clubs around Tokyo, as well as ice, hand towels, food, and drink— usually at inflated prices and it was said, at swordpoint, if necessary. The company had also, until recently, supplied similar services at some Rikidozan professional wrestling matches, until Yoshio Kodama struck a deal uniting the Tosei-kai, the 7,000-member Inagawa-kai, and the 10,000-member Kobe-based Yamaguchi-gumi in dividing up exclusive nationwide rights to professional wrestling—the deal leaving young Murata's organization out in the cold.

As the short but solidly built Murata was later to tell the story, Rikidozan was standing in the doorway to the men's room, talking to the hostess, when Murata tried to squeeze by and in the process accidentally made body contact. Words were exchanged, he said, and Riki uncorked a right hand that sent him flying several feet into the men's room, landing with an awful thud on the marble floor. As he lay flat on his back dazed, Rikidozan then leapt atop him and, crazy with anger and alcohol, began raining blows onto his face. Murata said he grabbed for the six-inch hunting knife he kept fixed to his belt and thrust the blade into his attacker's belly. As Riki rolled over in pain, Murata clambered to his feet and fled.

Holding his side, Riki got up and slowly made his way back to his table. He stood in front of his drinking companions, watching the blood gradually stain his clothes. Then, abruptly, he climbed up on the stage and grabbed the microphone from a singer who had been holding forth. Ordering the band to play "Mack the Knife," he began talking in a confused mixture of English and Japanese.

"There is a killer in this club," he was heard to say, a bit too nonchalantly some people thought for a man in his condition. "Look at what he did to me." Than he opened wide his jacket to display the growing swatch of red on his abdomen to the crowd.

There were several screams. Some customers fainted. Others started running out of the club, climbing over tables and chairs.

"You'd better be careful," Riki said, wagging his finger at them. "You'd better go home."

Some observers thought that Riki actually seemed to be enjoying himself.

Riki was taken to a nearby clinic for emergency first aid, then home. The wound would not stop bleeding, however, and the following morning he was taken to the American hospital, St. Luke's, for surgery. In a few days, he was up and about, telling everyone what he was going to do to Murata, who, in any event, had already been located and nearly sliced to death by a group of Tosei-kai gangsters before the police caught up with him. Accounts vary as to what happened next. Some reports say that Riki drank water from a bedside flower vase and developed peritonitis. Other reports had him ripping out his IV and his oxygen tube and downing a beer smuggled into the hospital. Still others said it was the milk and apples he had consumed—both forbidden, given the kind of wound he had. Whatever the cause, he was forced to undergo a sudden second operation and four hours after it was completed he was dead. At the inquest, doctors later testified that Rikidozan had died from the shock of the anesthetic;

because Riki was so much bigger than ordinary Japanese, he required a large dosage, but there had been a miscalculation and he had been given an overdose.

Almost no one thought the original fight with Murata had been unintentional, and the Japanese weeklies had a feast of lurid speculation over the incident. Some journalists, aware of the North Korean connection, believed Rikidozan was the victim of a U.S. CIA plot, that the CIA, under orders from the White House, no doubt, had hired a gangster to do the hit. It was more than a coincidence, conspiracy theorists noted, that Riki's stabbing occurred at a well-known CIA hangout and that he had also died in an *American* hospital . . . from an *overdose* of anesthetic.

The theory was believable enough to many knowledgeable Japanese, given the CIA's involvement in the LDP and the fact that the last thing the conservative leadership would want was Japan's national hero revealed as a North Korean and Communist sympathizer. The clincher to some was the fact that the knifing had occurred on the twenty-second anniversary of the Japanese attack on Pearl Harbor, as the Japanese counted time: That was the U.S.'s answer to those Japanese who had cheered Rikidozan's humiliation of the Americans in the ring.

However, there was no hard evidence that any of this was true. Skeptics pointed to the fact that in June 1963, Rikidozan had married the daughter of a police chief in Shizuoka and was investing in the development of a leisure country club, hardly the actions of a man who intended to defect.

Japanese prosecutors, for their part, had concluded that Riki had been killed as part of the ongoing underworld turf war between the Sumiyoshi and the Tosei-kai. They charged Murata with murder, and although Murata insisted it had all been an accident, a misunderstanding, that he'd only been acting in self-defense, a court found him guilty of manslaughter and sentenced him to prison for seven years.

After a funeral attended by hundreds of prominent people, including LDP cabinet ministers, as well as tens of thousands of mourners, Riki was buried in the cemetery at Ikegami Honmonji temple in Ota Ward Tokyo, in view of a five-story Buddhist pagoda. His tombstone featured a lifesize bronze bust, underneath which was his adopted Japanese name of Momota Mitsuhiro. Nowhere was there any mention of Kim Sin Rak, or of Korea—North or South.

His grave stood as a lasting reminder of the layers of deception that were helping to build the foundation for the "new Japan."

4. POST-OLYMPIC UNDERGROUND ECONOMY

The Tokyo Olympics were a watershed event, one that transformed the psyche of Japan as well as its physical image. All the world had been watching, and by universal agreement, the country had put on a flawless performance. Critics said they were the best-organized Games ever and that the structures built specifically for the extravaganza, seen on global television by millions, were among the most aesthetically impressive in the history of Olympic architecture. Kenzo Tange's National Yoyogi Sport Center, with its sweeping curved rooflines of tensile steel, suggesting some hi-tech Buddhist temple, won the Pritzker Prize for architecture in 1967—all of which served to greatly enhance the self-esteem of the Japanese people.

At the same time, the explosion of construction that accompanied the affair also altered the face of the nation's capital, almost beyond recognition. Nearly all of the city's canals were filled in with concrete and the shacks and mobile stalls of an earlier era turned into firewood. In their place were scores of new hotels (including the futuristic seventeen-story Hotel New Otani, showcased in the James Bond film *You Only Live Twice*), a network of modern roads and elevated freeways with protective steel-siding sound barriers, as well as gleaming new subway lines, a monorail, and a terminal for the world's first high-speed railway. So much of Tokyo, in particular the southwestern areas of Akasaka, Roppongi, Shibuya, and Aoyama, had been rendered unrecognizable from a decade before that a Tokyo gang boss, released from prison after seven years and reeling from confusion at what greeted him, was moved to say, "I feel as though I am returning to a completely different city."

This modern, post-Olympic, new Tokyo could not, by any stretch of the imagination, be called an attractive place. Away from the breathtaking Olympic sites, it was for the most part an amorphous assemblage of gray, boxlike office buildings of cheap reinforced concrete, utilitarian storefronts, and soulless "rabbit hutch" apartment blocks. The terrain was flat, the low-rise skyline monotonous, and the city's hubs, featuring as they did ubiquitous station-front pachinko parlors, "stand bars," and fruit shops, were boring in their uniformity. (Even the city's rebuilt shrines and temples were, in general, indistinguishable from one another.)

But the energy was palpable, especially during the morning
Tokyo rush hour when the millions of determined commuters
made long treks on unspeakably crowded trains to begin the
twelve-hour workday. The so-called Izanagi Boom, which
started in 1965 and was fueled by exports in motorcycles, transistor radios, television sets, and other manufactured products,
lasted fifty-seven months. It was the longest continued economic
expansion in the nation's history and turned Japan into the
world's third largest economy, doubling worker incomes in the
process. By the end of the decade, nearly every family owned a
color TV, an air conditioner, and a washing machine, and Tokyo's
main boulevards were one massive traffic jam from the explosion of privately owned cars—*Japanese* cars like the Datsun
Bluebird and the Toyota Publica. Automobile pollution was so
bad that in some areas street corner police boxes provided oxygen on demand to pedestrians overcome by exhaust fumes. A big
electronic board erected on the Ginza displayed minute-by-
minute PPM levels—alongside decibel levels of noise from traffic and the omnipresent construction machinery.

At night, Tokyo's new wealth was visible in another way, when
the neon signs were turned on—in a phantasmagoric explosion
of Chinese characters, Japanese *kana*, and Roman letters—and
the city's 25,000 bars and nightclubs came to life. Many of them
could be found in the booming Roppongi-Akasaka area, which,
with its international flavor, was becoming Tokyo's major nighttime center.

Roppongi's dusty main avenue was simultaneously gutted
with new construction and lined with pricey modern restaurants—among them the elegant two-story Seryna, where kimonoed waitresses served grilled steaks on heated stone, the Ile de
France, which served quintessential French provincial cuisine
on Japanese cedarwood tables, and the Crazy Horse club, with its

flashy Parisian ambience and live bands direct from Manila. In place of the streetcar was the recently completed Hibya subway line, shuttling in a fresh generation of youth, the first since the war with pocket money, who were anxious to experience the cosmopolitan atmosphere of this thriving hip area.

Nicola's was still the attraction. It now occupied an entire newly constructed three-story concrete building with forty large tables, two blocks away from its original location and a stone's throw from the opulent new Hotel Okura, modeled after an ancient Kyoto palace and adjudged to be the finest hotel in the world. The restaurant had made Roppongi synonymous with pizza. Although Crown Prince Akihito and Princess Michiko had subsequently curtailed their pizza-eating excursions to concentrate on the task of producing an heir to the throne, Nicola's remained a Who's Who of Tokyo and international society. On any given night, celebrities in full view might include: Robert Mitchum, Richard Widmark, and Cary Grant, who all filmed movies in Japan; Frank Sinatra, Sammy Davis, Jr., Billy Eckstein, and Xavier Cugat on concert tour; and even Ava Gardner, who came to town promoting *55 Days in Peking* (announcing that as long as she was in Tokyo she was going to sleep only with Japanese men).

It was neighboring Akasaka, however, with its bevy of expensive new hostess clubs that had sprung up around the New Latin Quarter, that offered one of the more interesting views of emerging "Japan Inc." Akasaka was where Japanese corporate executives took their prospective foreign clients, to soften them up with what amounted to a modern-day version of the old RAA (now retired with honors), one now applied to global commerce instead of domestic peacekeeping. Among Akasaka's popular establishments was the pagoda-like Mikado, the world's largest cabaret. Featuring splashy, Las Vegas–style shows in which scantily clad girls in feathers were transported overhead in pint-sized cable cars, the Mikado boasted 1,000 comely hostesses bearing numbered electronic pagers in their bras.

Said one American importer who was frequently taken to the Mikado by his Japanese associates on buying trips to Tokyo, "It was like a giant warehouse of sex. Your eyes would get tired from staring so much. You'd be out dancing with #832 and her beeper would go off and she'd leave you for another customer. But you didn't care, because the next one would be even better. It added a whole new dimension to doing business in Japan. I can't tell you how many contracts were signed because of that place."

Japan spent (and still does) 1.5 percent of its annual gross national product on declared "business entertaining," which is more than the country ever allotted per annum during the postwar era to the national defense budget; most corporate executives were given generous expense accounts for that purpose. The high figure was a measure of the special Japanese need to develop a relationship with their clients and partners in commerce that goes beyond the mere exchange of goods and services—in the interests of the long-term success of the alliance. It was a need that the Japanese government recognized, incidentally, by condoning tax laws that allow most entertainment to be written off as operating expenses (a policy that, in turn, helped keep the city's myriad watering holes in the black). Entertainment was said to be the adhesive that bound together Japan's so-called Iron Triangle of business, politics, and the bureaucracy and there was, naturally, often more going on than mere fun, games, and male bonding, as anyone familiar with the Akasaka Copacabana could attest.

The Copacabana was the most exclusive and expensive club in the city, by far, the most impressive place a Japanese could take a VIP from abroad. It was a successful attempt to create a Western-style *ryotei*—the name given to the old-style high-class

restaurants of polished bamboo where silk-robed geisha traditionally entertained Japanese politicians and captains of industry—and from where, it was said, Japan was really governed.
Located on an Akasaka back street near the New Latin Quarter,
the Copa offered an elite corps of beautiful bilingual young
women, flawlessly groomed and garbed in Givenchy gowns and
white enamel shoes. They poured drinks, hand-fed gourmet
snacks, flattered, caressed, and otherwise pampered clients in an
intimate setting of dimly lit tables and red velvet booths, while
noted performers from abroad like Nat King Cole and Dean Martin entertained on a small stage. (The Copa's owner, a former
dance hall hostess and prewar Shanghai dancer known as
"Mama Cherry," was famous for her discreet but eagle-eyed surveillance of her hostesses to see that the service was perfect.
When technology later allowed, she even enlisted the aid of
strategically placed TV cameras.)

Each night a steady stream of sleek black limousines glided
to a halt in front of the Copa's distinctive arched entranceway to
disgorge the rich and the famous. Private citizen Richard Nixon
was taken there whenever he came to Tokyo to discuss business
with the great trading house Mitsui Bussan, whose American affiliate he represented. So was King Faisal and Indonesian President Sukarno, among others. And it was a hotbed of espionage.

To cite one notorious example, as reported in 1966 by the
Shukan Gendai, a Copa showgirl known as "Dewi" (whose real
name was Naoko Nemoto), was hired by the Japanese Tonichi
Trading Company, under the baton of Yoshio Kodama, which
had developed several interests in Indonesia, to serve as a "secretary" for Sukarno. She did her job so well, she became the president's fourth wife and mother of Sukarno's youngest child.
Tonichi coincidentally or otherwise continued to reap financial
benefits in Jakarta until Sukarno's ouster from power in the middle of the decade.

It was, however, the budding military and commercial aircraft manufacturing industry that generated most of the action. The Copa was where the big trading houses took the unsuspecting executives from Grumman, Lockheed, McDonnell-Douglas, and Northrop, the major players in the aircraft sales business, where billions of dollars in contracts were up for grabs. And, as it turned out, the agents for the Japanese trading houses, the middlemen in the aircraft buying business, were paying the hostess girlfriends of the American aircraft executives to listen in on any business talk that took place in their presence. The agents had recruited and trained them to ferret out anything that would help in negotiations and the effort to obtain contracts. What they valued, in particular, was information that involved fuel consumption and maintenance or that involved rival government ministries and defense agency personnel (e.g., "Was it true that the Grumman airplane was having problems with its SFC [specific fuel consumption]?" "Was the finance minister in favor of x or y?" "What was MITI's unofficial position?" "Had Colonel So-and-So at the JASDF approved a certain plan or supported a certain strategy?"). Some of the girls, in fact, had developed considerable knowledge about aircraft and had grown into fairly skilled industrial spies. The Americans, not surprisingly, had little idea what was going on—at least not until a magazine article about the Copa entitled "The Nighttime Stage for the Aircraft Wars" appeared on the stands in the mid-1970s.

The intelligence gathered was valuable in determining strategy and decision making in regard to contracts. But there were other deciding factors, too. Like bribery. Which was the case during heated competition between Lockheed and Grumman Aircraft Corporation in 1959 to sell planes to the Japan Defense Agency, which had just begun to negotiate the purchase of jet fighters. The Defense Agency had initially decided to buy the

Grumman F-11 (F-11F1F), then suddenly and mysteriously reversed its decision and chose the Lockheed F-104 Starfighter instead. Said Jim Phillips, an ex-fighter pilot who joined Grumman in 1958, "It didn't make any sense. Grumman's craft was stable and Lockheed's was marginal in terms of safety. I thought I was a smart man but I didn't find out what was going on until much later."

What was going on was a lot. It was later documented that a secret donation in the neighborhood of $1.5 million had been made by Lockheed representatives to certain members of the Japanese government; the contribution had been engineered by—who else?—Yoshio Kodama, who received a fee of $750,000 from Lockheed for his efforts. The payments, it was reported by the *New York Times*, were made with the knowledge of the CIA, which kept that information secret from Grumman and the rest of the aircraft industry. (Lockheed was the firm that had built the U-2 reconnaissance plane for the Agency, and Yoshio Kodama, lest we forget, was an employee of the CIA at the time.)

A subsequent Diet inquiry into the affair had gone nowhere, thanks to Kodama's considerable powers of persuasion. After the Socialist in charge of the probe refused to accept a briefcase full of Patek Phillipe watches and, after that, refused to be intimidated by a sword-wielding Kodama associate, Kodama resorted to blackmail. He produced an embarrassing series of photos of the Socialist in secret trysts with his mistress, and that proved to be enough to do the trick. Kodama did his job so well Lockheed would turn to him again some years later—this time with somewhat different results.

If the business world was expanding its horizons in the new post-Olympic era, so was organized crime. An Olympic year crack-

down weeded out the more youthful offenders, cutting the number of badge-carrying yakuza in half, but its primary accomplishment was to further strengthen the ties between the
authorities and the underworld, already close, thanks to the "I-
Like-Ike" army. Many gangsters had volunteered to help police
clean up Tokyo and reduce crime during the Games so as to protect Japan's image before the foreign visitors. Ginza Machii, for
example, had ordered all his followers who had no regular jobs
and whose appearance was "not pleasant" to leave Tokyo during
the two months around the Olympic Games and go to the
seashore to undergo bodily and spiritual training. The result was
that during the Olympics it was almost impossible to find anyone who looked like a yakuza in Tokyo, offering yet another lesson in gang psychology, Japanese style. Afterward, the gangs that
remained consolidated their strength and increased their participation in the operation of legal businesses like taxi fleets,
trucking companies, construction firms, and entertainment
agencies, using front companies to disguise their ownership.
(90 percent of all the booking agents in Japan were run by underworld gangs; in fact, Japan's number one earning singer
throughout the decade called the boss of the Kobe-based Yamaguchi-gumi "Uncle." Many of the Akasaka-Roppongi—area
deluxe hostess clubs were backed by mob money, among them,
according to more than one report, the Copacabana.)

Tosei-kai boss Machii had reorganized his men into a "credit
union" formally known as the *Toa Yuai Jigyo Kumiai* (or East
Asia Friendship Enterprises Association). And had further established a corporation that now owned nineteen clubs in the
Ginza, including the Silk Road, where the cost of one drink in
the company of a hostess was equivalent to a month's salary for
ordinary Japanese men. He had also gone into the restaurant
business at Zappetti's urging, despite his protestations that he

didn't even know how to boil water. ("You got 1500 little yakuzas running around the Ginza that can bring you customers," the Nicola's boss had said. "Who's going to say no to a gangster?") The result was a small smoke-filled greasy chopstick Korean *yakiniku-ya* that was always full and, in a few short years, transmogrified to two haute cuisine Korean restaurants where the ingredients were imported directly from Seoul. Then, in 1966, in partnership with Kodama, Machii opened a restaurant in Roppongi called the Caravansary that had to be seen to be believed. It featured a Persian façade with Moorish furnishings and massive Arabic tents suspended over floors of polished Italian marble and had more than a million dollars of old Egyptian jewelry, tapestry, and artifacts hanging on the walls. Tuxedoed Korean gangsters greeted the guests, and fez-capped Caucasian waitresses dressed in black tights did the serving. The menu offered French food prepared by a Japanese chef with six years' experience in Germany (which as far as most Japanese of that era were concerned was close enough to France to count). Entertainment was provided by an Egyptian belly dancer and a Japanese quartet singing Spanish songs. If nothing else, it gave new meaning to the term "international dining."

In a press interview, Kodama, the director-general of the operation, announced grandly that the purpose of the restaurant was to "impress foreigners" and erase the postwar image of Japan as a country of prostitutes and bar hostesses.

"Foreigners believe that Japan is a paradise in which to obtain women," he said. "This I cannot tolerate. I wanted to help create this, the number one restaurant in the world, in order to show Japanese superiority to foreigners."

As Kodama gave this speech, he was proving Japanese superiority in another field as well, the recondite world of corporate extortion. He was in the process of bringing under his wing the city's 2,000 *sokaiya.* A concept invented in Japan, a *sokaiya* was a racketeer who specialized in corporate "security." The idea was to obtain enough stock to give him the right to question company officials at general shareholders meetings (*sokai* means "general meeting") and, for a price, agree not to. The *sokaiya* and his organization would bully malcontent stockholders, suppress unscripted comment, and otherwise control procedures to assure a brief, eventless meeting on behalf of management; or conversely, they might even stand up and question the performance of the board, depending on who was footing the bill. There were an estimated 5,000 *sokaiya* throughout Japan, and they also published scores of so-called black magazines, to which they persuaded reluctant corporate executives to subscribe—by fair means or foul (those who declined to purchase a subscription ran the danger of finding themselves the subject of a negative feature in the publication they had declined to buy). Another field Kodama was involved in was "solving" internal business disputes or resolving intra-boardroom power struggles by the use of unfriendly persuasion for a "mediation fee." He was being paid some 20 million yen a year as an "adviser's fee" from the giant brokerage house Nomura Securities, one of the many companies who paid him for his services and whose representatives claimed the investment was well worth the expense.

In the year after the underworld's Olympic hiatus, the National Tax Office estimated that the total annual income from mob activities was more than the annual Tokyo metropolitan government budget of roughly 2 trillion yen (1.5–2 percent of the GNP)—only one-fifth of which was from legitimate enterprises. But no one was exactly sure just how much that was. "The tax bureau asks us to provide a figure," said one police representative, "and we do. But we're really only guessing. The reality might be much higher." Indeed, some organized crime experts in Japan believed the total yakuza take to be about *seven* times higher. (For the sake of comparison, it is generally estimated that the Mafia accounts for some 2.5 percent of the U.S. GNP.)

The final figure, whatever it was, added up to tremendous economic clout.

KING OF ROPPONGI: MAFIA BOSS OF TOKYO

In this atmosphere of wealth and duplicity, the American Zappetti was right at home. By all accounts the richest foreigner in all of Tokyo, having long since supplanted Attorney Blakemore (when one included unreported income), he had opened his new restaurant in October 1964, and soon after he purchased a palatial new three-story, four-bedroom, Western-style concrete house in the same high-rent neighborhood. It came complete with sunken fireplace, grand piano, swimming pool, maid, and butler and encompassed over 10,000 square feet, not counting the driveway, which itself could accommodate up to twenty automobiles. In a city as starved for elbow room as Tokyo, that was saying something. It took seven complete lounge sets and a small fortune in expensive paintings and art objects to furnish all the other individual rooms. In short order, he also acquired a second smaller house in Roppongi as a "backup," a summer house in the historic templed suburban town of Kamakura, a seaside vacation home in nearby Zaimoku, a beachfront residence in Honolulu, a state-of-the-art yacht, and a fleet of cars that he replenished every year with the newest model Cadillac, imported at twice its Stateside list price because of import taxes and shipping charges. Not even the U.S. ambassador lived as well as he did.

Zappetti had gained his riches, he didn't mind boasting, through a combination of business skills and criminal cunning. An example of the latter came when officials from the Tokyo metropolitan government approached him about buying the land on which his first restaurant was situated in order to widen the street. They had offered to fully compensate him for all business losses he would suffer in the process of changing locations, so in the spirit of a born hustler, he hired nightclub hostesses from the area to come in and occupy all empty tables during the slack daytime hours to create the impression that his restaurant was always full. They sat there for several days in a row, doing their nails, waiting for the inspector from the highway commission to make his appearance. When he finally materialized, he was so impressed, he recommended a reimbursement of 97 million yen—more than twice what Zappetti had originally paid for the land and the building.

It may have been unethical and illegal, but, Zappetti argued, it was no worse than some of the other things that were going on around him—like the delegation of Tokyo snack bar operators who had come demanding he raise his prices. They complained that what Nicola's was charging for a small pizza was about half of what they were getting for something they called "pizza toast," which consisted of a slice of bread topped with tomato and locally made processed cheese, cooked in an oven— and was hurting their business (causing "confusion" was the term they had used, one that would be heard in the years to come whenever the Japanese government was asked to further open its markets). They wanted him to adopt their standard of ten times cost for something that was essentially a grilled cheese sandwich, which, of course, amounted to price fixing, collusion, and possibly attempted extortion. But he refused. He had his contacts on the military bases who provided him his supplies from

North America so cheaply (if illegally) that he could afford to charge reasonable prices.

Buying on the black market was, for him, more of a necessity than a luxury because the prices of imported products on the open market were prohibitively high. A can of tomato sauce bought in Japan cost five times what it did in the United States. So did a cut of pork, and a kilo of cheese. He had tried, on occasion, to import those items directly from abroad, in bulk, but there had always been some esoteric rule or law blocking him from getting the required permission. Once, for example, he had actually been told by a government official that the sauce tomatoes he wanted to import were not allowed in Japan because they had been grown in the sunshine, in violation of government regulations that permitted only hothouse tomatoes in that category of import. The economy was clearly rigged to protect those few domestic producers who had the market locked up from foreign competition that might otherwise come in and blow them away, because of the inferior quality of the homegrown product—the Japanese had only been making cheese since the nineteenth century and could not yet meet standards set by the Europeans. The needs of the consumer—the hard-working salaryman, the cash-strapped housewife—who had to pay through the nose, did not seem to matter. The consumer, after all, unlike the producer, was not a heavy political contributor.

He had also tried parallel importing—a system whereby one could claim shipments as unaccompanied baggage upon arrival in Japan. To get around the high cost of foreign whiskey—a fifth of imported Scotch cost a small fortune—he and a partner had imported 800 cases of liquor through the process, flying back and forth and signing the declaration sheets each time. It was considerably cheaper than going to the liquor store. But then someone in the Japanese government complained and the North

American supplier was ordered by Schenley, the company that controlled most of the liquor sold in the United States, not to sell in bulk to unauthorized agents anymore—meaning people like Zappetti and his partner—and that was the end of that. Thus did he return to the black market.

In time, he tried to produce his own materials, with varying degrees of success. He leased a huge plot of farmland in Hokkaido, that big, open, northernmost island, and started a dairy farm in order to make his own cheese, confident he could do a better job than any domestic producer. He purchased a herd of pedigreed cows and struck a deal with six local farmers to tend his farm while he was in Tokyo, the idea being they would clear the land, feed and milk the cows, and then make the cheese, which he would use in Nicola's pizza.

Zappetti had constructed an authentic American-style ranch house with five bedrooms and a new state-of-the-art barn and purchased an array of modern equipment, which included five ten-ton Komatsu bulldozers, a tractor, a pickup, a jeep, a snowmobile, and assorted other trucks. He even sent his farmers to bulldozer school.

Nobody had bothered to tell him that there was clay under the topsoil, which meant that it would be impossible to grow anything for the cows to eat, and that consequently Zappetti would have to *buy* all his feed. Or that sinkholes would appear as the hired hands began clearing the land—one of them swallowing up an entire bulldozer. And when his crew of farmers finally got around to making the cheese, it was all but inedible, which may or may not have had something to do with the fact that Zappetti's cows were beginning to keel over and die. A veterinarian from the local Farmers Association identified the malady by pointing to the word "neglect," in his Sanseido Japanese-English dictionary, hinting that the local farmers spent more time in the master's whiskey cabinet than they did tending to his livestock.

In the end, Zappetti was forced to shut down that operation. But a sausage factory he put up outside the city in the town of Atsugi proved less disastrous, and with the economy in overdrive, he continued to prosper. To keep up with demand, he added 3,500 square feet at his main restaurant, then 3,500 more, then put in a parking lot and a mini-sausage factory on the roof of the building in violation of a city ordinance. He hired new chefs, expanded his staff, opened more branches around the city, and built a frozen pizza plant in Yokota, with a fleet of four-ton trucks to deliver the wares.

Money was coming in faster than he could think of ways to dispose of it. He spent as much of every evening as he possibly could in the fleshpots of Akasaka and Roppongi. He boasted that he never went to sleep without a beautiful girl in his arms, sometimes two. The nightclub bartenders grew so accustomed to the concupiscent *gaijin* tycoon and his conquests that they would automatically point out the newest hostesses whenever he walked through the door.

"They called me the King of Roppongi," he would boast years later. "And that's what I was. I was the richest American in the country. I always had a knockout doll on my arm. And when I walked down the street, everyone turned to look."

Being the Mafia Boss of Tokyo provided Zappetti with other moneymaking opportunities of the type not normally discussed at meetings of the American Chamber of Commerce of Japan. Indeed, from the time Lee Mortimer's article came out, he found himself besieged by a bizarre stream of requests and business proposals. There were Americans who came in looking to peddle fake military ID cards, black market dollars, counterfeit yen bonds, stolen fur coats, and even smuggled rice—for which, incidentally, there was a strong market in Japan, given the strict price controls imposed by the LDP, which depended heavily on the rice-growing industry to stay in power. There were nightclub hostesses with "international" business secrets to sell—commodities futures prices, projected interest rate shifts, and other such data, pregnant Japanese women seeking to find departed foreign lovers, and sailors off ships parked in Yokohama Harbor with goods from the Golden Triangle for sale. There was even a retired mafia hitman who wanted to introduce cocaine to the Japanese public. Some proposals he took. Others he turned down because of the trouble or the potential danger involved. Still others he passed on to more qualified "business associates," like that of a high-ranking Latin American flyweight boxer, in Japan for an important match, who had offered Zappetti a million yen if he could arrange to "eliminate" his wife's lover—an unranked middleweight from South America who was also on the fight card. Zappetti took the latter to a certain smoke-filled Korean barbecue in the Ginza, and within two days, the middleweight was on a plane out of the country. It wasn't exactly what the flyweight had in mind, but he wasn't in a position to complain—especially since his wife had already taken up with someone else.

Being known as the Mafia Boss of Tokyo meant that Zappetti was usually surrounded by yakuza. In fact the Tosei-kai men dined at Nicola's so often that other habitués cracked that the gang's crest should be emblazoned on the front entrance next to the Nicola's logo—which now consisted of a large painting of a bulbous-nosed chef holding a stack of pizzas. It is safe to say that no other American ever saw as much of the Tokyo mobster up close as Zappetti.

The Toei Film Studios was in the process of glamorizing

yakuza in a long series of movies about the prewar and modern underworld. They starred heroic, taut-muscled figures elaborately tattooed and wearing colorful kimonos and carrying long swords (as later portrayed in the 1975 Sidney Pollack movie *Yakuza*).

However, what appeared at Nicola's every night was something else entirely. These gangsters dressed like Lee Marvin in the 1963 hit movie *The Killers*—black suit, black hat, sunglasses, crewcut, .38 in a shoulder holster. They were all in notoriously bad health, with toneless bodies and wan complexions caused by a steady morning-to-night diet of cheap sake, unfiltered cigarettes, and methamphetamines. Many of them suffered from diabetes and they talked incessantly of treatments for tooth cavities and hemorrhoids, afflictions for which medical care was denied in Japanese prison, where most of them wound up at one time or another. It was always easy to spot undercover policemen—members of the *sakurada-gumi,* or "cherry blossom gang," as the plainclothesmen were derisively called in the underworld—when they were trying to pose as mobsters. They were invariably ruddy-cheeked and looked as though they could run the mile in four minutes. (What's more, they always wanted to shake hands. Real gangsters just nodded and fixed you with a dark stare.)

Unhealthy though the modern day yakuza may have been, there was nothing wrong with their level of courage. Approximately one-third of all Tokyo gang members were walking around with self-amputated left pinkies, having atoned, as per yakuza custom, for some egregious sin. Among them was boss Machii himself. In 1963, after one of his men had flagrantly shot an important adviser to an Osaka gang with which Machii had just forged a key alliance, the TSK boss chopped off the top joint of his own little finger as penitence, performing the ceremonious amputation with a silver fruit knife. He'd had to cut the bone in two at the joint, as well as slice the flesh to get his grisly morsel, which he had then stuck in a formaldehyde jar and hand-delivered to the gang boss's home. Zappetti didn't know too many people back on Pleasant Avenue who were capable of doing that. Or taking fifty-three stitches without an anesthetic as one Shibuya gang boss had done after being slashed from ear to chin in a street fight. Or facing a man with a sword *unarmed,* as a Tosei-kai gangster named Kaneko, now minus a left hand, had done. That, according to the conventional wisdom, was the single bravest thing a yakuza could ever do. ("You see that sword glint in the light," a retired yakuza had confessed, "and you realize how easily it can open you up. It's the worst feeling in the world. If you get shot with a gun, it's over. Maybe you die instantly. But a sword . . . you just keep bleeding.")

More often than he would have liked, the *gaijin padrone* found himself involved in squabbles between the Western men who came to his restaurant and the gangsters who also patronized it. Although the soldiers of the Tosei-kai were Koreans who had suffered their share of discrimination at the hands of the Japanese and were thus not overly fond of the "pure-blooded yakuza," they shared with them a strong distaste for the *Ameko,* as Americans in the city were derogatorily referred to in demotic Japanese—because of what they perceived to be the tendency of the Yanks to walk around town as if they owned it, even though the Occupation had been over for twenty-five years.

A loud, boastful Nicola's customer named Dave, a big ex-GI who liked to preen, flex his muscles, and talk tough, was removed from his stool at the bar one afternoon at gunpoint by the aforementioned TSK captain Matsubara and escorted outside into a waiting car. Nobody knows exactly what happened next, but several hours later, Dave returned, pale and shaken, to retrieve his coat. He was never seen in Roppongi again.

Then there was the retribution exacted from a French judoist named Maurice, a casual drinking acquaintance of both Zappetti and Machii, who had made the mistake of snubbing the Tosei-kai gang boss one night. On this particular occasion, Maurice had walked into a Roppongi nightclub with the French ambassador, glanced at Machii and Zappetti sitting together in one corner, and without saying hello or even nodding, ushered his companion to a table on the other side of the room. Big foreign judoists were not very popular in Japan anyway, after a 6'7", 250-pound blond Dutchman named Anton Geesink had captured the Tokyo Olympics gold medal in the open weight division, easily defeating Akio Kaminaga and thereby shattering the myth of Japanese invincibility at the sport—causing, in turn, grown men watching on street corner television to break down in tears. Big, stuck-up foreign judoists were even less liked. Thus, a few minutes after Maurice's ill-advised entrance, the lights in the club were suddenly turned off and the Frenchman was escorted at gunpoint to a back hallway, where he was severely beaten.

When the lights came back on, Maurice reappeared, his face a bloody mess.

"Machii," Nick had cried. "What the hell is going on? Why did they do that?"

"Maurice *namaiki* [arrogant]," was Machii's reply, and he stuck his nose in the air to emphasize the point.

Zappetti was left with the task of explaining to Maurice what he had done wrong and why it was necessary for him to go and apologize, even though he was the one with the mashed-in face.

After Matsubara had come out on the wrong end of a brawl with an Australian reporter named Mike Sullivan and decided he wanted to kill him, Zappetti was forced to step in and broker a peace there, as well. Sullivan, who worked for a brief interlude at the *Stars and Stripes* during the 1960s, had been sitting in

Tom's late one night with a Japanese girl nicknamed "Crazy Emi" (she once appeared at Tom's clad only in a fur coat and her birthday suit, which she proceeded to reveal to the entire bar). In walked Matsubara, not entirely sober and looking for trouble. He approached Sullivan's table and invited Crazy Emi to dance. When she refused, he became belligerent.

He said a few choice words about arrogant *Ameko,* although Sullivan was from Down Under, and the two began exchanging punches, knocking over tables and chairs, snarling and shouting insults at one another—Matsubara yelling, "*Kono yaro*" ("You SOB"), and Sullivan repeatedly shouting, "*Saru no chimpira*" ("You punk gangster ape"). The brawl lasted fifteen minutes. As befitting a high-ranking captain in the TSK, the shorter Matsubara struggled mightily to hold his own, until finally Crazy Emi picked up a beer mug and smashed him over the head, making a big gash in his scalp and sending blood streaming down his forehead into his eyes. The police arrived to restore order, but the fight was far from over, as Sullivan would discover.

That a TSK captain had lost a fight was bad enough. That he had lost to a big white *gaijin* and that the big white *gaijin*'s Japanese girlfriend had contributed to Matsubara's injuries only made the humiliation worse. The word went out that Sullivan's days were numbered.

According to Zappetti, Sullivan then turned to him for help.

"You're the Mafia boss of Tokyo," the Australian reportedly said. "Can't you do anything?"

Zappetti held a meeting with Machii and Matsubara, which consisted mostly of him "kissing ass," as he put it. Finally, a deal was struck in which Sullivan's life would be spared. But there would have to be one more meeting with Sullivan at Tom's, where Sullivan would be expected to apologize.

On the appointed night, Sullivan duly made his appearance before a group of men waiting for him in the downstairs area.

As one of the men extended his hand in a feigned peace offering, two others suddenly pounced and held his arms. A man
behind Sullivan picked up a chair and crashed it over Sullivan's
head, making a large gash in his scalp. A fourth man hit him in
the face, breaking his nose.

Thus was Sullivan's "apology" accepted.

The Tokyo Metropolitan Police Department had made Zappetti
number one on their "*Gaijin* Enemies List," to use their term,
but they could never catch him at anything. Police officers had
arrested him several times throughout the 1960s on suspicion of
black marketeering. Raids on his palatial home produced, on different occasions, 30-30 shotguns, freezers, cases of brandy, and
other booty. But Zappetti was always able to come up with documents to show that the goods in question belonged to someone
else, not him, and the police had to release him.

The police knew that Zappetti frequently traveled to New
York, where he always paid his respects to the neighborhood
dons—which caught the attention of local authorities and the
Federal Bureau of Investigation and caused them in turn to send
queries to the Tokyo police about Mafia activities in Japan. After
Zappetti and a cousin from New York had been surveilled by an
FBI stakeout team in Fort Lauderdale in the company of a group
of anti-Castroite Cubans in the market for guns, the Bureau even
dispatched an agent to Tokyo to investigate and peruse Zappetti's
considerable MPD file in some detail. (Under questioning, Zappetti insisted, somewhat flippantly, that he and the Cubans had
not been talking about "pieces," as had initially been reported
by the Bureau, but "pizzas.")

On top of all that was the strong suspicion that in 1969 Zappetti had somehow been involved in the disappearance of a Por-
tugese-Japanese businessman from Macao who had bilked him

out of some money, but again, there was not enough evidence to file charges. The seeming ease with which Zappetti avoided prosecution was also further evidence to the Tokyo police that the American was indeed a Mafia boss. And they continued to believe it for years after.

Zappetti did nothing to discourage that belief. In fact, he had let it be known on the sly that he had ordered the killing of the missing Macaon—to show his power and to demonstrate that no one could cross him. He said that he had had the businessman tracked down in Manila, and through a contact at the Philippine Embassy had hired a gunman to do the shooting. It only cost him sixty dollars, he bragged in hushed tones, plus a finder's fee. (The victim's brother had even come to Zappetti and begged him not to seek further retribution from anyone else in the family.)

There was no proof that any of this was true. And close friends of Zappetti suspected that someone else had been responsible for the deed and that Zappetti had made his involvement up just to enhance his image, just as he encouraged people to believe he was a "made guy," even though he wasn't. (Japan seemed to bring out that trait in more than a few foreigners.)

Zappetti confessed to a friend that being known as the Mafia Boss of Tokyo was the highest honor a man like himself could aspire to. That the center of the new Tokyo should have provided fertile soil for his peculiar brand of the American dream says as much about the postwar relationship between the two countries as any economic or political history written on the subject.

LEGITIMATE SUBTERFUGE

Not every foreign businessman had special access to the Tokyo underground economy. There were approximately 2,600 members of the American Chamber of Commerce in Japan, and most of them could be heard grumbling in their beer about how hard it was to grab, legitimately, even a tiny share of the booming Japanese market. There were all sorts of roadblocks—tariffs, restrictions, bureaucratic regulations (one needed, for example, twenty-four separate licenses to sell meat or fish and had to pass a national examination just to open a laundry business)—and a complex nationwide distribution system in which products had to move through a series of warehouses, decreasing in size from large to medium to small and then smaller, before they reached the consumer, which dramatically increased the final sales price. With some 400,000 wholesalers and 2,400,000 retailers intertwined in a lattice of long-standing professional and social relationships, it was easy for the foreign product to get lost in the shuffle. Commercial lawyer Tom Blakemore knew of a case where one Japanese trading company sold two competing products—one Japanese and one U.S.—without revealing that fact to the American client with whom it had an exclusivity contract. It wasn't the only instance of a distributor in Japan handling competing products.

Coca-Cola had succeeded in the country only by setting up its own dealerships in order to circumvent the distribution system. The U.S. monolith joined forces with the powerful regional bottlers in Japan—the Daimyo bottlers, as they were known—offering a healthy percentage of sales to their distribution outlets as well as classy new shop signs. "We'll put your name on top of the sign," they said, "but underneath it, there has got to be 'Coca-Cola.'" They also set up a nationwide chain of their own *talking* vending machines, introduced a sweeter-tasting formula designed to suit the Japanese palate, and conducted a massive ongoing marketing campaign, which turned *Koku* into a household word. But few companies had Coke's unlimited resources.

One reason Americans found themselves in such a disadvantageous situation was the largely unspoken cold war arrangement the United States had made with Japan in the post-occupation era, whereby Japan would become the United States's main anti-Communist ally in Asia and in return Japan would get unconditional access to America's rich markets, along with the privilege of keeping her industries at home protected from foreign competition. To American businesses that wanted access to Japan, the U.S. State Department had essentially said, "Tough luck. Don't interfere with Japan's economic growth. Let them have their 100 percent tariffs on imports and sell them technology instead. We need a strong Japan for security reasons."

Because of this arrangement, IBM had been obliged to license its patents to competing Japanese firms at the very low royalty of 5 percent in order to get permission to manufacture in Japan; not surprisingly, Fujitsu and NEC were eventually able to surpass Big Blue in the computer sales market.

Imaginative attempts to bypass this system often backfired, as the American who parallel-imported whiskey via Hong Kong and was thrown in a Tokyo jail for his efforts. So did the man parallel-exporting TransAm sports cars to Japan, selling them at half the going sales price there. The exclusive TransAm agent in Tokyo complained to Pontiac, who in turn notified the Stateside dealer in question not to sell to the unauthorized Americans anymore.

Foreign companies also had to battle the perception among the masses that their presence was somehow harmful to Japanese society, that American executives were, in general, up to no good, an attitude reflected in the 1969 B-movie *Blood Toast*, which portrayed the American businessmen as the modern-day equivalent of the invading Occupation forces. *Blood Toast* starred retired Shibuya gangster Noboru Ando, a one-time mortal enemy of the Tosei-kai, whose face still bore the scars from the fifty-three-stitch knife wound he had received at the hands of a TSK foot soldier in the Ginza. After serving a six-year prison term, Ando had launched a film career in 1965, becoming known as the "George Raft of Japan." In *Toast*'s opening scene, set in the immediate postwar era, a frail shoeshine boy in the streets of Tokyo asks a passing U.S. soldier for some gum. The GI, (played by a blond German with a thick English accent) shouts an insult—"You stupid little idiot." The boy is infuriated. He chases the soldier and bites his hand, whereupon the GI, who is built like an Olympic weight lifter, knocks the boy to the ground. He climbs astride him, removes his gum from his mouth and begins to force the boy's jaws open. "You want chewing gum?" he snarls. "I'll give you chewing gum."

As he stuffs the wad of Doublemint down the boy's throat, the pint-sized Ando comes along to save the day. He pulls the boy's tormentor off and delivers several sharp punches to the face. The sergeant collapses in a heap. Later, Ando takes the grateful boy for a walk in the country; they sit by a river and the boy starts singing, in English, "You Are My Sunshine." Ando angrily rebukes him; he orders the boy to sing a Japanese song instead, and the boy dutifully complies.

In the second reel, set over twenty years later, a greasy-looking, shifty-eyed American businessman visits Tokyo and attempts to buy controlling interest in the stock of a company owned by one of Ando's friends. The friend turns to Ando for help. Ando pays a surprise visit to the businessman's room, where the unscrupulous American is busy sexually molesting a hotel masseuse. Ando pulls out his gun and comes to the rescue once more.

"You speak Nihongo?" he growls in stilted English, waving his pistol.

"No," says the man, quaking with fear.

"Japan small company," says Ando. "America big company. You go home."

"Y-y-y-y-y-es," says the American, cowering on his bed.

Heading for the door, Ando turns for one last admonishment.

"And when you come to Japan, learn to speak Japanese."

At the time the movie was made, one must remember, Japan already had the world's second largest economy.

For some American companies in Japan, success came ridiculously easy. Encyclopaedia Britannica made a killing in the 1960s and early 1970s selling English encyclopedias to education-conscious parents who believed that owning a set of such exalted English books would somehow help their children get into good universities—regardless of whether anyone in the family could read them or not. One Britannica salesman, arrested for late-night harassment of a recalcitrant customer, sold two sets of the $800 encyclopedias to jailhouse guards during his seventy-two hours of incarceration—a feat that helped him win the Salesman of the Month award.

But the Britannicas were the exception. In all, it took a certain mind-set to make it in Japan that not everyone had—a certain single-minded dedication and a willingness to undertake guerrilla warfare if necessary. Consider the case of one Ed Ransburg. Ransburg owned an Indianapolis-based company, Ransburg Electrostatic Painting; he had perfected and patented a spray paint gun, using an electrostatic process that caused the paint to wrap itself around an object and adhere to it. Ransburg had invented the process in 1942 and had been selling it to American manufacturers of cars, washing machines, and refrigerators. His company charged royalties on the basis of the percentage of the cost of paint saved: 10 percent for a large flat panel, and 30 percent for a round tubular object.

In the late 1950s, when it became possible for foreign companies to do so, Ransburg filed for a patent in Japan. He discovered, however, that many Japanese plants were already using his process, among them Matsushita Electric, Sanyo, and Hitachi. Those firms had sent representatives to the United States to see the painting process, they had taken samples of the equipment back to Japan, they'd broken it down, copied it, and began using it, without paying royalties. By Ransburg's count, there were 400 companies using his process without permission.

He went to see several of the larger firms and asked them to pay. All of them refused and even joined forces to form something called the Household Equipment Manufacturers Association to fight off potential lawsuits. So next the American went to the Ministry of International Trade and Industry. He asked officials there to order the Japanese manufacturers involved to pay a 30 percent royalty—standard in such cases. The MITI men rebuffed him as well. Japan needed to foster as much domestic growth as possible, they explained, and to avoid marketplace "confusion"—a term Japanese government officials were using increasingly more often to justify to their American counterparts what amounted to price fixing and market share allotment. MITI would only consider a figure of 5 percent.

Ransburg was furious. He engaged the services of attorney James Adachi, a Japanese-American from Wyoming who was one of a select group of foreigners granted special permission to practice in Japan. The first thing Adachi did was to talk him out of suing.

"You can't bang Japanese over the head," he said. "You need a more subtle approach. You can't hit a Japanese curveball with a big American-style swing."

Adachi looked around for a Japanese company that might be persuaded to form a partnership with Ransburg, and his eyes fell on a promising young motorcycle manufacturer named Honda, which had been using the Ransburg process to paint its bike fenders and tanks. Adachi paid the management a friendly visit and explained the situation. He appealed to their sense of fair play (something that many American critics of trade with Japan maintained did not exist) and suggested that some kind of joint venture with the American firm would prove beneficial to Honda's plans for expansion to the United States (and, it went without saying, would avoid possible lawsuits in *American* courts over sales of their vehicles in that country).

After giving the matter some thought, Honda agreed that they had an obligation to the American manufacturer. They agreed that paying a 30 percent royalty was only fair, given the circumstances and said they would be happy to do so.

Legally, however, MITI's permission was necessary for Honda to make the payments and Ransburg to receive them. Without it, nothing could be done, and Adachi doubted that that permission would be granted, given the powerful ministry's well known arrogance and intransigence in regard to matters of international trade. Adachi had to develop yet another scheme to deal with that problem, as well.

If a Japanese judge issued a ruling that Honda had to pay Ransburg, Adachi reasoned, then MITI would have no choice but to accept it. Thus, with Honda's consent, Adachi filed a pre-arranged suit against the bike maker on Ransburg's behalf, a suit that Honda, as privately agreed upon, did not contest in court. Instead, the two parties entered into a judicial compromise whereby Honda agreed to pay damages deemed appropriate by the judge hearing the case.

That set up phase 3 of the Adachi plan.

Since there were strict foreign exchange rules in effect at the time in regard to paying dollars and sending money out of the country, Adachi had to establish a Tokyo branch of the Ransburg

Co., as required by law, in order to receive money from Honda in yen and then file for permission from the Ministry of Finance for Ransburg Japan to legally accept said funds.

The Finance Ministry was as powerful and entrenched an institution in its own right as MITI. In fact, MOF and MITI often clashed in setting government policy, much to the consternation of the political leaders frequently caught in the middle. When MOF officials examined the court ruling and granted approval, having no real reason not to, MITI was forced to accede to Ransburg's wishes. In the face of dual opposition from its powerful rival MOF, as well as the Japanese courts, the ministry decided discretion to be the better part of valor.

The members of the Household Equipment Manufacturers Association, publicly shamed by press reports of Honda's magnanimity toward Ransburg, now suddenly began to experience pangs of guilt. One by one, they agreed they should pay royalties, too. Soon, everyone had fallen in line, and Ransburg was in business.

He bought land in Eastern Tokyo, where he put up an office building and opened testing facilities and an assembly plant. He formed a joint venture with a Japanese manufacturer of shock absorbers, brake drums, and auto parts and used that company to gain an introduction into the market, forming in the process the all-important *jimmyaku* (connections), with Japanese auto manufacturers. All this at a time when the nascent Japanese auto market was supposedly tightly sealed.

In time, the automotive companies became major users of the Ransburg paint spray system, and Ransburg dominated the industry until his death in 1991—a time when robots were using his spray paint and paint guns. Even after the patents had expired in fifteen years and they were not required to pay royalties anymore, Ransburg's customers remained loyal (including Toyota, which had its own paint department, developed through

Ransburg technology after a competing company they had owned was put out of business by Ransburg's patent case; they stayed with him when legally they did not have to).

Adachi liked to tell that story as an example of Japanese fairness and to refute those who claimed Japan was a totally closed country. To others it meant something else.

Thomas Blakemore, the doyen of the foreign commercial legal community, had a client list that read like a Who's Who of American industry. But even he was basically a skeptic about foreigners in business in Japan because of all the problems. There were just too many areas of the economy the Japanese had locked up, he would tell prospective clients, and they were not about to let foreigners in. He had his own story to tell to illustrate the difficulties of penetrating the Japanese market for potential new investors who came to him for advice: the tale of the Yozawa River Project and his efforts to introduce fly-casting to the Japanese.

Blakemore had been an avid outdoorsman back in his home state of Oklahoma, and sometime during the mid-1950s had fallen in love with a several-mile stretch of the Yozawa River, about an hour's train ride west of Tokyo and set in a valley among beautiful trees and alpine hamlets.

The only problem with the river was that there were no fish in it, only minnows and fingerlings. Blakemore, a devoted trout fisherman, sought out one of the local village heads and suggested the idea of stocking the river with startup trout and establishing a fly-casting operation. He offered to bear all the expenses himself, and later, when it was all up and rolling, the village could charge admission fees and keep the profits. By this time, Blakemore was already a very wealthy person and, being civic-minded, wanted nothing more for himself than the opportunity to use the stream.

The village head thought Blakemore was out of his mind. Japan was a nation that subsisted on fish. No one in the country had ever heard of fly-casting before.

"You catch a fish with a fly, not a worm, and throw it back?" the man asked skeptically.

"Yes," said Blakemore.

"And you have to pay for it?"

"That's right," said Blakemore in his Oklahoma-accented Japanese. "It's sport."

The man walked away scratching his head, muttering that this strange foreigner's suggestion was the craziest idea he had ever heard of.

Blakemore talked to a few other people in the area about the idea and they thought he was nuts, too. Who wanted to catch a fish he couldn't take home?

Blakemore went to the National Fish and Game Commission, whose officials had never heard of fly-casting either. He pored over National Fish and Game laws, which offered no help either. So he began a laborious process of persuasion and negotiation with the various villages located along the five-to-six-mile stretch of stream he had had his eyes on.

To get them all together in one group, he arranged for the Daiei Motion Picture Company to show, at his expense, their latest samurai sword-slashing thriller at a local schoolhouse. It required bringing in a generator by truck for the special show.

Knowing how valued the word of a *sensei*, or teacher, could be in such a status-conscious country as Japan, Blakemore had prevailed upon a Japanese diplomat he knew who had been fly-casting with him overseas to explain the sport to the audience. He also recruited a noted Japanese fishing writer who was in favor of the project to follow with a speech of his own.

The movie was well received. There was lots of blood and one good rape scene. But it was all downhill after that. The audience listened to the diplomat describe the joys of fly-casting and to the writer explain the technique. Then Blakemore got up to give his spiel. He related how the operation would be set up, that he would assume all financial responsibility for stocking the stream (making full use, he emphasized, of existing dams and a couple of natural breaks in the stream of water), and that a fee would be charged to fly-fish. Although in principle, only fly-casting would be allowed, as a special concession to the Japanese village, each person would be permitted to take home one or two fish: the rest, they would have to throw back. All profits would accrue to the villagers until the fish-for-pay enterprise was self-sustaining. At that point, they would take over paying the expenses from Blakemore.

The crowd was skeptical, to say the least. There was immediate opposition from many villagers who feared an invasion of fly-casters from outside. Younger people wondered where they would do their swimming. Women pointed out that Tachikawa and Fuchu U.S. Air Force bases were nearby. GIs there were always causing trouble, brawling, raping, and whatnot. What if they started coming around? More than one person thought the whole idea smelled of a scam. What was this foreigner up to?

Said Blakemore, "It was like I had dropped out of Mars with this proposal."

There were other problems. No one person or group was really in a position to control fishing in the stream. There was no one to issue the right to start the operation. There was no satisfactory answer as to who owned the fifteen-mile-stretch of stream because the question had never been asked before. There was no local government organ that covered fishing there because nobody had ever fished there before.

As it turned out, there was, oddly enough, a local Fishing Society, even though there were no fish in the river. But the society, Blakemore was told, never went fishing. It existed for the sole purpose of a sake bust once or twice a year. Nevertheless, Blakemore tried his luck there. He visited the Fishing Society and proposed giving them 10 percent of the gross receipts if they would confer the right of use of one section of the stream—even though they in fact had no authority to grant such rights. The board of the Society readily agreed, and finally the ball got rolling.

An association with no controlling legal authority gave permission it had no right to give in return for money it had no right to take.

Ultimately, the elements began to come together.

The five hamlets along the stream each designated a representative to form a governing body to run the new Fly-Casting Enterprise. However, Blakemore kept having to agree to pay additional costs: wages for a ticket seller, a salary for a night watchman and security guard, reimbursement to village youth for unloading a weekly stock of fish brought in by truck. He also had to agree to sponsor an annual Fishing Festival when the May–September fishing season was over, in which fishing prizes would be awarded—all bought and paid for, of course, by Tom Blakemore. Blakemore submitted a list of prizes but the villagers adjudged it to be too short, since it was regarded as inconsiderate not to have something for everyone. Thus, the list grew to include additional awards in such esoteric categories as the oldest woman to catch a fish and another for the best blindfolded fisherman, until there were enough to go around for all.

Finally, Blakemore had to donate toilets, build a new ticket office, and, to make sure the funds were being handled properly, hire a certified public accounting firm to come out to audit the books—with copies of the audit certificates being sent to each hamlet.

In the end, Blakemore gave up trying to keep track of how

much it cost him. He kept at it, if only to prove it could actually be done.

It took several years, but the Yozawa River operation became a success. By the end of the 1960s, Blakemore had become something of a local celebrity and was even given a special award from the prime minister's office for "helping to combat juvenile delinquency."

As it turned out, there were so many GIs patronizing his fishing pond that the twin evils of crime and public mayhem in the Tachikawa and Fuchu areas had declined dramatically. (And so, he was told at the award ceremony, had the VD rate. Said a sergeant from the Tachikawa Air Force Base who had attended the function, "Mr. Blakemore, thanks to you our GIs have a chance to catch fish instead of VD.")

To Blakemore, the moral of the story was clear. "If you have to go through all that trouble just to give something away," he would say to his new clients after telling them the tale, "you can imagine how hard it must be to sell something in Japan."

It was yet another lesson not being taught at Harvard Business School.

5.   MISS HOKKAIDO

There are those who came to Japan to immerse themselves in the culture and to find out what it was that made the Japanese tick. For these people the attractions were artistic and metaphysical in nature. They were drawn to the grace and dignity of Japanese calligraphy, the subtle beauty of a Japanese garden, the Zen suggestibility of Japanese art where empty spaces are just as important as the lines, and the inner harmony of Buddhist enlightenment attainable through meditation, among other such mystical enticements. Exposure to them was all the reward they sought in coming to Japan.

But the people of Nick Zappetti's world were a different breed altogether. Few individuals in that dissolute cast of characters had even seen a Kabuki drama or sat through a tea ceremony. They had zero interest in elevated states of self-awareness and suffered no treacly yearnings whatsoever to comprehend the subtleties of *wa* (harmony). The thinking of people like the American Buddhist priest in Kyoto, a shaven-headed six-footer from Nebraska in orange robes, who talked of a "destiny that was decided 10,000 years ago," was as incomprehensible to them as the books on *netsuke* authored by Tokyo attorney Raymond Bushell, who was assembling one of the world's most formidable collections of the tiny figurines. Zappetti's own appreciation of Japanese aesthetics ran to Copa hostesses who could satisfy him sexually with their toes while soaking with him in a hot bath or eat their fried eggs in the morning with chopsticks; to him, those were extraordinary acts of virtuosity—as were those of the nude performers in the live Shimbashi sex shows he occasionally attended, who somehow managed to keep their genitalia hidden from public view through the entire "show." Now *that*, he liked to say, was Oriental art.

What Nick essentially wanted from Japan was what most other foreign men in Japan wanted, if the truth be told: to make money and bed women. And of course, in his case, have people point as he walked down the street and say, "There goes Mr. Nicolas, the King of Roppongi," or "That's the Mafia Boss of Tokyo." It was attention of the type he would never get back in East Harlem. Historically, he had far more in common with the Dutch seamen on the trading ships that came to Japan in the sixteenth century than the missionaries, teachers, traders, technocrats, and students who came later.

In its own perverse way, his lifestyle was a singularly success-ful adaptation to life in a country that was as radically different from the United States as was his adopted homeland. Because of his simple straightforward priorities, he would never experience the disillusionment of those who searched for the soul of the Real Japan, only to find it had disappeared in the growing morass of pachinko shops, vending machines, fast-food stands, "pink sa-lons," and other icons of contemporary Japanese culture. Nor would he ever endure the bitter frustration of those who dis-covered that *gaijin* always meant outsider, no matter how hard they tried to assimilate. Zappetti simply didn't care.

A further irony of his situation was that he would spend nearly his entire adult life in Japan without any formal training in the language or in doing business there, yet still he would fare better in the Japanese marketplace than other supposedly "more qual-ified" individuals, including senior corporate go-getters and Ivy League MBAs. *His* success was based on raw intelligence, sheer energy, and an instinctive understanding of the way people really did business—not to mention a willingness to break the law.

He would suffer his share of setbacks, including one of mon-umental proportions—a takeover that would go down in Rop-pongi history. What caused his problems, however, was less his disdain for domestic customs or his peculiarly American way of thinking that Japanese (along with everyone else) should strive to emulate the United States in all things, but rather other more universal flaws like greed, arrogance . . . and lust.

He was married four times—thought to be a record in the an-nals of American-Japanese matrimony, and that would not prove helpful. Like thousands and thousands of other Western men who had been taken in perhaps by images of the submissive, docile female geisha doll as portrayed in movies like *Sayonara* and wed Japanese females, he found the reality of marital life not quite as advertised (as did, perhaps, the Japanese wives involved in such unions, who for their part had been equally deluded by the courtesy and gallantry American men showed during courtship, seeing in these foreign males liberation from the traditional bonds of female servitude that had been their lot).

Zappetti had married his first wife because she spoke fluent English, and because she was a practicing Catholic (one of the very few Christians in the country).

But there had been conflict almost from the beginning. His wife had been especially angered at the suggestion made by an Army officer, in one of several prenuptial interviews required by the U.S. government, that her sole motivation for marrying an American was a desire to live in the United States and escape the poverty of Japan. Because of that, she decided she would *never* go there. And not once, in all the years that followed, did she ever set foot on U.S. soil—not after both she and her husband had accumulated considerable wealth, not even after she had divorced him and reestablished her dental practice, which she had temporarily abandoned for the life of a housewife. She would travel all over the world, to Europe, to Southeast Asia, to Australia, but there was one country she steadfastly avoided. She would not even enter an American military club.

Of course, more troubling for her was her husband's view of matrimony, which allowed him to adopt the male Japanese custom of taking mistresses, which, in addition to his criminal tendencies, was what prompted her to file for divorce. In June 1957, she was awarded custody of their two children, along with the house in the suburbs and monthly support. It was an arrangement the children liked just fine because, they had let it be known, the fewer the people who knew about the foreign blood coursing through their veins the better. His eldest son, Vincent, fluent in both English and Japanese, had had his fill of being teased in school by his classmates. But then Zappetti discovered that his ex-wife had found herself a Japanese boyfriend and

alarm bells went off. He was sure he knew what would happen
if his wife married this man and had another child. A pure-
blooded Japanese child in a house with two half-breeds was, in
his opinion, a certain recipe for disaster, for it was not difficult
to guess where the next husband's affections would lie. So he took
the matter to the *katei saiban* (family court), where the presid-
ing judge—a holdover from the earlier divorce proceedings
named Kondo and a man who had become a regular customer at
Nicola's—awarded Zappetti custody.

Zappetti's next stab at domesticity came in December 1964,
when he married his cash register girl—a petite, determined,
and ambitious young woman named Yae Koizumi, the orphaned
daughter of an old family in rural Maebashi. He had hired her
when he opened for business because she had spoken the best
English of the half-dozen girls he had interviewed from the
labor office and because she had had the most poise as well. Although romance had somehow blossomed amid all the carnal
distractions of the city, Zappetti's second marriage, to the surprise of absolutely no one who knew him, did little to change his
lifestyle. He left his bride behind the register and continued his
nightly sexual prowling, his lone concession to matrimony the
renting of a room at Riki Apartments for his liaisons with assorted young women.

Once a very agitated young lady came into the restaurant, approached the second Mrs. Zappetti, and announced, "I'm pregnant and your husband is the one responsible."

"What are you talking to me for then," the new wife replied
with studied indifference and the learned forbearance of many
a Japanese woman. "I didn't get you pregnant. He did. Take your
problem to him."

To some observers, it seemed that Nick's second wife viewed
the marriage as more of a business opportunity than anything
else. Their union produced no children and she devoted herself

to running the restaurant and helping to oversee the empire of Nicola's enterprises. If business *was* her main interest, however, her choice was understandable, given the strictures of the limited options available to women in the Japanese marketplace.

Despite the prevailing (and generally overdrawn) picture of a Japanese female as a domestic slave, it was and is the wife who controls the family purse strings, who takes the husband's entire monthly paycheck and doles out an allowance, and who runs domestic affairs to such an extent that the bank and other sales organizations solicit *her* for business, not the husband. In the workplace, however, there was still much discrimination, especially on a corporate level.

Most women who had full-time jobs in respected corporations were expected to spend their days making tea and otherwise serving Japan's corporate samurai—before resigning at a reasonably young age, so they could get down to the serious business of child rearing and running a household. The American term "career woman," directly transliterated into Japanese, has only recently gained a purchase in the language.

Despite the great reforms of the postwar era—two out of every three women in modern postwar Japan worked at least part-time—Japan did not have an equal opportunity law until 1986, and even then it had little in the way of teeth. (As the century drew to a close, less than 3 percent of all management positions were held by women.)

Thus did many career-seeking Japanese females, looking for a place to demonstrate their capabilities, turn to foreign companies (not high on the list of desired places for Japanese male workers, whose pecking order started with the Ministry of Finance, MITI, the Bank of Japan, Mitsui, and Mitsubishi). And thus did the second Mrs. Zappetti use Nicola's as an outlet for her own career energies (and, as it turned out, the job offered almost unlimited opportunities for advancement—in family court, if nowhere else.)

Perhaps if Zappetti had somehow managed to stay married to Yae, his business affairs might have been far less tumultuous. But that would have been asking too much, especially after his encounter with a nineteen-year-old beauty pageant queen from Hokkaido.

Her name was Miyoko, and Nick had met her one day in 1968, on his way to his Hokkaido ranch, where he was now busy setting up a mink farm. It had been a warm spring afternoon in 1968, he was strolling down one of Sapporo's distinctive wide thoroughfares, and suddenly there she was, right beside him, one of the most devastatingly beautiful women he had ever seen. It was the summer of love, of long stringy hair and beads, of social protest and antiwar demonstrations, but Miyoko was a glamorous throwback to another era. In her tight black dress, thick makeup, and permed hair, she looked like she belonged on a Toho Movie Studios calendar.

Nick immediately said hello and Miyoko smiled in return. They walked together down the street, exchanging pleasantries, until they reached the train station, where she handed him her card, flashing him another smile, and went on her way. Several days later, after preliminary research in which he learned she had recently won a major Hokkaido beauty contest and still lived with her mother, he was sitting down with her over lunch at the Sapporo Royal Hotel, the leading Western-style hotel in the city. Before she was even finished with her soup, he had proposed marriage.

Nick had long been complaining to friends about wife number two, grumbling that she was more interested in the family business than in him. At age forty-five, he still cut an impressive figure. He was in reasonably good shape, always impeccably dressed, and had a smattering of gray in his short cropped hair that lent him a certain air of distinction. With his wealth, he viewed himself an ideal catch for any girl and had begun thinking that perhaps it was time yet again to make some changes.

He told his new inamorata he was known as the King of Roppongi and that he was the richest *gaijin* in all of Japan. He owned seven or eight companies, he said, a slew of restaurants and houses all over the place. He had limos, yachts, sports cars. He couldn't keep track of it all. He would share it with her, he said, if she would accompany him to a room he had booked and took what he called in Japanese the *Ii Ojosan Tesuto* (Nice Girl Test)—meaning the test to determine if she was still a virgin. He was Italian, he explained, and Italians only married virgins. It was a religious thing. Dating back centuries.

The outrageousness of what he proposed gave him not the slightest pause. His demands were no different to his mind than someone like Aristotle Onassis or Howard Hughes or Prince Charles might make. To such people the normal rules didn't apply. And he was in the same class, of that he was convinced.

History does not record how the *Ojosan* exchange ended. However, on June 25, 1968, Zappetti formally divorced Yae in Tokyo Family Court—in the presence of his old friend Judge Kondo—and on July 16 he married Miyoko in Sapporo.

The divorce settlement was a hint of things to come. The court awarded Yae the Yokota operation, along with one of Zappetti's smaller houses and 50 million yen in cash. The settlement made Yae a very wealthy woman. And she would become even wealthier in the years to come, as Japan's booming economy and real estate market added more zeros to the value of her land holdings—many, many, many more zeros. Given the going rate for the Fujisawa property, of which his first ex-wife was the proud owner, Nick imagined that he was now in a class all by himself where divorced *gaijin* men in Japan were concerned. Both his former wives were rich and getting richer by the day.

At first, despite the high cost of his freedom, Zappetti had been overjoyed with his young prize, whom he bragged about to his round table of friends in Roppongi. He had set up house-keeping with her in a two-story wooden traditional Japanese-style house in Sapporo so that Miyoko could be near her mother, with Nick spending weekdays in Tokyo, and he was boundless in his munificence. He gave his bride 1,750,000 yen each month for daily expenses (enough cash to last an ordinary Japanese house-wife two years) and lavished her with gifts—a new car, a mink coat, a sapphire ring. When she decided she wanted to wear noth-ing but white suits, in tribute to the all-female Takarazuka danc-ing revue of which she was a great fan, he bought her a complete new wardrobe: white pants, white shirts, white hats. When she said she wanted to open her own nightclub in Sapporo, he said, "Sure, no problem," and went out to look for the best site. He took to calling her Cinderella, because that's what she was: *Shin-dorera*. She had more going for her, he'd tell her, than any two dozen Sapporo girls combined.

But, trouble was inevitable. Miyoko was outgoing, adventur-ous, even "flirtatious," as more than one acquaintance described her. And Nick was the jealous type—extremely jealous. More-over, the fact that the unwelcome specter of middle age was mak-ing its presence known and preventing him from performing in a manner he would have liked only made things worse.

When the reports started coming in from friends in Sapporo that she was seen in the company of other men, among them her fortune-teller, and a popular singer, and that she was whiling away some of her free time in the evening at "host clubs," Nick went ballistic—although Miyoko denied doing anything wrong. To him, it was humiliating.

Host clubs were the latest phenomenon in Japan's profligate nightlife. They were institutions in which suavely groomed young men with impeccable manners and smooth conversational skills catered to mainly rich, bored middle-aged wives with absentee workaholic husbands. Male hosts served their customers drinks, danced with them, and, after closing hours, provided other services—if the tip was generous enough.

That was how his wife, possibly the most beautiful girl in Japan, had been whiling away her free time. A great deal of her free time, if what his friends said was true. He simply could not understand it. She was such a good-looking girl and still she paid men to cater to her. What was the appeal?

On impulse, he decided to go see for himself. With the name and address of one of Miyoko's "boyfriends" supplied by the manager of the Sapporo Royal, Nick made an unannounced visit to the man's residence—a modest but typical box-sized Japanese apartment not all that different from the type of accomodation most nightclub hostesses lived in.

The young man who opened the door was tall and thin with a wavy pompadour—good-looking, Nick had to admit, but in a creepy, pouty, narcissistic sort of way. Nick introduced himself and without hesitation asked the youth, who was in the process of putting on a tuxedo for the evening's work, point-blank, whether he had slept with Miyoko.

"I don't know," he replied matter-of-factly, not in the least ruffled. "Maybe."

"Maybe?" Nick repeated. "I ask you if you sleep with my wife and maybe is all you have to say?"

The man shrugged.

"I can't keep track of everyone," he said, affixing his bow tie. "Women pay me. I flatter some. I make love to others. That's that. It's business. Not personal."

Nick had to admit he admired the man's candor. And he was

not immediately sure how to proceed from there. How could Nick blame the poor guy just for doing his job?

In a way, he could even begin to understand his wife's feelings. A woman needed companionship, and Nick wasn't there much of the time. Even when he was . . . well.

On the other hand, what if word got around about what was "maybe" going on? The whole circumstance left him furious.

Thus, he wound up and slugged the carefully coiffed young man, knocking him out cold.

Eventually Nick moved Miyoko to Tokyo, where he could keep an eye on her.

With his son Vince having left home, it would be the two of them and his daughter Patti, now in her early twenties, plus the maid and the butler. But Miyoko would be under virtual house arrest, unable to go anywhere without permission and without being transported there and back by Nick's chauffeur, who also doubled as a watchdog. If she wanted a friend, then Patti would have to do.

It didn't take Miyoko long to violate the terms of her parole and, predictably, she moved back to Sapporo. In 1972, she filed for a divorce, and demanded 30 million yen in alimony.

THE TAKEOVER

Zappetti's initial decision to marry Miyoko had caused him more trouble than he had ever imagined, for in addition to all the emotional turmoil that ensued, it almost led to his financial ruin and, in the process, taught him some painful new lessons about business in Japan.

To begin with, after Nick had turned over to Yae the assets designated by the Family Court, the National Tax Office sent him a bill for the very large sum of 65 million yen—a tax on the transfer of property to Yae in the divorce settlement. When Nick protested that the transfer had not been a voluntary sale but rather one ordered by the court, the tax authorities replied that it made no difference under the law. Technically, as far as they were concerned, he had transferred property and received something in exchange for it—namely, his freedom—which in their estimation was taxable to the amount of 65 million yen—a sum they would be willing to reduce to 23 million yen if he paid it all immediately.

The 23 million yen was not an enormous sum of money, but Nick was painfully embarrassed to admit he didn't have the cash. He had lost over 200 million yen on a mink farm venture that everyone he knew had advised him not to undertake. Determined to get some use out of the land and equipment he had gone to such lengths to acquire, he had decided to raise mink in his barn, build a fur factory that processed the fur skins into coats, and sell them in Japan, despite objections from those who believed that introducing a new brand in a country that was rapidly becoming status conscious, and without connections to department store managers who sold most of the fur coats in Japan to boot, was far too risky.

Boasting that he was going to break the "the stranglehold the Norwegian Jews had on the world market," Zappetti then proceeded to lose over a million dollars in record time. Japanese buyers, who were indeed rapidly becoming increasingly status conscious, wanted little to do with an unknown label regardless of how high the quality of his garments was. (When Zappetti, desperate to make a sale, cut his prices to a third of the going rate, buyers took it all as evidence that the quality of his coats had deteriorated and paid even less attention.)

He had followed the mink farm fiasco with yet another calamity, importing frozen rabbit skins from France. In addition, he had made a number of sizable loans to people who could not afford to pay them back, and overextended himself in a couple of other investments. Suddenly he found himself leveraged all the way up to his newly receding hairline. His last big chunk of ready cash, 50 million yen, had gone straight into Yae's account.

He went to his regular banker, the Setagaya Trust Bank of Tokyo, for help, but officials there told him that the bank was prohibited from loaning money to anyone for the purposes of paying government taxes. However, they said that if he could manage to borrow the money elsewhere to pay for his tax bill, then the bank would be able to lend him the money to pay back *that* loan, which is when Nick made the fateful decision to go to the moneylenders, Tokyo's infamous, usurious, and entirely legal storefront loan sharks, who charged 30 percent per annum and more.

To get the 23 million yen in cash he so desperately needed, he was forced to borrow 34 million yen—the result of a standard three-month contract at 8 percent per month, the first install-ment of which the moneylender took off the top, along with a 5 percent *orei,* or "thank-you" fee. As collateral, Nick was re-quired to put up the title deeds to the building that housed his main restaurant and the property on which it stood. The requi-site cash now in hand, he paid his tax bill and then returned to the Setagaya Trust Bank to get his loan, only to be rebuffed a second time. Officials now informed him that bank policy specif-ically prohibited granting anyone a loan to pay off a money-lender.

Then he received a letter from the First National City Bank notifying him that a loan he had guaranteed some months ear-lier for a business acquaintance—a Chinese-American pots and pans salesman in Tokyo named Chester Yepp—was overdue. If he did not reimburse First National its 10 million yen immedi-ately, the bank would seize Nick's property. What this meant was that now he had to go back to the moneylender and ask for yet another emergency loan. *This* time he was charged an interest rate of 5 percent compounded *every ten days*. In all, it would cost him 18 million yen to get the 10 million needed to pay First National, and it would require him to mortgage even more of his assets.

Nick paid off First National, but now he owed a total of 53 million to the moneylenders and the interest was snowballing. Over the next six months, he paid monthly installments reaching a total of 48 million yen, but because of the crippling accumulation of interest, his total debt to the moneylender ballooned to 133 million (over $400,000). Paying the moneylenders every month was sucking up all his incoming capital, and consequently he had been unable to pay other bills, which were now piling up. He had been neglecting his suppliers. He found himself in a very serious bind.

If he had been smart, he acknowledged later, instead of merely stupid and greedy, he would have sold some of his property in the beginning to pay the original tax bill. He had more than enough to spare. In addition to the 170-*tsubo* (6,181-square-foot) plot of land on which his flagship restaurant stood, and his 275-*tsubo* (10,000-square-foot) main residence, there was the Atsugi factory, the fleet of four-ton trucks, the various other houses in and around the city, the cars, the yacht, the Hokkaido factory, the Hawaiian estate, and the smaller branch restaurants in the suburbs. There was also his newly opened pizza house near Roppongi Crossing, which encompassed the entire third floor of the six-story Hama Building next door to the elegant Seryna and which was doing a thundering business.

It was at this particular juncture that a representative of Nihon Kotsu (Japan Transport) had approached with an offer of "help." Nihon Kotsu (Japan Transport) was the largest taxi company in the city, with a fleet of 2,000 cabs. The representative had heard of Nick's difficulties through a Japanese business consultant Nick had hired and proposed a joint venture between

Nihon Kotsu and Nicola Enterprises to create a nationwide chain of restaurants under the Nicola logo. In return for a 70 percent interest in the venture, Nihon Kotsu would immediately pay off all the outstanding debt Nick owed to the moneylender, which by then, the summer of 1971, had swollen to 160 million yen. Nick would subsequently be allowed to reimburse Nihon Kotsu at the very reasonable rate of 8 percent annually.

Nick did not care for the 70–30 percent arrangement, but he needed money instantly. He replied that he would agree to go along with the deal if Nihon Kotsu would throw in another loan of 63 million yen, on top of everything else.

Done, said the NK executive.

(And the devil take thy soul, he might well have added.)

A joint venture was quickly set up and Nick was asked to sign an agreement promising to pay the 160 million yen by March 31, 1972, and the 63 million by December 31, 1972, with the land and building belonging to his main restaurant serving as security. The agreement was "just a formality," an NK executive assured him. If for some reason he was unable to pay at deadline time, the date could be extended. "Don't worry," one of the men said. "We're partners. We're in for the long run."

Indeed, the words "just a formality" should have triggered internal alarm sirens. Especially in Japan, where the spirit of a contract was more important than the letter of it and multi-million-dollar deals were often concluded with just a handshake (or bow). At a fateful meeting attended on one side of the table by Nick and his ex-wife Yae, who was still an officer in Nicola Enterprises because of her holdings, and on the other, a dozen gray-suited Nihon Kotsu executives, accountants, and lawyers, Yae urged him not to sign. Although devastated by the divorce, she still cared enough about her ex-husband's future to give him good advice. But Nick had ignored her and proceeded to put his signature on a document he could not read.

What did a woman know of such matters, anyway?

Nihon Kotsu quickly opened up a string of small Nicola's around the metropolis, then, ninety days into the joint venture, management had a sudden change of heart. A store manager in the seaside resort of Ito, southwest of Tokyo, had taken the liberty of adding squid and fish to his pizza, which, in turn, had spoiled, and done damage to the gastrointestinal system of one customer. Nihon Kotsu management shortly thereafter advised Zappetti that the company did not wish to pursue the joint venture any further and gave him notice to be ready to pay off his debts totaling 223 million yen, 160 million of which was due in less than six months. There would be no further discussion.

He sold one of his lesser Roppongi residential properties, for 120 million yen, with the idea that he would take advantage of a special bank system in effect in Japan whereby one could deposit 30 percent of the amount of a desired loan and borrow against it for the full 100 percent. But before he could do this the Nihon Kotsu executives somehow found out about the 120 million and demanded he immediately turn over the cash in his possession to them, which they had a legal right to do. He thought it curious they would make such a demand, thereby preventing him from going to the bank and immediately getting the full 223 million due them. But they insisted. So, after deducting 23 million yen to pay real estate broker's fees and urgently outstanding bills, he turned over 97 million yen to Nihon Kotsu. This reduced the balance on the 160 million yen loan due March 31, 1972, to 63 million (160,000,000 − 97,000,000) plus interest. Adding the second Nihon Kotsu loan of 63 million yen, due December 31, 1972, plus interest, meant that he now owed a total of 156,000,000. (230,000,000 − 97,000,000 = 126,000,000 + 30,000,000 interest = 156,000,000.)

In February 1972, just weeks from the March deadline, he decided to sell his Atsugi sausage factory. The buyer was the Higa family, connected to Domino's Pizza, in the process of establishing a foothold in Tokyo—much to Nick's dismay. The offer was 40 million yen, which, again, he could have taken to the bank and turned into 120 million yen. But Nihon Kotsu found out about that deal as well, somehow, and again demanded the cash. They had ears everywhere, it seemed. And he was forced to keep selling. He dumped the fur factory in Hokkaido. Then two more of his smaller houses and, finally, his prized home in the heart of Roppongi—moving to a house one-tenth the size and depositing his seven sets of living room furniture in storage. That put 120 million yen in the till. He refused to part with his hit pizza house near Roppongi Crossing, which was rapidly becoming his last refuge.

Nihon Kotsu made him one final offer. They would give him a flat 215 million yen cash for everything. In return, they would cancel all debts and assume full ownership of his flagship restaurant, as well as the building and the land on which it stood. Take it or leave it, they said.

Nick refused.

Enough was enough, he said.

It was time to make a stand. He was, after all, the Mafia Boss of Tokyo, he told friends.

"They'll never foreclose on me," he told a friend. "They wouldn't dare."

Right.

On April 1, the day after the first loan was due, the taxi monolith did indeed foreclose—and in a way no one expected. Nick arrived at his Gazembo-cho restaurant on that chilly spring morning to find fifteen rather big and very rough-visaged Japanese men occupying the main floor of his restaurant, glaring at him, and looking as if they expected trouble. They appeared to

Nick to be members of the Sumiyoshi gang. And they were being directed by a Nihon Kotsu representative with the help of a government bureaucrat, who informed Nick that Nihon Kotsu had taken over the building and the land and was now running the restaurant, too—waiters and waitresses included. They could do this, the man explained, by virtue of something called *daibutsu bensai*, a Japanese law on the books which meant "taking property in lieu of cash." It was legal, if not exactly customary, at least not that fast and not when the potential value of the property involved was exponentially higher than the cash owed.

It was a hell of a way to learn a word, Nick would remark later. What it all meant was that the flagship Nicola's, by then a Tokyo landmark and an operation that was grossing a million yen a day, was now under new management.

TOKYO DISTRICT COURT

It has been said that to file a suit in Japan is an act bordering on masochism. Under the Japanese system, there are no provisions for intensive criminal or civil trials as there are in the United States, where testimony is heard daily until the conclusion of the pleadings and discussions. If the participants are lucky, the plaintiff and the defendant might make one appearance in court a month. Usually, however, it is more like once every three or four months, because either side can delay matters by claiming illness, unavoidable absence from the country, or general inconvenience. The number of trial judges in Japan is far fewer than in the United States. Most judges preside over 300 cases at a time and are so overburdened with work that they find it impossible to move any faster. Although most simple cases of theft or assault might be adjudicated in half a year or less, the average run-of-the-mill civil case takes nearly two years on the average, and complicated ones take five or ten. Given appeals to the Higher Court and the Supreme Court, quite literally lifetimes can be spent in litigation.

Apologists for the system claim it is deliberately kept slow to apply pressure on the parties to resolve the problem harmoniously out of court in negotiated settlements. The longer the court takes, the better the chances that the parties involved in the conflict will be forced to settle out of court, and therefore preserve social harmony, or *wa*, the desideratum of virtue in Japan. And indeed, a high percentage of cases are settled informally, often with the direct participation and encouragement of the judge (whose promotion in the judicial system is partially determined by the number of settlements he elicits in or out of court).

However, a major unpleasant side effect of this system has been the involvement of the yakuza in civil disputes like those relating to traffic accidents or unpaid debts, "persuading" reluctant parties to settle on the side, through effective use of the midnight knock on the door and other tools of intimidation. It is estimated that Japanese gangsters forcibly collect one-half of all the debts in Japan—a service that provides them with some 20 percent of their overall *illegal* income.

The legal profession does not have a long history in Japan. Before the Meiji era, there were no lawyers. Criminal and civil matters involving merchant and farmer classes were settled in the Court of the Feudal Lord by a prefect known as a *bugyo*. (Samurai, being a notch higher on the social scale, were exempt from such judgment.) Commoners considered the court an unfriendly and often frightening place, a feeling that has carried over somewhat into the modern day. When lawyers finally did appear on the scene, they were regarded as being in much the same category as geisha, yakuza, and *kisha* (reporters), people to whom no self-respecting landlord would ever let a room. (Only judges and prosecutors, members of the elitist bureaucrat class who managed the country's day-to-day affairs, commanded respect.)

The status of lawyers began to change with the institution of a new postwar system—and a very difficult bar exam. But even so, few people put much stock in lawsuits. Many Japanese pointed to a famous case involving the aforementioned greenmailer Hideki Yokoi, victim of the first postwar mob "contract" shooting, as one very good reason why. In 1950, Yokoi had borrowed a large sum of money from an aristocrat who went by the title of the Duke Hachisoka—a distant member of the Imperial Family—and refused to return the money. Yokoi was sued and ordered by a district court to pay. He appealed to a higher court and lost. Then he appealed to the Supreme Court, which also ruled against him in 1958. Still, he refused to pay. Yokoi took advantage of a Japanese law that does not obligate the defendant in a debt settlement suit to pay if he has no money in his name. Yokoi, an extremely wealthy man who owned a department store and a leisure shipping line, simply had all his assets transferred to his wife's name, effectively voiding the court's verdict.

Yokoi's outrageous behavior led to the pistol attack on him in 1958, ordered by yakuza boss Noboru Ando, who had been asked to intercede in the matter by a friend of the Duke's family. It may have been the first attempt in history by a member of the aristocracy to use the mob as a collection agency. Yokoi survived the attack, despite taking a .32 caliber bullet in the lung, to become even wealthier. Ando, as seen earlier, emerged from prison to become a movie star, his first film *Chi to Okite* (Blood and Law) reenacting the attack on Yokoi. But no one from the Duke's family ever saw any of the money.

At the time of the Nihon Kotsu takeover, Japan had roughly 10,000 lawyers, compared to the United States's half a million. (By the end of the century, the figures would be 15,000 and

780,000.) The system was set up so that only about 600 people a year, or 3 percent of the 23,000 Japanese who annually applied, were able to pass the rigorous bar exam to win a place at the Legal Training and Research Institute, the state-run training facility for attorneys. Of those who passed, two-thirds became practicing lawyers; the rest became prosecutors or judges.

Because of all this most disputes between Japanese businesses never go to court in the first place—the parties instead referring to published guides to determine negligence and calculate damages. And that is how many Japanese believe it should be. To them, the American adversarial system where people routinely sue each other, often over trivial matters, is simply insane—it is unpleasant, expensive, and unnecessary.

Zappetti's lawyers initially advised their client to try for a cash settlement—to see whether Nihon Kotsu's previous offer of 215 million was still on the table—and save himself a lot of grief. That way, at least, he would be debt free, with a large injection of cash in his bank account, and he would still have his booming Roppongi Crossing branch.

"Give up your name. Give up your trademark," they urged. "Take the money and start over again."

Nick adamantly refused.

"Why doesn't Nihon Kotsu give up my name and my trademark and start over again?" he said. "They're the ones with all the money."

The lawyers tried reasoning with Nihon Kotsu. They argued that what the company had done was not necessarily 100 percent in accordance with the law, even given the validity of *daibutsu bensai*, because there had been no sales contract—no *bai-bai-keiyaku*, in the parlance—and because there was no *bai-bai-keiyaku*, Nihon Kotsu did not have the right to touch the restaurant, Nicola's staff, or the company logo. Legally, they were only entitled to the land and the building. Even then, propriety

169

dictated offering Zappetti a rental agreement so he could continue to run his business.

The lawyers elicited a vague promise from a Nihon Kotsu official that the company would give Zappetti one more chance to somehow pony up the money he owed, and if he could do that, the executive said, the company would relinquish the property in full and put an end to the matter.

In desperation, Zappetti went back to see the original moneylender—the one who had started his vertiginous descent into debtor's hell with the original package of 34 million yen—and proposed a deal whereby the lender would pay off the entire Nihon Kotsu debt, which had now grown to 265 million yen, in one fell swoop, and assume 50 percent of the property in question. Zappetti would continue to run his business and at some future mutually agreed on date they would sell the land and split the profits.

The moneylender agreed and supplied a check, which Zappetti carried to the head offices of Nihon Kotsu in Akasaka, a new corporate tower of steel and glass. But there he could not find anyone to take the check from him. No one would even acknowledge knowing him. Finally, a security guard asked him to leave.

So much for Plan B.

In a rage, Zappetti called East Harlem. He hired two men to fly to Tokyo and "do a job" for him and wired a $4,500 advance for air tickets. The day before the men were scheduled to fly in, however, Zappetti's lawyers discovered that Nihon Kotsu had already reregistered ownership of the land and the building at the property registration office under the Nihon Kotsu name and had also transferred the title deed of the restaurant to one of their development companies: Nikko Kaihatsu. They had even used the Nicola Enterprises company seal to do it, with the help of a turncoat within his organization.

His business was now firmly in the grip of enemy hands. They had even raised the salaries of his staff—or rather what was now his former staff—to keep them from quitting. Nothing any gangster—foreign or Japanese—could do would change that or help him get his property back now.

"Sue us" was essentially what the folks at Nihon Kotsu were saying.

So he switched his headquarters to his Roppongi Crossing branch, renamed it "Nicola," and decided to take up the challenge.

Nick saw parallels between his situation and that of the Tokyo Hilton Hotel in 1967, in a case that garnered much notoriety—and actually turned out favorably for the international hotel management chain. In 1963, the Hilton had signed a twenty-year contract to manage a hotel in Akasaka built and owned by the Tokyu Hotel chain of Japan. Four years later, however, Tokyu decided to stop paying Hilton's management fee and assume management of the hotel themselves. One day when the Hilton representatives were away at lunch, Tokyu executives walked into the hotel offices and installed their own manager. When the Hilton men returned that afternoon, they found that they and their staff had been ejected, their desks and office furniture moved into the parking lot, and a cloth sign hung over the entrance to the hotel bearing the Tokyu name. The Hilton men were physically barred from reentering the premises.

Tokyu justified its actions by citing recent changes in the Hilton corporate structure, which included a planned merger of a subsidiary, Hilton International, with Trans-World Airlines. The move, in Tokyu's eyes, invalidated its contract with Hilton; the conditions under which the original agreement had been made had changed; therefore, their contractual obligations no longer existed.

The dispute reflected a fundamental difference between Japanese and Americans in regard to the concept of written contracts. Whereas Americans adhere verbatim to the letter of an agreement and go to court if there is any deviation, Japanese believe it valid only so long as the conditions under which it was reached continue to hold true. If not, they will rewrite the contract to suit the changing circumstances. It was the difference between the American practice of trying to close every conceivable loophole versus the Japanese practice of viewing contracts in general with some suspicion, assuming from the beginning there will be flexibility on the part of both parties involved, should conditions change.

To foreigners in Tokyo, however, the Hilton affair also reflected something else—a familiar pattern of deception. As the complaint frequently went, the Japanese, in the beginning of a relationship, would welcome foreign partners, learn as much as they could, then, once they thought they had acquired enough expertise and needed no further instruction, start looking for a way out of the deal. (It did not escape Nick's attention that Nihon Kotsu was still running the small chain of medium-sized Nicola restaurants set up under the original joint venture deal.)

The Hilton corporation had immediately hired Thomas Blakemore, who, the next morning, filed a request for an injunction in the Tokyo District Court, claiming that Tokyu lacked just cause for its actions. Although most observers expected the court to procrastinate and then, after a long delay, rule in Tokyu's favor, the district court judge surprised everyone by granting the injunction—one of the few times the Tokyo District Court had ever done so.

After the Hilton staff moved back into their offices, Tokyu took a page from the Hilton book and filed a suit of its own. But in the end, in still another surprise, the court ruled Tokyu would have to abide by the contract. There was widespread speculation that pressure had been put on both Tokyu and the court by the Japanese government because of the implications that a ruling against Hilton would have (i.e., that it would be futile for a foreign company to enter into a business agreement with the Japanese because the latter might not stick to it).

In Nick Zappetti's case, however, the Tokyo District Court reverted to form, ruling that too much time had passed between the actual land seizure and the filing of the injunction some days later.

And thus did he press on with his suit.

There was, of course, no evidence of any ulterior motive on the part of Nihon Kotsu when the company originally entered into the agreement with the big, rich white *gaijin*. Yet, the takeover kept Roppongi buzzing for months. It was viewed as more than just a business deal gone awry. It was a highly symbolic act. Many Japanese saw it as putting the arrogant American in his place—and as yet another step in taking back their country from the conquerors. The company could have had Zappetti continue to run his business and arranged to take a percentage of the profits, but chose not to. It seemed clear they wanted the business as much as the property.

Coincidentally, *The Emerging Japanese Superstate,* by Herman Kahn, had just been published, outlining how Japan would eventually be overtaking the U.S. economically. It was a revolutionary idea to the ordinary Japanese man in the street, perhaps unimaginable to most, but to those familiar with the substantial trade surpluses Japan was beginning to build up with the United States and the rest of the world, and the growing realization that the yen was vastly undervalued against the dollar, Kahn was considered most prescient.

For an Occupation-era American to own such a valuable and visible plot of land as Nicola's had, a slab of real estate that was destined to become one of the most expensive pieces of property in the world (worth nearly $150 million twenty years later, when Japan would be at the height of its economic power) was unseemly, especially when the owner was so ostentatious about his wealth and so arrogant. It was just one of the vagaries of postwar misfortune that had to be reversed, one of the many wrongs to be righted as Japan reasserted itself.

Proceedings began on March 13, 1973, in a sparse, utilitarian, oak-paneled room in the Tokyo District Court, closed, as was customary, to photographers or TV cameras. There was one black-robed judge to hear the arguments and render a decision. In their opening statement, lawyers for the plaintiff presented their argument that Nihon Kotsu had no right to take over Nicola's restaurant because there had been no bill of sale, no *bai-bai-keiyaku*, and that the loan agreement had been intended to refer only to the land and the building—not the actual business.

Lawyers for the defense retaliated that Nihon Kotsu did indeed have the right to take over the business, as well as the land, according to the way *they* interpreted the contract, because the business was so closely connected to the land and the building.

It would take two years for the first witness to get on the stand.

It would take fifteen more to adjudicate the dispute and reach a decision.

By the time a final settlement was reached, Nick Zappetti would be an old man.

6. BEHIND THE SHOJI

Over the years, Japan developed a reputation, internationally, as a place of high ethical standards. And justifiably so in many respects. It was a place where shopkeepers found it unnecessary to chain down their goods, where lost wallets inevitably made their way back to their original owners, the cash inside untouched, and where hardly anybody tried to run out on a bill. It was a model society, visiting foreign journalists and sociologists in the post-Olympic era gushed. It was peaceful and affluent and the people were moral and *yasahii*—a word meaning meek, gentle, and kind, and one, incidentally, that Japanese especially liked to use to describe themselves.

The other side of the coin generally escaped notice—except in certain circles like Roppongi Nicola's. The proprietor, to be sure, had seen his share of astonishing displays of integrity: Once, when a Tokyo post office mistakenly sent an express mail package of Zappetti's out by regular mail, the regional postal director paid a personal visit to Nicola's to refund the money, apologize, and present *"Meesuta Neecola-san"* with an elaborately wrapped package of soap to boot. However, the longer Zappetti stayed in the so-called straight world of business, the harder it became to square the reputation for Japanese honesty with what he witnessed going on around him—and that wasn't even counting his experiences in litigation, in which he remained deeply enmeshed.

In his two decades as a restaurateur, he had had to fire cooks for taking kickbacks from the food suppliers, he had had to discipline waiters for hawking TV sets and stereos of dubious origin to his foreign clientele on the side, and he'd had to ferret out employees who robbed him of everything from cash to a brand-new copying machine he was renting. Among his competitors, price fixing and collusion were commonplace, and *every* independent businessman he knew cheated on his taxes. It was the national pastime. Near the end of every fiscal year, for example, there was a mad rush among Tokyo entrepreneurs to generate false "entertainment" receipts in order to take advantage of the Tax Bureau's liberal allowances for such deductions. He guessed there were more tax cheats per capita in Japan than in any other country of the world. And, he would readily admit, he was one of them.

There was more. Visiting boxing promoters from Manila routinely complained to him of having to intentionally drop matches if they wanted to get invited back—that Japanese still had to win. Racetrack aficionados who patronized his restaurant frequently spoke of rigged horse and bicycle races, and even the *gaijin* professional baseball players, who had made Nicola's their hangout, had talked of being offered money by gamblers to participate in a fix (500,000 yen per player was the going rate). One of his regular customers, an up and coming young sumoist, suddenly confessed to him one day he had been ordered to start losing more often by his stable master; his success was upsetting the senior wrestlers in the stable.

Then, too, the underground government was as entrenched as ever, and the United States continued to be involved in its tangled skein. It was an open secret among a certain segment of Nicola's clientele that the CIA was continuing to funnel U.S. aid to the ruling LDP to the tune, it was said, of about $1 million a month (a practice that continued until Japan's growing trade surplus with the United States became a serious issue). It was another open secret that LDP politicians were taking the money and using it to buy votes, the going rate being 10,000 yen a head in a national election. And it was also common knowledge that the mob was supporting the LDP right along with the party's friends in the CIA and big business—especially the gang-controlled industries that were dependent on government contracts in public works and construction. It was quite a coalition.

A walking symbol of this shadowy web of connections was a curmudgeonly LDP Dietman named Koichi Hamada, who could frequently be seen cavorting in Akasaka-Roppongi area nightspots. Hamada was a former member of an affiliate of the Inagawa-kai, the nation's third largest gang and a man who had done time in prison for assault and embezzlement before turning to the more lucrative field of politics. He was a protégé of onetime CIA employee and political fixer Yoshio Kodama, an avowed disciple of then Inagawa-kai boss Kakuji Inagawa— a person whom Hamada openly said he respected more than anyone else. Hamada reportedly received assistance from his former colleagues during election campaigns. During one awe-inspiring trip to Las Vegas in October of 1972, Hamada lost $1.5 million playing baccarat at the Sands Hotels Casino. However, his debts were conveniently paid by his travelling companion, a hotel and transportation tycoon named Kenji Osano, yet another Kodama business associate, who had links to the highest levels of government on both sides of the Pacific (during the September 1972 summit in Hawaii between the new prime minister of Japan, Kakuei Tanaka and U.S. President Richard Nixon, Tanaka stayed at a hotel owned by Osano), not to mention a wide assortment of underworld characters of both Japanese and American pedigree.

Osano and an Inagawa gang underboss named Susumu Ishii had been running gambling tours to Las Vegas for well-to-do Japanese—an activity which, in turn, prompted Caesar's Palace of Las Vegas to open an office on the Roppongi strip to collect unpaid gambling debts. By 1975, the total Caesar's tab in Tokyo surpassed 150 million dollars, which caused three Japanese employees of the Caesar's Palace East operation to begin threatening overdue clients with death at the hands of the American mob—a collection tactic for which they were eventually arrested by Tokyo police.

There was wide, if unproven, speculation that Hamada's baccarat losses represented a secret way of circulating funds back to the United States, funds that had originally been supplied by the CIA for use in Japanese political campaigns. Such speculation was perhaps natural given the colorful backgrounds of the per-

sonalities involved and further fueled, possibly, by the fact that
the casino in question was owned by Howard Hughes, whose
right-hand man was Bob Maheu, an ex-CIA employee. (Interestingly enough, some $200,000 of the loot used to pay Hamada's
gambling debts was eventually traced back to the American aircraft manufacturer Lockheed, which made the U-2 spy plane for
the Central Intelligence Agency—but that is a tale which comes
later).

The quality of crosscultural decadence in the Roppongi-
Akasaka area was further enhanced by the entirely new phenomenon of high-priced Caucasian prostitutes who exclusively
solicited monied Japanese. They charged outlandish fees—
50,000 yen for thirty minutes in a backstreet "love hotel" called
the *Chanté*—and had more business than they could possibly
handle. Their leader was a busty, blue-eyed German blonde in
her thirties named Maria Sojka Hannelore, who came to Tokyo
by way of Hamburg, London, and New York. She was featured
in a Japanese magazine article, which introduced her as the
"Queen of the Tokyo Night World" and the richest, most successful *gaijin* hooker in the history of Japan.

"Japanese men are not used to a woman like me," she was
quoted as saying. "Sometimes all I have to do is undress and
kaput. I'm in and out of the room in ten minutes."

She became famous in Roppongi for the time when, needing
a new permanent base of operations, she paid for a half interest
in a local bar called Danny's Inn, by dumping a paper bag filled
with a quarter of a million dollars in cash on a table where the
owner was sitting.

Prostitution was illegal in Japan, but the law against it was
hardly ever enforced. The Akasaka police had thick files on
Maria and all of her friends but left them alone as long as they
did not solicit on the street—perhaps because so many LDP

politicians could be seen at Danny's Inn, stopping off to get serviced on their way to the Copa.

Maria earned enough to buy a town house in New York and her own real estate firm, in preparation for retirement. But she never got a chance to enjoy the fruits of her labor. In November 1978 she was discovered strangled to death in a room at the *Chanté*, her assailant, a dissatisfied customer and fringe underworld figure.

Perhaps no area of international commerce matched the aircraft industry for corruption, and it seemed to get worse by the year. The major U.S. aircraft manufacturers, along with the trading companies that represented them, and the Japanese officials and industrial leaders they solicited, were all up to their necks in bribes, payoffs, and whatnot because of the lucrative contracts available.

It is worth noting that while there was a growing trade imbalance between Japan and the United States and complaints about Japan's closed markets were beginning to be more loudly voiced, there was hardly any grumbling at all from the civil or military aircraft interests in America. In fact, the United States had a virtual monopoly on the sale of military aircraft and equipment to Japan. Japan Self-Defense Force organizations were constructed and patterned after their U.S. counterparts. JSDF officers were bred in a near carbon copy of the U.S. system, and they were sent to the United States for training. Thus, it was only natural to buy American.

Moreover, the system was set up to the benefit of Americans in a number of other ways as well. The U.S. Defense Department decided which configurations it would give Japan and which it would hold back. It arbitrarily decided what price Japan would be charged without giving any advance notice. It also had *free* access to any advances in technology that the Japanese might happen to make in the course of using the equipment, under a Flow Back Technology clause. Along with American-imposed restrictions prohibiting Japanese from developing their own aircraft, it was the price Japan had to pay for being "protected" by the United States under the Security Treaty—although no one seriously believed that the United States could possibly prevent a massive nuclear first strike on Japan.

The Copacabana remained the favorite hangout of the American executives from Grumman, Lockheed, McDonnell-Douglas, and Northrop, and because Zappetti remained a Copa regular and over the years had developed special relationships with some of the Copa hostesses, he kept up to date on the goings-on in the air industry. He had made an arrangement with them to bring their well-heeled patrons to his restaurant on their after-hours dates, and he padded the bill with a "service charge" that he made certain found its way into the hostess's purse. Many a grateful hostess bedded him free of charge by way of thanks for the extra income, filling his ear with the latest Copa gossip in the process.

There was an old saying in Japan to the effect that the ideal woman is one who is dumb on the outside and clever underneath. And that description certainly fit the Copa girls, especially those in the secret employ of the trading houses. There were girls who could charm a man with mindless flattery in one moment, providing the sort of "adult nursery service" that such places demanded, and in the next launch into a discussion about turbine surges, maintenance hours per flight hours, and the three axes of stabilization required in the F-104—pitch axis, roll axis, and directional axis. Talking to them, Zappetti thought, was sometimes like talking to an aircraft sales rep; half the time he couldn't figure out what they were saying.

Zappetti toyed with the idea of setting himself up as an aircraft consultant, in partnership with one of the Copa girls, selling what she learned to the highest bidder. He gave the idea up when he realized how much trouble it would be to learn all the jargon.

As it turned out, there were some Americans who played the aircraft sales game better than anyone ever suspected. One was Copa regular Harry Kern, a former *Newsweek* foreign affairs editor and lobbyist with the postwar ACJ. The Washington-based Kern was a close associate (and English tutor) of ex-prime minister Nobusuke Kishi, whose career Kern had helped resuscitate while with the ACJ and whose blood brother Eisaku Sato was prime minister of Japan from 1964 to 1972. The Sato faction of the LDP also supplied most of the subsequent PMs. Kern became a highly paid consultant to Grumman—which hoped to take advantage of his connections in high places in the LDP—while simultaneously working for the Nishho Iwai trading company in a second secret deal. It was in this capacity that Kern arranged for the Japanese government to purchase Grumman's E-2C early warning patrol plane through Nissho Iwai in exchange for a substantial secret kickback—40 percent of Nissho Iwai's commission from Grumman (a portion of which was paid to former defense chief Raizo Matsuo and other Japanese officials as a "reward"). Kern eventually lost his job with Grumman when executives there discovered what he was doing and reported him to the SEC. However, an astonished Japanese press memorialized Kern in a series of feature magazine articles, nicknaming him "The Blue Eyed Fixer" and "The White Wirepuller." After all, it wasn't often that a Japanese firm hired an American to gain access to the halls of power in Tokyo.

The Japanese had a well-known philosophy of life that related to such goings-ons. They called it *tatemae* and *honne* (principle and reality), which, to give one interpretation, meant: Say what is necessary to maintain face before society, and then do what you want on the sly. The duality of human nature was, of course, universal, but the contradictory aspects of man's behavior were more recognized and seemingly more marked in Japan, where there is such a surface premium on *wa*. Japanese professional baseball stars would sign for modest salaries each year, declaring to the press how important self-sacrifice and the concept of "the team" were, all the while taking huge secret bonuses under the table—an arrangement which helped ownership keep the rest of the payroll down. Nowhere was this dichotomy between words and deeds more astonishing than in a striking new building up the street from Nicola's where Zappetti's old gangster friend Ginza Machii had set up his headquarters.

From his perch in Roppongi, Zappetti watched in awe as the one-time street fighter climbed to heights of power and legitimacy most underworld figures only dreamt about. The leisure industry magnate had unveiled his crowning glory in July 1973, on a sidestreet corner less than a minute's walk from Roppongi Crossing, a new billion-dollar membership club called the TSK.CCC Terminal; the first three initials stood for *Toa Sogo Kigyo* (Eastern Mutual Enterprise)—Machii's post-Olympic corporate name, carefully chosen to match the initials of the gang's old acronym itself, while the second set represented Celebrities Choice Club. Housed in a six-story edifice of polished Italian marble and stone, it was by common agreement the most elegant building in all of Tokyo and, observers said, the ultimate symbol of Japan's postwar recovery—more impressive even than the cluster of new earthquake-proof high-rise office buildings and hotels in western Shinjuku, which was by now beginning to resemble L.A.'s Century City.

Contained in the building's 19,000 square meters was an array of Dionysian delights—a cabaret, a disco, restaurants specializing in Chinese, Korean, Japanese, and Continental cuisine, banquet halls with authentic rococo, Spanish, German, and Roman motifs, wedding salons, private lounges with deep leather armchairs, tatamied mah-jongg parlors, and a sauna imported from Finland. The lobby and various sitting areas were outfitted with expensive furnishings imported from Europe and the Middle East, while priceless ancient Korean vases, porcelains, stoneware, and calligraphy were showcased in alcoves along the building's many lushly carpeted corridors and caverns. On display in the main vestibule, lit by an enormous chandelier, was a giant Picasso.

Machii, now in his fifties, had personally overseen every aspect of the design, which, with its incongruous blend of Eastern subtlety and Western garishness, was an appropriate metaphor for what was happening in Japan in general. The popular weekly magazine, *Shincho,* summed up the public verdict: "The most glorious, splendidly appointed undertaking in all of Asia. It sings to the spring of our world." Added the English periodical *The Tokyo Weekender,* which did a large spread on the opening, "Truly one of the most exciting enterprises anywhere."

The opening ceremony, attended by a Who's Who's of Tokyo celebrities and politicians, was an exercise in unintended hyperbole. The chairman of the Tokyo Bar Association gave the keynote address, describing the oft-arrested host with the missing fingertip as a "decent and successful businessman." This paean was followed by similar bromides from the presidents of the great Mitsukoshi and Seibu department stores, the president of Tokyu Railways, and the political editor (and future president) of the Yomiuri Shimbun, who were all incidentally members of the TSK.CCC operations committee. Even the Greek ambassador stopped by to lead a toast and drop an encomium or two.

Machii's climactic welcome speech could have been borrowed from Dale Carnegie. He talked of benefiting his fellowman and declared he had built the TSK.CCC not to make a profit but rather to create an "oasis for human communication in the desert of modern society."

"A free society is liable to cause the loss of intimate human relationships as it progresses," he had said, "which is why the world needs a place like the TSK.CCC—a place where people can relax and communicate and understand each other's responsibilities and sense of values." Nick, sipping a glass of beer in the back of the room, wondered what Maurice would have thought.

The office of the gangster-turned-philanthropist was a further testament to how far he had risen in the so-called straight world. On one wall was a certificate of honorary citizenship in the city of Los Angeles, along with a photograph of Machii and a former California state assemblyman named Kenneth Ross, his partner in a U.S. oil venture that would grow to thirty-four wells in Texas, New Mexico, and other states. On another was a plaque from ROK President Park Chung Hee for "meritorious service in promoting friendship between South Korea and Japan"—referring perhaps to the casinos and cabarets that Machii had built in the Republic of Korea and his new Kampu Ferry Line connecting western Japan with the South Korean port of Pusan. Also displayed were letters of commendation from dignitaries around the globe, including members of the U.S. House of Representatives, who swelled the chorus of praise for his role in normalizing relations between Japan and the ROK.

Machii had even delivered an impromptu lecture to reporters on the lofty theme of Pan-Asianism. Noting that even he had suffered decades of hardship because he was a "third national," and that Japanese society was still far from being open and free

("If Rikidozan were alive today," he wondered aloud, "would he proclaim his Koreanhood? I doubt it."), Machii urged that Japanese start honoring their joint Asian heritage with Koreans and Chinese.

"Get over this complex toward the West and especially toward America," said the honorary citizen of L.A. "By copying America in music and dress so much, you are aspiring to a false lifestyle. Love Asia first and be yourself."

Over the next couple of years, the TSK.CCC became one of the busiest social spots in the city, limousines arriving every evening with VIPs of all types—government leaders, business executives, entertainers, diplomats, and U.S. Army officers. It outdrew the American franchised Playboy Club, which had recently opened up in a tony new ten-story edifice facing Roppongi Nicola's from across the strip. Underneath it all, however, were indications something else was also going on. The soft, deep leather armchairs of the TSK.CCC lounge were frequently occupied by crewcut-wearing, hard-bitten men in sunglasses, eyeing the lobby for signs of trouble, while in the rear office, the aging captains of the old guard sat idly scrutinizing visitors from behind gunmetal gray desks—as they performed mundane tasks like ordering chopsticks. The boss himself lived in the fortress-like penthouse, accessible only through a tightly guarded security gate and a locked private elevator.

Whenever Zappetti went to pay his respects, a pair of tight-lipped strongmen with fireplug necks would check him for hidden weapons before unlocking the elevator and taking him upstairs. Two more gangsters would greet him at the landing, then escort him down the hall—an elegant passageway of inlaid stepping-stones and Japanese lanterns—to a heavy metal door bearing the shape of a lion's head in perforated brass. There, yet another set of hoods would open the door from inside, lay out slippers, and usher him to a rooftop terrace adjoining a tennis court where the Master of the House, clad usually in kimono, would serve coffee. More henchmen scanned the Roppongi skyline, on the lookout, perhaps, for snipers.

The juxtaposition of cosmopolitan business veneer and underworld menace could be jarring, as an American businessman and Zappetti associate named Richard Roa would readily attest. Roa was a quality control systems engineer who had come to Japan in 1968 to work for the U.S. military and then stayed on in Tokyo to go into the P.R. business. He had been hired by the TSK.CCC to put together a multilanguage brochure that would introduce potential overseas investors to a new leisure center the company was developing in Nasu, where the Imperial Family kept its summer vacation home. The project required Roa to meet several times a week with the vice-director of overseas projects, a diminutive, dark-suited man in his fifties named Junji Tanaka.

Tanaka was Machii's interpreter and one-time chauffeur. He had learned his English as a young man working in the motor pool of a U.S. military base, and he had learned it well enough to help put together the Machii–Ross oil deals in the United States, as well as to arrange the purchase of a beautiful home in Beverly Hills for his boss. He could also type 100 words a minute.

One night, after a conference at TSK.CCC, Roa had gone out drinking by himself in Roppongi, barhopping along narrow back streets. He wandered into a closet-sized place named Cupid that had a bare concrete floor and nude photos on the wall, sat down on a vinyl-covered stool, and ordered a beer. An anorectic, middle-aged woman with a heavily painted face slid alongside him and plied him for a drink. Roa, in a tipsy, generous mood, bought her a *mizuwari* (highball), then another, plus a second round for himself. Then he got up to leave and was presented with a bill for 60,000 yen, enough to pay for 100 drinks at most other bars. When Roa protested, a very unpleasant-looking man with scars on his face appeared out of nowhere. He grabbed Roa's shirt, demanded the money, and called to someone in a rear room for help. The woman seized one of Roa's arms and held tightly.

Roa was a physically big man in his early forties who hailed from a tough neighborhood in Brooklyn, but he decided he was not sober enough to put up a fight. He paid the 60,000 yen, which was all the money he had on him, and walked home.

At the TSK.CCC the next day, he related the unpleasant experience to Tanaka.

"Where's the place?" asked Tanaka. "Show me."

Roa took him outside, around the corner, down a side street, and pointed to the Cupid, now tightly shuttered in the noontime sunlight. Tanaka sighed and wagged his finger.

"Roa-san," he said. "You have got to be more careful."

Two days later, Roa was at home when a call came from the TSK.CCC. Could he please come at once? There was an urgent matter to discuss. When Roa arrived by cab half an hour later, Tanaka was waiting in the lobby and took him to an upstairs mah-jongg room. He sat Roa down on the tatami in front of a low-slung table, picked up a phone, and grunted into the receiver.

A few minutes later, a sallow-faced middle-aged man wearing a suit and tie was shoved into the room and the door closed behind him. Roa watched, mouth agape, as the man dropped on his hands and knees and began crawling across the floor to where Tanaka stood glowering, hands on hips.

"Not me," Tanaka growled, pointing to Roa. "That's the guy over there."

The man shifted direction, crawled over to where Roa sat, and fumbling inside his coat, produced a brown envelope. He held it out to Roa in both hands, palms facing upward, bowing his head so deeply at the same time that his forehead touched the floor.

"*Suimasen*/I'm sorry," he said, in a guttural, barely audible voice. Then he crawled back to Tanaka, bowed his head again, and waited.

"Get out of here," Tanaka commanded.

The man crawled backward across the room to the door, reached behind him, and turned the doorknob. Then he backed himself out. From his seat at the mah-jongg table, Roa could see the man pull the door shut, still on his knees in the hallway.

"Count the money," Tanaka said.

Roa opened the envelope to find six crisp new 10,000-yen bills.

"That was the manager of the Cupid," said Tanaka, answering Roa's unspoken question. "We own it."

Roa was stupefied. He had never seen such a vivid exercise in raw power.

"Now I know where I am," he thought to himself.

It also dawned on Roa that the TSK had made an unnecessary concession. Not wanting to become any more obligated than he already was, Roa treated Tanaka to a night on the town, blowing the entire 60,000 yen and more.

Tanaka never mentioned the incident again, and when the Nasu project manual was finished, Roa respectfully declined the offer of a permanent job with the TSK.CCC. He figured he was better off that way. And he was right. The company was about to implode in the biggest scandal ever in the history of U.S.–Japan relations.

LOCKHEED AND LITTLE NAPOLEON

The director general of the TSK.CCC, Yoshio Kodama, was an elusive figure who kept a low public profile and did not eat a lot of pizza. He was involved in a number of shady lucrative deals with Machii—real estate and land development projects like the one in Nasu where mob muscle was needed to persuade recalcitrant farmers to sell their land, as well as assorted ventures on the Korean peninsula—casinos, hotels, cabarets—where his gangland associate was well connected. (Police noted a substantial increase in the use of metamphetamines when the Kampu Ferry, owned by the TSK group, began operations. The ROK was manufacturing about 70 percent of the *shabu,* as it was called, that was sold in Japan and consumed by an estimated million consumers—mostly overworked students, cab drivers, salarymen, and bored housewives.)

What only a handful of people knew, however, was that Kodama had once again become a secret sales agent for Lockheed. The aircraft maker was in trouble. It had lost a key sales race in 1968 when the Japan Self-Defense Force opted for the new McDonnell-Douglas F-4 Phantom and was facing a further decline in sales of military aircraft with the coming end of the Vietnam War. Lockheed needed the burgeoning civilian market in Asia to survive, and to get it the company needed Japan. With Japan Air Lines and All Nippon Airways preparing to buy a new generation of wider-bodied planes, Lockheed launched a massive three-year sales effort on behalf of its new Tri-Star passenger jet, signing up Kodama's public relations firm, Japan Public Relations, to a consultancy contract . . . and thus tapping once more into the underground government.

Kodama started off by lobbying his old friend, Kenji Osano, the tycoon extraordinaire who happened to be the largest individual shareholder in JAL *and* ANA and who was also said to be the single most influential decision maker in the selection of civilian aircraft in Japan. Osano was a big, bald-headed man described by one journalist as a "restless gorilla" who, like so many of his peers, had risen from shady Occupation beginnings (Osano's forte had been black market gasoline). He was also partners with Kodama and Machii in several ROK business ventures and was not averse to under-the-table payments and other forms of arm twisting. He set about engineering a scandal which would result in the ouster of a certain ANA executive who was steadfastly opposed to buying the Tri-Star.

Lockheed president Carl Kotchian made several trips to Tokyo to concentrate on the sale, staying at a luxurious suite in the Okura where, as one reporter wryly noted, his total bill must have exceeded the cost of one Tri-Star. He met secretly with Kodama several times at out-of-the-way spots—in parked cars and in darkened office building stairwells—to receive progress reports. At the same time, as added insurance, he plotted with top executives of Lockheed's Japan representative, the Marubeni Corporation trading house, who had its own direct route to the office of the prime minister, then occupied by newly elected Kakuei Tanaka. Tanaka, an earthy, horse trader's son who had just replaced Eisaku Sato in the top spot, would take the art of political corruption and kingmaking, already highly refined in Japan, to a new level.

Back in the United States, Lockheed representatives went a step further and lobbied the White House for help. In September 1972, U.S. President Richard Nixon and Tanaka met in Hawaii. Nixon suggested Tanaka could help reduce the burgeoning U.S.–Japan trade deficit, then about $1.3 billion, by buying U.S. aircraft. Tanaka responded by pledging Japan to buy $320 million worth of large civilian aircraft from the United States.

According to some Japanese reports, Nixon then suggested the Japanese chief of state might also use his influence to get ANA to buy the Tri-Star, which Tanaka was in a position to do since Osano, the ANA's leading shareholder, was a close friend as well as his biggest campaign contributor. The reports of the Nixon request were unconfirmed but not difficult for journalists to believe since Nixon came from California where Lockheed was based and employed 60,000 people. In fact, he had already rescued Lockheed from bankruptcy a year earlier by pushing a $250 million loan guarantee through Congress.

Whatever the truth, in the fall of 1972, ANA, in a move that shocked everyone, suddenly dropped previously announced plans to replace the airline's aging Boeing 727s with new McDonnell-Douglas DC-10s and formally decided to purchase a fleet of Lockheed Tri-Star 1011s instead. This was all the more surprising given the fact that the airline company had already made down payments on three DC-10s.

Evidence later came to light that Lockheed had employed middlemen to pay some $12.5 million, much of it in bribes, to various Japanese government officials and political leaders in order to ensure the sale of $700 million worth of aircraft in Japan. The money was funneled through Kodama and the trading house executives, who earned several million dollars in commissions and service fees. Some of the more questionable disbursements were delivered in secret nighttime transfers of wooden orange crates and suitcases full of cash, conducted in underground garage lots, deserted side streets, and even the parking lot of the Hotel Okura, directly across the street from the residence of the U.S. ambassador. Half a billion yen worth of loot went directly to Tanaka himself, while other emoluments went to the secretary-general of the LDP, officials in MITI and the Ministry of Transportation, ANA executives, and Osano himself.

As we have seen, such payoffs were almost standard operating procedure in Japan. Most of the nation's postwar prime ministers, in fact, despite their ceaseless talk of trust, integrity, and the democratic process, had had run-ins with the law over corruption. Both Tanaka and Osano had done time in their younger days for bribery and embezzlement, respectively, and Tanaka himself had once said, "You can't be called a man if you are afraid of going to jail once or twice."

Tanaka, it was widely acknowledged, had essentially bought the premiership by purchasing the support of the large Nakasone faction of the LDP in the 1972 LDP presidential election. (In practice, the president of the majority party becomes prime minister.) It was the most expensive intraparty election in history, and while Tanaka had extracted hefty donations from numerous wealthy industrialists in return for big development contracts, Osano's money was the single biggest reason Tanaka was able to win. Witnesses saw Tanaka make an unscheduled visit to Osano's private office near Tokyo Station on the day he was elected, and there, in an act unprecedented for a man of his position, he bowed deeply in gratitude. Later he awarded his benefactor a key spot on the management committee of Nippon Telephone and Telegraph, Japan's national telephone monopoly. Other supporters got pork in the form of big development contracts, vast land reclamation projects, and construction projects for new railways, bridges, and highways whose main utility, in some cases, was confined strictly to the area of political infrastructure.

The fact of the matter was that the cost of engaging in politics in postwar Japan had become progressively more prohibitive with the rapidly increasing population. Although TV advertising was limited and door-to-door canvassing restricted, the amount of cash a politician was required by tradition to dispense regularly in the form of wedding gifts and funeral solatiums for people in his ever-expanding constituency was now, by itself, enough to bankrupt most wealthy men. Also increasing was the amount of funds the several hundred members of Parliament were expected to contribute to the campaigns of politicians in their local districts, including the prefectural assemblymen, mayors, village and neighborhood heads, constituency support group leaders, and others on the food chain—in addition, of course, to paying for their own elections. So entrenched had this trickle-down system become that many elected officials at the lower levels actually borrowed money in advance of the expected political donations.

Some students of Japan viewed this all as a natural outgrowth of the nation's long feudal history, where what mattered most was personal allegiance on the home front rather than ethical principle, the strict letter of campaign donation law, or one's duty to society at large. Others cited the gerrymandered electoral scheme, both pre and postwar versions, where rural areas had several times the voting power of the large cities, in a multi-member system of small constituencies that made it easy to dispense patronage and rely on personal appeal. Others even blamed American influence for coarsening the system by greatly increasing the number of local elective positions and opening up politics to any ambitious scoundrel who wanted to run for office. Whatever the reasons, politics had become first and foremost a sort of money game rather than a form of national service. It naturally followed that those with the most skill in raising money rose to the top. Hence the birth of the term "money politics" to describe the system.

Tanaka himself broke new ground when he got major banks, automakers, steel producers, and construction companies to sponsor select conservative politicians and "sell" them to the voters. In one instance, the Mitsubishi Group rallied to raise funds and votes among its several hundred thousand employees to support one LDP candidate. Although Tanaka was forced to resign as prime minister in 1974 after a magazine article ran a lengthy exposé of his shady financial dealings, revealing that he had bought stock worth $425 million in 1973, even though his declared income had been only $260,000, he blithely continued to wield power behind the scenes because of an overflowing war chest.

Finding himself in such an environment, it was not difficult to understand why Kotchian, the man most responsible for authorizing Lockheed's payoffs, had naturally come to consider bribery as a Japanese business cost—sort of like fire or life insurance—necessary if one wanted to succeed. Japan was run by a small, close-knit group of people in business and government, he said in Senate testimony, and if you wanted to enter that group, you needed help. He was also quoted as saying that he kept the CIA informed of his movements and that "if they wanted to, they could have stopped it." Agency spokesmen naturally denied any knowledge of involvement.

Lockheed's extracurricular activities in Japan remained secret until February 1976, when a U.S. Senate investigation committee chaired by Senator Frank Church exploring bribery by U.S. firms overseas compelled Kotchian and two other Lockheed senior executives to give detailed testimony about their firm's lobbying activities in Japan and reveal the role Kodama had played.

The bombshell revelations that *Americans* were casually bribing leading figures in Japan's government and industry stunned the Japanese in much the same way as the Watergate scandal had shocked U.S. citizens a couple of years earlier. Although certainly not unaccustomed to corruption in their system, the authorities in Japan were humiliated that a foreign country—and not just any foreign country but Japan's closest ally—had been the one to uncover such massive wrongdoing. A widespread investigation was triggered, and in late July Tokyo prosecutors ordered the arrest of Kakuei Tanaka on charges of accepting the 500 million-yen bribe, then about $1,666,666 at the prevailing exchange rate. (Released on bail in mid-August, an indignant Tanaka was quoted as saying, "How dare they arrest me over such a trifling sum?") Many others, including Kenji Osano, Marubeni trading house executives, and government bureaucrats, were also arrested and indicted on various charges, which, in addition to bribery, included perjury, and violation of foreign exchange laws. The strict legal requirement in Japan that for a bribe to be proven, monies paid had to be specifically reciprocated by a favor and *clearly* understood by both parties as a bribe, not a gift (as compared to America where the mere act of a payment to an official is considered bribery), made it necessary for the prosecutors to go after the lesser offenses.

Kodama was indicted for the more easily proven charge of tax evasion. Prosecutors conducted an intensive search for hidden assets and found accounts in twenty-three different banks, along with five different safety deposit boxes containing diamonds, emeralds, sapphires, and other gems, and a safe containing a pile of stock certificates a foot high. The procurator's office impounded all his assets, including substantial real estate holdings, and determined he owed $13 million in back taxes.

Police raided the ornate new offices of the TSK.CCC in search of evidence related to the case, and although none was found the fallout was considerable. The names "Kodama" and "Machii" were frequently linked in the media coverage of Lockheed, which, by midyear, had escalated into dramatic nationally televised hearings in the Diet. Since no one of any standing wanted to be seen as being remotely connected with the affair, the regular TSK.CCC crowd vanished almost overnight.

By June 1976, the handwriting was on the wall. The company owed billions of yen in unpaid loans; its credit, theretofore guaranteed by the Japan Real Estate Bank, one of the many institutions Kodama was affiliated with, was now suddenly cut off.

Kodama embezzled millions of dollars from TSK coffers and the company was forced to file for bankruptcy—on the very same day, coincidentally, that Kodama, suffering from a sudden attack of deteriorating health, was wheeled into Tokyo District Court to start his long and lengthy trial.

THE ENIGMA

Just exactly why some people in Washington decided to open an investigation into bribery by U.S. corporations overseas and publicly reveal the Lockheed payoffs was something many people in Japan wanted to know. It was certainly the subject of much debate around Nicola's tables, especially among the foreign journalists who dined there. Some of them cited the new so-called post-Watergate morality as the main motivating factor, rectitude in politics having become the new fashion in Washington, while others claimed an internal CIA rift as a factor. Still others, however, believed the reason was simple revenge.

The Watergate scandal that forced U.S. President Richard Nixon out of office in 1974 had brought about a change in the U.S. power structure. It had meant the end of what some writers called the "Southwestern Money Nexus" ("Southwestern" being a reference to Nixon's California roots), which included the disgraced ex-president, Lockheed, the Pentagon, and the CIA. Taking its place was the "Eastern Establishment Nexus," which included the Rockefeller Group, the Eastern seaboard multinationals, and McDonnell-Douglas. Since Tanaka, Osano, Kodama, and the others were known to be tied up with Southwestern Lockheed money, they had to go.

A noted believer in this theory was Kodama himself. Up until the time of his death in 1984, he had been trying to find out why he and his cronies had been singled out for prosecution while others equally guilty—namely, those involved in bribery with Lockheed's rivals—went scot-free. *Mitsui* author John Roberts, a Tokyo-based journalist and an acknowledged expert on the Lockheed scandal, helped prepare a written appeal by Kodama to a U.S. court for an explanation and reported that Kodama seemed to think it had been a political move by the Rockefeller clique. "The best answer he could offer up," Roberts said, "was that he had egregiously offended the omnipotent Rockefellers by successfully persuading the government to cancel the purchase of McDonnell jet fighters . . . and buy Lockheed instead."

It may be worth noting that the ranking Republican on the Church Committee was married to a Rockefeller and that the new vice president of the United States, after Nixon's resignation and Gerald Ford's assumption to the presidency, was Nelson Rockefeller.

It may also be worth noting that Tanaka himself had suspected that the Rockefellers were out to get him. When subjected to hostile questioning about his political irregularities at a 1974 press conference at the Foreign Correspondents Press Club of Japan, Tanaka angrily stormed out of the room, remarking loud enough to be heard, *"Kore wa Rokafera no shiwaza"* (This is Rockefeller's doing).

In any event, the complete truth of the Lockheed scandal was never revealed. Then U.S. Secretary of State Henry Kissinger obtained a court order that prevented full disclosure of the affair on grounds that revealing certain U.S. government documents would damage the country's foreign policy interests. For years afterward, Lockheed attorneys would still be arguing that disclosing certain matters would adversely affect the reputations of foreign officials important to good relations with the United States.

An enduring enigma was the fate of bearer checks issued by Lockheed totaling $1.6 million and intended for Yoshio Kodama and Kenji Osano. The checks had mysteriously disappeared and were cashed before Lockheed could cancel them—Kodama's explanation being that they were stolen while in his possession. Although not obligated to do so, Lockheed then issued another set of checks which Kodama managed to hold on to.

The question naturally, was, why?

There are some people who suspect the original $1.6 million wound up in the re-election campaign coffers of President Richard Nixon. Their line of reasoning was that Lockheed felt obliged to help out at election time with a nicely laundered donation because Nixon had saved the company from bankruptcy. They found it a curious coincidence that the $1.6 million was approximately the same amount of money that mobster-turned-politician Koichi Hamada had lost at the Sands Hotel in Las Vegas at approximately the same time the checks had vanished.

Interestingly, in April 1984, the Tokyo High Court determined that Kenji Osano had actually used Lockheed money to pay Hamada's gambling debts. According to the verdict, Osano received the money in an attaché case from a Lockheed executive at 5 P.M. on November 3, 1973, at the Los Angeles airport and within an hour was on an airplane to Las Vegas, where he turned it over to Sands personnel on Hamada's behalf, to cover the final installment of what Hamada owed.

The money was believed to have been a final payment to Osano for his role in persuading ANA to buy Lockheed Tri-Star airliners as well as Orion P3C antisubmarine patrol planes (later). Journalist Takashi Tachibana, in his four-volume work on Lockheed, *Rokuiido Saiban Bochoko* (A Record of the Lockheed Trials), *Asahi Shimbun* 1994, the most thorough and reliable work on the subject, noted that the amount, $200,000, was significant. It reflected a difference caused by a fluctuating yen-dollar exchange rate to wit: 300 yen to the dollar when the first "stolen" $1.6 million was paid as opposed to 260 yen to the dollar when the second $1.6 million was paid. Lockheed, claimed Tachibana, agreed to add on the extra yen and give it to Osano, because there was still work to be done involving the P3C.

However, speculation that the Lockheed money was used for secret campaign contributions has remained, over the years, only that—despite the incongruity of the lost checks and their speedy replacement. Subsequent investigations by SEC and the Justice Department over the missing checks were inconclusive and no one has ever satisfactorily explained the Lockheed-Osano-Hamada-Sands Casino link and what, if any, the CIA's and/or CREEP's involvement was. In fact, U.S. federal courts have blocked full disclosure of the details of the Lockheed case since Kissinger's court order. Osano went to his grave steadfastly denying the charges against him. Hamada, who resigned from his Diet seat when his high stakes gambling adventures became public (he was re-elected in 1980), has frequently been quoted as saying *"Shinde mo ienai,"* meaning, basically, "I'll die before I tell what really went on."

No doubt the timely demise of several key people helped keep secrets safe. Tanaka's chauffeur, eyewitness to some of the late-night payoffs, was found in his car, dead from carbon monoxide poisoning in what was adjudged to be a suicide, much to the surprise of everyone who knew him. However, a close relative was overheard saying that if she dared to pursue an inquiry into his demise that she would be "next." The head of the Kodama-owned company Japan PR, which formally represented Lockheed, a Japanese-American named Taro Fukuda, who also knew where all the skeletons were kept, died of heart failure while in the hospital being treated for cirrhosis of the liver. During his hospital stay, he had expressed fear of being poisoned and even had mapped out an escape route from the building. Members of his family reportedly did not believe his death was due to natural causes, although they too shied away from speaking out on the matter.

Still another mysterious death was that of a political reporter for the *Nihon Kezai Shimbun*, Japan's leading financial paper, who had closely followed the Lockheed scandal and who had conducted an in-depth interview with Lockheed chief Kotchian during one of the latter's final trips to Tokyo before the scandal broke. The reporter was only forty years old and in good health when he collapsed and died one evening—some ten days after the Church hearings had begun. He had left work, stopped at the Copacabana for a drink, then returned home, where he took a bath and ate dinner. Lighting up a post-meal cigarette, he suddenly complained of a severe headache. His wife called an ambulance, which rushed her husband to the nearest hospital, but he was pronounced dead on arrival. The attending physician listed the cause of death as heart failure but could not give a satisfactory response to the wife's questions as to why heart trouble would cause headaches.

It was still two months before Tanaka's involvement would be revealed and some 2,000 pages of SEC material delivered to Tokyo. Yet when a close friend of the reporter heard the news of his death, his immediate response was, "They got him."

Who "they" were never became clear.

When all was said and done, not one person charged in connection with the scandal ever did prison time. Kodama escaped full prosecution under the law. He was too ill, his doctors conveniently concluded, to testify at his trial, and court findings on his involvement were accordingly kept under seal, as required by Japanese statute when the defendant cannot physically present himself before the judge. Kodama would spend the rest of his life at home "convalescing" for another eight years before passing away at age seventy-two. Unlike his American counterpart Richard Nixon, who was disgraced and dispatched into political oblivion for some years by the Watergate scandal, Kakuei Tanaka remained a mightily influential figure. Out on bail and awaiting trial, he was not only overwhelmingly returned to his seat in the Diet but also maintained control over the largest single faction of the ruling LDP. This allowed him to allocate cabinet posts, choose party leaders, dispense patronage, and otherwise run the show from behind the scenes. It was said that during the decade following his arrest, he handled 1,000 "cases" a year. He was once quoted as saying, "A prime minister is like a hat. You can change it as you wish." His influence over his protégé Yasuhiro Nakasone, the former JPWA board member who was prime minister between 1982 and 1987, was so great that a cynical press corps devised the sobriquet "Tanakasone" to refer to him.

In 1983, Tanaka was convicted of bribery (specifically of taking money in exchange for influencing All Nippon Airways to buy Lockheed planes) and sentenced to four years in prison. He thus became the only postwar prime minister in Japan to be convicted of a crime. However, Tanaka appealed and during the lengthy appeals process was again re-elected to the Diet by his rural constituents, ever grateful for the new highways, high-speed trains, and other material benefits he brought them. He claimed that the overwhelming margin by which he had won constituted vindication.

Of the other thirteen people indicted in the Lockheed scandal, all were found guilty. All appealed, were found guilty again, and appealed a second time, to the Supreme Court. It took nineteen years for the case to drag itself through the legal system before all the appeals had been rejected, during which time the accused successfully continued their careers. Final sentences were suspended for reasons of advanced age and ill health, thereby illustrating the difficulties of prosecuting political corruption in Japan. Tanaka remained in power until a stroke felled him in 1986; he died in 1993. Kenji Osano, convicted of four counts of perjury that included lying about receiving Lockheed money and denying he had conspired with Yoshio Kodama to help Lockheed vis-à-vis the P3C (there were no counts of bribery because the three-year statue of limitations in effect in Japan had expired), continued to accumulate wealth until his death in 1987, adding more hotels to his Waikiki collection (which already included the Surfrider and the Royal Hawaiian) and running his gambling tours to the States with Inagawa-kai sub-boss Susumu Ishii.

ANA's chairman Tokuji Wakasa, who was convicted of perjury and of receiving a secret 160 million yen in kickbacks for purchasing Tri-Star planes, as well as for bribing government officials, remained the firm's chairman. Said an ANA spokesman after the seventy-seven-year-old Wakasa's verdict was upheld by the Supreme Court in 1996 (the sentence being three years at hard labor, suspended for five years), "the firm regrets the ruling. Honorable Chairman Wakasa is highly respected by our employees. He remains our spiritual pillar."

If nothing else, the Lockheed affair ultimately reinforced the idea that contemporary Japan was a society with no guiding moral purpose—and one that like its feudal and prewar predecessors did not question what was going on. Tanaka showed how a duly elected Diet member can form and maintain his own power structure, inside a duly constructed constitutional parliament, despite breaking the law. All he had to do was drag the legal process out and keep getting re-elected.

A TV journalist reporting the convicted politician's last electoral victory, barely controlling the tears in his voice as he stood under klieg lights before the National Diet building, asked, "How can this happen? After all the painstaking labors of a free press, all the revelations—what does something like this say about our Japanese democracy?"

Prize-winning author Inose Naoki had the following answer:

> Democracy is merely the voice of the people and our postwar value system and that's what Tanaka used as his biggest weapon. . . . (It) was not an incident in which democratic values were overturned by nondemocratic values. It was an incident created from inside of the system—a system which Tanaka only mastered.

CITIZEN NICK

The Lockheed disaster helped to profoundly alter the power structure in the Roppongi underworld—not to mention the makeup of the clientele at Nicola's. Machii and his gang simply disappeared from public view. One Friday night in 1977, Nick Zappetti, curious as to what had happened to his former customers, took a walk over to the TSK.CCC, still operating as bankruptcy litigation continued, and what he found astonished him. In the entire moribund building—the very same structure that journalists four years earlier had been hailing as the most magnificent in all of Asia—he could count only six customers. The rest of Roppongi, on the cutting edge of Tokyo nightlife and fashion, was teeming with people mirroring a booming new Japan, brimming with confidence from sustained double-digit growth that had continued unabated despite a 1973 oil shortage crisis that temporarily dimmed the city's ubiquitous neon lights. The pink and white Almond Coffee Shop on the southwest corner of Roppongi Crossing had become one of the most popular meeting spots on earth—the waiting crowds of people on the sidewalk fronting it so thick they blocked pedestrian traffic. But the expensive restaurants and lounges of the TSK.CCC were all embarrassingly empty. Waiters and waitresses stood yawning. Cobwebs gathered in the corners; men from the TSK were nowhere to be seen.

The TSK slide into oblivion had received an additional, if unneeded, kick when a U.S. congressional investigation team visited Tokyo to probe suspicions that a wealthy Washington-based lobbyist named Park Tong Sun, at the center of an influence-peddling scandal known as "Koreagate," had entertained American lawmakers at TSK nightclubs. (Soon after that, a Socialist member of the House of Councilors would charge that girls working for the TSK had been trained by the KCIA in political operations and, intentionally or otherwise, had given VD to at least one leading LDP figure.)

"Ginza Machii" himself had slid into a kind of Howard Hughes-like existence, holed up daily in his penthouse and refusing contact with the outside world. It was said that he feared being killed—especially after a story appeared in the *Weekly Yomiuri* magazine about a CIA plot to assassinate Yoshio Kodama. In fact, in March 1976, Kodama had miraculously survived a kamikaze attack in which a deranged rightist had crashed his Cessna into a deserted second-floor section of Kodama's huge home. Cynical Japanese journalists said it served Machii and Kodama right for ever getting in bed with the Americans in the first place.

However, Zappetti had other things on his mind besides the

shifting power structure in the Roppongi underworld, which was in the process of being taken over by the Sumiyoshi.

He was about to stretch the concept of *tatemae* and *honne* to new boundaries, by applying for Japanese citizenship, something most people thought he had no chance of ever achieving.

He was about to stretch the concept of *tatemae* and *honne* to new boundaries by applying for (and receiving) Japanese citizenship—something most people thought he had no chance of ever achieving. The Japanese Nationalist Law was first and foremost based on bloodline, and it was generally acknowledged to be extremely difficult for a Caucasian foreigner to be naturalized. Moreover, under the criteria outlined by the Ministry of Justice, one also had to be able to read and write the Japanese language, to be of "upright conduct" (which meant, of course, no criminal record), and meet a number of other requirements, including making a loyalty pledge to the Japanese government. Final approval or disapproval of an application for Japanese citizenship and the length of time it took for the decision to be made was entirely at the "discretion" of the justice minister, who was not normally prone to granting such requests, especially where Caucasians were involved. The wait could take years or even a lifetime—even for someone without Zappetti's obvious handicaps.

There were deep historical reasons for Japan's general ambivalence toward Westerners. Japan had only opened up her doors to the world in 1853, after centuries of feudal isolation, and although the Japanese were eager to modernize and to catch up with the more industrialized countries of the West, they were at the same time leery of too much Western influence. The Japanese philosophy was encapsulated in an oft-repeated slogan:

Wakon-Yoshi (Japanese Spirit, Western Skill) which essentially meant, "Give us your technology, but don't disrupt our national spirit of *wa.*" (Meiji-era scholar Seishisai Aizawa wrote: "Barbarians are, after all, barbarians. It is only natural that they have their hearts set on transforming our civilization to barbarism.") Meiji-era technocrats, imported from North America and Europe to help modernize Japan, were forbidden to proselytize or even socialize with the populace, under penalty of deportation and being forced to pay their own passage home. Remnants of such contradictory attitudes could still be found in modern-day "democratized" Japan, where there were more private English conversation schools per square kilometer than anywhere else in the world. Elvis Presley, James Dean, and the Beatles were icons, but where prosperity and the trappings of Western culture did little to change the insular attitudes toward the *gaijin* themselves. Foreigners who spoke Japanese *too* well were often regarded with a jaundiced eye.

Zappetti's unlikely—and to some observers, galling—request for entry into such an exclusive club was for him nothing more than a necessary, if troublesome, business tactic, one prompted by yet another court battle he had entered into. Awaiting a verdict in the interminable litigation with Nihon Kotsu, he became embroiled in a dispute with his ex-general manager, a man named Fujita, which had started when the latter approached retirement age and asked for his *taishokin,* the customary lump-sum retirement bonus paid out by Japanese companies. An astonished Zappetti had angrily rebuffed the request.

"What the hell do you mean, *taishokin?*" he had said. "I paid you a good salary, didn't I? That's enough. Americans don't pay a retirement bonus."

That turned out to be an irreparable mistake. Now Zappetti was not without his generous side. He once gave an ailing, alcoholic American writer who was broke and down on his luck a plane ticket to Hawaii and several thousand dollars' worth of pocket money with which to get his life back in order. He paid the medical bills for an old friend from the black market days who was suffering from a bad heart. And, over the years in Roppongi, it was known that if a man needed a loan of money and a free hot meal he could always get one at his place—for Zappetti remembered all too well what life had been like back in his post-Tokyo jail, Turkish-bath days. By the time the 1980s had rolled around, he calculated that he had lent friends and employees a total of over a million dollars, money he never expected to see again. His neighbor, Dr. Eugene Aksenoff, termed Nick a "soft touch for any bum or con artist with a hard luck story."

Moreover, as an American boss employing Japanese workers, he had other virtues as well. He demanded none of the excessive formality and discipline that typified many Japanese-style establishments—some Tokyo bars required bartenders to bow at a certain angle, to slide the customers' drinks across the counter with just the right "whoosh," and then stand at something approximating parade rest while awaiting the next order. At Nicola's there was no standing at attention for daily inspection. No lists of rules to memorize. No "self-reflection conference" at the end of each day to go over misdeeds, real or imagined. You showed up to work on time, cleanly dressed, and did your job. Period. You could stand there and chat with the customers without fear of recrimination. As longtime Nicola's waiter Akio Nomura put it, there was no *burusheeto*—which was why he liked working there.

(More important, but seldom noted in a society where human rights were not a frequent topic of discussion, Nick was an equal opportunity employer. He hired Koreans, Taiwanese, Indians, and others to work as waiters or managers and gave them the same pay he gave Japanese nationals—which separated him from other indigenous employers, for whom employing minority workers was only primarily a way to save on labor costs.)

Unfortunately, however, the master had his weak spots, and one of them was his total lack of interest in bonding with his employees. Typically, the Japanese expected a work environment that fostered a sense of belonging and gave them a say in how things were done. This meant periodic group parties, company outings, and frequent staff meetings to hear employee opinions. To Nick, however, *that* was all *burusheeto*. And he said as much to anyone who would care to listen. "We don't need a relationship," he would tell his waiters. "I'm the one who is paying. Just do your job." No matter how much anyone tried to talk to him about changing his ways in that regard, he refused to listen. In fact, he became notorious in Roppongi, as years passed, for his increasing bluntness and his bad temper. More than once, in a pique over bad service or incompetence, he fired a worker, which is something Japanese managers simply *never* did. In Japan, one took a bad employee aside and with the help of a friendly third party persuaded him to find another job, one that suited *him* better. Face was all-important and the cardinal rule was you never made a man lose it.

Another notably weak area was his dismissiveness of the Japanese custom of paying bonuses—the annual summer, winter bonuses and, as in the case of his former GM, the traditional retirement bonus. Had he taken a cue from Grolier International, the American encyclopedia company down the street from his restaurant, when it decided to drop a massive Japanese *Americana* translation project and fire all the editors hired for that purpose in the process, he might have saved himself some grief. In what became a notorious case, Grolier was sued by its own in-house union—over *taishokin*—and a long court battle ensued, lasting several years, during which Grolier was forced to rehire the *Encyclopaedia Americana* Japanese translation team and keep them on the payroll—even though there was no work for them to do. It was a painful reminder that in Japan employees were supposed to be considered family and one did not lightly let them go. (*Reader's Digest* later tried to close down shop in Japan without notifying its union and became embroiled in a similar battle.)

Instead Zappetti offered his GM a post-retirement job in lieu of cash. He sent Fujita to buy the land in Hokkaido he had been leasing, because Japanese law prohibited foreigners from owning farmland. Zappetti's idea was for Fujita to set up residence on his ranch, qualify as a homesteader (meeting the legal requirement for a landowner to actually live on the land before being allowed to buy it), and thereby gain the legal right to purchase the land on which the ranch stood from its original Japanese owner. Upon completing this assignment, Fujita was then to have held the land for his master until such time as it became legally feasible to transfer the title, either directly to Zappetti or to Zappetti's company. Fujita purchased the land as requested, and then, in a sudden, vengeful act, claimed the land as his own. Zappetti found himself with no choice but to file yet another lawsuit to recover his property.

Including a countersuit filed by Fujita for his retirement pay and a countersuit Zappetti himself had filed against his third wife for damaging his manly honor (a suit he would, to his great surprise, win), it would be Zappetti's sixth lawsuit of the decade. That was believed to be a record for an individual *gaijin*, as was Zappetti's third divorce from a Japanese woman and as was Zappetti's fourth marriage in late 1975, when he remarried Yae.

He could fill a page in Guinness all by himself.

Zappetti filed suit over the Hokkaido property in 1982, just as the long-awaited decision in his Nihon Kotsu case was handed down. After nine agonizing years in litigation, the judge deliberating that suit delivered a terse five-word verdict: "Mr. Nicolas cannot be believed." Period. Given all that he had invested, Mr. Nicolas had no alternative but to appeal that case, meaning that he would now have three court cases going simultaneously—another first for an American in Japan.

At the rate he was going, one page in Guinness might not be enough.

It was at this juncture that his Japanese lawyers, fearful he would lose again, twice, suggested he become a naturalized citizen and thereby increase his chance of winning, and in the hope it might help his cause, Nick took them up on the idea.

That the semiliterate white *gaijin* Zappetti, with a police file a foot thick, no less, actually managed to pull it off causes people in Tokyo even today to scratch their heads in amazement. In 1983, when he first filed his application for naturalization, he had yet to take a single lesson in the Japanese language and could barely put together a grammatically correct sentence. What Japanese he knew, he had picked up on his own, and it was a specialized and unique lingo, to say the least. He could easily translate *chobo* to hectares, *tsubo* to square meters, and give yen or dollar values on them in either English or Japanese; he could also shift from counting years in the Gregorian system to the *Showa* system, which was based on Emperor Hirohito's reign from 1926 to 1989, without missing a single beat, and he knew words that could stump most foreign linguists—like *dai-butsu bensai*—terms which he had picked up in the course of attempting to conduct his affairs. Although such knowledge was of little use in a language proficiency test, he did have a keen visual memory for names written in *kanji* (Chinese ideographs), which had come from dealing with the business cards he had received over the years. Banking on this skill, he arranged, through an influential politician's lawyer—one he had met through an introduction from his wife's family—for a special language test to be given him, in the comfort and privacy of the lawyer's office, where he would identify family names printed on business cards randomly handed to him. He passed with flying colors.

His criminal record was another hurdle. Fortunately, his lawyer's expertise encompassed crime as well as language. The influential politician the lawyer represented was the LDP's Yasuhiro Nakasone, who was about to become prime minister and a man with his own ties to the underground. Interestingly, Nakasone's history as a member of the JPWA during the Rikidozan era, a rising star in the outer constellation of Yoshio Kodama, and a protégé of Kakuei Tanaka was a thread that wound its way into the Nick Zappetti story as well, ending as a neatly tied ribbon on the gift box of his naturalized citizenship.

On a bitingly cold afternoon in January 1983, he formally became a Japanese citizen and officially changed his last name to that of his fourth wife, as "recommended" by Japanese authorities. Then he went to the U.S. Embassy to surrender his passport—his U.S. passport, one of the most coveted documents in the world—and verbally renounce his U.S. citizenship.

Nearly all of the minuscule handful of Westerners who applied to become naturalized Japanese citizens in the postwar era did so out of their love for the culture and perhaps their desire to be accepted on equal terms with the rest of the general populace. But none of them ever did so lightly. Jesse Kualahula, a popular 300-pound sumo wrestler from Maui, obtained Japanese citizenship at approximately the same time as Nick because without it the Sumo Association would not allow him to start his own sumo stable. He called surrendering his U.S. passport the most difficult move he had ever had to make. He consulted often with then U.S. ambassador Mike Mansfield and cried all night after making his big decision.

Nick Zappetti, however, did not shed a single tear.

For the man who had just turned sixty and who from then on would be known as Nicola Koizumi, thereafter requiring a visitor's visa to get back into the land of his birth, it was, he insisted, just another business day. After he had signed all the papers, he simply went back to work.

DEA CULTURAL WALL

Like novice American businessmen in Japan trying to figure out the distinction between a gift and a bribe, U.S. crime investigators on the trail of lawbreakers in Japan encountered their own cultural brick wall. Chasing down drug dealers was a particularly difficult task. FBI Director William Sessions would later testify to a Senate committee that U.S. authorities believed that Japanese gangs were controlling 90 percent of the stimulant trade in Hawaii—peddling drugs brought in from the Golden Triangle and using the profits to buy back firearms, which they would sell back home at a 1000 percent markup. In fact, Attorney General Robert Mueller told the committee that the Hawaiian branch of the TSK, or the *Toa Yuai Jigyo Kumiai* (East Asia Friendship Enterprises Association), as it was now known, controlled most of the business in crystal methamphetamine or "ice" produced in Korea and Taiwan—which, interestingly, answered the question of what *some* members of that organization had been doing with themselves in the years since Lockheed bust. But authorities in Japan were little help in investigations.

For example, Japanese police did not follow the practice, routine in North America and Europe, of carrying out "controlled deliveries"—persuading drug couriers whom they have caught to carry on with delivery to the next person in the chain. Nor did they conduct "controlled buys." They did not even purchase drugs on the street to gain an accurate idea of the supply available. Japan's Criminal Code prohibited the authorities from participating in such activities and from conducting any other sting-type operations, including for most intents and purposes wiretapping. They were even averse to wiretapping. Undercover cops could observe and prevent. That was all. And then they were required by law to put perpetrators behind bars immediately, as one Nicola Koizumi was to discover a second time.

Upset because a member of his family had become ill from drug addiction and hepatitis (from an expedition to the Golden Triangle), he had decided to take action when the son of an ambassador from a Southeast Asian country approached him with three kilograms of white powder in search of a buyer. In a misguided effort to lay a trap, he took a plainclothesman to the dealer's residence, introduced him to the dealer, and was promptly arrested. He spent three days in the Tokyo Detention House trying to convince police he was not an accomplice.

The Japanese police believed that American-style undercover tactics would also upset the underworld *wa*—thereby lessening the chances for the poor misguided but redeemable criminal ever to be steered back onto the straight and narrow. Moreover, there was the implicit belief that a policy of self-regulation by organized crime, as much as was reasonably possible, had its uses in maintaining order and discipline in certain fields like the gang-run entertainment industry.

Thus, the Japanese police naturally resented a U.S. Drug Enforcement Agency sting conducted in 1984 on Osakan gangsters who had been selling amphetamines for guns in Honolulu.

DEA agents had entered Japan without requesting the approval of Japanese authorities. Then, posing as promoters, they approached the Osaka mob bosses for help in financing a fictitious tour of the country by Michael Jackson. They were so successful in winning the mobsters' trust that, several months later, eleven of the Osaka yakuza were indicted in Honolulu over a $350 million gun-and-drug smuggling deal. However, as a result, the Japanese police were slow to cooperate when, several years later, popular Japanese film actor Shintaro Katsu was arrested for bringing cocaine into Hawaii and DEA officials visited Japan to try to investigate his background.

What further complicated the relationship was the fact that, even as international drug traffic increased, the Japanese police were reluctant to accept suggestions of the visiting DEA agents from America that Japanese gangsters, bound as they were by the unique yakuza code of honor, would be so vulgar as to deal in "hard drugs" like cocaine and heroin, rather than their usual traditional trade in the less harmful amphetamines. The Japanese authorities preferred to blame the newly rising trade in such "bad" drugs on the increased presence of foreigners attracted to Japan by its new economic wealth. It was all the fault of the quarter of a million illegal immigrant laborers in the country, or the Cali cartel, or whomever. Anybody but the proud descendants of the old *bakuto* and *tekiya.*

In 1991, for example, Japanese authorities would insist that a shipload of cocaine in Yokohama Harbor had merely been in transit from the Golden Triangle to the United States. They were forced to admit otherwise only when they received a handwritten letter in Spanish threatening terrible retribution unless their investigations were called off. The letter was signed with the name of a South American drug cartel that nobody had ever heard of. The clincher was the fact that all the r's and l's in the letter were reversed—a mistake a Japanese would make, but not a Latin American.

Chasing down dirty money posed another set of problems for the Americans. RICO—the Racketeer Influence and Corrupt Organizations Act—passed by the U.S. Congress in 1970 was a new legal tool to deal with organized crime. It was designed to control a specific organization or family by focusing on a systematic pattern of criminal activity, like murder, extortion, loan sharking, illegal gambling, hijackings, narcotics trafficking. It made it a crime for someone to receive or invest in a legitimate enterprise, or otherwise utilize ill-gotten gains, even if not personally or directly involved in the related crime. RICO also allowed victims of organized crime to sue those responsible for punitive damages.

Japan had a marked absence of such money-laundering laws, making it extremely difficult to crack financial crimes. The mob could invest drug and prostitution money in the real estate and financial markets and the police could not track it down. Money-laundering statutes for drug-related crimes were finally enacted in 1991, but even then Japanese privacy laws were such that relevant information could not be given to outside parties. In fact, Japanese attitudes and laws to protect privacy were so stringent that gang members actually sued the Japanese National Police for releasing information on them to other Japanese officials.

It was a wonder anyone was ever arrested.

Outdoor markets in Tokyo were up and running almost from the moment hostilities ceased, and well before the conquering Americans had set foot on Japanese soil. Operated by gangsters, the black markets, like the one shown here in Shinjuku (which belonged to the mob boss Kinosuke Ozu and peddled supplies stolen from the Japanese Imperial Army), were for a time the only thing that kept the war-ravaged, impoverished populace from starvation. (*Mainichi Shimbun*)

It didn't take long for the initially wary American soldier to start relaxing and enjoying what Japan had to offer. In addition to rickshaw rides and government-sponsored hostesses supplied by the Japanese Recreation and Amusement Association to satisfy the Yankee libido, this could also mean highly lucrative participation in the underground markets. (*Mainichi Shimbun*)

Postwar economic hardship forced many Japanese to find new ways of making a living. A top-ranked but financially strapped sumo wrestler named Rikidozan, shown here in 1950 in formal sumo garb that dates back centuries, turned to the crass imported American "sport" of professional wrestling and, in the process, ignited an extraordinary craze. (*Mainichi Shimbun*)

Stirring performances against larger American opponents turned the new *puroresura* into a wildly idolized figure and made him one of postwar Japan's first multimillionaires. Rikidozan displayed his revamped public persona in this 1956 photo in front of his new home. Guard dogs and armed watchmmen kept the un-invited away, especially during secret, nighttime, illegal gambling sessions which Riki liked to organize for his influential political, corporate, and underworld friends—members of the emerging ruling class in Japan. (*Mainichi Shimbun*)

The repeated sight, however scripted, of foreign foes like Killer Kowalski being cut down to size by homegrown grapplers, never tired Japanese fans. Such displays helped restore the wounded national psyche bruised and battered by defeat in war. (*Kyodo*)

Rikidozan's wedding to the daughter of a police inspector in June 1963. In six months he would be dead from a gangster's knife. Japanese historians would later hail him as one of the most influential social figures of the twentieth century in Japan because of his electrifying impact on the national spirit. At the time, however, the public was largely unaware of his non-Japanese origins (a fact intentionally kept secret by Riki's handlers), as well as his clandestine honorary membership in one of Tokyo's largest criminal organizations. (*Kyodo*)

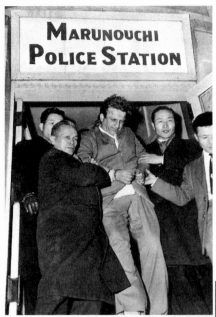

American John MacFarland, a popular professional wrestler in Japan known as "The Wild Bull of Nebraska," is shown here being arrested by the Tokyo police for his role in the Imperial Hotel diamond robbery.

MacFarland's escapade stunned a nation of neophyte wrestling addicts, who jammed public squares to watch matches telecast live on outdoor TV. Some cynics cracked that MacFarland was merely carrying to its logical extension the role of villain that was thrust upon the American wrestler as a foil for his pure-hearted and inevitably victorious Japanese opponent. These enormously popular morality plays did more than lift the country's mood. Among other things, they sparked a huge nationwide boom in television sales, which helped to rejuvenate the postwar Japanese economy. (*Mainichi Shimbun*)

The New Latin Quarter, one of Tokyo's premier nightclubs, was a notorious watering hole for the foreign intelligence community and the Japanese underworld. (*Kyodo*)

Katsushi Murata, a young foot soldier in the Sumiyoshi crime syndicate, fatally stabbed Rikidozan during a bloody encounter in the New Latin Quarter men's room—a deed that earned Murata enduring fame in Japan. Some suspected it was all a part of a CIA plot. (*Kyodo*)

Matura's star power was evident in this March 1989 edition of the *Yukan Fuji*, Japan's leading tabloid. With a great front-page flourish, it reported the arrest of Matura and his wife for extortion and for the assault of a nineteen-year-old woman. Matura, who by this time had risen high in the Sumiyoshi hierarchy, was released without being charged after he formally denied participating in any of the violence. Noticing how weakened Matura had become from a case of diabetes, the leading *yakuza* affliction, a police officer commented, "He doesn't look like he is going to hit anyone anymore." (*Kyodo*)

Hisayuki Machii, the Crime Boss of Tokyo, in 1966. One of his many nicknames was *Fanso* or "violent bull," in tribute to what lay underneath his calm outward demeanor. He is said to have killed at least two men with his bare hands. He once worked for American Intelligence. (*Kyodo*)

Machii later became a successful international businessman and was made an honorary citizen of Los Angeles. Still, he continued to pay his respects at formal *yakuza* functions like this 1981 funeral of his blood brother Kazou Taoko, gang boss of the Osaka-Kobe.

Inside the Mikado, once described by an American visitor as "one giant glorious warehouse of sex." The largest cabaret in the world, with 1,000 hostesses and lavish Las Vegas-style stage shows, the Mikado was a den of international intrigue, where a broad spectrum of female talent, from bare-breasted dancers to coquettish kimonoed companions, used their charms to soften up unsuspecting foreign clients for Japan, Inc. (*Mainichi Shimbun*)

Sojka "Maria" Hannelore, also known as "The Queen of the Night World," claimed to be the most successful foreign call girl in Tokyo history.

Maria plied her trade at the "Chanté Akasaka," a "love hotel" in demotic Japanese. The Chanté was a monument to a certain kind of western-style, Disneyesque architecture that took root in postwar Japan. Maria was murdered at the Chanté in 1978, at the age of forty: she was found strangled to death in one of the rooms, the victim of an unsatisfied customer. Her life story was later made into a TV movie by the Tokyo Broadcasting System. (*Mainichi Shimbun*)

Nick Zappetti, the mafia boss of Tokyo, on the day in 1982 that he became a Japanese citizen and changed his name to Koizumi. He is posing in a formal Japanese kimono at his Roppongi restaurant, Nicola.

Nicola, shown here renovated in 1998, was famous for helping to create the international nighttime playground of Rappongi. The restaurant was a magnet for Hollywood movie stars, Tokyo gangsters, and lawsuits. (*Gregg Davis Photos*)

NICOLA
KOIZUMI
ITALIAN RESTAURANT
& PIZZA HOUSE
Est. 1956

- Tokyo Roppongi   03 ⟨401⟩6936
- Ginza Printemps ⟨B-2⟩   03 ⟨567⟩0077
- Omori Station Bldg.   03 ⟨764⟩3212
- Chuo-Rinkan Station Bldg.   0462⟨75⟩0775
- Yokota   0425⟨51⟩0707

A 1988 ad for the Nicola restaurants lists Nick Zappetti's restaurant holdings—which by then had divided to less than half of his former empire. His Japanese partner had taken the rest.

A menu from Nicola's restaurant, under the proprietorship of Nick Zappetti's former partner.

共Ａ３Ｔ５０７電説０４９Ｓ　97年08月12日　（東京）

◎日本の黒い構造の原型　ロッキード裁判の児玉被告

１９７７年６月２日、雨の中を東京地裁に入る、ロッキード事件の児玉誉士夫被告

Yoshio Kodama was a man of many masks: feared right-wing
fixer, founder of the ruling Liberal Democratic Party, confidant
to *yakuza* kingpins, CIA advisors, and linchpin of the Lockheed
Bribery Scandal. Kodama is shown on his way to the Tokyo District Court for his day of reckoning in 1977. (*Kyodo*)

Kakuei Tanaka, Japan's most powerful postwar politician, on the day of his arrest for accepting a bribe from Lockheed Aircraft Corporation. While out on bail, Tanaka continued to run the ruling Liberal Democratic Party from behind the scenes, as he fought his conviction in the higher courts. He died in a Tokyo hospital in 1993 at the age of seventy-five, while the Supreme Court was still hearing his appeal. (*Kyodo*)

Tanaka's disciples hard at work running the government for him in 1986. In the middle is his handpicked heir, Yasuhiro Nakasone, prime minister of Japan from 1982 to 1987. On the far right is Shin Kanemaru, who would soon be forced to resign his Diet post because of his relationship with a leading gang boss named Susumu Ishii. To the left of Makasone is Ryutaro Hashimoto, who would oversee a variety of corruption scandals, first as Finance Minister in the early 1990s and then as Prime Minister from 1996 to 1998. (*Kyodo*)

Susumu Ishii, boss of the second-largest crime syndicate in Japan, in 1989. Among Ishii's many business associates was Prescott Bush, brother of the then-president of the United States. (*Kyodo*)

In Tokyo in March of 1992, Japanese gangsters protest the passage of new legislation designed to limit their ability to formally organize and perform activities as a group. "Gangsters have rights too!" says one placard. (*Kyodo*)

Ryuichi Koike, a *sokaiya* (financial racketeer) who, in 1997, helped cause the downfall of Japan's oldest brokerage house, Yamaichi Securities. (*Kyodo*)

American entrepreneur Richard Roa advised Tokyo *yakuza* on business matters and got caught up in the gangland "Bob Hope Golf Club" scam.

7. THE GREAT

TRANSFER

OF WEALTH

The term "Japanese juggernaut" began to make its appearance in the early 1980s, after Japan had captured the global market for cars, motorcycles, TV sets, semiconductors, and VCRs. Thanks to a disciplined workforce and the highly effective practice of selling products low abroad to capture market shares while keeping prices high at home, the country that had always seemed to be struggling to catch up with the United States was actually on the verge of passing it in a number of important categories: productivity, per capita income, current accounts surplus, and a host of other esoteric economic indicators. America itself, once responsible for half the world's economic output during its golden era in the 1950s and 1960s, was fighting a reputation for being fat and lazy and making overpriced products that broke down. All around the world, people were talking breathlessly about the incredible East Asian export machine that was flooding the world with its products and wondering when, if ever, it would run down.

In a memorable effort to temper the effects of Japan's booming economic growth, representatives of the G-5 nations met at New York's Plaza Hotel in 1985 and collectively agreed to orchestrate the yen's rise against the dollar and the other major currencies of the world, so as to make Japanese exports more expensive and those of the United States, Canada, and European countries cheaper. Over the next two years, the yen would double in value against the dollar (from its 1985 level of 240 yen, to 120 by 1987), but so would Japan's trade surplus with the rest of the world. In the case of the United States, it rose from $25 billion to $60 billion.

Japanese manufacturers used the high yen to their advantage, setting up factories overseas where costs were lower, importing materials more cheaply, and streamlining production at home. The Bank of Japan dramatically lowered interest rates to spur domestic demand, and with credit cheap and capital easy to obtain, people began to borrow money to invest in the stock and real estate markets, which, in turn, caused share and land prices to rise rapidly. Investors then borrowed against their newly appreciated holdings to buy even more. In the ensuing spiral of wealth, many people became millionaires overnight.

The geometric progression of it all was staggering. At the peak of what became known as the Japanese economic bubble, Japan would possess nearly half of all the cash in the world. One economist would call what had happened "the greatest transfer of wealth in the history of mankind."

Tokyo began to reek of money and wretched excess: high-rise "intelligent" buildings of glass and steel, huge state-of-the-art TV screens filling the night sky and BMWs clogging the streets; restaurants that dished up sushi flaked with gold dust, private nightclubs serving cocaine and Ecstasy in back rooms, and even twenty-four-hour vending machines that sold the used underwear of high school girls. In Roppongi, new yuppie eating and drinking establishments were spreading like wildfire in all directions along the strip, lining every available side street, stacked on top of each other in a blaze of neon signs, among them the Tokyo Hard Rock Café, Spago's, Tony Roma's East, and half the city's discos. According to one middle-of-the-decade count, there were more than 2,000 licensed purveyors of alcohol and food within a 200-yard radius of the Crossing, which represented the highest density of nightspots in the world.

For the first time in Zappetti's long memory, the Japanese around him were talking openly about the ultimate superiority of their system. Japan, they pointed out, also had the longest life span in the world, the highest literacy rate, and the highest universal level of education. The United States, by comparison, had a 20 percent functional illiteracy rate, a 30 percent high school dropout rate, and a drug and crime problem of seemingly insurmountable proportions. The translated edition of *The Rise and Fall of the Great Powers* by Paul Kennedy, describing the end of the American century, was a huge best-seller in Japan.

As the money moved from East to West with a sense of gloomy inevitability, North Americans and Europeans who assumed they were born to rule were, for the first time in modern history, being forced to come to terms with an Asian culture from a position of weakness.

This largely unforeseen turn of events was the leading topic of discussion among expatriates who gathered around the red-checkered tables at Nicola's, among whom the most disgruntled was, not surprisingly, the proprietor himself. He watched with growing dismay as rising real estate prices and the skyrocketing yen caused rents to double, then double again, and forced more and more U.S. corporations to move their Asian base of operations out of Tokyo. Many of his patrons on dollar-based incomes found they could no longer afford to live in the city and pulled up stakes. By the end of the 1980s, Tom Blakemore's client list had dropped by 75 percent and even U.S. Embassy personnel in Tokyo were pinching pennies.

Zappetti could not understand how America could allow itself to fall so low, how it could trash its currency as easily as it had in the Plaza Accord and permit the selling off of its proudest assets. He thought the U.S. government should have blocked the sale of Rockefeller Center. It was an American symbol, he railed, in what was becoming a nightly tirade, an *American institution.*

"When we came here in 1945, we came to help them," inveighed the man who made a fortune on the Tokyo black market. "We were generous to them. We paid for their goddamn defense. Now, they're buying us out and making us second-class citizens. Shit."

One might forget that the speaker was himself now a Japanese citizen.

It was ironic that most of the leading Japanese industrial movers and shakers who were seizing markets in the United States were the firms descended from the *zaibatsu*—Mitsubishi, Mitsui, Matsushita, Yasuda, among others, who together accounted for a fifth of all Japan's liquid assets—were those very people whom big American business had helped to depurge long ago in efforts to further its own parochial business interests in Japan.

It was also an effect that was purely unintended by the liberators. As the American author John Roberts once put it,

> The people who helped the zaibatsu reunite were focused on their own narrow interests and didn't think the Japanese had it in them to become an economic power. They were essentially racists. They didn't think a country demolished by war and one with no oil, and no natural resources, could, in the span of a generation, achieve what Japan did. They had no idea that the economic ship of state they had helped launch into the harbor would go all the way across the Pacific Ocean and crash into the U.S. For Americans to cry foul after helping it all to happen was hypocritical.

Japan was actually the globe's largest importer of American goods as well as the second largest market in the world overall. But that fact somehow always got lost in the ballooning trade surplus, which had captured everybody's attention. The Americans and Europeans shrilly branded the Japanese as protectionist and made repeated demands for more access, ignoring Japanese claims that their allies were just not trying hard enough.

In reality, both sides had valid arguments. Japanese companies had succeeded in America because they had learned English, had done their R&D, and had tailored their products, like gas-saving compact cars, to suit Western tastes. Far too many American executives in Tokyo, by contrast, could not be bothered to study the Japanese language or acquire the knowledge and vital contacts necessary to operate in the domestic market, preferring instead to spend their brief three-to-four-year tour of duty within the cozy confines of the American Club.

Moreover, many of the U.S.-made products simply did not fit the Japanese market. American washing machines, air conditioners, and freezers were all too big for Japanese houses, American automobiles had the steering wheel on the wrong side, and the traditional sets of six American-made coffee cups, glasses, silverware, and such were considered too many for the average Japanese family—in Japan it was impossible to sell even a set of six chopsticks. Procter and Gamble made a classic blunder when it tried to market All-Temperature Cheer, a product the advantages of which were not readily apparent in a society where people did all their washing in cold water, in a box that was too big to display on the smaller Japanese supermarket shelves. They compounded their error by promoting the product through confrontational ads, which the more genteel Japanese consumer—used to harmonious social relations in the marketplace, at least on the surface—found offensive. (P&G changed its approach and finally succeeded, after developing a special concentrated detergent, packaging it in a small plastic container, and running "friendly" rather than comparative ads. McDonald's saw sales rise when it came up with a burger slathered in teriyaki sauce, as did Kentucky Fried Chicken when it began serving fried rice balls.)

It was also telling that compared to the few thousand American businessmen based in Tokyo, there were some 60,000 Japanese businessmen stationed in New York, and they were not just there eating sushi. An oft-told story involved the Mitsubishi executive in New York who ate *three* times a night: first he would dine from six to eight, then from eight to ten, entertaining two consecutive sets of foreign clients at expensive French restaurants. His last meal came at home in response to his wife's insistence he have Japanese food. "Americans won't go to those lengths to develop business contacts," the well-fed executive said. "They want to go home at 5:00 to their families." And *that* was why, in his opinion, America was the country with the trade deficit.

But the Americans had an argument too. Because of government controls, restrictive bureaucratic regulations, red tape, and other barriers, visible and invisible, there remained all sorts of salable American products that were kept out of Japan—a full two decades after capital liberalization and market-opening measures had begun under pressure from foreign governments. A U.S.-made muffler was a quarter the price of an identical Japanese-made item, but you couldn't find one in most supply shops because shop owners were pushing the wares of domestic automakers, with whom they had long-standing strategic ties. Can crushers, Peerless pumps, and garbage disposals, which were ideal for a country like Japan with no space, sold for several multiples of their U.S. retail cost because somebody was controlling the distribution rights. Through the 1980s, the era of "open Japan," Motorola arguably had the best cellular phone in the world but was kept out of the lucrative Tokyo and Osaka markets by Japanese government restrictions until Japanese makers were in a position to face the competition.

The fact of the matter was that there was just too much going on behind the scenes for an outsider to compete on an even keel—manufacturers and distributors in cozy relationships, corporations closing ranks through cross-shareholdings, powerful industry associations lobbying and scheming. No better example of this existed than in the construction industry, which was and is almost totally devoid of foreign participation

Perhaps the single most striking thing about Japan over the

last half of the twentieth century was the sheer amount of construction that was constantly going on. Everywhere one looked there was a building in the process of being torn down or put up, a new subway being dug, a bridge being built, highway sound barriers being put up. Construction investment had increased sixfold in the years since the great Olympic buildout, which itself represented a sixfold increase over what had come before. By the late 1980s, someone had estimated that the average life of a structure in the city was only seventeen years. And a national fondness for new architecture had little to do with it.

Consider the following statistics. As this book is being written, there are approximately 500,000 construction companies operating in Japan, which employ some 6 million people, or roughly 10 percent of all the workers in the country. Construction investment annually accounts for 20 percent of the GNP, which means that Japan, as a country, spends thirty-two times as much as the United States does in the same sector of the economy, when the size difference of the two nations is factored in.

Much of the construction is not even remotely essential. Great sections of the coastline are covered with unnecessary concrete and sea breaks, the remote rural stretches dotted with paved hillsides and useless highways. Tokyo, which spends roughly half of its annual budget on public works and construction, has become a city in which almost all the green has been replaced by concrete and wire.

What has caused it all is money. Construction companies have been among the largest of all political campaign contributors. They also have deep ties to organized crime, which controls work crews and supply companies and in some cases owns construction firms outright. The relationship between industry and the government represents what one analyst has called the "largest instance of official corruption in the advanced world."

Public works have long been parceled out by a collusive bid-rigging system called *dango*, in which the contestants for a public works project decide in advance among themselves which company will get what contracts and even determine what the respective bids will be. It is a long-imbedded system designed, in part, to make sure everyone gets a piece of the pie, therefore maintaining harmony in the marketplace and avoiding the much-dreaded onset of "confusion." If there is disagreement among the contenders, politicians and ministry officials make the final decision, for a "mediation" fee, the arbiters not required by law to reveal their criteria for choosing the winner on any given bid.

The results doubled and tripled costs for the taxpayer—and a market closed to outside competition. Angry U.S. trade representatives, alarmed that Japanese construction companies rake in $100 million a year from U.S. government projects, have officially deemed *dango* a trade barrier, a move that has done absolutely no good because LDP politicians are getting too much money under the table in kickbacks from contract bid winners. Better the Japanese demand that the U.S. federal government get the Mafia out of New York.

The bubble economy of the eighties, with its sudden jump in real estate prices, just made things worse, for it gave rise to a new mob activity called *jiyage*—meaning the business of persuading recalcitrant owners to sell their property so that the mob could consolidate it and sell it for the construction of million-dollar office blocks. Popular techniques of persuasion included dead cats at the doorstop, midnight visits from mean-looking thugs, and bombs in the mailbox. By such tactics, *jiyageya* (specialists in the practice) helped create one of the toniest new addresses in the city, Ark Hills, a stone's throw from the original site of Nicola's. A high-gloss complex of high-rise red brick and marble buildings and outdoor pools, it showcased the All Nippon Airways Hotel, with its polished marble lobby, shimmering indoor waterfall, and glistening high-tech studios of Asahi Television. Its smooth, glamorous exterior was in sharp contrast to the brute force that had, at times, been necessary to create it.

The bubble economy had its own impact on the affairs of Zappetti. Almost overnight, the cost of his rent doubled, as did the price of meat, vegetables, hot towels, and other supplies he regularly bought. He found it difficult to raise his prices because so many of his regular customers were foreigners on dollar-based incomes, the value of which was rapidly eroding. Instead, he decided to go back into the farming business. And thus did he get yet another lesson in how things really worked under the surface in Japan.

Allowed by the court to use his Hokkaido land while the lawsuit with his former general manager was being litigated, Zappetti decided to take up hog breeding. He would raise hogs to sell and make a profit and, at the same time, provide himself with a steady access to cheap pork and sausage for use in his restaurant.

The pig farm had originally been the suggestion of a Hokkaido neighbor whom Nick had hired to look after his empty state-of-the-art barn. The man's name was Kobayashi, but Nick dubbed him "Farmer Brown" because Kobayashi bore a strong facial resemblance to Nick's long-deceased cousin "Three-Finger Brown."

"Pigs are better than cows—or mink or rabbits," Farmer Brown had said. "See, you only have to keep them around for six months of the year and you can get your initial investment back fairly quickly. All you have to do is buy piglets, feed them, and sell them when they get big. Since the major pork producers overcharge, you can undersell them and still make a profit."

It seemed to make sense, given that pork was 2,300 yen a kilo (nearly $10 a pound) and rising. But Zappetti should have known better, given all that he had been through before. And, in fact, his friends tried to warn him.

"What the hell do you know about pigs?" chided his neighbor, the White Russian doctor Eugene Aksenoff, from behind his desk at Roppongi's International Clinic. "What are you doing back up in Hokkaido anyway? Your place is in the restaurant. Put your chef's hat back on. Stand by the door and greet everybody in your funny Japanese. The Japanese love that kind of thing. That's where the money is. Forget this other stuff."

Aksenoff knew whereof he spoke. Born in Manchuria and educated in Japan, he had paid his way through medical school in Tokyo by playing the role of enemy Americans in wartime propaganda films. Venal, stupid enemy Americans, it went without saying.

But Zappetti, a born enemy of common sense, refused to listen. Thus, in 1982, in his first official act as a Japanese citizen, he purchased thirty White Landraces and bred them over three generations, producing something called the F-1 pig, which he has been informed, was the most coveted type of pig in the marketplace. In the process, he made a number of interesting discoveries. One was that pigs were very delicate creatures. They had to be given all sorts of inoculations to prevent disease and they had to be handled very gently. Ushering his porcine charges into his barn one day, he whacked one of them with a stick and the startled swine collapsed and died of a heart attack on his mud-covered galoshes, the sudden coronary representing a loss of several hundred dollars.

The biggest surprise of all was the trip to the slaughterhouse, where a price would be offered only *after* the pig was slaughtered. Workers would hoist the pig up on a chain, slit the throat, and cut the arteries to the heart. Then, they'd put it on a roller conveyor, cut off its feet, skin it, and cut it in half lengthwise. Only after that would the appraiser examine the meat and determine a price. If the seller thought it was too low, he couldn't very well say he was going to take his pig home.

There were also pages of rules to follow. The pig had to have a certain girth and a certain length. There were upper limits on fat content. Fines were imposed for each violation, which served to lower the final selling price. A pig that was too long, too short, too fat, or too skinny was penalized. Since the appraisers also had quotas of fines they had to fill (another belated discovery), sooner or later they got Farmer Koizumi for some transgression or another. By the time they were finished, Nick's profit margin had almost disappeared.

It all became more understandable when Nick discovered that the slaughterhouse and its staff, including the appraiser, all belonged to Nippon Ham, Japan's leading pork producer.

For a time, Zappetti took to bringing gifts to the slaughterhouse officials, because, as he was frequently told, gift giving was the Japanese way. Gifts helped form human bonds. They were the grease that smoothed social and commercial intercourse, which was why twice a year, during the year-end and midsummer months, the Japanese went on a nationwide binge of giving gifts, sending bath soap, boxes of fruit, Scotch whiskey and such to everyone of social or professional importance in their lives. In fact, half the families in Japan never bought bath soap because they were given so much on those occasions.

The custom of gift giving demanded that certain forms be observed. One had to give to match the recipient's status, which in Nick's case meant buying from the most exclusive and expensive department stores in Sapporo, the gifts wrapped in paper that advertised their origins to everyone.

Thus laden with Napoleon brandy and other presents did Zappetti go calling on the officials at their homes, hand-delivering his gifts to demonstrate even more "sincerity." In turn, the officials began giving better prices on his pigs.

The idea of it all irritated Zappetti, however. He got tired of having his arm so subtly twisted. One night during a drunken session with an appraiser, he lost his temper. "You ought to be ashamed of yourself," he said. "You're always on the take."

That was the end of the special deals.

An independent breeder couldn't win. If he bought baby pigs in the spring, they were ready for sale in October, which, not surprisingly, was when the price went down. If he kept the pigs longer and waited for the price to rise again, he had to pay more to feed them. In the end, it was difficult to make a profit.

Nippon Ham knocked everyone out of business in one way or another. Nick was not surprised when Nippon Ham started its own pig farm in the area some years later. From that point on, the regional slaughterhouse, where he had been going, refused to take his pigs. He had to travel to Hakodate, several hours away, which was an even bigger expense than before. Finally, he had to quit. And he wasn't the only one. Eighty percent of the hog raisers that existed in Hokkaido when Nick started up his farm eventually went out of business, even though the total number of hogs raised on the island increased during that same time span.

"Americans had the wrong idea about Japan," Nick took to saying when it was all over. "The Japanese weren't just vicious competitors in trade with the United States. They were even worse with each other."

KEIZAI YAKUZA

The new economic might of Japan also gave birth to what became known as *keizai yakuza* (financial gangsters), bubble-era mobsters who distinguished themselves more in the area of white collar crimes. Among other things, they profiteered from insider trading on the ever rising Tokyo Stock Exchange, as they learned to translate brawn, connections, and cash into important investment tips. They also set up specialized finance companies called *jusen* to borrow money from the banks for the purchase and development of real estate. In the heated competition for business that marked the bubble era, bankers even began to approach them, offering cheap loans, while brokerages urged them to buy securities. As long as they had land, which was soaring in value, for collateral, the banks and brokerages would give them anything they wanted.

The men from the local chapter of the Sumiyoshi, the gang that had seized control of the Roppongi-Akasaka area in the wake of the Tosei-kai's decline and became regular customers at Nicola's, were exemplars of the new breed of racketeer. They arrived to dine at Nicola's in a convoy of black stretch Mercedes with opaque tinted windows, sporting double-breasted Italian suits and designer sunglasses and carrying cellular phones. Seated in groups of twenty to thirty, they would order pizza, filet mignon, and the best imported Chianti on the menu. Then, lighting up post-dinner cigars, they would lean back to discuss stock options, futures, and their overseas investments. This crime-on-the-half-shell modus operandi also described the men from the newly opened branch of the Inagawa-kai in Roppongi as well as a local branch of the Kobe-based Yamaguchi-gumi, which also held periodic dinner parties at Nicola's.

All of them were tanned, from periodic visits to Hawaii, and remarkably healthy looking. It was quite a change from the days of pasty-faced, hollow-cheeked, noisy goons dressed in loud checked jackets and baggy pink pants with wads of 10,000-yen notes protruding from their shirt pockets. If the model had once been Marlon Brando in the 1955 movie *Guys and Dolls,* it was now more like Michael Douglas in *Wall Street*. There was even a marked absence of clipped pinkies, because a missing finger-tip, it was now widely recognized, adversely affected one's golf swing. To avoid the slice—in both instances—therefore, every-one was on his best behavior.

One high-ranking captain named Tani could have passed for a Harvard graduate. He was fluent in French, English, and Chinese. He was an expert calligrapher who inkbrushed his own name cards (which carried the title of "corporate vice-president") and was as knowledgeable about classical music as he was about rock and roll—his favorites being Claude Debussy and Mick Jagger.

A tall, well-groomed man in his early forties, his hobbies in-cluded astronomy (a large telescope stood on the balcony of his $20,000-a-month red-brick Roppongi apartment) and collect-ing cars (a Karman Ghia, a Benz, and a black stretch Cadillac were among his possessions). His specialty, the *sokaiya* business of corporate extortion, was seeking out companies that were breaking the law—either by evading taxes, excessively padding expense accounts, or making illegal stock transactions and under-the-table donations to politicians—and then shaking them down. He would trade his silence for large blocks of shares, which he would later sell. To this end, he assiduously studied commercial law and subscribed to all the major dailies and eco-nomic journals (which offered quite a contrast to the yakuza of old, whose reading material had usually consisted of comic books and the horse racing news). He hired himself out to the corpo-rations he had just extorted—as an "honorary board mem-ber"—and advised them how to protect themselves from future extortion by other yakuza like himself. The longer he stayed, of course, the more evidence he collected of his new partners' mis-deeds that could be used for further extortionary purposes.

"It's the nature of human beings to be corrupt," he told Nick, explaining his philosophy of life. "If the companies didn't have anything to hide, people like me wouldn't be in business. The special weakness of the Japanese businessman is that he will do anything to help the company, even if it means breaking the law and risking going to prison. They do it out of loyalty. Or out of fear of being shunted aside. That's a weakness you can take advantage of. The American businessman breaks the law to line his own pockets and is thus harder to catch. That's a fundamental difference."

Another rising star was a man named Tomonao Miyashiro of the Kobayashi wing of the Sumiyoshi-kai. He was a slender, intense, articulate young man who had an MBA from a state college in California (along with an arrest record there that included charges of conspiracy, extortion, and assault with a deadly weapon—pleaded down to misdemeanors in exchange for Miyashiro's departure from America's shores). He had started Japan's first skateboard company before moving on to bigger things. His title was technically *hishokan*, or "secretary," to Kusuo Kobayashi, titular boss of the 300-member Kobayashi faction, but he wielded considerable influence, and some even viewed him as the de facto leader of the gang.

Miyashiro eschewed the practice of wearing tattoos, as well as finger shortening, and preached the need for modern-day yakuza to keep up with new developments in the world by reading the papers and watching CNN. He even appeared in numerous media interviews, including the U.S. TV programs *Moneyline* and *60 Minutes,* where he was seen sporting a Mephistophelian goatee, expensive gold jewelry, and suits out of *GQ.* He boasted of his friendships with Hollywood figures like Diana Ross and Frank Sinatra.

Miyashiro's boss, the man whose underlings had once tried, years ago, to shake down Nicola's restaurant and had fought the

Tosei-kai in hand-to-hand combat for control of Roppongi, had gone on to bigger things. In his sixties, wearing three-piece suits and designer sunglasses on a string, Kobayashi was a prime candidate for nationwide leadership of the massive 8,000-member Sumiyoshi crime syndicate and was nurturing ties to the highest levels of government. One of Yoshio Kodama's ex-disciples, Kobayashi had helped elect Yasuhiro Nakasone prime minister in 1982 by throwing the support of a several-thousand-member rightist organization he controlled behind the LDP politician. (A 1985 police investigation uncovered over 100 instances of extortion by the Roppongi office of the Kobayashi-kai alone.)

To Nick, the New Wave yakuza that appeared before him was all a bit perplexing.

"What the hell is the point of being a yakuza," he asked one well-tailored mobster, "if you act like everyone else? You guys use electronic calculators instead of swords. You talk about derivatives. Your name cards say corporate vice president instead of captain or elder brother. You're trying too hard to be respectable."

The mobster gave Nick a strange look and said, "What about you?"

Then he asked for the wine list.

The old breed of mobster, slowly dying out, still existed in the form of an aging Sumiyoshi underboss who ran an office a few doors from Roppongi Nicola's. He was none other than Katsushi Murata, better known as the man who killed Rikidozan.

Murata had served seven years inside the high grim walls of Fuchu Correctional Facility for his infamous act, and in between return visits, made possible by other convictions for gambling and arms possession, he had risen high in the ranks of the Sumiyoshi. By the mid-1980s, at age fifty, he had ascended to the post of director in the Kobayashi gang and been awarded his own personal *kumi*, or sub-gang, of fifteen men—an honor not lightly bestowed and one which meant that Murata now had men providing him with a share of their earnings as *jonnokin*, or tribute.

Murata, a familiar sight in his frizzy punch perm, was one of the most highly regarded yakuza in the city. There had been numerous media accounts of his exploits, especially the encounter with Rikidozan and its aftermath. After leaving the New Latin Quarter that blood-spilled evening, Murata had gone with his boss, Kusuo Kobayashi, and three other gang members to Riki Apartments in Akasaka—to apologize and negotiate some sort of monetary settlement, as was often the case in such instances, before turning himself into the police. Ordered by Kobayashi to wait in the downstairs parking lot and avoid violence at all costs while the matter was being discussed in Rikidozan's penthouse apartment, Murata found himself confronted by an angry band of Tosei-kai soldiers loyal to the famous wrestler and, rather than disobey his boss's order, he stoically allowed himself to be slashed several times in the face and chest with a butcher knife. It was only when his companions were attacked that Murata finally swung into action—making a foot-long gash in the abdomen of one opponent with the weapon he had used only hours earlier in the Latin Quarter men's room—before police arrived to impose order.

Murata was a gangster with an old-fashioned sense of honor in more ways than one. Whenever the anniversary of Rikidozan's death came around, he never failed to pay his respects. On those occasions when he was incarcerated, he had the prison Buddhist priest come to his cell to light an offering of incense and say a prayer for the repose of Riki's soul. When he was out among the general populace, Murata would visit Riki's grave in the Ikegami Honmonji Cemetery in Eastern Tokyo, to bow and pray before the life-size bronze bust of the wrestler. He would always go on the day before the anniversary or the day after, so as to avoid meeting Riki's family members.

But Murata was suffering from the old gangster disease of diabetes, for which he had to inject himself with insulin every day. Worn and flabby, he was sliding into the sedentary life of a middle-aged man. He lived comfortably in a tenth-floor 400,000-yen-a-month luxury apartment in the upscale residential area of Minami-Azabu with his young wife—the attractive twenty-seven-year-old madam of a high-class Roppongi hostess club—and a menagerie of pets, which included four Siamese cats, two mynah birds, four monkeys, four dogs, a parrot, a raccoon, and a tank of tropical fish. Neighbors would see him taking afternoon strolls in a nearby park, occasionally with a monkey perched on his shoulder. To casual observers, he looked more like a retired salaryman than one of the city's most feared gangsters, and he remained distinctly out of place among the new *keizai yakuza*.

The question of traditional values aside, the fact remained that the yakuza never had it so good as during that era, when the United States of America became a new money-laundering and investment haven for them. Zappetti flew back and forth between Tokyo and Hawaii all the time; he spent most of each winter at his house on Oahu with his wife, and the number of yakuza flying with him had increased dramatically during the eighties. It seemed that half the seats in the first-class section of the Japan Air Lines Friday evening flight from Narita to Honolulu were occupied by mob bosses and underbosses. In fact, there were so many gangsters on the flight that some people had taken to calling it the "Yakuza Express." The price of real estate consequently soared in Hawaii and on the West Coast as gangster types bought up U.S. property, and there was so much mob money being laundered in the United States each year via land deals and dummy corporations that by the end of the decade the total annual revenue involved exceeded that of all organized drug trafficking in America. In response, the FBI started conducting investigations into yakuza cash laundering in Honolulu, Los Angeles, Palm Springs, and Las Vegas. The yakuza had certainly come a long, long way from the days of peddling money orders on the Ginza black market.

A common method of money washing was one in which funds were lent to an "investment company," which used the cash to buy a golf club or a resort in the United States. The club or resort collected fees from new members, and the "clean money" was funneled back to the original investors. Eventually, the investment company sold the property—sometimes at a loss. An informant with ties to the yakuza told a Senate subcommittee in August 1992 that the Japanese firm which had bought (and since sold) the famed Pebble Beach Golf Course in California had borrowed funds from a bank with links to the yakuza, and noted several other properties in Hawaii bought with money generated illegally by the Borkyokudan.

One of the more closely watched players in this high stakes game was a character named Ken Mizuno, who owned a golf club, a real estate company, a Las Vegas restaurant, and a posh Indian Wells resort. Mizuno became something of a legend at the Las Vegas Mirage Hilton for his outlandishly lavish spending. He would regularly charter a DC-9 to fly in with a group of guests on gambling tours. Over a two-year span in the late eighties, he dropped $66 million at the gaming tables.

U.S. and Japanese law enforcement officials, it was reported, were convinced the cash was not his to spend and that Mizuno was a yakuza front man, or a *"paipu"* (pipe) in the parlance, who was losing intentionally at Vegas casinos with Japanese mob connections in order to wash illicitly obtained funds. In fact, in a report issued in 1992 by a U.S. Senate subcommittee probing Asian crime, Mizuno would be identified as an "associate" of the Yakuza. West Coast investigators said he was of Korean ancestry and had special links to the *Toa Yuai Jigyo Kumiai* (East Asia Friendship Enterprises Association), a yakuza gang of ethnic Koreans active in Southern California that was a branch of the Tosei-kai (also operating under the name *Toa Yuai Jigyo Kumiai,* and active in Shinjuku, Seoul, and Honolulu). Japanese journalists and authorities, on the other hand, saw greater significance in his relationship with Kusuo Kobayashi, the Sumiyoshi strongman—Mizuno being a noted guest at the huge wedding of Kobayashi's son in 1988.

Mizuno himself strenuously denied having any underworld alliances, as well as possessing any Korean blood. Although the suspicions of the authorities were never proven, a Ministry of Finance investigation in 1992 found Mizuno had illegally funneled over 32 billion yen to the United States, and the year after that, a U.S. federal court would indict him for money laundering. By that time, however, Mizuno had already been arrested in Tokyo for another crime: the fraudulent selling of golf club memberships. In one of his numerous golf course development projects, he had sold 52,000 memberships to an exclusive Japanese country club that claimed to allow only 2,800 memberships, raking in over a billion dollars—a crime for which he would eventually be convicted and sentenced to prison.

Mizuno's choice of careers in Japan was especially telling. During the roaring eighties, the business of developing new golf courses, or rescuing financially distressed ones, was notorious for being under the influence of organized crime, leaving golf entrepreneurs often at the mercy of mob-run real estate firms and underground money lenders.

BANKS, BOB HOPE, AND PRESCOTT BUSH

Americans, in or out of Japan, were not immune to the sting of the *keizai yakuza,* as a series of notable incidents in the 1980s demonstrated. Notable among them was a scam perpetrated on the Tokyo branch of a leading New York–based bank.

It all started when a private communications company approached the bank for a loan of $20 million. The company had been given official approval from the Post, Telephone and Telegraph Ministry to establish a series of new satellite broadcasting receiving stations; the money was needed, the company executives said, to buy trucks and other equipment and to begin the construction. The request came complete with the approved architect's drawings and specifications for each site. Since all the documents were in order and bore the ministry's stamps of approval, the loan was granted.

The new director of the bank's Tokyo branch, a tough-minded American who, by law, must remain nameless, along with his bank, waited in vain for several months for the first payment to come through. After several attempts to extract information from company executives, he hired a team of private investigators, who eventually discovered the entire project was a myth. Even the receipts for trucks allegedly purchased from Toyota and offered as evidence of good faith to gain an installment on the loan turned out to be fraudulent. Toyota reported it had never made trucks with such serial numbers. The private detectives also uncovered the interesting fact that two high-ranking members of the LDP were major shareholders in the firm.

The bank manager decided to sue and filed preliminary court papers in Sapporo, which was the prefecture in which one of the mythical satellite receiving sites was to be located. It was then that the American was summoned to the Ministry of Finance, of all places, to receive a long lecture about how he did not "understand" Japan and how it would be best for his bank's future

238

in the country, not to mention his career, if he withdrew the suit. He refused and was thereafter summoned several more times for additional warnings, which he also ignored. During one such visit, at a time when the manager's wife was visiting Hong Kong, a MOF official remarked that if the American continued being so obtuse, the wife might never be allowed to return to Japan.

Then he began getting anonymous threatening calls at home.

"You don't know what you're getting into," a strange-sounding man would say in English. "You're in over your head. You're in dangerous waters. Think about the welfare of your family."

To keep up the pressure, the lawyers on the other side kept delaying the start of the trial, but finally, after several months, they ran out of legal maneuvers and a definite date was set to begin the hearings. It appeared the whole incredible fraud, together with the involvement of its prominent LDP participants, was about to be revealed to the public, when the nefarious but influential borrowers caved in. After a number of clandestine meetings, they agreed to repay the $20 million in return for the withdrawal of the suit and a legally binding agreement never to reveal the details of the case. The final $250,000 or so of the repayment, in bundles of 10,000-yen notes in a paper bag, was passed between two cars in Tokyo's Hibiya Park at 10:00 at night. To this day, the American banker involved refuses to discuss the case.

Then there was the yakuza-backed company that in 1985 began selling memberships in a yet unfinished "Bob Hope Golf Club," which Zappetti's friend, the American Rick Roa, worked for. In 1985, he became sales director for the new Tokyo-based corporation, "Bobu Hopu Eiko Kaihatsu," commissioned to solicit clients for the projected Bob Hope Golf Course scaled to be built in Ibaragi, to the northeast of Tokyo.

Hope was famous in Japan for the film *Road to Bali*, among

others, and the entertainer, Roa was told, had been paid $500,000 for the use of his name.

The company chairman was a short, chubby Japanese man in his fifties named Zenya Hamada. On the walls of his office in Harajuku were photos of him with Hope in a reception at the Hotel Okura and another one with the Roman pope—the executive decked out in a formal kimono with white socks, a *geta*, and a fan in the belt. There were also photos of the beautiful piece of land where the golf course would be located, while brochures on the table listed the names of the members of the honorary board of governors; included were Alan Shephard, Henry Ford, and the presidents of Coca-Cola and American Express.

Roa recruited and trained a sales force, comprised mostly of the wives of foreign businessmen, who had wearied of *ikebana* and tea ceremony lessons, Tokyo Tower tours, and lunches at the American Club. Then he discovered that (a) the aforementioned members of the board had not given permission to use their names; (b) the property for the golf course had not even been bought yet; and (c) the real backers of the company were an organized crime group. Yakuza.

The catalyst for these revelations was a Japanese magazine article about the chairman and a similar verture he had run years before, at that time with an unsuspecting Jack Nicklaus, in which a small fortune had been wasted. When that story came out and Bob Hope's lawyers started calling, Hamada, like many other Japanese gangsters, politicians, and businessmen accused of a crime, checked into a private hospital room, where he slipped into his kimono, turned on the TV, and sipped *mizuwaris,* remaining incommunicado with the outside world.

When the Hope side terminated the relationship, Roa was left with the unpleasant task of ensuring that those who had bought memberships were reimbursed. For help, he was forced to turn

to his old friend, Mr. Tanaka at the TSK organization, who somehow pulled some strings and got the job done.

Scam number three involved the tall, courtly, silver-haired
Susumu Ishii, who had taken over as boss of the nation's second
largest gang, the Inagawa-kai, after his release from prison in
1985. A veteran of the Pacific War, where he had served in the
human torpedo unit of the special forces, Ishii had also been a
disciple of Yoshio Kodama, fighting against the leftists in the
1960 Security Treaty disturbances before going into the tourist
business with his friend, the transportation and hotel tycoon
Kenji Osano.

Ishii was the quintessential *keizai yakuza*. On becoming boss
of the 7,000-member Inagawa gang, he formed an investment
company called Hokusho Sangyo, soliciting large sums of capital from major business firms in return for his "protection,"
which he then invested on the gang's behalf in land and securities. His insider trading schemes brought billions and billions of
yen into the gang's coffers.

Like the Sumiyoshi's Kusuo Kobayashi before him, ganglord
Ishii had played his own role in electing a prime minister, when
he stopped a neofascist right-wing group from disrupting the
1987 campaign of LDP presidential candidate Noboru Takeshita
(a member of the Kakuei Tanaka faction); Takeshita was subsequently victorious. Ishii was also instrumental in arranging for
millions of dollars in illegal donations to LDP politicians,
through a trucking company he was affiliated with, known as
Sagawa Kyubin. One of the beneficiaries of the largesse was an
aging, dour, behind-the-scenes kingmaker named Shin Kanemaru, who had helped Takeshita take over the powerful Tanaka
faction in the wake of Tanaka's failing health. It was later re-

vealed that Kanemaru received some 500 billion yen from Sagawa. (In one transaction, 500 million yen of it, in cash, was loaded onto a dolly and hand-delivered to Kanemaru's office.)

The way that legitimate and illegitimate forces intertwined in the Ishii universe was truly fascinating. At the subsequent trial of an executive from said trucking company, there was open court, matter-of-fact testimony by an Inagawa gang associate as to the intimate relationship that existed between the LDP and the yakuza underworld. "It is," he testified without batting an eyelash, "one of help, friendship, cooperation, and support."

It was also very Byzantine. Consider the 1986 takeover by the powerful *zaibatsu*-owned Sumitomo Bank of the smaller Heiwa Sogo Bank, with which Ishii was deeply involved. The Heiwa Sogo had initially hired Ishii at considerable cost to "protect" it from just such a takeover attempt. But Ishii had been prevailed upon to go along with the Sumitomo merger by the former prime minister and still influential LDP figure, Nobusuke Kishi. (It was as if Ronald Reagan, in retirement, had brokered a deal between the Gambino Mafia family of New York and the Chase Manhattan Bank.)

In return for his acquiescence in the Sumitomo mugging of his client, Ishii was offered the as yet unfinished Iwama Golf Course north of Tokyo and granted a low interest loan to pay for the completion of the development work. The purchase of the golf course by Ishii was financed by the trucking delivery company, and the development loan was supplied by the Nippon Credit Bank, an institution where Yoshio Kodama had once served as director. The chief auditor of the Heiwa Sogo bank, Shigaki Isaka, the man whom Ishii ultimately betrayed to achieve the merger, was a former public prosecutor who also happened to be Ishii's lawyer.

Ishii immediately printed up club membership certificates for the undeveloped public golf course and used them as collateral to secure some 300 billion yen more in loans from the big Japanese brokerage houses and various non-banks. The Big Four Security giants, Nomura and Nikko (the largest in the world, with ten times the employees of Merrill-Lynch), Daiwa and Yamaichi, controlled up to three-quarters of the market volume in Japan and seemed to be able to drive prices up virtually at will—by ramping a given stock. Ishii used the money he had borrowed from the brokerages to purchase 24 million shares of equity in the Tokyu Corporation, a private railway, hotel, and department store conglomerate, knowing from inside sources that the stock would rise because of imminent policy and managerial changes. Within weeks of making his block purchase, in the fall of 1989, the price of a single share of Tokyu did indeed rise from 1,700 to 3,060 yen.

Those who wondered how it was that Ishii would be able to secure such huge loans on such questionable collateral—Nomura alone ponied up $14 million, despite the fact that the golf memberships would have no resale value until the club was completed—got their answer when it was discovered that the major brokerage houses involved also bought the Tokyu stock and then sold it for a tidy profit.

Given the vast riches they were accumulating, it was not surprising perhaps that Ishii and the Inagawa-kai would branch out to the United States, with its wealth of new opportunities. There they would purchase a reported several billion dollars' worth of real estate, among other things. What was surprising, perhaps, was the unprecedented aim that the organization would take at the highest levels of the American social and political structure.

In February 1988, representatives of a Tokyo-based real estate company, West Tsusho, which was a front for the Inagawakai, approached Prescott Bush, the elder brother of then U.S. vice president and soon-to-be president George Bush, who ran a prestigious consulting and real estate firm based in Manhattan. The president of West Tsusho, one Sampei Koyanagi, had been introduced to the elder Bush by a mutual acquaintance, a New York City jewelry store manager.

Bush signed on as a consultant, and in July 1989 he arranged for West Tsusho to buy into a New York-based international financial services company called Asset Management International Financial Settlement (AMIFS). He received a $250,000 fee for his services and then took a position as a senior adviser to the firm, supplying a $2.5 million corporate guarantee that the initial investment made by West Tsusho would be recovered within five years.

Bush also helped his new corporate client to purchase 1 million controlling shares of a Houston-based software company, Quantum Access and, after that, to buy 100 acres of land in New York's Rockland County for development into a golf course, which would be designed by Gary Player for a fee of $500,000. The auspicious occasion was celebrated with a posh reception held at New York City's exclusive 21 Club.

Bush even came to Japan in March 1991 and was feted at a lavish dinner held at the Hotel Okura's luxurious Chinese restaurant by executives of West Tsusho's parent company, Hokusho Sangyo.

It was then that Hokusho Sangyo president Munenobu Shoji suggested Prescott arrange a White House audience—"president to president," as it were. Prescott refused, adding that he was "appalled" by the request, whereupon, according to court papers, West Tsusho executives threatened to withhold further investments—"unless Bush showed proper respect by complying with their leader's wishes."

What Bush did not know was that both his client company and its parent were Inagawa-kai fronts, which meant, in effect, that he was employed by the third largest crime syndicate in Japan.

It was only several weeks later that Bush learned of his unwitting yakuza ties when Japanese police began investigating Hokusho Sangyo for violation of foreign exchange laws and the press began publishing details of the unusual relationship. He quickly backed out of the venture, only to find himself sued by his former employers for a $2.5 million breach of contract. The brazenness of the new *keizai yakuza* knew no limits.

It was truly amazing to contemplate. The brother of the chief executive of the United States had effectively handed over stock and real estate to a company with ties to Japanese organized crime, thereby helping it expand its web of influence, and had accepted a large payment for his efforts. The Japanese mob, whose forces had once been marshaled to protect the U.S. president, had now very nearly made it to the doorstep of the White House.

CRAZY WONG AND THE GOLD SCAM

It was not unrealistic to suspect that Nick Zappetti, given who he was, would get caught up in the web of deception that characterized the era of the *keizai yakuza*. What was unexpected was the way it all happened.

It all started one evening in 1989 when Franco and Roberto, from Rome, walked into his restaurant, completely out of the blue. They were short, stocky men in their forties wearing expensive leather jackets, fashionable three-day beards, and strong-smelling cologne. They introduced themselves and said they had a proposal.

"We hear you're the man to talk to around here," Franco had said in heavily accented English. "We got some biscuits we want to unload, *paisan*."

Franco produced a gold piece that weighed about 50 grams

and handed it to Nick. They had a whole shipment of them, he said, which they would be willing to sell below the going market price of $12.95 a gram—$11 perhaps. Maybe $10. Or best offer. Since Nicola was a *big man* around town, said Franco, perhaps he could arrange for a suitable buyer.

Nick knew that at the prices they were talking about, the gold was obviously stolen, but his curiosity had also been aroused and he arranged for another meeting at his restaurant early the next morning before opening hours.

Franco and Roberto showed up at the appointed time carrying a large Boston bag and Nick ushered them into his tiny office. Franco unzipped the bag to reveal a small safe filled with gold coins, each encased in transparent plastic wrapping. Franco pulled out a fistful and handed them to Nick.

"Check 'em out," he said.

Nick pulled the plastic off of one of the coins and ran a thumbnail across it to satisfy himself that it was genuine.

Then, in a demonstration of God knows what, Franco and Roberto counted out all the coins for him.

"It should have tipped me off," Nick was to lament later.

Tokyo, with all its wealth, certainly attracted its share of foreign con artists. In his time, Nicola had played host to many of them: a fake French socialite trading on nonexistent connections with European royalty who bilked the Hotel Okura out of 10 million yen, which she claimed had been stolen from the room where she had been staying for two months, without paying her bill. A retired Air Force captain who opened the "How to Diet and Quit Smoking Clinic" in Roppongi, appearing in TV ads in a white suit and smock warning of the dangers of tobacco, while chain-smoking up a blue storm in a back room office, behind locked doors. A civilian butcher at Grant Heights military housing complex who was selling meat on the side on the black market and making up phony ID cards. The American English school principal whose school was a front for recruiting illegal labor from Southeast Asia. The bogus CIA agent compiling reports for a Japanese government intelligence agency. An executive of a fictitious Hollywood entertainment firm bilking starry-eyed investors out of their money. A Nigerian posing as an American jazz musician living off wealthy female Japanese music buffs. A Texan selling counterfeit *Japanese* government bonds. All of them had wandered through Nicola's at one time or another.

Nick was fully aware of the risks in dealing with strangers —especially those who appeared suddenly to propose what amounted to a criminal transaction—but he rationalized his way around it. Franco and Roberto were fellow paisans. They were from the old country, and unless he misread his guess, they were also Mafiosi. If he could not trust them, then who could he trust? Besides, hadn't they said that *he* was the man to talk to in Tokyo? Hadn't they referred to him as a "big man"? He hadn't heard that in a while. And it felt good. Also, he was just recovering from a heart attack, which had laid him up for several weeks. He needed to get back in the swing of things.

Thus it was that Nick took five random samples of the gold and grabbed a cab for Okachimachi to look up an old gem dealer he knew. Okachimachi was a teeming commercial area of narrow streets and tiny shops situated in Eastern Tokyo beneath the elevated rails of the Yamonote Line, which passed through the area. It was the city's diamond center and the heart of Tokyo's underground jewel business.

There one could buy just about any kind of precious gem— diamond necklaces, emerald pendants, jade brooches—and all at handsome discounts, thanks to their illegal origins. A diamond-encrusted wristwatch normally priced at $2 million in a luxury Ginza department store, for example, could be had in Okachimachi for as little as $200,000—if it had been stolen.

Nick's acquaintance was an aging Taiwanese nicknamed "Crazy Wong" who ran a jewelry store not much bigger than a large closet, a few meters from Okachimachi Station, but one whose window display alone could ransom the Queen Mary. Wong was well known throughout the Tokyo underworld as the man to talk to if you had quality merchandise to sell. Nick had had a passing acquaintanceship with him for thirty years. Wong had even bowled on a team Nicola's had sponsored in the Tokyo Bowling League during a brief boom that sport enjoyed back in the late 1960s and early 1970s in Japan. In fact, it was Nick who had dubbed him "Crazy" because of all the bizarre things Wong did: he bowled sidearm, he chased his beer with whiskey, and he carried around a briefcase that was always filled with expensive gems—which, in Nick's opinion, was Wong's craziest habit of all. Wong was only 5'2" and lucky if he weighed 100 pounds soaking wet. He never carried a weapon, didn't know karate, and to Nick's mind was just begging to be robbed. In the States, they'd have cut off his arm to get the bag. Yet, in Japan, in all those years, he had never had anything stolen. Nick could only chalk it up to cultural differences or dumb luck. Or perhaps having the right kind of friends.

Wong inspected the gold coin samples Nick presented and verified them as legitimate. He offered to buy all the merchandise the Italians had, which amounted to twenty kilos (forty-four pounds) of gold coins at $9.00 a gram and pay Nick a commission of $2.00 per coin for brokering the deal.

With the price agreed to by Franco and Roberto, Nick engaged the services of a young down-on-his-luck American named Zack, who frequented his restaurant and who, for a spell, served as a late-night manager-cum-watchman. Zack arranged for

everyone to meet and conclude the transaction at his tiny apartment in residential Azabu.

When the brothers arrived at the appointed midday hour carrying their Boston bag, they subjected everyone to a rude body
search for hidden weapons. "I not thief," Wong had cried indig-
nantly. "I businessman. I gentleman." Then they opened their
portable safe and deposited five bags of gold coins, each weigh-
ing four kilos, on the living room floor. Crazy Wong produced the
$200,000 he had procured and started to undo the wrappings to
inspect the rest of the gold, but the brother immediately stopped
him.

"No touch," said Franco, wagging a finger angrily. "You don't
do that."

Wong protested, naturally, and Zappetti stepped in to medi-
ate.

"It's okay," he said to the jeweler, flashing a reassuring, knowing wink. "They're *paisan*."

Wong calmed down, but then Franco called a sudden halt to
the proceedings.

"I can't give you the key to the safe here," he said. "How do I
know somebody's not waiting outside to split my head open once
I take the money?"

This called for more discussion and, finally, a new, somewhat
more elaborate course of action was concocted in which Crazy
Wong, Zack, and Franco would stay in Zack's apartment and
jointly guard the safe while Nick and Roberto would go to the
Royal Park Hotel, on the other side of the city, where the brothers were staying. There, in the hotel coffee shop, a public and
therefore secure location, Nick would hand over the cash to
Roberto, who would then telephone Franco and signal the okay
to come down and give Nick the key to the safe. When Nick had
possession of said key, Nick would call and inform Crazy Wong

and Zack, who would proceed to carry the safe to Wong's Okachimachi office. Nick would then taxi over to unlock it.

It took several hours to carry out this complicated plan of action, and by the time Nick's taxi had finally made its way through the rush hour traffic to Wong's jewelry shop it had grown dark and Wong was waiting impatiently—alone.

Producing the final link in the labyrinthine scheme, Nick was given his broker's commission of $40,000 and unceremoniously shown the door. Zack had already signed a receipt for the commission on their behalf before leaving, said Wong, so the deal was concluded and now he would like to open his safe in private, if that wasn't too much to ask. Nick said no, it wasn't, and returned to his restaurant, where he ensconced himself at a back table and treated himself to a cold self-congratulatory draft beer, in defiance of doctor's orders. Only briefly did he wonder what had possessed Zack to sign for the money before Nick had even received it.

Then, the next morning, came the angry phone call.

The key did not fit, Crazy Wong yelled into the phone. He had had to call a locksmith to pry the door of the safe open. Inside, he had said, were five real pieces of gold and 395 counterfeit ones. He had called the brothers at the Royal Park, but they had already checked out. It appeared, Wong said, that he had just been cheated out of $200,000 and he wanted to know what Nick was going to do about it.

Nick could not have been more embarrassed. He, the King of Roppongi, and one of the city's great bullshit artists, had been duped. And for the life of him, he could not figure out how it had happened. Nick immediately offered to return the commission, but Crazy Wong was by no means satisfied. He demanded Nick also take responsibility for the $160,000 he had lost. When Nick refused, Crazy Wong announced he was going to sue Nick for *selling counterfeit merchandise.*

Jesus Christ, Nick wondered. How in the hell could Wong sue him over counterfeit merchandise when the goods involved had been smuggled into the country in the first place? Then he made an interesting discovery. On the receipt Wong had in his possession—the receipt for Nick's broker's fee which Zack had signed on Nick's behalf—was a handwritten notation in Chinese ideographs that the amount received, the $40,000, was *not* a commission but a *down payment* for "twenty kilos of gold worth $200,000."

That was how in the hell Crazy Wong could sue.

Nick contacted Zack, who insisted that the only writing on the receipt when he signed it at Crazy Wong's request had been the word "Receipt," the date, and the broker's fee figure of $40,000. That business about down payment must have been added later, he said, but unfortunately he had neglected to get a copy of the original. Then Zack abruptly left the country, leaving Nick to face the litigatory wrath of Wong all by himself, who was now calling Nick's employees at their homes in an effort to find out about Nick's worth.

To get out of his jam with Crazy Wong, Nick decided to approach someone from one of the gangs that now frequented his restaurant. He felt he had a right, at least, to ask for a favor because, for one thing, they were constantly borrowing his in-house cellular phone, calling all over Japan, discussing their business deals. As a result, he had an enormous monthly phone bill, which he diplomatically paid without comment.

The prime candidate for the favor Nick wanted to request was a man who introduced himself as the new boss of Akasaka. A robust-looking man in his forties—about 5'9", 190 pounds—who abstained from alcohol because of chronic diabetes and who could be seen jogging around the streets of Roppongi in a training suit buying his daily copy of the *Asian Wall Street Journal* at the Crossing bookstore, he was always very cordial. More than once he had told Nick, "If you have any problems, let us know."

Well, now Nick had a problem and he decided to let the guy know. The next time the boss came in, Nick sat down at his table, presented him with a drink on the house, and popped the question.

"Can you do something for me?" he said. "I need a 'hammer,' if you know what I mean."

"A hammer?" the man asked looking up from the pizza menu.

"Yeah. A guy's beating me out of some money and I would like him to meet with some personal misfortune. You know, maybe he could have an accident. Somebody could ransack his office. Maybe he could be mugged on the way home. It doesn't matter as long as he gets the message to stop fucking with me."

"Who's the guy?" he man asked.

Nick told him and the man replied that he would do some checking and get back to him.

Several days later he reappeared with an answer that left Nick slackjawed.

"Sorry," the boss said, "but, we can't help you. Your guy is under our protection. There's nothing we can do."

Then he sat down to order his dinner.

Nick already knew he'd been set up. Now he'd begun to wonder how far the sting extended.

In Japan, it was just one layer over another.

8. BLACK RIDER

Nicola Koizumi entered the last decade of the twentieth century—and the final years of his life—a sick and embittered old man. He had been hit with a sudden succession of debilitating ailments—heart trouble, diabetes, and failing vision, among them—which, Japanese doctors liked to remind him, were a natural outcome of the debauched existence he had led for so long.

Worse yet, at an age when most of his contemporaries were relaxing and enjoying the fruits of their lifelong labors, he remained enmeshed in endless litigation. His lengthy appellate court battle with Nihon Kotsu, which had been interrupted by a heart attack that nearly killed him, had become so complicated that his own lawyers had filed lawsuits against him. His Hokkaido land case, which had gone against him after eight tortuous years of legal wrangling, was bogged down in appeals, along with the *taishokin* case, and Crazy Wong was starting up the court machinery for his own attack on Zappetti's dwindled fortune. It all left him brimming with hatred for the Japanese and their system of justice.

"In any other country in the world I would have won hands down," he would rage darkly. "Ghana. Timbuktu. No problem. But here? Never."

If he had not had his stroke, he mused, things might have turned out differently. In the Nihon Kotsu appeal, the legal team of four lawyers he had assembled over the course of that case had adopted a new approach, arguing that his flagship restaurant, including the building in which it was housed and the land on which it stood, should *all* be returned because their combined value had multiplied over the years to an amount far, far in excess of their worth at the time of the takeover. The increase was so great, their brief stated, that it was now impossible to claim that seizure of the property constituted fair repayment of the original loan.

After four years of plodding through appellate court, it seemed to Nick, at least, the judge might actually be buying that argument—if the sympathetic looks he was getting from the berobed figure on the bench were any indication. It was a view, it might be noted, that was not wholeheartedly shared by his counsel. But then Nicola went into a hospital in central Tokyo for minor surgery to correct a bad back that was hampering his golf game and suffered a bizarre heart attack, which served to hopelessly confuse his situation.

It had come on a warm night in June 1986. He had been lying down in his expensive second-story hospital suite, thinking about the operation scheduled for the following morning, when suddenly he began to perspire and tremble; he felt a terrible pain in his chest and was overcome by a wave of nausea. He got up and went into the bathroom where he was racked by alternating bouts of vomiting and diarrhea. When he finally came out, pale and shaken, he looked out the window and what he saw caused him to rub his eyes in disbelief. There, bathed in the moonlight, he later told friends, was a rider on a black horse coming through the front gate of the hospital grounds, heading up the driveway toward the main entrance. The rider was wearing armor, like the knights of old, and his face visor was down. He was holding a sword in one hand and a deck of black cards in the other, which he began flinging in Nick's direction, one by one. Clearly visible in the dim light was the English word "Death" scrawled in yellow ink on each card.

"So this is death," Nick muttered to himself, wondering at the same time what a medieval English knight was doing in a twentieth-century Tokyo apparition.

"Well, I'm not ready to die just yet," he said aloud.

The rider kept coming.

"Fuck you, death!" he yelled out the window. "Go to hell."

He stood there cursing. Then suddenly the figure vanished.

Nick got back into bed and pressed the call button.

Soon the room was filled with doctors, more nurses, and equipment. A grim-looking Japanese heart specialist examined him and informed him he had had not one but two myocardial infarctions, which had caused 75 percent of his heart muscles to stop. He was immediately moved to the intensive care unit, where he was dosed with glycerine pills and told to keep as quiet as humanly possible.

Nick thought he was probably going to die. So, it appeared, did everyone else. His wife, his son Vince, who came the next day, the entire medical team—they all had that *look* on their faces. The chief of his legal team had even showed up to see him. He sat by the edge of Nick's bed and said, "I can get you a settlement of 5 *oku*—500 million yen right now."

Nick stared at him dully. He'd been fading in and out of consciousness.

"Plus legal fees," the lawyer added.

Nick grunted.

"All right," he managed to say weakly.

The figure the chief lawyer had cited—at the time the equivalent of roughly $4 million—was but a fraction of the total value of the property. But Nick had been thinking about something else. In his twilight zone haze, it occurred to him that it might be possible to use the Nihon Kotsu offer in court as evidence against the defendants. If they were willing to give up that kind of money—insufficient as it may have seemed to him—to settle the case, then, he asked himself, wasn't that an indication in itself that the defendants believed deep down in their hearts of hearts that they were wrong and owed something to the plaintiff?

That was what Nick's "all right" had meant.

"All right" as in "All right! Now we can get those bastards."

Of course, Nick's legal chief had an entirely different take on the conversation. He was increasingly of the opinion the case was unwinnable and that reaching such a harmonious conclusion would constitute a major feat of legal skill on his part. He believed he was doing his client a huge favor by convincing the other side to settle. However, since no one could read Nick's mind and Nick was incapable of uttering much more than a few unintelligible grunts at a time, no one disputed the "agreement." And thus while Nick was still bedridden, his fourth wife used his company seal to approve the contracts and the money was paid.

Much to everyone's surprise, Nick began to recover. And when he was well enough to realize what had really happened, instead of being grateful as his lawyer had anticipated, he was livid— or as livid as his delicate medical condition allowed him to be. He accused his lawyers of selling him out, of striking a quick deal to get their money before he bit the dust. He had had a chance for victory, he rasped, but the goddamn lawyers had snatched it from him.

The matter of legal fees was the breaking point. Nick had been given a bill of 15 million yen by his legal chief, which he interpreted as payment for his entire team of four lawyers. This was on top of a retainer of five million yen a year he had already been paying them all in toto. (That was the system in Japan. One paid retainers. Then one paid legal fees, which were decided after a settlement was reached.) But the chief counsel said no— the 15 million applied only to him. There would be more invoices coming from the desks of the others and that was between them and Zappetti.

The subsequent bills were perhaps not unreasonable in the Japanese context, but Nick was in no mood to listen. He refused to pay a single yen more. His legal chief took him to arbitration, while the other attorneys flat out sued him—three separate suits, one after the other, for several million yen. For a lawyer to unilaterally sue his client was almost unheard of in Japan. But Nicola Koizumi had managed to make it happen. Three times. He could have written a manual on ways to get into trouble.

Nick's health eventually improved to the point where he was able to leave the hospital, but he was not exactly in peak condition for courtroom warfare. He had a hacking cough. He needed to use a cane to walk because one of his legs had atrophied, and he was popping glycerine pills like candy to control what was literally only half a pulse. His doctor had told him that if he ever really lost control of his temper, he ran the risk of blowing out what remained of his heart. His blood pressure would rise, his heart would expand, and—poof! Sayonara Nick-san.

He had also managed to lose most of the vision in his left eye with the assistance of the staff at aging prewar Toranomon Hospital, the venerated caregiver to Tokyo's diplomatic corps. A few months before his heart attack, doctors there had diagnosed him with diabetes; they informed him he had "blood on his eyeballs," that the arteries around the edge of each eye had become brittle from high sugar content, and that he would need laser treatments to cauterize the veins. Under doctor's orders, he began making regular visits to the Toronomon laser room—from which he would stagger each time, seeing blurred spots of red, yellow, and blue for the rest of the day.

During one session, a junior technician had unwittingly trained the laser beam directly on the retina of Nick's left eye. The slip created an instant blind spot—a missing center of vision in the orb. After that fateful afternoon, if Nick looked at someone's face with his right eye closed, the person's nose was blocked out—like the genitalia in a censored pornographic movie—and the area around it fringed with colored polka dots.

The vision in his right eye had also deteriorated. In optical tests, he could barely make out the top line of the chart. To read a newspaper, he needed a magnifying glass. He was forced to wear an audio watch—one with a computerized voice that announced the time—because he was unable to read a conventional timepiece. Driving a car was totally out of the question.

When the expurgated vision in his left eye failed to improve, he complained to the doctor, who conducted an internal investigation and reported back, huffily, that his staff had done nothing wrong. It was the patient who had moved his retina into the path of the beam, not vice versa. The hospital was, therefore, not responsible.

How things had changed, Nick thought. In the old days, back when he was The King, the hospital would have come up with a new eye for him. But not anymore. Now, it was Fuck you, *gaijin*. He toyed with the idea of suing the hospital, but he was running out of energy. He did not think he could handle any more law suits, especially one he probably wouldn't win. In fact, he had growing doubts about his ability to withstand his present legal calendar, busy as it had once again become.

"I'm coasting on the gasoline fumes in the tank," he would croak. "I can't get it up anymore. It's just a question of time until I keel over."

But then he appeared before the judge in 1990 to hear the formal reading of the first complaint against him—"Failure to pay ex-lawyer 15 million yen for settling the case, as agreed"—and he felt a reawakening of resolve. "Settling the case?!" The dirty son of a bitch had some nerve. His heart began to beat faster as he sat there. He could feel the expansion. He clenched his fists, took a few deep breaths, and swallowed a glycerine pill.

The newly hired Japanese counsel, a young attorney not long out of law school, scribbled him a note in English which urged him to keep his calm, to answer all questions posed to him rationally, and to avoid making his usual remarks like, "I was blackmailed," or "My money was hijacked."

Nick read it twice, then popped another glycerine pill.

All right, he *would* keep his cool, if that's what it took. And to start things off, he would also scare the piss out of the cutthroat sons of bitches—that very day. He would teach the Japanese legal profession what it meant to mess with Nick Zappetti. At eight o'clock in the evening, he took a cab to his erstwhile attorney's downtown office. He limped down the dimly lit and deserted marble hallway, stopped at the glass door that bore the name of his legal firm in black stenciled letters. He turned the knob and slowly opened the door. The outer office was in shadows, but he could see lights and hear voices coming from an inner conference room. He rang the bell and in short order one of the men appeared. Nick smiled at him, malevolently, through the gloom.

"How do you like the way I come here and visit you? Eh?" he said, tapping his cane on the floor. "One of these days somebody is going to come here like this and kill you—before you know what's happening. So from now on you better lock your door and be careful how you open it—especially at night."

He was pleased to see the men cringe and take a step back.

It seemed to him he had lost everything to the Japanese. Once he had had eleven different restaurants. Now they were all gone except for the Roppongi Crossing branch, where he spent his afternoons and evenings commiserating with fellow expatriates. His wife Yae owned and ran three of them. Her sister ran one more. And the rest of his former empire, including the old flagship building in Gazembocho and several other small-sized restaurants around town, belonged to his one-time Japanese partner, Nihon Kotsu. Their menus were even enscripted with "Nicola's, since 1956."

Oh, the slings and arrows.

He calculated that had he been able to keep everything—all his restaurants, all his land, all his buildings—he would have been worth a billion dollars, bare minimum. That, as he liked to note, was the equivalent of the entire budget of the United Nations. The value of all the property he had lost in Roppongi alone came to nearly $500 million in 1990 prices. Add to that an annual gross of several million dollars over thirty-five years in service revenue and accounts receivable and he'd be in Ross Perot territory.

Now, however, someone else was the beneficiary of his labors. He had less than $1 million in the bank and only two houses— a new four-bedroom 10,000-square-meter place he had bought with the Nihon Kotsu settlement, and a $700,000 home in Hawaii. In Nick's view of the world, he was nearly poverty stricken.

What was happening to him after some forty-five years in Japan was not unlike what was happening to the United States in its relations with Japan.

RIO BRAVO

Now that the Japanese possessed half the world's money, they were spending it on buying up America, reeling in many high-profile American properties: Rockefeller Center, Columbia Pictures, Universal-MCA, Pebble Beach, and the Riviera Club, among others. Even ordinary office girls found themselves able to buy condominiums in Hawaii and New York. Japanese tourism to the United States had also exploded with millions of travelers annually invading the West Coast or New York City, where they stayed in Japanese-owned hotels, ate at Japanese restaurants, rode on Japanese-owned buses, and bought their souvenirs in Japanese-run trinket shops (many, incidentally, run by yakuza groups). Hawaii was jokingly referred to in some circles as Japan's forty-eighth prefecture; California as her forty-ninth. Fifth Avenue was starting to look like the Ginza.

America's reduced status in Japanese eyes was beginning to be reflected in the eyes of Japan's leaders. "Lazy and illiterate" was what the speaker of the Japanese parliament had only recently termed the Americans, while Nakasone had termed their intelligence level "low." (Even Nick's own son had joined the enemy camp, so to speak. "Who's Nicola?" he once said dismissively, referring to the Roppongi operation. "Who knows you now?")

As American complaints about "unfair trade" escalated, accordingly, the intensity of emotion surrounding matters of international commerce between Japan and America was ratcheted up to all-time highs. In 1989, for example, a famous article on trade in the *Bungei Shunju* bore the indignant title *"Warui No Wa America!"* ("It's America That's Bad!"). A year later Dietman Shintaro Ishihara's saber-rattling polemic, *The Japan That Can Say No,* urging that Japan stand up to the United States, sold a million copies, as did two sequels in the early 1990s. A noted Japanese psychiatrist, summing up the national mood, likened America to a bullying corporate executive driven by some inner psychotic need to intimidate his subordinates and declared that America, as a whole, was suffering from a disease called obsessive neuropathy.

America, which had once relegated the subject of Japan to the back pages, now was experiencing its own brand of paranoia, a prime example being the best-selling 1992 novel *Rising Sun,* in which Japanese characters in pursuit of American technology were unflatteringly portrayed, including one who liked to slice up women with a sword during sex. (Said a perplexed *Bungei Shunju* editor after reading *Sun,* "In my whole life as a Japanese, I've never met anyone resembling the people portrayed in that book. I must be missing something.") There was also the Japan expert who warned that Americans were all doomed to be enlisted men in the Japanese Imperial Corporate Army if something wasn't done soon.

The marriage of Nick and Yae Koizumi was symbolic of the U.S.–Japan relationship—two countries bound by a treaty and divided by a vast cultural gulf. They were a distinguished-looking couple when greeting guests at the entrance to the Roppongi restaurant—she elegantly dressed and bejeweled, he sporting a thick white mustache and dapper blue serge suit and cane of polished oak; they could have been hosting a diplomatic reception. When sitting together in a back corner of the room, however, they were often engaged in heated argument.

They fought about everything from household medicine to the auto industry. If he had a headache, he would take Tylenol brought from Hawaii, a brand-name pharmaceutical, she might note, that was not approved by the Japanese government. If *she* had a headache, she would put magnetic patches on her temple—something he referred to as a "quack" cure. If the subject was which new car to buy, he would lobby for a Cadillac Seville, in his opinion, the best car in the world, while she might argue for a Japanese or European model; after all, the word around town was American cars were so poorly made you might cut your finger opening the hood. She was inclined to agree with the Mitsubishi executive who opined that America ought to give up making cars because they just weren't capable of doing it well.

More often than not the bone of contention was the management of Nicola's empire, the major portion of which his wife now controlled—much to Nick's unending vexation. In fact, the only restaurant over which Nick exercised complete authority was the only Nicola's in existence losing money, a state of affairs that galled him even more and one that his wife did not fail to remind him of periodically. All the restaurants Yae's company owned and operated were raking in yen, as were the Nihon Kotsu-owned branches. But the Roppongi Crossing branch—his baby—was in steep financial decline. Except for Friday night, when the expatriate community came out in force, business was mortifyingly behind the curve.

Modern Roppongi and its environs now offered too many other more fashionable spots. The ballplayers, the mobsters, and the politicians still came around. The slick-haired future prime minister, Ryutaro Hashimoto, then biding his time as a cabinet minister, came in. Hollywood actor Tom Selleck, filming *Mr. Baseball*, also graced his portals. But younger Japanese preferred the trendier places like Ristorante Sabatini, on the top floor of the nearby Ibis Hotel, with its house wines and *canzone* singers straight from Rome or the deluxe Le Patio in the ANA Hotel featuring an Italian chef who also sang opera. The new glossy Il Forno with its original menu of California Italian cuisine was turning people away at the door.

Without red brick walls, medallioned waiters, and wandering minstrels to attract diners, Nicola's was starting to look old-fashioned. Unlike Nihon Kotsu, Nick did not have a fleet of 4,000 taxi drivers to turn to as potential "voluntary" diners when business was slow.

He had tried a number of tactics to reverse his moribund business—sponsoring a late-night television show aimed at younger viewers, installing a large new neon sign in his third-floor window, and erecting a life-size poster of himself at the front door—standing there, pizza in hand, next to a beaming nubile model, looking like some jolly old bald-headed Santa Claus. He also invested millions of yen in a large flat-paneled TV screen system so his customers could watch sumo wrestling and pro baseball games. But nothing happened.

In 1990, Nicola's Roppongi lost over $700,000, the fifth year in a row Nick was in the red. By contrast, his wife had shown a profit of over $1 million in the Yokota operation alone, which she was running all by herself, and where the clientele was now 98 percent Japanese. It pained him greatly to admit it, but she was now worth far more than he. In fact, she had become one of the wealthiest women in Japan. Her Yokota interests amounted to $30 million, her Roppongi property worth nearly as much. She possessed five or six luxury golf club memberships, one of them valued at more than $500,000 and a million-dollar jewelry collection.

His wife told him that his present sorry state had come about because he failed to keep up with changing Japanese tastes. With Pizza Hut down the street, Domino's starting the home delivery market, and Shakey's operating branches all over town (serving eggplant and mushroom pizza made especially for the Japanese), he needed something different to compete.

You had to Japanize the product, his wife said, reciting the Japanese trade mantra. Nicola's anchovy dressing was too strong for the Japanese palate. So was his sausage spice. Didn't he know that Nihon Kotsu now served pizza with soy sauce? It was time that Nick started paying attention.

She herself had a tie-in with Tokyu, a major department store chain, for whom she supplied year-end holiday pizza with colorful pineapple and cherry toppings, as befitting the season. Nick said he had never seen anything so grotesque, but the department store people had been ecstatic and sales were terrific.

It was also an absolute must, she kept saying, to give *o-chugen* and *o-seibo*, summer and winter gifts, to business associates. She *always* did it. It was how she maintained and serviced business relationships in Japan and one reason why she kept getting repeat department store orders. It was something that Nick had always stubbornly refused to grasp. But he could not continue to dismiss such important customs as bribes if he wanted to revitalize his business.

Nick listened as much as he could, then told her to shut up and mind her own business.

He was the one who had started Nicola's. He had taught her everything she knew. Who was she to tell him how to do things?

She replied that there was a limit to how Westernized Japan could become. The Japanese had accepted a massive infusion of bread and milk into their diets and adopted other radical changes into their daily lives in the wake of the Occupation. Would Americans ever tolerate a similar shift? Would they commit to a regimen of raw fish and rice every day? Would they start wearing kimonos instead of suits? The Japanese were flexible—a lot more so than the Americans, in her opinion. But there were limits, and it was time he learned that.

At the very least, she said, do something about the lighting and the music. Most Japanese people liked their restaurants brightly lit. They didn't feel right eating in darkened rooms. They wanted to be able to see their food clearly as well as look at the faces of their dinner companions. And as for the music, it was much too soft. Japanese diners liked it louder. Everyone knew that.

He refused, and thus was the battle of the lights and music engaged. Growing ever more assertive and determined to help him turn things around in spite of himself, Yae would arrive at the Roppongi Crossing branch and turn the light rheostats all the way up. At the very first opportunity, Nick would turn them back down again. In the course of a two-hour meal, patrons might experience several levels of illumination. This continued for some time until finally, in exasperation, Nick put cloth covers over each individual lightbulb.

The music, which was piped in from a local Roppongi service, experienced similar oscillations. Nick would be sitting at a back room table, squinting up at his giant TV screen, when suddenly the volume of the Muzak would swell. "Turn that goddamn music down," he'd yell at the nearest waiter, "I can't hear a damn thing." And everyone in the restaurant would turn to stare.

Said long-time headwaiter Akio Nomura, who witnessed it all, "It drove me crazy after a while. His wife would give an order to turn up the sound or the lights, and thirty minutes later, Nick would countermand it." Nomura had seriously considered quitting, but his boss, in a pique over some minor insubordination, fired him instead, before he had a chance.

An argument erupted over the decor as well, which Yae thought all wrong for the times. The red-and-white checkered tablecloths, the Chianti bottles with the candles stuck in them, the trellises with their artificial grapes—they were all passé in her opinion and even looked cheap amid the new wealth and glitter of the city. Redecoration was a must, she said, to get the customers to start coming again. Nick resisted fiercely. He believed that once the new fads ran their course, "traditional quality" would come back into fashion. What worked before would work again. All that was required was a little patience.

Some of the more cynical observers of their union believed that Yae had remarried him primarily to torment him about his business failures and remind him that she was now the more successful of the two, thereby exacting some measure of revenge for the way he had treated her over the years. Those same observers also believed that Nick had remarried her only in an attempt to get his property back. Nick encouraged both points of view in his fouler moods.

Increasingly, he took his frustrations out on lovestruck young Western men who brought their Japanese girlfriends in for dinner.

"Did you know that the only reason a Japanese woman marries an American or a European is that she wants to dominate him?" he would say with malicious delight. "If she marries a Japanese man, she has to be an obedient, stay-at-home wife. But if she can marry a foreigner, she can control him."

"One of the reasons I stayed in Japan in the beginning was because I was attracted to the women, too," he would add. "Now, four marriages later, it's one of the reasons I'm anti-Japanese."

His wife insisted to friends that she loved him, despite all the pain he had caused her, and wanted only to help him enjoy what was left of his old age, while Nick, in his rare, reflective moments would say, "Well, now, you don't spend the rest of your life with someone you don't have feelings for, do you?"

But such reflective moments were indeed rare.

He was too busy being angry.

It seemed that not a day went by without something occurring to arouse his bile and make him reach for another glycerine pill. The TV talk shows were now full of opinion makers running America down, and when U.S. President George Bush came to Japan hat in hand to try to open the market for auto parts, they had openly ridiculed him (much as Americans a generation earlier had ridiculed Japanese leaders as "transistor salesmen"). That ridicule turned to laughter when Bush became ill at a state dinner and vomited on Japanese Prime Minister Kiichi Miyazawa.

High on Nick's list of peeves was the new self-assertiveness of his Japanese customers. He could remember not so long ago when the Japanese businessmen who came into his restaurant sat there unobtrusively and ate their dinners. Now, it seemed to him, they were all puffed up with self-importance, shoulders thrown back in the manner of some ancient TV Daimyo, talking loudly enough for everyone to hear. One night a group of executives in his restaurant had been especially annoying.

"Japan is now number one," he could hear them bragging drunkenly from across the room. "Japan can do everything better than anyone. Who are the Americans to criticize us when it is we who are more economically powerful?"

Limping over to their table, Nick launched into a tirade: "We gave our markets to you and paid for your defense. And now you think you're hot shit, just because you got some money in your pockets? If you're so wonderful, why is it you can't even put a man in space? How come Hitachi's got to steal its technology from IBM? To me, you're like a banana republic, except you're a TV republic, because all you can do is make TVs."

Then he turned and limped away.

It was no wonder business was falling off.

To Nick, the whole city was going to hell. It pained him to witness the profound changes that were taking place right outside his window, starting with the new wave of discotheque doormen who barred all non-Japanese men from entering and including the unseemly spectacle of North American and European peddlers hawking cheap jewelry and trinkets on the streets of Roppongi. For some reason, this seemed especially galling to the former black marketeer.

Tokyo had once been a wonderful place to live in Nick's view. Back in the old days they had called him "The King," and they got out of his way when he came walking down the street. But not anymore. Now the shoe was on the other foot. They just brushed him aside as they sped past—many of the young men a head taller than he—and they didn't even say excuse me.

"You ever see that movie *Rio Bravo*?" Nick would say to his foreign customers. "You remember the scene where the leering cowboy throws the money into the spittoon? And Dean Martin, who's the town drunk, crawls after it? That's Japan's fantasy image of us. They want us to crawl and beg like Dean Martin."

To the King of Roppongi, abandoned by his subjects and hounded by tormentors, for the Japanese to crow over their success was, for them, to disdain America's might and its largesse to them. He took it all very personally.

On a trip to Hokkaido he nearly got into a fistfight. He had been sitting on a bench at Sapporo Station, waiting for a train, holding on to his cane, when an elderly white-haired man wearing traditional *hakama* robes and a straw fedora approached him. The approach, of a sort experienced at one time or another by many foreigners in Japan, was not friendly. The man stopped in front of Nick and offered his hand, as if in greeting. Nick grasped it halfheartedly.

"*Yowai ne* (You're weak)," the man growled, giving Nick a sour expression. "*Anta kaere*," he then added. "Go home."

The two of them were soon standing toe to toe, Nick leaning on his cane for support, exchanging insults in two broken languages. Fifty years after Pearl Harbor, forty-six after Hiroshima, the insults escalated into crisis, the two unsteady-looking men getting on in years, one American (if a naturalized citizen) and one Japanese, venting their antipathy across an unbridgeable gulf—a gulf widened further, ironically, by the more than four decades of common experience. With the two ranting, shaking fists in the air, and threatening each other with bodily harm, the confrontation might have been a Punch and Judy show on the whole bitter, dark, unreconciled side of the bilateral relationship, but the King of Roppongi was too lost in his ire to notice any ironic symbolism.

If it had not been for three Japanese youths in black cadet school uniforms who happened along, their mouths agape at the two haranguing, frail-looking, aged men, and persuaded Nick's nemesis to leave, there's no telling what might have ensued.

When he thought of his children and grandchildren, his mood did not improve. His son Vince (who had made it clear he wanted nothing to do with the family business, at least as long as it meant taking orders from his stepmother), had obvious Occidental features and, it seemed to Nick, mixed feelings about his American genes. Married to a Japanese woman and the father of two girls, for a time he had avoided PTA meetings at his children's school. He had done this, Nick was certain, because if it became known there that the daughters, who looked Japanese, were in fact biracial, the other students would give them a hard time. The mother had also let it be known she did not want Nick visiting his grandchildren at school for the same reason. In response, Nick had sent an emissary to talk to the school's principal, who had sympathized, but pleaded helplessness. "People don't want their relatives to be *gaijin*," he had said, as if to contemplate otherwise was outside the realm of human thought.

Gaijin, a compound of two ideographs—the first meaning "outside," "external," "off the mark," "out of place," the second meaning "person," "human," "mankind"—inherently implied a sense not only of Japanese uniqueness but a definite qualitative distinction vis-à-vis everyone else, which was why, even in the nineties Japanese who lived in New York continued to call the Americans they lived and worked among *gaijin*. Non-Japanese, even in their own country, were thus defined first and foremost by their otherness.

His daughter's children—three from two failed marriages—had similar problems assimilating, but she solved them by simply packing up and moving everyone to New Zealand.

What bothered Zappetti most of all, perhaps, was what he saw as the submissive attitude of his fellow Americans in this new era. There was a new phenomenon in his restaurant that he absolutely hated: apple-cheeked *gaijin* yuppies, speaking fluent, super-polite Japanese—young stockbrokers and security analysts for Japanese firms, living in $20,000-a-month apartments. They would come to dine with their Japanese bosses, kowtowing and bowing, as Nick watched with great displeasure.

"Their bosses would insult them all evening, just by their arrogant manner," he would say in disgust. "And these Western yuppies would just sit there and take it. These kids actually acted as if they believed the Japanese were superior."

Nick did not mind letting them know how he felt, either.

"How do you like kissing the ass of your Japanese boss?" he would whisper, cornering his prey by the cash register or in the rest room. "Is it worth all that money they're paying you?"

He looked at such people, and he saw American lobbyists in Washington, D.C., selling their services to the Japanese car companies, or even former U.S. President Ronald Reagan taking $2 million from a Japanese media conglomerate for a two-week series of public appearances in Japan in the fall of 1989.

What America needed, Nick thought, was an active right wing, like the militant Japanese thugs who rode around Tokyo in their olive gray trucks with the flags and loudspeakers, shouting antiforeign slogans. If he were younger, he swore, he would go back to New York and organize his own rightist group. Nicola's Army, he'd call it. He would put a truck outside of Rockefeller Center, displaying a big banner that said, "Down with Japanese corporations in America."

He was turning into a raving lunatic. This naturalized Japanese citizen would buttonhole anyone who would listen and regale him with tales of how great America really was. He'd remind one and all that during World War II Americans produced a 10,000-ton Liberty ship a day, that they had outfitted the entire Russian Army with Lend Lease—supplied them with every damn thing they had, clothing, uniforms, guns, helmets, and delivered it all to their goddamn doorstep. All America needed was a little kick in the ass to get back on track.

He even wrote U.S. real estate tycoon Donald Trump about the "Japan problem." Trump's representatives had been peddling high-priced suites in the new Manhattan Trump Towers to potential Japanese buyers in Tokyo at $2.5 million per unit. The Tokyo-based American Richard Roa had arranged for one of Trump's top salespeople to rent Nicola's restaurant for an afternoon to put on a seminar for a group of wealthy Japanese. Nick had sat and listened uncomfortably to the ensuing spiel and the next day wrote his letter to The Donald, urging him to stop selling to the Japanese. "They're buying us up and laughing at us, Mr. Trump," he wrote. "We've got to put a stop to this."

He was not pleased to discover later that the American billionaire had become a joint owner of the Empire State Building with the infamous Japanese greenmailer Hideki Yokoi.

THE FALL

The road to truth has many turns, to misquote an old Japanese proverb, and with his losses continuing to mount, Nick Zappetti had rounded *his* last bend. Unable to afford to hold out any longer, he capitulated—and took his wife's advice. He invested the equivalent of a million dollars—the last million, incidentally, in Nicola Roppongi's once overflowing coffers—and redecorated his restaurant in modern Tokyo kitsch. He replaced the furniture in the main dining room with rococo-like lounge sets of marbled granite tables, beige chintz tablecloths, and studded leather chairs. He scrapped the canned music in favor of a computerized karaoke set and player piano. He put in a cocktail lounge by the entrance, which he furnished with white marble tables, a polished black marble floor, and a multimillion-yen Yamaha piano on which a pianist imported from New York would play pre-dinner music. An enormous backlit color blowup of Italy's Porto d'Fino harbor filled the side of one wall. Then, Zappetti added designer snacks like white pizza and tiramisu dessert specials to the menu, turned the lights up, and sat back to wait.

The great remake of his restaurant might possibly have worked. But then the bottom fell completely out of the Japanese economy. The Nikkei Stock Index, which had risen from 13,000 yen at the time of the Plaza Accord to an all-time peak of 39,915 in early 1990, began a slide that took it all the way down to 14,000 in three years and helped precipitate the worst recession to hit Japan since the war. Bonuses dropped, entertainment expenses for executives dipped, and the crowd on the Roppongi strip began to thin out. For the first time since the brief 1973 oil crisis, night-clubs in the area found themselves in the red.

There were many reasons for this disastrous turn of events, which dimmed the lights of the city. Chief among them was a series of interest rate hikes and other credit-tightening measures by the Bank of Japan, necessary to control the wild overinvestment and rampant speculation that had created a dangerously inflating bubble. Unfortunately, in its latter stages, this bubble economy had been based so much on borrowed money using real estate as collateral that when the value of land dropped in the wake of the newly falling securities market, it became difficult or impossible for many people to pay back or even service their debt.

But there were also a series of big financial scandals, of which the *keizai yakuza* were part and parcel. The meteoric rise of the aforementioned Tokyu stock, for example, had prompted an investigation by Japan's harried prosecutors which, in turn, led to the public revelation in the summer of 1991 of what the crime lord Susumu Ishii and Japan's most trusted brokerage houses had been doing together. At around the same time, it was also discovered that Nomura, Nikko, and the others had, in addition, been routinely *compensating* their biggest customers—the major institutional investors—for stock losses incurred during the market's fall, paying billions of yen at the expense of the small individual investor (who only accounted for some 20 percent of the market). It was not yet known that Japan's major banks secretly were holding trillions of yen in bad debts, much of it issued by the middleman housing financial companies affiliated with the yakuza, known as *jusen.*

One of the biggest losers in the economic downslide which would last the rest of the decade was Ishii himself. Despite his penchant for high-tech finance, Ishii was also a practicing member of the Nichiren Shoshu Buddhist sect. He prayed morning and night, he believed in divination, and he frequently consulted a shaman about business moves. When at year's end he asked his shaman what to do about his Tokyu holdings, the shaman advised him to hold; the stock was going to rise to 5,000 yen a share, he predicted. Ishii dutifully held and the stock plummeted to 800. Ishii had a stroke and died. And the Inagawa family, 10 billion yen in debt, was forced to declare bankruptcy.

The collapse of the Japanese bubble was accompanied by signs of a comeback in the U.S. auto, IC, and other industries, thanks to corporate restructuring and improvement in quality control. For Japan to regain her clout, it was now being said, long-time dictums of Japanese industry such as lifetime employment and seniority-based promotion would have to be modified, as would the highly regulated, export-driven economy. While this millennium was being awaited, however, even the more lavish free spenders would find it prudent to curb their profligacy.

As several neighboring discos metastasized into karaoke boxes, many commercial rental units in the area emptied out. Nicola's entire yearly gross dwindled to less than half a million dollars, which didn't even begin to cover overhead. He watched glumly as the Domino's Pizza franchise took over the emerging new Japanese $400 million home delivery market, opening over 100 outlets, which would bring in total annual sales of $100 million. He himself couldn't even keep his one remaining restaurant afloat anymore. Although Nick slashed his prices, even his old regulars stopped coming. On one forgettable Monday evening, he served a total of nine customers in his newly refurbished restaurant.

He was forced to suffer the ultimate humiliation of asking for a loan from his wife—who, in a feat of excruciating irony, had just finished redecorating the suburban bed town branch in Chuo Rinkan and had seen revenue double as a result.

"Why should my company have to help yours?" she had sniffed before finally forking over the money.

"*My*" company.

There was no end to life's injustices.

In the summer of 1991, the Higher Court had rejected Zappetti's appeal in the Hokkaido land case. The appellate court judge ruled that the plaintiff's Japanese citizenship in itself was not enough of a factor. Nick would also have to obtain a national farmer's license if he hoped to reverse the original decision. To get that, he would have to take permanent residence on the land, which, given his age and health limitations, he was obviously not inclined to do.

Then, a few weeks after that depressing event, a Tokyo District Court suddenly ordered him to pay two of the lawyers who had sued him in the Nihon Kotsu mess. By District Court standards it was warp speed. It was just a matter of time, he was certain, before the judge ruled in favor of the third and final litigator. There was, of course, his share of the Nihon Kotsu settlement, which he had no choice but to take. But he had used that money to buy a huge home in the suburbs. And costs were beginning to mount in the Crazy Wong case.

His defense in court was to claim that Wong had switched the gold—that the gold had originally been authentic, then sold by Crazy Wong and replaced with counterfeit gold. It made sense whether it was true or not, and it was certainly plausible given the ease with which a man could buy fake gold in Okachimachi. The judge was bound to ask why anyone would pay $160,000 and not immediately get a receipt for it—which was a good question, because it is essentially what had happened.

But Nick was getting tired of going to court. He was running out of attorneys willing to defend him. In fact, one of his own ex-lawyers was even being quoted around town as saying that Mr. Nicola was the most unreasonable *gaijin* he had ever met and that he had never hated anyone more. At the same time, Nick

also guessed that in the end, he would probably lose—again—
no matter who defended him or what the argument was. A Chinese versus an American before a Japanese judge? He had no
doubt who was worse off, especially considering the insults that
Japanese and Americans had been slinging at each other across
the Pacific. For example, when Shintaro Ishihara offered the
view that Japanese could always make a better product than the
Americans, U.S. Senator Ernest Hollings retorted that they were
forgetting who made the atomic bomb. They ought to be sent a
reminder, he suggested, a mushroom cloud image with the legend affixed, "A quality product made in the USA and tested in
Japan." (Hollings later apologized.)

The Crazy Wong proceedings had just gotten started when
Nick received a bill for 6 million yen (almost $60,000) for hav-
ing the first batch of court-related documents translated. By the
time the case was over, given such prices, he might very well be
bankrupt. With the recession looking as though it was never
going to end, he was in a hopeless sinkhole.

Enough was enough, he decided. It was time to pack up and
move out of Tokyo.

He would sell his restaurant, leave his wife to manage her do-
main, and move to New Zealand, where his daughter and her
three children were living. There, maybe he would buy some
land, open a golf course, and make new millions. The King of
Auckland—that had a nice ring to it.

Nick made one last trip to Hokkaido. On the lone night he spent
in Sapporo, he had a car take him for a final nostalgic spin around
the city, despite a cold, driving autumn rain. At one point, he
passed the wood frame house where Miyoko and her mother had

resided and saw a light on inside. On impulse, he had the driver stop and back up. He got out, limped hatless through the downpour, and rang the doorbell. To his surprise, Miyoko answered. She was carrying a small child in her arms.

He flashed her his old devil-may-care grin and explained that he'd just been passing by and wanted to say good-bye. He was getting out of the restaurant business, he said, moving on to New Zealand to become a golf magnate. But he couldn't leave without seeing her once more—to say thanks for all the good times they had had together and to tell her he had forgotten about the bad ones.

He thought that, after her initial surprise had worn off, she actually looked happy to see him. She told him she had gotten married to a man who worked at the local cemetery, that she had joined a religious order, and that life was good, if not as exciting as it used to be. Then she flashed him a big, warm smile. He peered through the rain at her, leaning on his cane. She had put on considerable weight, and he thought she looked a bit like a middle-linebacker. But with her huge breasts, she was still a knockout. He leered at her. He had the feeling that Miyoko wanted to ask him in.

"I'd fuck her," he thought to himself, "even though she's the woman that cost me a billion dollars. Hell, I'd fuck all my ex-wives. One big farewell salute. If only I could get it up."

But getting it up was no longer an option. Neither was walking normally or reading or driving, for that matter. So after chatting for a while, he said his good-byes and left.

The next day, he had his barn and silo torn down.

In January 1992, he sold Nicola's Roppongi to the Moti chain of Indian restaurants for a million dollars. He paid off his staff, gave some money to his children, and kept the rest. Then he sat down to plot his first post-retirement move.

He had promised himself that he would settle the various accounts that had built up over the years.

All of them.

Just as Michael Corleone had done in the last scene of *The Godfather*. He would hire some men and have all the people who had screwed him wiped out in a day: the Nihon Kotsu people, the lawyers, Crazy Wong. Then, that very same evening, they would all get on a plane and disappear. Nick's enemies would never know what hit them.

The assassins would not be anyone in the Tosei-kai, although that idea had a certain poetic appeal to it. The criminal division of the TSK was not very active locally, as far as Nick could see. According to Nick's sources, Machii was in such poor health that he was unable to even receive visitors anymore, let alone physically run such an enterprise. A mutual acquaintance had espied him some years earlier at Tokyo Station on his way to Kobe to attend an important mob funeral. "He could barely make it up the stairs," said the man. "His *kobun* had to help him. He had a bad liver from drinking too much, as well as a bad heart." Most all the other gang members Nick had known had retired, or moved their base of operations to California, Hawaii, or some location in Asia—some of them just disappeared. Only occasionally did he run into somebody from the old days, like the afternoon in 1991 when he had played a rare game of pachinko and went to exchange his winnings for cash. He had been directed by a parlor employee to an alleyway near his restaurant; there, waiting at a window by a row of blue plastic garbage cans was an elderly man whom Nick recognized as a one-time TSK soldier under Matsubara.

"Hey, *Neeku-san*," the man had said, waving a gnarled hand, bereft of the tip of one little finger. "*Genki desu ka?*"

They stood and exchanged pleasantries and reminiscences.

TSK yakuza had a small operation in Shinjuku, the man told Nick, something in Ginza, and that was about it. There were only 500 gang members in the entire city, and in Roppongi some other group was collecting the protection money.

The man said that Matsubara was in the Tokyo Red Cross Hospital, seriously ill, and he wanted to know if it was true that Matsubara's one-time nemesis, Mike Sullivan, was now a TV personality living in the United States. Nick said yes. The TSK man shook his head in wonder and said that this was news they would have to keep from the boss. It would upset him too much.

There was a growing selection of foreign thugs in the area—young men from Southeast Asia, Iran, India, and so on, who formed a pool of foreign migrant labor. They had let it be known that they were available to perform certain tasks. In fact, he had gotten an estimate of $17,500 for his *Godfather* scenario from Filipino contact. It was a group rate, the man had said, although he wasn't sure what the $500 was for. But in the end, Nick ruled that option out. He was swimming in uncharted waters, and besides, it seemed more fitting somehow to have the New York Mafia handle this particular chore.

He swore that's just what he would do.

Then he had his third heart attack.

He clung to life in a bed at Dr. Aksenoff's clinic for several days, his fingernails turning black from poor circulation, his wife Yae constantly at his side.

And, on June 10, 1992, at the age of seventy-one, he died.

Among his last words to Yae were, "I never thought you'd be such a good wife."

The funeral was held at the austere Franciscan chapel in Roppongi, 200 yards east of the former site of Tom's, where Killer Ikeda had once held a gun to Nick's head. Several hundred people attended, a cross-section of Tokyo society that included busi-

nessmen, diplomats, entertainers, expatriates, ex-black marke-
teers. A delegation from the Tosei-kai also put in an appearance.

As Nicola Koizumi was laid to rest in a cemetery in Fujisawa,
letters and cards poured in from the States to his widow. Many
people wrote to express memories of the old days and their long-
ing for an era that did not exist anymore. Some of Nick's friends
were of the opinion that he had simply died of a broken heart.
He had no more restaurants to run. He wasn't *Nicola* anymore,
and that was too much for him to bear. Others believed that it
was his rage at Japan that killed him. Retirement had just given
him that much more free time to dwell on all the perceived injustices his adopted home had visited upon him. His heart was
too weak to stand up to the strain of it all.

The suit by Crazy Wong remained unsettled, as did other
outstanding claims against him. Nick's criminal file was transferred to the inactive section of the Tokyo Metropolitan Police
Department. It was, said a police representative, the thick-
est file ever assembled in the history of the department for an
American.

He left behind a number of other records as well. He had
made and lost more money than any other American in Japan.
He had been married to and divorced from more Japanese
women than any other American. He had been involved in more
civil suits than any other American and had spent more years in
court.

And, of course, he had been the only *gaijin* King of Roppongi.

EPILOGUE

Japan, for all its strides as a constitutional democracy, was still a country of secret meetings and back room deals made by faceless, colorless fixers, a society where one never knew what was going on until after the fact—if then. Any hopes that this modus operandi would soon disappear were certainly dampened by the events of the 1990s, which culminated in the 1998 election of a prime minister, the LDP's Keizo Obuchi, who took office with the lowest public support rating in the postwar history of the country, one that was barely in double digits. (Obuchi's election was masterminded by the aforementioned Noboru Takeshita, a former PM who went on to become the leading backstage wirepuller in the LDP.) LDP power broker Kanemaru was forced to resign his Diet seat in 1992 when it became known he had a "relationship" with the gang boss Susumo Ishii and that one of Ishii's corporate arms, Tokyo Sagawa Kyubin, had inundated him with cash and gifts. In 1993, Kanemaru was indicted for tax evasion and a search of his home by prosecutors uncovered enough cash, bearer bonds, gold ingots, and other booty to ransom the island of Honshu. Prosecutors also discovered evidence that Kanemaru owned $440 million worth of Hawaiian real estate. However, Kanemaru died during his trial, and aside from the Tokyo Sagawa Kyubin president, nobody involved in that scandal went to jail—an outcome not surprising to those familiar with trying political bribery cases in Japan.

The financial scandals involving the compensation of big investors and the granting of interest-free loans to mobster clients were also resolved in what might be described as a less than satisfactory manner. Nomura and the other brokerages received only light punishments—a suspension of trading for three months on the average—and after serving their sentences took up where they left off. Senior executives who had submitted ritual resignations to take "responsibility" for the problem then returned through the back door as "advisers." The first Tokyu stockholders meeting held since the scandal broke was an indication of how unlikely a change in the status quo really was. Held in a Shibuya movie theater in June 1992, it took all of twenty-six minutes. There was an apology for all the "confusion" that had been caused. A *sokaiya* rose to shout, "No questions." And then the gathering was treated to a free showing of the film *Basic Instinct*. Such breathtaking brevity was typical of most other shareholders' meetings which took place at the time. A Securities and Exchange Law, revised in 1991 in response to public anger, was largely ignored, as the under-the-table payments to preferred customers continued, a state of affairs explained perhaps by the discovery some years later that several senior bureaucrats in the Ministry of Finance and Bank of Japan had accepted bribes and hospitality from the executives they were supposed to be policing.

The adverse publicity that surrounded these scandals did cause the 1992 ouster of the LDP from power in a no-confidence vote for the first time in nearly forty years, after a group of rebellious Young Turks deserted the party. A new reform-minded government was installed behind a youthful, fashion-conscious prime minister, Morihiro Hosokawa, descendant of a feudal prince and a provincial governor thought to be outside the maelstrom of brokered politics. Some optimists in the media and on the political scene hailed this as a sign that a new corruption-free Japan was finally emerging, U.S. ambassador to Japan Walter Mondale even compared this new administration to "Camelot." Yet, in 1994, in a turn of events reeking with irony, it was revealed that Hosokawa had had his own illicit financial dealings with the infamous Sagawa trucking firm and he was forced to resign. Mondale, along with so many others, was compelled to reexamine his grasp of politics in Japan. Within three short years, the LDP would be back in power.

Predictably, attempts were made to blame the United States for Japan's economic woes. During the spectacular plunge of the Nikkei Dow, for example, it was the foreign brokerages that came in for much of the blame for selling borrowed stock, thereby inducing it to fall further. When Japanese regulators cited firms like Salomon Brothers and Morgan Stanley for their use of arbitrage and futures markets in the spring of 1992, hate mail aimed at the *gaijin* investment houses, (sometimes accompanied by bomb threats) began to appear (e.g., "Foreigners Beware. You have plotted to send stock prices lower and have thus profited greatly. This has already caused hundreds of people to commit suicide . . . the pained souls of those who have committed suicide are wandering around your offices. The country is now caught up in a vicious circle, where companies go into the red and bankruptcies greatly increase, unemployment rises, robbers cheat and murders multiply, suicides rise and numerous other incidents occur. All of this because of foreigners. . . . Foreigners, employees of foreign firms, get the hell out of Japan."). Conveniently ignored in the correspondence was the fact that everyone from Japanese insurance and trust companies to the big brokerages were themselves talking down the market as well, essentially doing the same thing.

Some Japanese economists were tracing the roots of the recession to Japan's acceptance of a series of U.S. demands, starting with the 1985 Plaza Accord. It was U.S. policy, they said, which led to the waves of speculation in Japan and the ensuing bad loan problem. This was an argument that had more merit than the one expressed in the above circular. Indeed, if U.S. policy helped to create the Japanese juggernaut (or "Frankenstein monster" as one author preferred to put it) through a preferential trade and security policy, then it might also be said that the United States helped create the conditions for cheap borrowing in Japan by engineering the rise in the yen. (However, the U.S. government did not advise the Japanese banks to engage in irresponsible lending practices.) Both of these courses of action, ironically, wound up adversely affecting the U.S. economy.

Eventually, however, the economic malaise that gripped Japan for the rest of the century, one in which the yen would lose over half its value, came to be known in many circles as the "Yakuza recession." It was gradually discovered that the major banks held billions of yen in bad debts, a significant portion of which were housing loans channeled through middleman financing companies *(jusen)* that were involved with organized crime. The money had been used to buy overpriced real estate, condominiums, and golf courses, investments that soured in the recession of the 1990s. Prompting a reverse of the sell-off of U.S. real estate purchases (including the Tiffany Building in New York) and other corporate acquisitions began in earnest, and the specter of a Godzilla-like Japan gobbling up America faded almost overnight.

Efforts by bankers to collect this sour debt showed just how overmatched their institutions were in dealing with their recalcitrant clients. In 1994, the manager of Sumitomo's branch in the city of Nagoya, who had sought to retrieve billions in overdue *jusen* loans, was shot in the head outside his tenth-floor apartment as he responded to an early morning knock at his door. The year before, the vice president in charge of loans at Hanwa Bank near Osaka had been murdered. Government money subsequently had to be used to rescue the leading failed housing loan corporations, making the bailout, as one magazine put it, "The first ever taxpayer-financed debt forgiveness of a nation's criminal underworld."

The highly touted enactment of antigang laws and outlawing organizations with over a certain percentage of members having arrest records and electoral laws that increased somewhat the power of the urban voter, modifying somewhat the old multi-member district during the nineties, did little to dislodge the black streak of corruption and influence peddling embedded within the system. Although a wave of FTC investigations into construction bid-rigging, for example, actually led to the indictment and conviction of an ex-construction minister in 1994 for taking a bribe—an eyewitness insider in another more important case was "persuaded" to recant his accusations against thirty-one other *dango* participants. Thus were collusive arrangements among industry construction heavyweights able to continue.

With only 2,000 prosecutors in the entire country, the approximate number that serves an average big city in the United States, there was simply not nearly enough honest manpower to investigate all the corruption that continued to go on, so relentless was the circulation of back-door gelt.

In 1997, the big story was that the chief brokerage houses were paying record amounts of cash, secretly, to corporate extortionists, to keep them from revealing facts about hidden debt, illegal loans, and secret accounts the houses held for VIPs in the Japanese government. One of the VIPs, according to the *Shukan Gendai,* was the then prime minister, Ryutaro Hashimoto, while another was a cabinet minister who had once solicited gangsters to suppress a book exposing corruption in his district. In the ensuing turmoil, the nation's oldest securities house, Yamaichi Securities, was discovered to have billions of dollars in hidden debt and forced to declare bankruptcy, leaving 6,000 workers jobless and helping to send the Nikkei Stock Index, which had been showing signs of recovery, into another tailspin. This was not beneficial to the financial currency crisis that struck Asia in the fall of that same year, the repercussions of which were felt all the way back to Wall Street.

The *sokaiya* at the center of it all, a smiling, *keizai yakuza* with designer glasses and fashionably long hair named Ryuichi Koike, was yet another by-product of the environment created by U.S.–Japan "cooperation" that allowed organized crime and the government to join forces and flourish. He had been able to get close to the companies involved because of links to the infamous Yoshio Kodama Sokaiya group, still going strong despite the master's demise.

Koike, arrested and accused of receiving nearly 700 million yen in illegal payments from the securities houses and 12 billion in illegal loans from a Dai-Ichi Kangyo subsidiary, was released on 40 million yen bail—not even 1 percent of his total take. The harshest penalty was given to Nomura, a five-month suspension this time. Two more officials subsequently committed suicide.

In October of that year a politician in the ruling party, sitting for a magazine interview, openly expressed his view that cutting the links between the world of the gangs and conservative politics was impossible given the close ties that bound certain underworld and political losses. He even boasted that he did not have to engage in vote buying because he could rely on the Yamaguchi-gumi to get the vote out for him. As he offered these remarks, a nationwide shoot-out involving rival factions of the nation's largest gang was going on.

It was an admission that surprised no one, save perhaps the U.S. government, which had been loudly complaining about "discriminatory" port charges imposed by the Japan Harbor Transportation Association and had leveled retaliatory fines against Japanese vessels using American harbor facilities. The effort was, of course, doomed to failure since the United States was taking on a formidable featherbedding source of post-retirement positions for government officials—and an organization controlled by organized crime in Japan. It was as if MITI had decided to take on the New York City Harbor Dockworkers Association.

In March 1997, the Tokyo District Court sentenced Ken Mizuno to eleven years in prison and a fine of nearly 70 million dollars. This came some eighteen months after the U.S. Customs Service auctioned off Mizuno's Los Angeles mansion (used in the movie *Beverly Hills Cop II*). It was the last of Mizuno's U.S. assets, including properties in California, Hawaii, and Las Vegas, auctioned as part of a plea bargain with U.S. Federal authorities in which Mizuno's firm plead guilty to fraud and money laundering. The money was to go to the U.S. Treasury Asset Forfeiture Fund, to be divided between the fraud victims and Mizuno's creditors. U.S. law enforcement officers said they had obtained unprecedented cooperation from the notoriously secretive Japanese police in their investigation of Mizuno's money laundering and that Japan's Finance Ministry had identified some $250 million in fraudulent funds he transferred to U.S. banks.

However, the FBI and Japanese police would continue to have their hands full. The last two years before the millennium, as Japan began implementing a program of deregulation known as the *biggu ban* (big bang), were witness to the unusual spectacle of U.S. financial companies buying up substantial amounts of bad Japanese real estate—backed loan portfolios (in January 1998, the Ministry of Finance had pegged the size of bad loans at well over $600 billion, larger than the U.S. S&L crisis), thus putting themselves on a collision course with the *keizai yakuza,* who owed much of the debt in question and who, in some cases, were occupying property facing foreclosure in the wake of the deals with the Americans. Amid media cries and rightist protests that Japan was "selling out" to the United States, the head of the Sumiyoshi was standing by to offer his assistance to any American firm that had difficulty collecting its money—for a commission of only 40 percent. Back in Los Angeles, an investigator associated with the LAPD, long familiar with the scene in Japan, was shaking his head in disbelief at the risks being taken.

"One would think," he said, "that these American financiers would have more sense."

Then again, one never knew. Perhaps they knew more than they were letting on.

Thomas Blakemore died in 1996 in Seattle, where he had moved to be treated for the onset of Alzheimer's disease. He was seventy-seven. But he left behind a legacy that is not likely to be

matched by any American in Japan. In addition to ably representing the fortunes of many U.S. firms for forty years, including GE (a company that remained the largest single investor in
Japan, with 13 percent of Toshiba's stock), he was decorated by
the Emperor—receiving the "Third Order of the Sacred Treasure," in 1989—for legal services Blakemore had contributed to
the Japanese Supreme Court over the years.

Blakemore had been a perpetual goodwill machine. He and
his wife Frances set up an experimental farming project on five
acres of agricultural land outside Tokyo where they introduced
short hybrid fruit trees, a series of miniature orchards that grew
apples, loganberries, raspberries, blueberries, and cherries,
among other fruit. ("The Japanese people know what starvation
is," he said, "and this is one hedge against it.")

Moreover, he also identified two species of Iriomote Wild Cat
from the Ryukyus and a species of bear from Hokkaido, passing
on his discoveries to the Museum of Natural History of New
York. He sponsored adventurer Naoki Uemura for membership
into the New York Explorer's Club. (His wife, in addition to introducing many young artists in her Okura gallery, authored several books on Japanese prints.) Before moving back to the States
to battle his illness, Blakemore used much of his wealth to set
up a foundation in his name to provide scholarships for aspiring
students of Japan.

If Blakemore was the symbol of one side of the U.S.–Japan
dynamic, Nicola Zappetti was certainly the symbol of the other.
Although *he* had never been in danger of receiving an imperial
decoration, he had indeed left his own unique legacy: Roppongi.
When he first opened his tiny eight-table bistro, Roppongi was
little more than a military camp. By the end of the century, it
stood in the same league as the Champs Elysée, the Via Veneto,
and other famous international playgrounds. Many long-time

observers of the Tokyo scene gave Nicola's much of the credit for that happening; his restaurant became such a lodestone for Tokyo night owls that it caused the creation of other nightspots in the area. By the time Tokyo Tower had gone up in the neighborhood, 1959, with a big television studio opening up a year later, Roppongi had come to stand for the exotic and the advanced. As *Tokyo Rising* author Edward Seidenstecker would write about the area—"young people went to ogle and to imitate, and to dance and eat pizza."

By the late 1990s, there were enough restaurants serving ethnic delicacies in the quarter to please even the most serious gourmets, and there were perhaps more places per square kilometer to sit down and eat Italian food than any other area of the world—even New York City and Rome. At the same time, Roppongi had also became a magnet for Southeast Asian drug dealers, prostitutes, illegal workers, and foreign college girls seeking work as lap dancers to earn their tuition. Notable in the new landscape was One-Eyed Jack, a casino club that had opened in the early 1990s. Outside stood a tall white American doorman dressed in a tasseled greatcoat and cap who greeted one and all in flawless Japanese: "*Irrashai. Irrashai. Wanu-aido-zyaku e dozo.*" Inside, operating roulette and blackjack tables, where customers could gamble for ostensibly worthless chips, were attractive Caucasian female card dealers and croupiers—who plied their trade in perfect Japanese, to a clientele that was almost exclusively young and well-heeled Nipponese male. In an adjoining room was a large circular bar surrounded by a number of private booths occupied by some seventy-five imported *gaijin* women—Americans, Australians, Canadians, New Zealanders, British, and Russian—clad in miniskirts, fishnet stockings, and low-cut silk blouses. A seminude revue of Las Vegas dancers helped liven up the proceedings every half-hour, while gangsta rap played in the background. It was the largest assemblage of Caucasian hostesses in the history of Tokyo—not to mention Japanese-speaking Caucasian hostesses—and was a stunning example of the power of the yen, even with the long recession.

The club, managed by an American, occupied the former site of the fabled Caravansary and was so successful that several sister clubs popped up in the vicinity, all of them in buildings owned outright by the TSK or TSK affiliates. One of the operations, *The Pharoah*, was closed down in 1997 for illegal gambling. A casual observer might think *Toa Sogo Kigyo* was making something of a comeback.

The TSK still owned a number of cabarets and hotels in Seoul, a resort in the Philippines, interests in Okinawa, casinos in the Marshall Islands and, of course, the *Toa Yuai Jigyo Kumiai* (East Asia Friendship Enterprises Association), as the criminal wing was now formally known, had made it into the U.S. congressional record, having been cited in a 1993 U.S. Senate report as being behind most of the crystal methamphetamine business in Hawaii. It was quite an achievement for a group that did not even constitute 1 percent of all *boryokudan* members. A representative of the Los Angeles Police Department's Organized Crime Intelligence Division told the *Mainichi Shimbun* in 1994 that he had a strong suspicion that the Santa Monica-based Machii-Ross operation was now a money-laundering cover for the yakuza, something which the company's spokespeople strenuously denied. (Ross, now involved in gold mining in Liberia, had always firmly denied any wrongdoing and had expressed his belief that his partner's criminal activities were a thing of the past—something which had occurred well before their company was ever formed.) The 500-some active Tosei-kai yazuka operating as the *Toa Yuai Jigyo Kumiai* (East Friendship Enterprises Association) were showing renewed signs of life on the homefront as well as abroad. In 1994, a forty-four-year-old TSK captain named Hiroji Tashiro stormed into the Tokyo headquarters of the *Mainichi Shimbun* and fired three .38 bullets into the ceiling. Tashiro was upset with an article published by the *Mainichi* weekly magazine that described the Tosei-kai as "over the hill." The article concerned a new skirmish between the Tosei-kai and the Sumiyoshi-kai in Shinjuku, which was ignited when a TSK soldier was stabbed to death for kicking a Sumiyoshi car that had honked at him. The offending article quoted a police detective as saying that the TSK of the nineties was as nothing compared to the much larger Sumiyoshi, which had just signed a "gangster's constitution," or peace treaty, with the three other big gangs of Japan, the Inagawa-kai, the Yamaguchi-gumi, and the Kyoto-based Aizukotetsu, to peacefully divide up territory around the four main islands. The author of the *Mainichi* piece added sarcastically that perhaps even the new Chinese gangs in the city were scarier than the TSK, which caused Tashiro to shave his head and launch his one-man assault on the nation's third largest newspaper.

Then, in March 1995, a high-ranking member of the Toa Yuai Gang, Kenji Jojima, was shot in the back four times in front of a Roppongi pachinko parlor by a man police identified as a member of a gang affiliated with the Sumiyoshi.

It was just like old times.

The year 1995 marked the fiftieth anniversary of the end of the war and the occasion inspired a wave of nostalgia in Tokyo for the past. For a time, in the mid-1990s, the popular Roppongi Crossing bookstore was filled with memorial tomes about Rikidozan. The respected publishing house Bungei Shunju produced and telemarketed a retrospective four-hour video package on the most important figures of the postwar era, devoting one complete tape to Rikidozan.

"No one," said the narrator in a glowing summation, "had ever had as great an impact on the Japanese in such a short time as the great Rikidozan."

(Not once in the entire sixty minutes was a reference made to Rikidozan's Korean background. A study published that same year showed that roughly 80 percent of Korean youths living in Japan used Japanese names.)

It was fitting perhaps that 1995 was also the year that an athlete from Japan finally appeared who could be termed Rikodozan's equal. Hideo Nomo, pitching for the Los Angeles Dodgers, became the first Japanese to star in the U.S. major leagues. He won the Rookie of the Year award and led the National League in strikeouts (then followed that in 1966 by winning seventeen games and pitching a no-hitter).

Nomo's success ignited a wave of nationalistic pride the likes of which had not been seen since Riki's heyday. Every game Nomo pitched was telecast nationwide *twice* in the same day on NHK. Huge Hi-Vision screens around Tokyo had replaced the *gaito telebi* of Riki's era, but the crowds were just as rapt. During the All-Star Game break, some fans even camped out in tents to catch the big-screen early morning telecasts relayed back to Japan. One radio station broadcast every game Nomo pitched, but only those half-innings Nomo was out on the mound. The rest of the time, when Nomo was on the bench and his teammates were batting, normal programming was resumed. It was a display of single-mindedness matched only by the TV station that ran an eleven-hour special on Japan's new national idol.

In the years since his death, Rikidozan had also become a full-fledged North Korean hero and tool of the state. Celebrating in its own way the fiftieth anniversary of the end of Japanese rule, the Democratic People's Republic of Korea issued a Rikidozan "autobiography" entitled *I Am a Korean,* which topped the charts in Pyonyang; an English version went on sale in the Pyongyang Airport departure lounge, alongside a popular liquor for foreign consumption, "Rikidozan Drink."

In 1995, Riki's one-time "disciple" Kanji "Antonio" Inoki, who was now, improbably, a member of the Japanese Upper House, representing the "Sports-Peace Party," visited Pyongyang on a public relations pilgrimage to participate in the festivities celebrating the fiftieth anniversary of the end of the war. At the behest of the Pyongyang government, Inoki traveled to Rikidozan's boyhood home accompanied by Riki's daughter.

While in Pyongyang, Inoki took part in a highly touted East vs. West wrestling exhibition. He propelled an outdoor audience of 100,000 North Koreans—supposed bitter enemies of Japan—into fits of confetti-scattering delirium when he handily dispatched an aging, pot-bellied, blond American wrestler.

That too was just like old times.

Aficionados of Roppongi history noted with interest the reopening on November 16, 1995, of the newly remodeled Nihon Kotsu Nicola's, which had been closed for three years. The original plan had been to raze the building to make way for the construction of a new complex to rival Ark Hills—another grand *jiyageya* plan from the bubble era. But somehow in the yakuza *jusen* recession that had not been possible. And so after being closed and standing silent and empty for three years, Nicola's was renovated.

It boasted a sparkling new entrance, a six-car parking lot, a sign proclaiming it as the oldest pizza restaurant in Japan—"in business since 1954 [sic]," and advertisements assuring customers of a "bright, airy interior."

The main dining room would have made Zappetti's widow

proud; it was well lit and decorated with thin beige strips of chiffon suspended from the ceiling. The tablecloths were so white they almost hurt the eyes. On the second floor was a party room complete with *karaoke* equipment, for "group or corporate rental." Outside in the parking lot were plastic round white picnic-style tables for dining al fresco—the latest Tokyo rage. The menu promised "light, sweet cuisine," including a wide variety of different colorful mixed pizzas (olive oil on the side) and a diminutive thirty-dollar steak.

It was impossible to miss the huge painting of a bulbous-nosed black-mustachioed Italian chef holding a tall stack of pizzas that adorned one whole side of the two-story building, accompanied by a huge encircled "R" informing everyone that the logo was duly "registered." It was also downright impossible to ignore the complete absence of foreign diners inside, a phenomenon perhaps caused by the fact that the pizza was nearly inedible to the Western palate—even the ones that weren't topped with tuna and squid—or that a medium-sized pizza, a "Nicola's Classico" as it appeared on the menu, was three times the cost of a pizza in America and approximately one-third the size.

The new Nicola's proved so popular with Japanese businessmen in the area that the sushi bar down the street suffered a precipitous drop in business.

Lamented the shop's proprietor, "It's hard to compete with foreigners in Roppongi."

Guide maps were handed out to all customers introducing them to the seven other Nicola branches Nihon Kotsu was running, which, added to the Yokota and Chuo Rinkan branches, made for a total of ten Nicola's restaurants in the Tokyo area.

In 1994, a half-block from the former site of Nicola's Roppongi Crossing branch on the main drag, a cavernous new pizza joint with street-side seating and 1960s pop decor opened for business. It offered a smorgasbord of brawny pizza, all-you-can-drink sangria, and a rack of comic books for diners to peruse at their leisure. A year later, on the second floor of Nicola's former building, the Il Cardinale, specializing in Italian cuisine *de la mare* made its debut, while around the corner above the Kentucky Fried Chicken outlet, Gino's seafood Italian opened its doors. Then near the southwest corner of the Crossing a young American named Brenden Murphy opened up a tiny second-floor pizzeria with flowered tablecloths and a giant pizza oven imported from Canada where he mixed five different kinds of flour to get a unique pizza crust. At Pizza-la, a new pizza chain in competition with Domino's, it was possible to buy a bacon-lettuce-tomato pizza. S-barro's, another new addition to the pantheon of Roppongi pizza houses, became an instant gathering spot for hungry night club hostesses working in the area. And finally, just past the Crossing to the north, appeared the Zia pizzeria, in front of which stood a sketch of the "proprietor," a balding, mustachioed Italian man, drawn with hands out in a gesture of welcome. He looked just like Nick Zappetti.

ACKNOWLEDGMENTS

My first real exposure to the Tokyo underworld came in 1969 when I was living in Higashi Nakano, just outside of Shinjuku, in the western part of the city. I had just graduated from Tokyo's Sophia University and had gone to work in the editorial department of *Encyclopaedia Britannica*, Japan. Each evening on my way home to my tiny box-like apartment, I would stop at a neighborhood snack bar for a drink; there I made the acquaintance of a short, muscular, mean-looking young man with a crewcut and scarred eyebrows. His name was "Jiro," and, as I discovered from the membership badge he wore underneath the lapel of his suede leather jacket, he belonged to the Sumiyoshi-Rengo kai, the huge Tokyo-based criminal syndicate.

Jiro took an interest in me because he had been given the task of overseeing a Sumiyoshi-owned nightclub in Shinjuku employing English-speaking hostesses from Southeast Asia. Because he couldn't communicate with them, he offered me the job of assistant manager, six nights a week, for the monthly sum of 300,000 yen (then roughly about $1,000). Although I turned him down because of other commitments, Jiro and I developed a relationship of sorts, because believe it or not, of a shared interest in politics. I had studied Japanese politics while at Sophia and had written my graduate thesis on the factions of the ruling Liberal Democratic Party. At the time I was one of the few Americans alive remotely interested in such an esoteric subject—Japan was not yet the world power it was destined to become. In the course of my research, I had even met a young Turk named Yasuhiro Nakasone, then being touted as the "JFK of Japan," who would become prime minister from 1982 to 1987. Jiro thought that was just great. He was a strong supporter of the LDP, and so were all his fellow gang members. At the time, the LDP was in the midst of one of its many scandals (this one called the "Black Mist") and its nationwide approval rating had sunk to around 25 percent. Jiro said it was vital that he and his confreres help "get out the vote" at election time.

One of Jiro's regular duties was collecting protection money from the night-clubs, bars, and pachinko parlors in front of the Higashi Nakano train station. He frequently had envelopes full of cash in his coat pocket, but in all the time I knew him, I never ever saw him pay a bill. Periodically, he would invite me to one of the cabarets in the vicinity and casually offer me my choice of any host-ess in the house to spend the night with, if I so wished—no charge involved. (Or, if I preferred, a tête-à-tête right there on the spot in a back booth.) Every-one seemed terrified of him and willing to do anything to please.

Jiro was not the most psychologically stable person I had ever met. He had a razor blade secreted in his sleeve to be slipped between two fingers for use as a weapon in a fight, and a pair of sharply pointed polished ivory chopsticks con-tained in a case he carried in his inside coat pocket, which he explained could also be used in combat. After several drinks, he was apt to fly into a sudden, un-controllable rage triggered by poor service or some unhappy memory, and over-turn his table, sending beer bottles and glasses flying. Once, trying in vain to flag down a cab in the street around midnight—always a difficult task in a city like Tokyo—I saw him kick a dent in the side of a taxi which had slowed for a traf-fic light. When the driver got out to confront him, Jiro punched him in the mouth several times and kicked him in the groin. One memorable besotted evening, complaining that he was without friends or family, he pulled a jackknife out of his jacket and sliced his left cheek.

"I'm human trash," he moaned. *"Ningen Kuzu."*

He said that foreigners and yakuza in Japan had one thing in common. They were outcasts from proper society.

Jiro lived alone in a tiny six-mat room, but often he would wind up spending the night in some semen-stained back booth in a neighborhood cabaret, too drunk to move. Periodically, he would disappear from the neighborhood. Once, after an absence of several months, he returned with the tip of his little finger missing, which, he said, he had chopped off himself as penance for being ar-rested and sent to prison.

I lost touch with Jiro when I moved to New York in 1972 and when I returned to Tokyo four years later to work for Time-Life, he had simply vanished. No one knew where he was and I never saw him again. This time around, I was living in the quarter of Akasaka, near the city center in a Western-style apartment complex known as Riki Mansion—my new lodgings a seventh-floor one-bedroom flat with a panoramic view of Tokyo Tower and environs. It was there that Phase II of my education in the ways of the Japanese underworld began.

The complex—actually two separate buildings in one compound—"Riki Mansion" and "Riki Apartments"—was named after a postwar national wrestling legend, Rikidozan. By the time I came upon the scene, Rikidozan was dead, having met his fate at the hands of a Sumiysohi gangster in an Akasaka nightclub, the New Latin Quarter. My landlady was Rikidozan's widow, a po-liceman's daughter. My fellow residents and neighbors came from a wide range of Tokyo's nightlife. There were nightclub hostesses from the high-class clubs like the Copacabana and the El Morocco, as well as foreign models and foreign prostitutes—tall, long-legged blondes from Australia, New Zealand, Canada, and America, along with assorted drifters, con artists, hustlers, smugglers, and others. Frequently milling around in the lobby and outside in the parking lot were groups of dark-visaged, mean-looking, hard-bitten men wearing dark suits and sunglasses—men whom I later learned belonged to the Tosei-kai gang, a rival of the Sumiyoshi, especially in promoting professional wrestling. The parking lot through which I passed every day was the site of a famous bloody sword encounter in December 1963, involving foot soldiers from both gangs.

From Riki Mansion, it was a five-minute walk to Roppongi Crossing, the center of the city's nightlife. I usually spent my evenings there and, quite often, I wound up at an Italian restaurant called Nicola's for a late-night meal. The place was always packed with a fascinating mixture of foreigners and Japanese—movie stars, athletes, and others—and it vibrated with excitement. The proprietor was a bullish, arrogant-looking man in his fifties who was not infrequently in the company of underworld types. People referred to him in whispers as the Mafia Boss of Tokyo.

I gradually came to know Nicola Zappetti, for it turned out we, too, had certain things in common. He was a baseball fan and he had read numerous books and articles I had written about the subject. The ballplayers I knew and wrote about frequented his restaurant. He was also a fan of pro wrestling, another subject I had written about. We were both acquaintances of Richard Beyer, otherwise known as The (Masked Man) Destroyer. Beyer, an NCAA wrestling champion at Syracuse, had performed professionally in Japan for several years and had also carved out an enormously successful second career as a comic on Japanese TV—appearing in Nazi helmet, polka-dot shorts, waving a Japanese flag, and singing songs in fractured Japanese. Beyer had been one of the very few Americans to defeat Rikidozan and he was a close friend of Giant Baba, a 6'10" 250-pound wrestler who lived directly above me on the eighth floor, in the luxury penthouse Rikidozan once occupied. From time to time I could hear Baba practicing his back flips, knocking loose tiny pieces of plaster from my ceiling as he landed on his living room floor.

In time, I learned of the ties that had bound Nicola to Rikidozan and the Tosei-kai gang, as well as other elements of the Tokyo underworld, politics, and big business. I began to understand what a remarkable life he had led, dating all the way back to the postwar black market era when he had been one of the first Americans in Japan after the fighting had stopped. He seemed the very embodiment of a certain type of relationship involving Japanese and Americans that had sprung up in the wake of the Occupation.

In 1989, Zappetti, suffering from a heart attack that destroyed three-quarters of his heart and suspecting that he did not have long to live, agreed to cooperate on a vaguely defined book project about Tokyo I had started. In numerous tape-recorded discussions, he told me his life story in detail—which was so striking it turned out to be a substantial part of the manuscript.

What struck me most was his total candor. He talked openly about having committed robbery and doing even worse things. He admitted that he preferred a life of crime to any other; growing up in East Harlem, New York, he said the Mafia men in his neighborhood enjoyed the most respect, while the police were despised—this was why he gravitated toward gangsters in Japan, putting his freedom, and even his life, in danger at times. He confessed that he stayed in Japan because he had a chance to be somebody—to be a "king" or a "mafia boss," to accumulate enormous wealth and have beautiful women at his beck and call—what he revealed to be overcoming a complex about his size. (In high school he had weighed but one hundred and twenty pounds, filling out only after joining the Marines. He still walked with a chin up, chest out, shoulders back swagger not uncommon in shorter men.) He further confessed that decades of booze and debauchery and four marriages had rendered him impotent by the age of sixty-four.

His life was almost Shakespearean—filled with passion, intrigue, betrayal, and revenge. At the end he was left nearly bankrupt, broken in spirit as well as body, and consumed with hatred for the Japanese—even though by then he was a naturalized citizen of Japan, a white-haired, old foreign man who carried a Japanese passport with a Japanese name (as required by law), and who spoke the language so poorly, at times he needed an interpreter. One of the very last things he said to me before he died was that any man who left his own country to live in another was an "asshole," deserving of everything bad that happened to him.

It took me several years to check out the stories he told me, to track down and interview people in his circle who had known him, to read books on the era, wade through old newspaper and magazine files, and do other research. What I wound up with was not only a reconstruction of his bizarre, amazing life, but also a rare view of a half-century of U.S.–Japan relations, a special subculture without equal in the world for drama and color.

The result is *Tokyo Underworld*.

A number of people helped me in putting this book together and I would like to thank them all here, with the exception of the ones who understandably wish to remain anonymous. I am indebted to Kiyondo Matsui, editor-in-chief of the *Shukan Bunshun*, who helped to start me on the road to a structured understanding of the Tokyo underworld. He supplied me with numerous articles and books to read and study, as well as police records and other documents, and made many key introductions besides. I am also deeply grateful to Midori Matsui, Mr. Matsui's wife, a longtime friend and collaborator (she translated *Chrysanthemum and the Bat* and *Slugging It Out In Japan*, among other works I did for the Japanese market). Midori-san helped out with my research, and among other things, taught me how to give a proper speech in Japanese. And I am further indebted to veteran crime-journalist Hiroshi Sasaki, now head of the *Rokka-kan Bunko* Information Center, who provided a great deal of invaluable information and documentation on criminals and corruption in Japan.

Next, I would like to thank friend and author Masayuki Tamaki, translator of *You Gotta Have Wa* and an established novelist in his own right, who gave me advice, materials from his personal library, and took time out from his busy schedule to personally show me the ropes at the *Oya Soichi Bunko,* Tokyo's vast magazine repository. Thanks also to his wife Kyoko for her kindness and to Atushi Imamura of the Bungei Shunju, and Satoshi Gunji and Mr. Nakanishi of Kadokawa Publishing for their help in getting me started. Also a very special thanks to Jiro Kawamura and Ichiro Tsuge of the *Asahi Shimbun* Co.

I would like to express my appreciation to Takashi Shimada, a former Boston Consulting Group official, Kenichiro Sasae of Japan's Foreign Ministry, and William Givens of Harvard University and director of Twain Associates, for helping to educate me in certain matters of trade, to author Glen Davis for educating me on Japan's right wing and the activities of the American Council on Japan (few authors I have ever met have been as generous in sharing their time and information as Glen and his mentor, the late John Roberts), and to attorneys Thomas Blakemore, Rosser Brockman, Shin Asahina, and Ray Bushell, who kindly spent hours patiently explaining Japan's legal system to me. A special note of gratitude goes to Jim Phillips, ex-fighter pilot and Grumman executive who put in many afternoons at the exclusive Tokyo Club elucidating the complexities of the aircraft industry for me, and helping to put the Lockheed scandal in perspective. And another special word of gratitude to Fusakazu Hayano, Ph.D., vice president of Asahi Chemical, who explained technological differences separating Japan and the United States and to Professor Kan Ori of Sophia University and Tsuneo Watanabe of the *Yomiuri Shimbun*, who began my education in Japanese politics.

In addition, I am especially beholden to Hal Drake, the great *Stars and Stripes* reporter in Tokyo, for allowing me to rummage through the *Stripes* morgue, and also to his wife Kazuko for her hospitality and their friend Toshi Cooper for her cooperation. Thanks also to Dick Berry and Jim Blessin for rummaging through their attics for me.

Thanks to my old friend Kozo Abe, a longtime reporter and editor for the *Yukan Fuji* and the *Sankei Shimbun* who, over many drunken nights, provided information and insights and opened many doors. Thanks to yakuza expert Reikichi Sumiya of the *Asahi Geinno* for his informative conversation and his gift of the world's largest gangster encyclopedia, and to a Brooklynite named Rick for his seminar on Tokyo con artists and grifters.

Mark Schumacher helped out immensely in my search for old newspaper and magazine pieces. Mark also set up the Micron computer system I used to write this book. Also helpful were Willis Witter and Mieko Miyazawa. David Howell and Kagari Ando in Kamakura provided a friendly, sympathetic ear, useful advice, and countless weekend dinners. Thanks also to Joe and Leith Bernard in Washington, D.C., and Rosser and Yin-Wah Brockman in San Francisco. To attorney Richard Siracusa and Judge Edwin Torres for helping me understand the East Harlem (New York) mafia. And to David and Jean Halberstam in New York

City. Also thanks to the Kawamura family of Denen-Chofu, Koichi, Machiko and Reimi, Bob Spenser, Elmer Luke, Robert Seward, Akio Nomura. Skip and Miko Orr. Yoshiko Takaishi. Jack and Toshi Mosher. Eduardo Sanchez. Tim Porter. Mayumi Nakazawa. Nobuko Sasae. Hide Tanaka of the Asahi Shimbun and his wife. Vince Izumi. Michi and Toshi Naito; Eide and Michiko Haru. Lucy Craft. Rick Wolff, JB Burkett, Takao Toshikawa. Velisarious Kattoulas. Naose Inoki. Kimberly Edwards and Robert Richards.

My special appreciation goes out to Tom Scully for editing the first finished draft, to Greg Davis and Randy Ulland for reading it and offering many valuable suggestions and comments. And finally to the author of "Chrsyanthemum and the Thoroughbred," David Shapiro, for putting his life on hold for a solid week in December 1997 when I needed a fresh eye and literary expertise to help nail down the final draft. I owe David a debt of gratitude and, knowing Dave as I do, I'm sure he will never let me forget it. I would also like to thank Greg Davis, the noted *Time* photographer and longtime pal, and his wife Masako Sakata, the president of the Imperial Press, for helping me get photographs. Yae Koizumi kindly supplied photos of her husband.

I owe a particular debt of gratitude to my editor at Pantheon, the estimable Linda Healey, who deserves some sort of award for patience and perseverance. She never wavered in her support for me or this project, even though I kept missing deadlines. She was always willing and eager to set aside what she was doing to listen to my ideas, wade through extremely rough drafts, and offer clearheaded, incisive criticism of often unformed ideas. I spent many a pleasant evening with her and her late husband J. Anthony Lukas—something I will not forget. I would also like to thank Amy Gray for being right there all the time on top of everything, Paul Kozlowski for his support, and Kate Rowe for keeping me out of court.

I also want to express my deepest thanks to my agent Amanda Urban, who played an exceptionally active part in engineering this project from its very inception to its conclusion. Without Binky, this book would never have happened.

Finally, thanks to the Kondo, Kobayashi, Hayano, and Noble clans. And to Carmel Oendan, Mom and Dad, Margo and Buck, Ned and Joseph, Debbie and Tim, Matt, Gracie and Cody, Peggy and Glen, Ross and Tyler, Lesslie Steve, Stevie, Erin, and Mary.

And the hightest *arigato* of all to my wife Machiko for not divorcing me during this project.

NOTES AND SOURCES

In researching this book, I conducted nearly 200 interviews with participants, eyewitnesses, and others with firsthand information regarding the characters, incidents, and episodes described in these pages. I had some three dozen intensive sessions with Nicola Zappetti alone between the fall of 1989 and his death in 1992, as well as numerous other recorded conversations with the people—friends, relatives, business associates, and enemies—who went to make up his milieu.

Among them was Richard Roa, a fixture in Roppongi nightlife for the past thirty years and a man who has proved to be a fountain of information about the area's bars and nightclubs. No other Westerner I have met in Tokyo has worked in such a wide variety of jobs in the *mizushobai* ("water trade"), as the Japanese call it, ranging from part-time manager of Danny's Inn, one of Tokyo's most famous call girl operations, to business adviser in the gilt-edged inner sanctum of the TSK.CCC. Other sources included Katsuji Maezono and Akio Nomura, men with nearly a century's experience between them working in and operating Tokyo restaurants, snack bars, and pubs, Jim Blessin, the longtime military club manager in the city, and his wife Kyoko Ai, a famous TV personality in the 1950s who appeared in the first *Godzilla* film and who once dated Rikidozan, and longtime Nicola's patrons Hal Drake and Tom Scully, both veterans of the *Stars and Stripes* Roppongi headquarters.

Still other important interview subjects included attorney Thomas Blakemore, for fifty years the only American qualified to try a case in a Japanese court, his wife Frances Baker, a graphic designer who first came to Japan in the mid-1930s, commercial lawyers Raymond Bushell and James L. Adachi, aircraft consultant James Phillips, MPD official Yutaka Mogami, and Eugene Aksenoff, M.D., one of the few foreigners ever to graduate from a Tokyo medical school. All of these people had lived and worked in Tokyo since the end of the war, and their recounting of their many and varied experiences in extensive talk sessions helped me recapture the atmosphere of the times.

The process of piecing together a half-century's worth of history was a laborious one. Because memories fade and play tricks after so many years, I relied, whenever possible, on multiple sources as well as documentation for the factual basis of the book. Particularly valuable in this regard was the Oya Soichi Bunko in Tokyo, a repository of Japanese-language magazines and periodicals dating from the postwar era, which proved an enormous help in reconstructing a clear portrait of the city as it reconstituted itself. Also useful were the libraries at the International House, the Foreign Correspondents Press Club, the Foreign Press Center, and the National Diet in Tokyo, as well as the New York Public Library at 42nd Street. The archives of the *Asahi Shimbun* and *The Stars and Stripes* were an important source of newspaper articles, while other documents and information were provided by the Library of Congress, the U.S. Senate Library, the National Archives, the U.S. Marine History Office, the FBI FOIP Section, the DIA SVI-FOIA, the NYPD-FOIL, the Dudley-Knox Library in Monterey, California, and John Neuffer's informative Website "Behind the Screen," and the LAPDOCID.

The vast databank of the *Rokka-kan Bunko Joho Senta* headed by Hiroshi Sasaki was especially useful in creating the lives of Ginza Machii and other characters in the book. A personal seminar Mr. Sasaki conducted for me helped give me an understanding of what some people call Japan's Shadow Government I otherwise would not have had. The books of Yasuhara Honda (*Kizu*), Eiji Oshita (*Eikyu No Rikidozan*), and Hidehiko Ushijima (*Mo Hitotsu No Showa Shi*) brought that world into even sharper focus with an immediacy and emotion it is difficult to describe. I can only hope these works will someday be translated into English so that others can enjoy them as I did. (The same goes, I might add, for Noboru Ando's three-part autobiography, *Yakuza to Koso*.) Anyone who thinks the postwar history of Tokyo is boring would do well to seek these books out.

Lastly, the collections of John Roberts and Glen Davis proved to be an invaluable source of material on the ACJ, Lockheed, and the *Kodama Guntai.*

All the dialogue in the book that I did not witness personally is reconstructed from interviews and/or media reports and other documents. The bibliography lists the approximately 100 English and Japanese books I utilized in the research and preparation of *Tokyo Underworld.* A fuller, more detailed, section-by-section explanation of the sources I relied on, including the wealth of magazine and newspaper articles I consulted, follows.

1. THE FIRST BLACK MARKET

The Ozu notice was translated from the Japanese as it appeared in *Kizu,* a highly regarded biography of a postwar gangster by Yasuharu Honda, p. 132.

For descriptions of Tokyo as it appeared immediately after the war, the author relied on interviews with eyewitnesses James L. Adachi, Kyoko Ai, Shin Asahina, Frances Baker, Jim Blessin, Toshi Cooper, Tetsuo Sato, and Yoshiko Takaishi.

The description of the Ozu black market is based on accounts by Honda in *Kizu*, by GHQ government section official Harry Emerson Wildes in his excellent book *Typhoon in Tokyo* (pp. 171–76), and by GHQ labor official Theodore Cohen in his voluminous *Remaking Japan* (pp. 305, 336). Ozu is also described in the well-respected work *Yakuza*, by David Kaplan and Alec Dubro, pp. 50–51.

Historical background on the gangs is contained in *Ninkyo Dai Hyakka* (The Encyclopaedia of Chivalry), a massive, 810-page tome on Japanese gangsters.

A NOTE ON GANG CHARACTER

The *Ninkyo Dai Hyakka* noted that activities such as loan sharking, prostitution, and narcotics were considered beneath the dignity of a true prewar *bakuto* and delineated a Gamblers' Code of Behavior (pp. 62–81), which included the following instructions: Obey the *oyabun* and other superiors in all matters. Never reveal the secrets of the gang. Always be ready to defend the honor of the gang and never hesitate to put your life on the line, either in fights with other gangs or the police. Train every morning in the martial arts and learn to ignore pain. When you fight, always fight with someone important; never engage in a fight with an opponent who is outnumbered and never appeal to the police for help. Never sleep with a woman belonging to a fellow gang member and stay away from so-called straight women; if you must have a woman, buy one. Always keep your composure while drinking. Never sit with one knee drawn up, and if you commit a misdeed and have to apologize, do it with actions, not words. The encyclopedia also features an old yakuza poem:

> *Men who forget shame,*
> *Who dishonor their face*
> *Are not worthy of belonging.*
> *Know shame,*
> *Keep your face while knowing*
> *shame*
> *Stake your life on your face.*

The collaboration of the gangs and the Tokyo municipal government during the war and immediate postwar era is described by Wildes in *Typhoon* (see Chapter 16, "Underground Empire," pp. 171–80).

It should be noted here that although Tokyo entered the war with 5 million residents, which made it the largest city in the world, it finished it with only 1 million, as most of the population had moved to the countryside. It took some years for the population to reach its prewar level.

The 45,000 street stall figure is from a special dispatch issued by the International News Service, November 25, 1947.

The outdoor markets as Japan's first experiment in democracy is discussed by Honda in *Kizu* (p. 138).

The informal survey of the residents at the Nomura Hotel was taken by Jim Blessin, then a Navy enlisted man who later became the hotel's manager.

The establishment of the RAA, the encounter of the first Army ground patrol in Tokyo, and the workings of the International Palace were described in some detail by Cohen in *Remaking Japan*, pp. 125–26; by Associated Press correspondent Mark Gayn in *Japan Diary*, pp. 232–234; and by Wildes in *Typhoon*, p. 328. The experiences of the MAG 44 advance party were described in interviews with the author by First Sergeant Nick Zappetti who led the excursion. Zappetti was also a sometime patron of the International Palace. "Hooker Alley" was described by Adachi and Blessin. After talking to veterans of the Occupation, it sometimes seemed as though the sole purpose of the whole undertaking was the sexual gratification of the invaders.

A NOTE ABOUT PROSTITUTION

The world's oldest profession had always been legal in Japan. In fact, Japanese brothels were among the most extensive in the world, with thousands of young girls sold into the life each year by their impoverished parents, some as young as age twelve. A prewar tally of individuals working in brothels in Japan exceeded 52,000 (see John Gunther, *Inside Asia*). Prostitution was considered a kind of art form in some circles in which ladies of the night would tattoo the names of their favorite clients on their thighs. It was also a serious business, without the stigma attached to it in some countries of the West. Prostitution only became illegal in Japan after the Americans arrived. The anti-prostitution law, passed in 1948, but not promulgated until 1958, gave rise to a whole host of substitute enterprises, such as *torukoburo* (Turkish baths) and *osawariba* (touch bars), which served as a cover for the real business of sex for money. In the late 1980s, after several complaints by the Turkish Embassy in Japan, the term *Soapland* came into use and gradually replaced the term *toruko*.

RAA establishments, it should be noted, were equal opportunity purveyors of pleasure. They provided their services to anyone, regardless of race, creed, or color. It was only later that their proprietors learned prejudice from white American soldiers, who taught them about segregation. (A constant feature of life outside U.S. military bases in Japan over the years was the existence of white-only and black-only bars.)

The growth in illicit commerce was described by Occupation eyewitnesses Roger Suddith, Ernie Solomon, and Thomas L. Blakemore in interviews with the author.

Ozu was described as the "worst criminal in Japan," by Wildes (*Typhoon*, p. 175).

The $8 million figure was quoted by Wildes (*Typhoon*, p. 3), who wrote that during the first year of the Occupation it seemed impossible to find an American who had not been approached with some sort of deal by Japanese. New York Times correspondent Russell Brines, in *MacArthur's Japan*, pp. 293–95, reported that the Army lost "at least $70 million on illegal marketing" in the first eight months of the Occupation, the time during which troops could legally convert yen into dollars. Another good account of Occupation-era corruption appears in Mark Gayn's *Japan Diary*. The books of both Wildes (*Typhoon*, p. 36) and Gayn (*Japan Diary*, pp. 124–25, 178, 245–47, 262–63, 304–5, 307, 309–20) contain extensive descriptions of Akira Ando, as does Kaplan and Dubro's *Yakuza*, pp. 49–50.

Kades's press conference was held on November 10, 1947. In it he noted, "A vast and insidious network of feudal forces was undermining American democratic policy." Later, a GHQ officer in the Public Safety Division went so far as to warn that the "entire political, economic and cultural life of Japan is at the mercy of gangster groups" (Wildes, *Typhoon*, p. 179). A detailed description of the "underground government" was contained in a special report released by the International News Service on November 25, 1947. Also *Mo Hitosu No Showa Shi (1)* (One More History of Showa: I), written by Professor Hidehiko Ushijima, contains a comprehensive discussion of the underground government in its introductory pages.

The effects of the GHQ crackdown were discussed by Wildes (*Typhoon*, pp. 171–80) and in *MacArthur's Japan* by Brines, who wrote, "Criminal identification units devoted most of their efforts to large scale operations; several black market rings, feeding on stolen army supplies, were smashed but the battle was endless . . . the easy profits too alluring. Controlled black marketing continued almost openly, therefore, with each participant aware he was risking heavy penalties" (p. 294).

The history of corruption in Japan is delineated in *Political Bribery in Japan*, by Richard H. Mitchell. Also see *Jitsuryoku Nihon Oshoku Shi* (A History of Japanese Corruption: An Authentic Account), by Tetsuro Muroboshi, (which describes several dozen scandals that occurred between 1872 and 1963 involving many of Japan's leading statesmen and financiers, few of whom, incidentally, were ever tried or convicted). The Showa Denko scandal was described in Mitchell, *Political Bribery*, pp. 100–106; in Wildes, *Typhoon*, pp. 160, 164; and William Chapman, *Inventing Japan*, pp. 49–50. (Also see Karl Dixon, "Japan's Lockheed Scandal: Structural Corruption," *Pacific Community*, January 1977.)

Most studies of corruption in Japan compare the political sector unfavorably with the well educated civil service bureaucracy, which actually runs the country on a day-to-day basis and which has a somewhat better reputation for honesty and integrity.

A NOTE ABOUT THE VICKERS-SIEMENS SCANDAL

The Siemens affair was originally discovered by a Tokyo Thought Police agent who inadvertently stumbled upon it while pursuing a Mitsui Bussan trading house employee on another matter. During his investigation he found that a representative of the German company installing wireless equipment for the Navy was also blackmailing the Japanese manager of said company over the bribery. The agent filed his report to his superior, and soon after, a Mitsui executive advised him that the German had returned to Berlin and the matter had been settled. A series of secret meetings followed, involving the Japanese prime minister, the minister of the navy, the minister of justice, the German ambassador, and a man from Siemens, after which instructions were passed down to the prosecutor's office and the police board not to pursue the affair any further. (The PM, Gombei Yamamoto, was an ex-Navy admiral.) The police agent was instructed by his superior to keep his mouth shut and visited by thugs on more than one occasion to encourage him to keep that silence.

But early in 1914 the Siemens representative, on trial in Berlin for stealing company documents, testified that Siemens had been bribing the Japanese government, including certain high-ranking officials in the Ministry of the Navy, to win contracts. With the news out, the Japanese police were forced to act. Two vice admirals and three top Mitsui executives were arrested, and the prime minister's cabinet collapsed. The Siemens clerk for transactions was also arrested but did not go to trial because someone strangled him in the detention house (Mitchell, p. 20). There was public rioting, and shrill editorials decried the loss of national confidence in the government. (As one cynical observer put it, however, "'national confidence' was a journalistic exaggeration since the incidents . . . were only the most conspicuous symptoms of a disease which affected the entire body politic . . . a serious condition in which the several organs functioned independently [and exuberantly] without regard for the well-being of the body as a whole." [John Roberts, *Mitsui*, pp. 186–88.)

The GHQ crackdown on crime by its own personnel is described in Cohen, *Remaking Japan*, pp. 128–31. An author interview with Occupation businessman Jack Dinken, whose company helped rearm the MPD, confirmed the account of the disappearance of the original armory and provided additional background on the black markets.

THE BANK OF TEXAS
Several contemporaries of Zappetti confirmed facts about his black market activities, among them, fellow CPC workers James L. Adachi, and Reid Irvine, Jim Blessin (friend and manager of the Nomura Hotel, where Zappetti stayed), and Dr. Eugene Aksenoff. Aksenoff, a White Russian native of Manchuria who practiced medicine in Tokyo for more than half a century, provided further information on the workings of the black market, the Ginza-based smugglers of the era, and the White Russian members of Lansco, whom he knew well.

An unpublished manuscript of an interview with a one-time member of the Tosei-kai gang conducted in the early 1970s, when the gangster had relocated to Seoul, confirmed details of the illegal check and money order business on the Ginza during the years following the end of the war. (The manuscript was provided by journalist Hiroshi Sasaki.)

Adachi summed up the general opinion of Zappetti among the Occupation-aires (as some of them liked to call themselves) when he said, "He was a typical New York wop. He talked out of the side of his mouth and he bragged about his black market activities. A lot of people played the black market in those days, but quietly, on a small scale, and didn't talk about it. But not Nick. He had everyone scared. We all thought he was dangerous." Added Blessin, "Nick was flashy, a fast mover, and disdainful of people. There was talk about him and the gangs. He was involved in things we didn't want to be part of." Said Aksenoff, "He was well known and he was a little scary in those days."

Zappetti was deported after being fingered by a teenaged Ueno black market courier who had been caught *in flagrante delicto* by a conscientious Japanese undercover detective and enticed to talk by a princely seventy-five-cents-per-day CID government witness fee. Before leaving, Zappetti said good-bye to his wife and kids and then accosted his accuser, a pouty-looking anorectic youth, in the elevator of the Teikoku Building, a seven-story, prewar, marble and stone structure facing Hibiya Park and the Palace grounds, where the CID was located. He grabbed the youth in a hammerlock and took him to the roof. With the charred skyline of Tokyo serving as backdrop, Zappetti methodically went to work. He broke the young man's nose, cracked several ribs, and closed both eyes, leaving his victim lying in a crumpled, bloody heap on the concrete. "That's what we do to squealers back in New York," he said.

It was the general consensus within the U.S. Embassy proper in Tokyo that, while in New York, Zappetti had struck a deal with the Mafia to look after their interests, in return for which they helped him get a visa and passport. That was what Barry Nemcoff, U.S. Embassy press official in Tokyo from 1963 to 1968, believed. And it was the belief of the Tokyo Metropolitan Police Department, although nobody could prove it.

Crime journalist Rekichi Sumiya confirmed details about the Ginza gangs of that era, the Sumiyoshi and the Tosei-kai, as did the aforementioned ex-Tosei-kai soldier in his unpublished memoirs. The sale of a fake $30,000 "Chase Bank" check is a matter of public record (as is the three-year prison term served by the seller). *Asahi Shimbun* journalist Shigeo Fujita confirmed details about Huff and the Evergreen.

A longtime Tokyo-based accountant from England, William Salter, provided information on the Hotel New York.

OCCUPATION LEGACY

The 10 percent estimate appeared in the leading weekly *Shukan Bunshun* on October 4, 1979, in an article entitled "*M-Shigen No Ura No Shinjitsu*" ("The Truth behind the M-Fund"). The $200 million figure was quoted by Wildes in *Typhoon*, p. 168.

The existence of a secret slush fund, known as the "M-Fund" in many circles, has been the topic of much discussion over the years. Some say it was created with the cooperation of the U.S. government. A good summary of all the gossip and speculation on the subject is the above M-Fund article, which was actually a three-part series appearing in the *Shukan Bunshun*, October 4 and 25 and November 1, 1979.

There is a wealth of excellent books on the Occupation as a whole. Among them are Cohen, *Remaking Japan*, Wildes, *Typhoon in Tokyo*, Brines, *MacArthur's Japan*, and Gayn, *Japan Diary*.

SCAP's demotion of Emperor Hirohito from his previous post as a god under the Shinto state religion to figurehead was made abundantly clear in the first meeting between the Emperor and General MacArthur. The Emperor had arrived in full regalia, only to be greeted by MacArthur in an open-necked shirt with no tie, no medals, and no campaign ribbons. The Japanese put great stock in symbols, and to see news photos of the two men together—the informally dressed MacArthur, hands in his back pockets, towering over the Emperor, who was standing at attention in his best uniform displaying all his decorations—was an enormous shock. The Sun God looked like an ordinary little man trying to appear important while standing next to someone much taller. The scene conveyed more than any SCAP declaration ever could have. It was clear beyond the shadow of a doubt who the most powerful figure in the country was.

The general consensus of the people I interviewed was that the Occupation GI was a much-better-mannered animal than his successors. The former came from a poor Depression-era background. He made a decent living in the Army and did not want to lose it.

Especially offensive in the list of new restrictions imposed in late 1947 was the issuance of a new SCAPIN (SCAP Instruction), "Fraternization without conversation is not fraternization," which, in effect, was a bow to the impossibility of controlling the sexual urges of so many GIs. It showed Japanese that Americans could be every bit as bureaucratically ludicrous as anyone else. Under SCAP Order 3-11, an American caught talking to the Japanese girl he had just slept with could be court-martialed for violating fraternization laws. Moreover, the girl could be arrested by the Japanese police for "endangering the solemn mission of SCAP." Only married couples like Nick Zappetti and his wife were immune from such prosecution.

The activities of the American Council on Japan have been documented in great detail by the late University of Maine scholar Howard Schoenberger, who published a number of articles on the subject. See, for example, "The Japan Lobby in American Diplomacy, 1947–1952," *Pacific Historical Review* 46, no. 3, August 1977, pp. 327–59; and "Zaibatsu Dissolution and the American Restoration of Japan," *Bulletin of Concerned Asia Scholars*, September 1, 1973. Also see Glen Davis and John G. Roberts, *An Occupation without Troops*. GHQ labor official Theodore Cohen had several unkind words to say about the activities of ACJ lawyer James Lee Kauffman in *Remaking Japan*. Sources for Rockefeller-related businesses in Japan included "An Untitled Essay, The Rockefellers in

Japan," a thesis submitted to John Dower in the Department of History, University of Wisconsin, 1974, and *The Rockefellers,* by Collier and Horowitz. On March 15, 1994, NHK aired "The Japan Lobby," a documentary on the ACJ.

At the end of the Occupation, there were 3,760 American men and 453 American women employees in the GHQ, a discrepancy that helped to account for the large number of marriages between Japanese women and American men.

2. OCCUPATION HANGOVER

The two drownings and other "unpleasant occurrences" (including the robbery of a Fuji Bank branch in Tokyo in 1952 by three GIs armed with shotguns and rifles) were described in the *"Gaikokujin Makaritoru"* [The Foreigners Have Their Own Way], *Shukan Yomiuri,* October 10, 1954, pp. 4–11. The article ran with a two-frame cartoon: the first depicted wartime GIs dropping bombs on Tokyo; the next showed peacetime GIs terrorizing peace-loving citizens with spears and gleefully picking their pockets with fishing hooks. The Lucky Dragon incident is described in David Halberstam's *The Fifties,* pp. 345–47.

Voice of America excerpts and other related material are from Ushijima, *Mo Hitotsu no Showa Shi (1)* (pp. 110–16).

Descriptions of Tokyo in the immediate post-Occupation era came from Hal Drake, Tom Scully, and Richard Berry, who all worked in the *Stars and Stripes* Roppongi office at the time. Lawyer Tom Blakemore, who lived on the economy, also provided his recollections, as did Richard Roa, then an Army private.

Tokyo-based commercial lawyer Ray Bushell was a close acquaintance of Ted Lewin and provided background material on the gambling czar, including the $25,000 bribe that Lewin confided to him. Descriptions of the Mandarin were provided by Jim Blessin and Jack Dinken, who were occasional visitors. For additional material on Lewin, the author relied on interviews with Jim Phillips, a longtime Tokyo resident and aircraft consultant, who knew him, as well as *"Gaikokujin Makari Doru,"* and *Shukan Yomiuri,* October 10, 1954, *Mo Hitotsu no Showa Shi (1).*

Longtime Tokyo entertainment columnist "Shig" Fujita, who designed the logo for the first Latin Quarter, jointly owned by Lewin and Yoshio Kodama, and did public relations work for the Mandarin as well, provided background, as did acquaintance Dr. Eugene Aksenoff. Aksenoff also provided a description of the time in the mid-'50s he operated on one Jason Lee, a Korean-American "business associate" of Lewin's. Lee had been shot in the side and he demanded Aksenoff remove the bullet in the doctor's Tokyo clinic without using an anesthetic; he did not want to be rendered vulnerable to enemy attack. Lee later gained notoriety when he was arrested in Monte Carlo for gambling with loaded dice at the famous casino.

A NOTE ABOUT GAMBLING

Gambling has been illegal for centuries in Japan. The feudal lords of centuries past banned it because they did not want citizens making money too easily. Tough anti-gambling laws were a way of controlling the populace on the one hand and instilling a strict work ethic on the other, a philosophy followed by modern-day bureaucrats in Japan. However, the old *daimyo* often held private gambling sessions for their own amusement and called in the local *bakuto* to help organize them. Although the anti-gambling laws remained in effect into the modern era, public betting on horse racing and motorboat racing appeared after the war as municipally sanctioned activities, providing a much-needed source of income for local governments, which split the take with private entrepreneurs. (Perhaps the biggest beneficiary of this postwar phenomenon was a man named Ryoji Sasakawa, an eccentric right-wing activist and one-time Mussolini supporter who had spent time in Sugamo Prison with Yoshio Kodama and Nobusuke Kishi. His Japan Motorboat Racing Association, which put on the races, made Sasakawa a multimillionaire, enabled him to build his own private army and claim, in 1974, that he was the "world's wealthiest fascist.") The rise of this type of public gambling caused much hand-wringing among purists, who saw it as evidence that the moral fabric of Japanese society was being torn asunder.

For the police raids on the Mandarin and their aftermath, the author relied on the following newspaper reports: *Yomiuri Shimbun*, July 17, 1952; *Asahi Shimbun*, July 18, 1952, March 17, March 31, and July 18, 1953, and August 3, 1954. The Lewin swindle was reported in Shinsuke Itakagi, *Kono Jiyuto* [This Liberal Party]. Vol. 2, pp. 214–15.

Descriptions of the Latin Quarter were provided by Ushijima, Blessin, and Bushell.

Itagaki also reported that Lewin was being "manipulated" by the FBI, under the control of a Colonel Diamond, who was representing the FBI in Tokyo, at the same time Lewin was running the Latin Quarter in a consortium with former Japanese nationalists, whom he had met during the war in Manila, agents of the GHQ's G-2 Intelligence Unit, and agents from the CIA. Ushijima reported that during the war, when Lewin managed the Riveria Casino, he had become involved in the opium trade and had maintained a business relationship with the Japanese military—specifically, with an ultranationalist leader named Yoshio Kodama, who ran one of the most effective wartime procurement machines in the Co-Prosperity Sphere. Kodama, wrote Ushijima, helped Lewin establish the Latin Quarter.

Itagaki reported that, after the war, Lewin hooked up with U.S. intelligence, helping agents trace money-laundering operations in Asia and uncover Communist operatives working in the region—all while he was running a gunsmuggling ring for Japanese underworld and right-wing groups. Lewin's interpreter, Carey Yamamoto, was associated with the Tosei-kai.

Another Tokyo club Lewin owned was the Golden Gate in Azabu, which was a hangout for pilots of the CIA-run Civil Air Transport, an airline service running troops between Taiwan, Hong Kong, and Tokyo, and which was famous for its backroom, high-stakes poker games.

For the history and background of Japanese pachinko, the author relied on the excellent book *Winning Pachinko: The Game of Japanese Pinball*, by Eric C. Sedensky.

The arrest of Vladimir Boborov and his accomplices, including Leo Yuskoff, was a major story in the *Asahi Shimbun*, March 17, 1953. See *"Kokusai Tobaku"* [International Gambling]. Also see the March 31, 1953, and July 18, 1953, editions for follow-up articles on the deportation. (Also *Asahi Shimbun*, February 3, 1954.)

GORGEOUS MAC

There is a wealth of material in Japanese on Rikidozan and the professional wrestling boom that hit Japan in the 1950s. One of the best is the biography of Rikidozan written by Eiji Oshita, *Eikyu No Rikidozan* [Rikidozan Forever]. Another valuable source was the 700-plus-page history of pro wrestling, *Nihon Proresu Zen-shi* (Baseball Magazine Co.). Also useful were *Rikidozan* by Noboru Kurita and *Yobo No Media* (Ambitious Media), by prize-winning author Inose Naoki, as well as two hour-long film documentaries available on videotape: *Rikidozan to Sono Jidai*, Bungei Shunju, and *Rikidozan*, Pony, Canyon.

The Indians-as-bad-guys quote is from Hidehiko Ushijima, *Mo Hitosu no Showa-shi (1); Shinso Kairyu No Otoko: Rikidozan* [One More Showa History, I; Rikidozan: Man of Deep Currents].

IMPERIAL HOTEL DIAMOND ROBBERY/TOKYO JAIL

The diamond robbery at the Imperial Hotel was widely covered in the Japanese media. Magazine articles dealing with the robbery at length include *"Nokoru Hoseki Ten No Ikikata," Sunday Mainichi*, February 5, 1956, and *"Hoseki Goto 'Gomenasai,'" Sunday Mainichi*, March 25, 1956.

MacFarland's bizzare personality quirks and sexual preferences were attested to by Nick Zappetti and the *Sunday Mainichi* pieces. Raymond Bushell, who represented MacFarland after his arrest, also provided colorful accounts of MacFarland's odd behavior.

MacFarland's six-month hospitalization and insulin shock treatment were reported by the INS, March 22, 1956. His suicide attempts were reported by the INS, January 27, 1956. His indictment was covered by the *Mainichi Daily News*, February 8, 1956, and his confession, by AP, March 9, 1956. INS correspondent Leonard Saffir wrote several pieces on MacFarland, including the numerous suicide attempts in January and February 1956 (see " 'I'm Crazy,' says Sick Jewel Thief," INS, March 22, 1956).

On March 7, 1956, MacFarland issued a lengthy letter of apology to the court and sent a copy of it to the Kyodo Wire Service, which published it in full. The last paragraph is excerpted here:

> I'm deeply sorry to the people I've wronged, to my own government for the embarrassment I've put upon them, and to you the Japanese people for my

lack of respect for your laws and honor. I pray that the courts and you the people will allow me to stay and make my home here in Japan. I honestly feel that if this is allowed, my future actions will show that I was worthy of the consideration.

So I now ask you, the people, to have "Mercy on Me, a Fool."
Humbly,
John M. MacFarland

MacFarland's sentence was announced on May 27, 1956, in Tokyo District Court. See INS dispatch, May 27, 1956, and the AP report of May 28, 1956.

MacFarland's apology was prompted perhaps by his learning of an interesting aspect of the Japanese criminal justice system, whereby truly repentant criminals come clean and admit guilt and get lenient treatment. (In fact, one-fourth of all criminals in any given year are sentenced merely to write "I'm sorry" at the bottom of their confession.) In any event, in MacFarland's case, it didn't work.

MacFarland's male paramour, who abetted MacFarland's robbery, was identified by Zappetti and Bushell, MacFarland's lawyer. Mori's activities were described in the various media accounts in Japanese and English, but referred to only as "M" at the time of the robbery because he was still under age. (In Japan, one reaches majority at age twenty.)

Shattuck was implicated in various news accounts (see INS, May 8, 1956, for example). Bushell was a witness to MacFarland's face-to-face accusation of Shattuck, and Zappetti, who testified at Shattuck's trial, maintained that Shattuck was framed. Bushell privately believed that Shattuck had really bought the jewels but then lied about it.

Dr. Aksenoff, a highly respected member of the foreign community in Japan by the mid-1950s, related the story about introducing Shattuck's wife to the judge, who was Aksenoff's friend. Bushell told a similar story, without mentioning the judge, who, in any event, is now deceased. Doris Lee and Shattuck have long departed Japan and are believed to have retired in Mexico in the late 1950s.

The details of Zappetti's incarceration and excursions to American Express were verified by one of the official police interpreters assigned to the case, a man who wishes to remain anonymous. Incidentally, the regimen Zappetti endured remained essentially unchanged thirty years later when ex-Beatle Paul McCartney spent a week in detention after being arrested at Narita Airport for possessing 225 grams of marijuana.

The *Jimbutsu Orai* article, "*Tekikoku Hoteru Hoseki Gyangu*" ("The Imperial Hotel Jewel Gang"), was by Yoshino Saburo (March 1956, pp. 164–67).

U.S. Embassy official William Givens visited MacFarland every month during the six years the jewel thief was incarcerated in Fuchu Prison—a grim, unheated place with high gray walls located outside Tokyo. On each visit, Givens hand-delivered MacFarland's lone request, a copy of *Gourmet* magazine. "He was sick of fish and rice," said Givens. "He had lost about 100 pounds. He fantasized all day about gourmet food."

3. SUCCESS STORY

Descriptions of Roppongi in the mid-1950s are from Tom Scully, Hal Drake, Richard Pyle, Richard Roa, Minoru Sasaki, Reikichi Sumiya, Dick Berry, William Givens, and Thomas Blakemore.

Crime journalist Minoru Sasaki wrote the first article about Nicola's restaurant. He described his impressions in an interview with the author of this book. Akio "Frank" Nomura, the first waiter to work at Nicola's and a man who would work on and off there for some thirty years, provided additional information and background color on the restaurant and its clientele.

TV sales figures and ratings for the era are from *Nichiroku 20 Seki, Shukan Yearbook* series, *Dai 38 Go*, published by Kodansha, and by the wrestling encyclopedia *Nihon Puro Resu Zen Shi.*

All of the books on Rikidozan mentioned in the bibliography describe bizarre behavior. His antics were quite well known in Japan. Nick Zappetti and Nicola's headwaiter Frank Nomura were also eyewitnesses.

A good description of gang life in that era is *"Hi wo Haiita Koruto!"* [The Colt That Spat Fire], *Shukan Tokyo*, June 28, 1958 (pp. 4–9), which describes the shooting of Hideki Yokoi.

UNDERGROUND EMPIRE

The underground empire of Yoshio Kodama has been described in many works. Foremost among them is the work of journalist Takashi Tachibana, in particular, his lengthy article, *"Kodama Yoshio To Wa nani-ka?"* [What Is Yoshio Kodama?], for the respected monthly *Bungei Shunju*, May 1976, pp. 94–130. Also see the multi-part series in the weekly *Shukan Bunshun, "CIA to Yoshio Kodama"* [Yoshio Kodama and the CIA], published April 15, April 29, May 13, May 20, and May 27, 1976. Also the *Shukan Asahi* weekly magazine article, *"GHQ Johobu, CIA, Soshite Uyoku To No Setten Wo Arau"* [Laundering the Connection between the GHQ Intelligence Wing, the CIA and the Right Wing], April 23, 1976, pp. 173–76.

Also revealing was a report by Jinkichi Matsuda, "How Yoshio Kodama Behaved Himself on the Continent: History of Crime of the Shanghai Adventurer," IPA Case No. 194, U.S. National Archives. And Soichi Oya, *"Kodama Yoshio,..."* *Bungei Shunju*, January 1961. Another interesting source is Yoshio Kodama, *Akusei, Jusei, Ransei*, which describes his early years as a young nationalist.

The definitive work on the relationship of Kodama and Machii is a long (15,000-word), two-part article published by the prestigious but now defunct weekly, *Asahi Journal, "Kodama no Kage De Odoru Aru Fuikusa"* [The Fixer Who Danced in Kodama's Shadow], published in two parts on October 1 and October 8, 1976. Authorship was credited to the magazine editorial staff. It describes the gang boss's youth and rise to power in great detail. Also see the *Shukan Bunshun* series, *"Kankoku Kara Kita Otoko"* [The Man from Korea], June 23, June 30, and July 7, 1977. The Tokyo Metropolitan Police Department file on Machii, to which the author had access, confirmed many facts, as did crime reporter Hiroshi Sasaki and a confidential interview with a former member of the Tosei-kai.

Ushijima's *Mo Hitosu no Showa Shi (1): Shinso Kairyu No Otoko: Rikidozan* was a valuable reference in that it explored Rikidozan's political connections, which, the author wrote, represented a map of Japan's underground government.

There are numerous references to the Machii and Rikidozan relationship in Honda's *Kizu* (a highly regarded biography of a famous Shibuya gangster who was assassinated in 1963 by a pair of Tosei-kai soldiers wielding *yanagi-bo*, thin but deadly willow-branch-shaped swords, in a decisive turf war) and also in *Eikyu No Rikidozan*, by Eiji Oshita. Ex-gang boss Norboru Ando's three-part autobiography, *Yakuza to Koso*, describes how his face was slashed from ear to chin by a Tosei-kai soldier. Both Honda's and Ando's books describe the postwar growth of crime and the gangs. So does *Ninkyo DaiHyakka* [The Great Encyclopaedia of Chivalry], an 800-page colossus on crime and gang history and culture in Japan, and *Koan Hyakunenshi* [The 100 Year History of Public Security].

Machii's finger mutilation episode is described in the above *Bunshun* series and the *Asahi Journal* article. It is also described in Kaplan and Dubro's *Yakuza*.

The nightclub incident with Maurice was related by eyewitness Zappetti.

Ginza Nippo—a gang-run magazine—was just one of many, many such "magazines" in Japan that were sold by the "direct sales" method, so to speak, and were not available on newsstands. They represent a well-known type of extortion racket in Japan.

The CIA's interest in Kodama as delineated in the previously referenced articles was twofold: as a string puller for the LDP, and as a quiet leader of the extreme rightist elements in Japan. ACJ co-founder and ex-State Department official Eugene Dooman carried out a covert CIA-funded operation to smuggle tons of tungsten—a strategic metal used for hardening missiles—to the Pentagon from Japanese military installations. Yoshio Kodama was the man hired to accomplish the task. (The Kyodo News Agency reported on October 16, 1994, that Kay Sugahara, an official of the OSS [the predecessor of the CIA] procured tungsten from Japan through Kodama and paid $2.8 million to the rightist; this according to Howard Schoenberger, late professor at the University of Maine, in an unpublished manuscript.)

There are numerous references to the Machii and Rikidozan relationship in *Kizu* and in *Eikyu No Rikidozan*. Machii's real name, according to his file in the Tokyo Metropolitan Police Department, is Cheong Geong Young.

Descriptions of Kodama in English include several pages in *Yakuza* by Kaplan and Dubro.

The activities of the Tonichi trading company vis-à-vis Sukarno and Dewi were described in the weekly *Shukan Gendai*, February 28, 1966. Also see Yoko Kitazawa, "Japan-Indonesia Corruption: Bribe, It Shall Be Given You" (part 1), by *AMPO* 8, no. 1, 1976.

The Diet protests against the renewal of the Security Treaty were described in detail to me by Dr. Fusakazu Hayano, a chemical engineer for Asahi Chemical, who participated in them when he was a student at Tokyo University. William Givens, a U.S. Embassy official at the time, also witnessed them and related his impressions.

The formation of the gangster patriot army is described in detail in *Koan Daiyoran* [Great Directory of Public Security]. Other good descriptions are found in *Yakuza to Nihon-jin*, by Kenji Ino, *Mo Hitotsu No Showa Shi (1)*, *Black Star Over Japan*, by Alex Axelbank, and *Yakuza*.

The quote, "Even in dirty swamps," is from a fourteen-part *Mainichi Daily News* series on gangs, "Organized Violence Pattern in Japan," which began July 18, 1964, and ran through August 22 of that same year.

Secret meetings involving Kodama, Machii, LDP officials, and ROK representatives are described in detail in *Mo Hitosu No Showa Shi (1)* and also in the aforementioned *Asahi Journal* article, "*Kodama No Kage De Odoru Fuiksa*" of October 1 and 8, 1976. Machii himself mentioned them in a rare interview with the *Shukan Gendai*, June 23, 1966.

A NOTE ABOUT GUN CONTROL LAWS IN JAPAN

Possession of firearms has been illegal since the Tokugawa era, when guns were introduced by Portugese traders. The shogunate banned them because they were fearful of what might happen with such weapons in the hands of the populace. A famous feudal lord named Toyotomi Hideyoshi (1537–1598), who unified the nation, began a campaign in which all swords and other weapons owned by civilians were confiscated, assuring people their safety was guaranteed as long as they paid their taxes. The police system developed in this vein over time, and a certain awe of law enforcement and authority was engendered along with it. The legal prohibition of individual ownership of handguns has continued.

The relatively low number of violent crimes in Japan is considered the result of this historic absence of a custom of armed self-defense, as well as the result of certain cultural traits in regard to a sense of public decorum and an aversion to publicly shaming one's family name, which some regard as particularly strong among the Japanese.

MAFIA BOSS OF TOKYO

The Club 88 typhoons were described by eyewitness Zappetti. The close friendship of Zappetti and Rikidozan and Machii has been described to me by the chief waiter Nomura, the cash register girl Yae Koizumi (who later became Zappetti's wife), and Yutaka Mogami, formerly of the Tokyo Metropolitan Police Department, who called Rikidozan, Machii, and Zappetti the "leading enemies of the Tokyo Police."

The Tanashi gang encounter was described by Zappetti and Yae Koizumi.

Numerical data on gang membership appear in *Koan Daiyoran*. Also see the fourteen-part series on gangs appearing in the *Mainichi Daily News*, beginning July 18, 1964, entitled "Organized Violence . . ." And the round table discussion, "*Henshin Suru Boryoku Shudan*" [The Changing Organized Violence Gangs], in the weekly *Shukan Yomiuri*, October 15, 1978, pp. 28–40. In it, a police official is quoted as saying, "We really don't know how many yakuza there are. The government asks us to make a count, so we do. But it's only a guess."

The "Wash Blood with Blood" incidents were taken from *Kizu* and police reports.

The standoff with the Kobayashi-kai men was described by Zappetti and his cash register girl at the time, Yae Koizumi.

The twenty-man battle between the Sumiyoshi and Tosei-kai took place in 1962 in front of the Chako nightclub in Roppongi, prompted by an argument over an unpaid bill. The club was operated by the TSK. The customer who refused to pay was from the Sumiyoshi. The details were verified by a police report of the incident.

KILLER IKEDA

The encounter between Zappetti and Ikeda and henchman was related by Zappetti and by eyewitness Frank Nomura. Some secondhand accounts dispute certain details, such as Ikeda leaving his gun on the counter.

KIM SIN RAK

The facts about Rikidozan's true identity were first revealed to the public in 1973, in print, in the aforementioned Ushijima book.

A NOTE ABOUT KOREANS IN JAPAN

The term *sankokujin* (third country people) was used to refer to the Koreans and Formosans who had been brought to Japan to work in the coal mines and factories during the 1920s and 1930s, when Korea and Formosa belonged to the Japanese Imperial Empire and, after years of oppression and harsh treatment, liberated by the Occupation forces. Although a postwar repatriation program resulted in over 2 million going home, 600,000 Korean imports, along with some 100,000 Taiwanese, chose to stay in Japan and enjoy the new liberated status granted them by the GHQ, which exempted them from the legal authority of the Japanese police. Some of them formed gangs, set up their own markets in the burned-out areas around the train stations, and with better access to American goods than the Japanese, began to expand their influence, a state of affairs that was not welcomed by the pure-blooded Japanese gangs despite the demo-cratic spirit supposedly in the air. What one Japanese gang boss of the era wrote of their incursions in his autobiography some years later was typical of the at-titude toward the *sankokujin:*

> Thinking back, for those people who had been treated like slaves and beaten by the Japanese military, the time was for them like a spring which came in the 100th year. They wanted to behave as they wish and that may be a reflection of their feelings of revenge, as well as an inferiority com-plex.
>
> They would drink on the train, annoy Japanese women and take up too much space, occupying 2 seats or even lying down during the rush hour.
>
> Using their special privileges, they got access to rationed goods and sold them on the black market . . . going into places like a thief.
>
> Although it was understandable, it was also unbearable to see in front of us: our own people being treated badly and for us not to do anything about it and to pretend as if we were not seeing it. (Ando, *Yakuza to Koso,* vol. 1, p. 119.)

In the end, the Japanese gang bosses did do something about it, in several bru-tal clashes (in Shibuya, Ueno, and Shimbashi) when the American MPs were not around, using swords, handguns, and, in one instance, a machine gun, slowly gaining the upper hand over the upstart outsiders.

The battle for territory between Korea and homegrown mobsters was sym-bolized by the rivalry between the Tosei-kai and the Sumiyoshi. In the after-math of war, the Sumiyoshi grew to several thousand members citywide, becoming Tokyo's largest gang, and expanded into other spheres of activity once disdained by the true *bakuto.* They gained control of the Tokyo docks, moved into the amphetamine trade as well as the entertainment business, and even took up handling the promotion of Rikidozan pro wrestling. But the Tosei-kai was not easily displaced.

The Sumiyoshi influence in the Ginza was seriously eroded one afternoon in March 1956, at a gangland funeral in the old quarter of Asakusa. Four men in the crowd at a seventeenth-century Buddhist temple where the services were being held drew .38 caliber pistols from their morning coats and began firing at the Sumiyoshi-Ginza head, who was in attendance. When the smoke cleared, he was dead and the TSK's Ginza position had been solidified. A Shibuya gang boss found this out one evening when he took a stroll through the West Ginza and neglected to pay his respects to a TSK foot soldier as he passed by and was slashed from ear to chin.

As he grew in power, Machii developed a friendship with Rikidozan, whom he knew as a fellow Korean, and eventually took over the promotion of all Riki's Tokyo matches, much to the chagrin of the Sumiyoshi, assuming the post of au-ditor in the JPWA. In return, Machii quietly installed Rikidozan as a formal member of the Tosei-kai, with the high-ranking post of *saiko komon* ("supreme adviser"), a rank beneath only that of the boss. For Riki, who had a bizarre fascination with mobsters, it was an honor in the same league with winning the WWA championship. Soon, the police began calling his Club Riki a "branch office of the TSK" in their internal reports.

Descriptions of Riki's character came from the plethora of books about him as well as several people the author interviewed who knew him. In addition to Zappetti, there was Richard Beyer, who wrestled in Japan as "The Destroyer," Carl Goch, also a professional wrestler who knew Rikidozan, Roger Suddith, who managed the Nomura Hotel, which Rikidozan often terrorized, and Y. Mogami from the Tokyo Metropolitan Police Department. Beyer recalled traveling with Rikidozan on tour in the months before his death, staying in Japanese *ryokan* (inns). Riki had taken to sleeping with a gun under the futon, while gripping tightly a briefcase containing the evening's take. A knock on the *shoji* would bring Riki to his feet, gun in hand. He frequently moaned that someone was trying to kill him.

In *Yakuza to Koso,* his autobiography, former gang boss Noboru Ando describes his ongoing war with Rikidozan, including an unsuccessful attempt to have Rikidozan killed and the brief kidnapping of three of Rikidozan's top wrestlers, which Ando had ordered. (Ando was upset because Rikidozan had opened a bar in the major Tokyo entertainment hub of Shibuya, which Ando's gang controlled. Also Rikidozan had assaulted a nightclub hostess who then turned to Ando for retribution. Rikidozan actually went into hiding until the matter was resolved—through the payment of a sum of money.)

Rikidozan's ROK trip was reported in *Sports Nippon,* January 11, 1963. The *Tokyo Chunichi Shimbun* translation of the AP story on Riki's trip revealing his identity was published on January 11, 1963.

The North Korean magazine article was written by Rikidozan's daughter from his first marriage, who was then living in Pyongyang. It was first published in *Ryuitsu Hyoron,* March 9 and 16, 1984. It appeared in Japanese in June 1984 under the title, *"Rikidozan Ni Mo Sokoku Ga Atta"* [Even Rikidozan Had a Homeland], in the monthly *Tong Il Hyoron,* pp. 118–35. By then, the daughter was married to the president of the National Physical Education Committee of the Democratic Republic Committee of North Korea, a union strongly blessed by Riki's number one fan on the peninsula, Kim Il Sung.

The knifing of Rikidozan was reported extensively in the daily newspapers and later in the numerous books written about Rikidozan. The most complete account of the knifing was given by the assailant Murata himself, in an interview with the *Shukan Shincho* weekly, February 9, 1989 (pp. 127–28), entitled, *"Hanin Ga Kataru Rikidozan Sasatsu No Shinwa"* [The Criminal Tells the Truth about the Stabbing of Rikidozan]. Also see *"Jiken No Ato"* [After the Incident], *Shukan Sankei,* pp. 176–79, which quotes Murata on the stabbing, and *"Pro-Resu Sankoku-shi," Asahi Geinno,* August 15, 1992, pp. 60–64.

Conspiracy theories were mentioned in *Mo Hitosu No Showa Shi (1), Eikyu no Rikidozan,* and *"Rikidozan Ni Mo Sokoku Ga Atta."* Rikidozan's daughter did an interview in the August 1, 1991, issue of *Yukan Fuji* (p. 1), in which she laid all the blame for her father's death on the Japanese yakuza without mentioning the CIA.

Nick Zappetti's private eulogy of Rikidozan was this: "Rikidozan was a nice guy, a really nice guy when you got to know him. And he was the greatest friend in the world; he'd do anything for you. It was only when he was drunk that he turned into a mean son of a bitch. Of course, the problem was, he was drunk all the time."

4. POST-OLYMPIC UNDERGROUND ECONOMY

"I feel I am returning to a completely different city," Noboru Ando, quoted after his release in 1964 from six years in prison. See *Yakuza to Koso* (vol. 3, p. 126).

Economic data on the Olympic boom are from the annual *Japan Almanac.* The 25,000 bars figure comes from the Leisure Development Center White Paper.

Descriptions of Roppongi in the 1960s are from firsthand experience as well as from interviews with Zappetti, Tom Scully, and Hal Drake. The Mikado description is from Grolier Japan President Hiroo Nakao, Richard Roa, Dwight Spenser, and, again, firsthand experience.

Defense and entertainment expenditures were drawn from *Japan Almanac* (data provided by the Defense Agency).

Description and background of the Copacabana comes from *"Copacabana To Rikon Nyobu No Mise"* [The Copacabana and the Club of the Manager's Ex-Wife], *Shukan Shincho,* May 25, 1978, pp. 40–44. *"Seizai Kai no Naisho wo Shirisugita Otoko* [The Man Who Knew Too Many Secrets about the Political and Economic World], *Shukan Sankei,* August 9, 1979, pp. 24–27, and *"El Morocco," Shukan Bunshun,* April 5, 1979. All of these referred to club's mob connections in one form or another. Another source of information was crime journalist Hiroshi Sasaki, who also frequented the Copacabana.

Further Copa descriptions came from Grumman aircraft consultant Jim Phillips, Hiroo Nakao, Richard Roa, and nightly fixture Nick Zappetti. The author has also paid his own visits to the Copa.

Tonichi trading company's procurement of women for Sukarno was described in the February 28, 1966, issue of the weekly *Shukan Gendai* (p. 51), as well as in the aforementioned *Shincho* piece of May 25, 1975, which credited Tonichi with helping to arrange Dewi's marriage to Sukarno and also by journalist Hiroshi Sasaki in interviews with the author. Tonichi's activities became a scandal in the 1960s and subject of many other newspaper and magazine articles. The president of Tonichi trading was Masao Kubo, an intimate of Machii and a man whose company was backed by Kodama and LDP bigwig Ichiro Kono. Whenever Sukarno was in Tokyo, he stayed at Kubo's palatial home in Takagi-cho.

The Tonichi–Dewi relationship was reported in the February 28, 1966,

Shukan Gendai article, the aforementioned *Shincho* piece, and in Yoko Kitazawa, "Japan-Indonesia Corruption: Bribe, It Shall Be Given You (Part I)," *AMPO magazine* 8, no. 1, 1976. "The Structure of Sponging (1)" by Eiji Tomonomiri, in the *Asahi Evening News,* March 19, 1976, describes the activities of Tonichi's main competitor and subsequent partner in Indonesia, Kinoshita Shoten.

Material on Copa hostesses as industrial agents came from journalist Hiroshi Sasaki, aircraft consultant Jim Phillips, and Nick Zappetti—all regular visitors to the club. The activities of the hostesses was also revealed in May 25, 1978, *Shukan Shincho* article, in which the Copacabana was referred to as the "night-time stage" for the "aircraft wars."

The 1958 Lockheed bribe is described in detail in "Japan's Lockheed Scandal: 'Structural Corruption,' " by Karl Dixon, in *Pacific Community* 8, no. 2, January 1977. It is also described in Anthony Sampson, *The Arms Bazaar: From Lebanon to Lockheed,* as well as by Takashi Tachibana in the aforementioned *Bungei Shunju* article, "*Kodama Yoshio to wa Nanika*" (The latter piece also described the Patek Phillipe watch incident with Kodama.)

Ginza Machii's order to those followers whose appearance was "not pleasant" was published in the aforementioned July–August 1964 *Mainichi Daily News* series on organized violence.

The Caravansary was introduced in the *Shukan Bunshun* article, "*Yoru No Kanko Ni Noridashita Showa No Kaibutsu,*" June 9, 1966, pp. 38–42. Further description came from firsthand experience and from one-time patrons Hiroo Nakao, Rick Roa, and Dwight Spenser. Kodama's quotes were taken from the Bunshun article.

Data on Kodama and the *sokaiya* are from Takashi Tachibana, "*Kodama Yoshio to wa Nani ka?*" *Bungei Shunju.* The Nomura Securities "adviser's fee" paid to Kodama was reported in the *Japan Times,* June 12, 1977. (It states, "Kodama was getting 2 million yen as a summer gift and 3 million yen as a winter gift from Nomura.") The article entitled "*Black Current,*" issued by Kyodo News Agency on April 1, 1992, cites a 20 million yen fee the brokerage paid to Kodama in the mid-1970s with a quote from Minoru Segawa, chairman of Nomura Securities. Segawa was quoted as telling an LDP staff worker, Katsuyoshi Hayashi, "Even publicly owned companies have both public and private faces. We pay Kodama-*sensei* 20 million annually in an adviser's fee. In return, he fixes problems of all sorts for us. I consider the fee well worth it."

There were an estimated 5,000 *sokaiya* throughout Japan. Some were of the type that specialized in peacekeeping operations at shareholder meetings, others' main area of interest was corporate extortion through their own private publications. Before his influence waned, Kodama managed to bring some 75 percent of them under his control.

The police representative's quote and other related estimates are from "*Henshin Suru Boryoku Shudan*" [The Changing Violent Gangs], *Shukan Yomiuri,* October 15, 1978, pp. 28–40.

KING OF ROPPONGI: MAFIA BOSS OF TOKYO

Descriptions of life at post-Olympic Nicola's came from Zappetti, Frank Nomura, Eugene Aksenoff, Marty Steinberg, Larry Wallace, Loren Fetzer, and Joe
and Leith Bernard, all of whom were habitués at the time.

The Machii finger-amputating incident was described in several publica-
tions, including "*Kodama no Kage De Odoru Aru Fuikusa*" [The Fixer Who
Danced in Kodama's Shadow], *Asahi Journal*, October 1, 1976, and also the
Shukan Bunshun series, "*Kankoku Kara Kita Otoko*" [The Man from Korea],
June 30, 1977. It is also described in Kaplan and Dubro, *Yakuza*.

In his autobiography, *Yakuza to Koso*, Ando vividly describes the knife attack
on him and how his face was sewn up with no anesthetic. The incident in which
a TSK soldier faced a man with a sword and had his left hand lopped off is described in the Tokyo police file on the Tosei-kai. The "You see that sword glint
in the light," quote is from an author interview with ex-gangster turned novelist Joji Abe, who once belonged to Ando's gang.

Dave's kidnapping was described by eyewitness Frank Nomura. The incident
with Maurice was related by eyewitness Zappetti. The Mike Sullivan story was
related by Nick Zappetti. Witnesses to Sullivan's fight with Matsubara were Akio
Nomura, who was working behind the bar at Tom's that night, and Hal Drake,
a *Stars and Stripes* reporter who was present, sitting at one of the tables. The
aftermath was described by Drake and Tom Scully, who worked with Sullivan
at the *Stripes*. Scully sent whiskey and other supplies when Sullivan was in hiding from the Tosei-kai. Sullivan, who is now at the New York *Post*, refused to
grant an interview.

Zappetti's arrests were verified by the Tokyo Metropolitan Police, Azabu
Precinct; the shotgun raid by U.S. Embassy attaché Barry Nemcoff. The FBI visit
was described by Yae Koizumi and Zappetti. Zappetti was characterized as "Gaijin Enemy Number One" by Yutaka Mogami, a member of the Tokyo Metropolitan Police Department's Foreign Affairs Division. Zappetti's offenses were
many and varied. He once flew into a rage at a policeman who had arrived with
a light meter to gauge the darkness level of Nicola's restaurant. Angry over having his dinner interrupted, the proprietor threw the light meter, and the policeman, down the stairs of his restaurant, which earned him a huge fine by the
Tokyo District Court. Zappetti also had a habit of getting drunk while out on
the town and forgetting where he had parked his car. He would call the police
the next morning and demand they track it down for him. Yutaka Mogami had
struck up a friendship of sorts with Zappetti after his first incarceration in the
Tokyo Detention Center, when Mogami belonged to a team of interpreters
tasked with interrogating foreign criminals. Mogami thought that Zappetti was
one of the strangest people he had ever met. Mogami ran occasional small er-
rands for him, tracking down old girlfriends, and got all the free pizza he could
eat in return. Mogami also did occasional translation assignments as well. But
Mogami's honesty was beyond question. He once turned down an extremely
handsome offer from a representative of Lucky Luciano's gang who wanted

Mogami's help in setting up a casino in Japan. Instead, he reported the man to his superiors, and the Luciano mobster was deported. Mogami's relationship with Zappetti eventually deteriorated. It wasn't just the fact that Mogami's fellow police officers looked askance at it. The problem was also Mogami's wife, who told him she did not want him associating with "that crook."

In regard to the murder of the man from Macao, Zappetti admitted to the author in an interview that he had commissioned it.

Zappetti told Askenoff that being a Mafia boss was the highest that anyone from his background could aspire to.

Barry Nemcoff, press officer at the U.S. Embassy (from 1963 to 1968), affirmed in an author interview that throughout the 1960s Zappetti was still regarded as the Mafia Boss of Tokyo by U.S. Embassy officials and Tokyo Police and that the prevailing belief was that Nick was still in the employ of the New York Mafia, looking after their interests in the Far East.

LEGITIMATE SUBTERFUGE

Business data here were supplied by the ACCJ, the Coca-Cola story by Thomas Scully, a former Burson-Marstella official, and the IBM story by representatives of IBM, Japan office. IBM's efforts in Japan are also described in *Nippon: New Superpower*, by Horsely and Buckley (pp. 141–147).

Blood Toast was released by the Shochiku Film Studios in 1969.

The author worked for Encyclopaedia Britannica from 1969 to 1972 and is familiar with that company's sales history. Additional information came from interviews with Toshiro Suzuki, EB general manager.

The Ransburg story was related in its entirety by attorney James Adachi, whose office holds the relevant documents.

The Yozawa River project was related by Thomas Blakemore, Frances Blakemore, and Jim Phillips, with background information provided by Rosser, Yin-Wa-Mah Brockman, and Tetsuo Sato.

A NOTE ABOUT THOMAS BLAKEMORE

Blakemore was the most successful foreign attorney in the city's history. Blakemore translated the Japanese Civil Code and Criminal Code into English. He knew the law so well that he was the only Westerner who could presume to lecture Japan's implacable bureaucrats on the finer points of their own voluminous statutes.

An oft-told tale concerns the time Blakemore, a hunting enthusiast, neglected to register the offspring of two blooded Irish setters he owned and had bred. The required time to register such pups was six weeks from birth, but Blakemore had let a full six months elapse before he took the documents to the appropriate government office to file an application. When the official in charge of dog registration told Blakemore that he was too late and that nothing could be done, Blakemore retorted that something certainly *could* be done. He produced a copy of the Japanese Civil Code, opened it to a dog-eared page, and read in his fluent, Oklahoma-accented Japanese: "The subsequent marriage of the parents provides for the legitimization of the offspring."

"This law applies to animals as well as human beings," he explained patiently, "by analogy, what is applicable to humans is applicable to animals too."

Blakemore informed the clerk that he was a full-fledged American lawyer who had passed the Japanese bar, and to his legally trained mind the pups' parents were in the truest sense married—under "common law." They had been living together with him on his Chiba farm for several years; he could attest to this personally. Thus, for the dogs' sake and for the sake of their offspring's future, something had to be done.

Although the government official was dubious, in the end, he bowed to Blakemore's obviously superior knowledge and validated the dogs' papers. It was a feat the likes of which no other foreigner was ever capable of duplicating.

5. MISS HOKKAIDO

The American Buddhist priest's name was Robert Wheeler; he adopted the Japanese pseudonym Shuzen, meaning "absolutely excellent."

The "What are you talking to me for then?" quote came from an interview with Yae Koizumi and Nick Zappetti.

The data on careerist women in Japan are from Patrick Smith, *Japan: A Reinterpretation,* pp. 158–159; and *Japan Almanac,* 1998. For an excellent essay on the role of women in Japanese society, see George Fields, *From Bonsai to Levis,* Chapter 3.

The source for the virginity requirement and other details of the Zappetti-Miyoko marital life came from Zappetti himself, who freely admitted the most sordid facts of their relationship. Miyoko declined to be interviewed when Zappetti asked her to cooperate. She has since remarried and joined a religious order.

Zappetti's daughter Patricia confirms the general gist of the relationship, including her father's keeping Miyoko under "house arrest."

Details of the mink farm came from Zappetti and Eugene Aksenoff, who also watched another Zappetti disaster, a nutria farm in which the American had invested only to see it completely wiped out by a typhoon-induced flood that scattered hundreds of the furry little creatures across the countryside.

For details of the Nihon Kotsu takeover, the author relied on interviews with Zappetti, Yae Koizumi, and Vince Iizumi, who was an officer in Nicola's enterprises at the time, Yutaka Mogumi, and court documents. The chief Nihon Kotsu executive is deceased. It is Vince's conviction that once the deal had been entered into and the people at Nihon Kotsu saw how profitable Nicola's restaurant was, they began looking for ways to drive Zappetti out of the pizza business in Tokyo because they effectively blocked Zappetti from using his name. After the takeover, only Nihon Kotsu was allowed to use "Nicola's," by court order, and Zappetti thus had to start calling his restaurants "Nicola." Dr. Aksenoff watched all this from his perch next door at the International Clinic and provided additional background, as did Y. Mogami, who interpreted in court and translated the legal documents.

TOKYO DISTRICT COURT

For information on how the Tokyo legal system works the author relied on interviews with Tokyo attorneys Thomas L. Blakemore, Raymond Bushell, Rosser Brockman, Shin Ashina, and James Adachi.

Yokoi's fraudulent concealment of assets and his subsequent shooting were described in Noboru Ando's autobiography, *Yakuza to Koso,* and in *"Ando Noboru To Yokoi Hideki 7 nen me No Taiketsu"* [7th Year Confrontation of Ando Noboru and Yokoi Hideki], *Shukan Bunshun,* August 1, 1965, p. 75. Also see *"Futatabi no Taiketsu"* [Second Encounter], *Heibon Punch,* August 2, 1965, p. 29. The facts behind Hachisoka's friend hiring the mob to collect the debt was described in *Yakuza to Koso*

The shooting of Yokoi was one of the more bizarre incidents of the postwar era. How the gang boss Noboru Ando, angered over Yokoi's rude dismissal of his efforts to collect the aforementioned debt, came to order it done is described at great length in the above autobiography. Also, Ando explained his motives, in an unusual essay written by Ando shortly after his arrest, in the *Bungei Shunju* monthly, October 1958, pp. 232–237. Ando made it clear he ordered his hit man to shoot Yokoi in the right shoulder—only to wound him, to "teach him a lesson." Unfortunately, the hit man's aim was bad. The bullet hit Yokoi in the left side and traversed several of his internal organs, nearly causing his death. At the time of the attack, Yokoi had been conferring with two business associates, one of whom was a black belt in judo. "If you help us in the project," the man had been saying, "I will risk my life for you." When the gunman burst into the conference room, however, the judoist-turned-businessman immediately dove under the table, leaving Yokoi and the other party to face the assailant. Said Yokoi later (during the *Shukan Bunshun* interview in August 1965, when Ando and Yokoi met in a restaurant to have dinner to promote a movie, *Chi to Okite,* about the affair), "You just can't trust people nowadays."

Ando went into hiding at the Pan American employee dormitory in Izu, eluding a nationwide manhunt for two months, before an eagle-eyed resident of a nearby town recognized him from his picture on the wall of the local post office and turned him in. While incarcerated in the Tokyo Detention Center, Ando wrote his famous *Bungei Shunju* mea culpa, in which he bemoaned the economic violence that was supposedly crippling postwar Japan.

Chi To Okite [Blood and Law], which devoted several scenes to the incident, was produced by the Shochiku Film Studios and released in 1966. Hachisoka is dead. As of this writing, Yokoi, eighty-three years old, is in prison and in failing health. Ando, still alive, runs a film company. He was arrested twice for illegal gambling after his "retirement" from organized crime.

The date on lawyers came from the *Japan Almanac* (Ministry of Justice), the Tokyo Bar Association, and the American Bar Association. Also useful was an in-depth special report, "A Survey of the Legal Profession," *Economist*, July 18, 1992. So was Jack Huddleston's *Gaijin Kaisha*, chap. 4.

The Hilton-Tokyu affair was described to me by Thomas L. Blakemore, who handled the case. It was also reported by Richard Halloran in *Japan—Images and Realities*, pp. 154–55.

The Nihon Kotsu case court procedures were related by Zappetti and Y. Mogami, court interpreter and document translator.

6. BEHIND THE SHOJI

In 1969, three players were suspended for life after it was discovered they had participated in fixing games. In fact, fixed matches in sumo were an open se-cret, and in 1996, in fact, a former sumo wrestler blew the whistle on stable mas-ters who ordered their underlings to lose for money. The two authors of the book died of the same mysterious illness within twenty-four hours of each other. (Po-lice ruled them both natural deaths.)

Talk of the CIA funneling money to the LDP had been around for years in Tokyo, but the party had always vigorously denied it. The New York *Times* re-ported on October 9, 1994, that the conservative Liberal Democratic Party had been funded by secret payments of millions of dollars from the CIA. The pay-ments were part of a major covert operation during the cold war to make Japan a bulwark against communism in Asia, to check opposition led by the Socialists, and to fight off Socialist-led public resistance to building U.S. military bases in Japan.

"We financed them," the *Times* quoted Alfred Ulmer, Jr., who ran the CIA's Far East operation from 1955 to 1958. "We depended on the LDP for informa-tion." He said that CIA had used the payments both to support the party and to recruit informers within it from its earliest days.

By the early 1960s, said Roger Hilsman, head of the State Department's In-telligence Bureau in the Kennedy administration, the payments to the party and its politicians were "so established and so routine" that they were a fundamen-tal, if highly secret, part of U.S. foreign policy toward Japan.

Hilsman, as assistant secretary of state for Far Eastern affairs, was quoted in the New York *Times*, April 2, 1976. "The principle was certainly acceptable to me," he said.

In response to the revelation, John Dower, a leading Japan scholar at MIT, said, "This story reveals the intimate role that Americans at official and private levels played in promoting structural corruption and one-party conservative democracy in postwar Japan, and that's new. . . . We look at the LDP and say it's corrupt and it's unfortunate to have a one-party democracy. But we have played a role in creating that misshapen structure."

Reports in the *Asahi Shimbun* (October 10 and 12, 1994) identified an LDP official as a *madoguchi*, or conduit. So did "CIA Had Japan Funding Group," *Asahi Evening News*, October 10, 1994.

Also see the multi-part series, "*CIA to Yoshio Kodama*" ("Yoshio Kodama and the CIA"), in the weekly *Shukan Bunshun*, April 15, April 29, May 13, May 20, and May 27, 1976, and "*GHQ Johobu, CIA, Soshite Uyoku To No Setten Wo Arau*" [Laundering the Connection between the GHQ Intelligence Wing, the CIA and the Right Wing], *Shukan Asahi*, April 23, 1976, pp. 173–76.

Even after the 1996 *Times* report, the LDP had steadfastly refused to admit taking any CIA money. (See the front pages of the *Asahi Shimbun, Japan Times*, and other Japanese- and English-language dailies, October 11, 1994.)

For material on vote buying, see Eiji Tominomori, "Structure of Sponging," *Asahi Shimbun & Asahi Evening News*, March 19, 1976.

Mob support of the LDP has been an open secret ever since its inception. The LDP kingmaker of the 1950s, Bamboku Ono, was an adviser to the longshoremen's association, controlled by Kobe yakuza boss Kazuo Taoka, of the Yamaguchi-gumi. When the police raided Taoka's house in the 1960s, they found the name card of the prime minister, Eisaku Sato, in his desk. LDP members like ex-PM Kishi were not averse to attending gangster funerals, weddings, and other mob gatherings. (In fact, more than one gang boss kept an office next door to that of his friendly local parliamentarian.)

In 1989, according to the *Far Eastern Economic Review* (November 21, 1991), the secretary of a large factional leader in the LDP, Hiroshi Mutsuka, solicited gangsters to suppress a book exposing corruption in his district. The same issue reported that in 1990, Shintaro Ishihara, the Man Who Could Say No to Americans, was accused of accepting illegal political contributions from notorious gangland figures like Ken Mizuno. An unidentified mobster was quoted in that *FEER* issue as saying, "The Yakuza are part of the LDP" (p. 30).

For an interesting discussion of vote buying *within* the party in Japan, see Karl's Dixon's essay on Structural Corruption in *Pacific Community*, January 1977.

For material on Hamada, see "Black Current," *Kyodo*, April 1, 1992. A good profile of Hamada appears in Kaplan and Durbro's *Yakuza*, pp. 110–11. In March 1980, it was first disclosed in a Tokyo courtroom that Kenji Osano had received $200,000 in Lockheed money at Los Angeles Airport, money that Osano used to cover some of Hamada's gambling debt. For reports on the disclosure, see *Asahi Evening News*, March 14, 1980, and the follow-up on March 25, 1980, and the article "Lockheed Payment Used to Cover Hamada Losses" in the *Yomiuri Daily News*, March 7, 1984, and the long article "Black Current," *Kyodo, Japan Times*, April 1, 1992. The *Yomiuri Shimbun* of March 11, 1977, reported that a joint FBI, IRS, and Immigration Service investigation had uncovered Osano links to the American Mafia in Las Vegas.

Media reports on the arrest of Caesars Palace Tokyo employees and death threats they were charged with making can be found in the *Yomiuri Daily News*, June 21, 29, 30, and July 11, 1975. Also see *Japan Times*, June 21, July 13, October 19, and December 19, 1975. Among those arrested and indicated were the ex-president of the Tokyo Bar Association and a Toho movie producer named Okuda, who was an associate of Frank Sinatra; the two had met while he was associate producer for *Never So Few*.

For material on Maria Sojka Hannelore, the author relied on interviews with Richard Roa, who was a part-time manager of Danny's Inn and knew Maria extremely well, along with a number of foreign patrons, who, for understandable reasons, do not wish to be identified. The original proprietor, Danny Stein, is dead. Danny's Inn is long defunct.

The *Asahi Shimbun* of November 11, 1978, carried a detailed description of Maria's life, "*San Men Kyo*" [3-Sided Mirror], p. 2. Also see *Asahi Shimbun*, November 10, 11, 19, and 28, 1978; *Mainichi Shimbun*, November 11 and 28, 1978; and *Yomiuri Shimbun*, November 11 and 28, 1978. Also see *Japan Times*, November 11, 1978, for articles on her murder and the arrest of her assailant. The *Asahi Shimbun* evening edition of November 28, 1978, carried a report on the assailant's confession ("In the room, she asked for more money. I refused and went into the bath, and when I came out, I saw her rifling through my wallet. I got angry and before I knew it, I strangled her.")

A 1977 crackdown by Akasaka police on Maria and her confreres had resulted in the arrest of several of the girls, but all were released and the charges dismissed. Few Japanese men, it turned out, were willing to testify they had engaged the services of the young ladies. Further attempts by Japanese undercover police to entrap the young ladies failed, because it was all too obvious they were policemen in disguise.

For explanations of the aircraft business, the author relied on interviews with Jim Phillips a former fighter pilot, Grumman executive, and longtime aircraft consultant in Japan.

For material on the Copacabana as a favorite hangout of the aircraft executives, the author relied on interviews with Phillips, journalist Hiroshi Sasaki, Richard Roa, and Nick Zappetti, and on personal experience.

Kern's negotiating the Grumman kickback was reported in the *Mainichi Daily News*, October 17, 1980, p. 17 (Kyodo News Service): "In the libel case Nishho-Iwai and the former Grumman consultant (Kern), were found to have concluded a secret contract for payment of substantial kickbacks to former defense chief Raizo Matsuno and others in reward for sales of Grumman's E-2C early warning patrol plane to Japan." Kern died in 1997 in Washington, D.C. The author also relied on "Harry Kern: A Man behind the Scenes of Postwar Japan's History," *Asahi Journal*, February 2, 1979; "*Nazo No Otoko*" [Mystery Man], *Gekan Gendai*, February 5, 1979; by John Roberts and Takashi Tachibana, "*Shiroi Kuromaku*" [White Wirepuller], *Bungei Shunju*, March 1979. Also see "*Aoi Me No Fikusaa*" [The Blue Eyed Fixer—Sensational Scoop Rewrites Japan's Postwar History], *Shukan Posuto*, February 2, 1979; and "Japan Inc. Exit Harry J. Kern," *Insight*, April 1979.

The first reports of the Grumman scandal appeared in *Form 8-K, Current Re-*

port for the Month of January, 1979, Grumman Corporation, Washington, D.C., Securities and Exchange Commissioner, Commission File No. 1-302.

Also see Davis and Roberts, *An Occupation without Troops,* pp. 32–33.

The quotes and other descriptive material about TSK.CCC came from magazine articles about the opening day reception in the *Shukan Shincho, "Machii Hisayuki to iu Otoko"* [A Man Called Hisayuki Machii], July 26, 1973, pp. 32–34; and the *Shukan Bunshun* series article, June 23, 1977, pp. 152–57, June 30, 1977, pp. 146–50; and July 7, 1977, pp. 144–49 entitled *"Kankoku Kara Kita Otoko"* [The Man Who Came from Korea]. The author also relied on interviews with Zappetti and Roa and his own firsthand experience. The book *Yakuza* contains a summary of Machii's career (pp. 191–97).

The description of the *Cupid* incident and its aftermath was provided by Richard Roa.

The Lockheed scandal and Kodama's role in it are discussed extensively in a number of excellent works, not the least of which is Anthony Sampson, *The Arms Bazaar: From Lebanon to Lockheed,* and Inose Naoki, *Shisha Tachi no Rokkuiido* [The Lockheed Dead].

Also see, *"Rokkuiido Kenkin"* [Lockheed Donations], *Shukan Yomiuri,* special issue, February 28, 1976. Koichiro Yoshiwara, *"Burakku Rokkuiido"* [Black Lockheed], *Shukan Yomiuri,* April 3, 1976, pp. 42–45; Takashi Tachibana, *"Kodama Yoshio to wa Nanika?"* [Who Is Yoshio Kodama], *Bungei Shunju,* May 1976, pp. 94–135; Tad Szulc, "The Money Changer," *The New Republic,* April 10, 1976; *"Kimi Wa Kodama Wo Mitaka?"* [Have You Seen Kodama?], *Asahi Journal,* June 11, 1976; and the *Hearings Before the Subcommittee on Multinational Corporations of the Committee on Foreign Relations,* U.S. Senate, 94th Congress, February 4 and 6, and May 4, 1976.

In addition, there is the aforementioned Dixon piece, in the January issue of *77, Pacific Community; "Hawaii Kaidan Kuirima Hotel No Hishitsu De nani Ga Atta Ka"* [What Happened in a Private Room at the Kurima Hotel during the Hawaii Conference], *Shukan Bunshun,* February 1, 1979, pp. 156–60; "The Selling of Japan," *The Nation,* February 13, 1982, pp. 171–78; and "Black Current," *Japan Times,* April 1, 1992. Kotchian's exorbitant expenses are noted in Inose Naoki, *Shisha Tachi no Rokkuoodo Jiken* [The Lockheed Dead], pp. 223, 224.

The "bribery, as a business expense" quote appears in Sampson's *The Arms Bazaar.* Bribes are also described in Williams Horsely and Roger Buckley, *Nippon New Superpower,* p. 129; and in the aforementioned Dixon article on structural corruption. Also see the excellent *Shadow Shoguns,* by Jacob M. Schlesinger, for an in-depth study of Tanaka's highly suspect political fund-raising tactics.

The "If they had wanted to, they could have stopped it" quote is from Sampson, *Arms Bazaar,* p. 223. The April 2, 1976, edition of the New York *Times,* quoted a CIA agent as saying that the agency "was checking with headquarters every step of the way, when the Lockheed thing came up. Every move was approved by Washington."

"How dare they" quote is drawn from Horsley and Buckley, *Nippon New Superpower*, p. 129.

See *Rukuiido Saiban Bochoki [A Record of the Lockheed Trials] Asahi Shimbun*, 1994, vol. 1, pps. 132–35; 184–86; 196–99 for Tachibana's analysis of the missing bearer checks and the $200,000 Osano payment at LAX. Also see interview with Takashi Tachibana in the monthly magazine *Ushio*, November 1976. For a discussion of the theory on secret campaign donations as well as an article in the *Mainichi Daily News*, March 15, 1976, p. 4, "Nixon Said Implicated in Lockheed Bribery."

The Lockheed aftermath is discussed in the aforementioned Naoki, *Shisha Tachi no Rokkuiido*. Its effect on the Machii organization is described in the *Shukan Bunshun* series (*Kankoku Kara Kita Otoko*) and in "*Ginza No Senryo No Shussen Wo Tsugeru TKS.CCC no Banka*" [The Elegy of the TKS.CCC's Postwar Occupation of the Ginza], *Shukan Shincho*, May 26, 1977, pp. 42–46; and in "*Kurabu*" [Club], *Shukan Shincho*, January 8, 1977, pp. 130–31.

Also see Yoichiro Tanaka, "*Rokkuiido Jiken Wa Sagi Jiken?*" [Was the Lockheed Incident a Sting Operation?], *Shukan Bunshun*, March 1, 1979, pp. 46–47.

Kissinger's court order was discussed in Tad Sculz, "The Money Changer," *New Republic*, April 10, 1976.

The *Mainichi Daily News* of June 13, 1976, listed eight people related in one way or another to the payoff scandal who died under "mysterious circumstances," including a police inspector investigating Lockheed who killed himself by leaping into Tokyo Bay. The excellent book *Shisha Tachi no Rokkuiido* describes them in detail.

(See *Asahi Shimbun*, evening edition, April 27, 1984, p. 1) for reports on Osano's conviction.

The Supreme Court verdict of ANA's Wakasa was upheld in 1996; it was widely reported in all the Japanese newspapers, as was his company's response.

For an excellent essay on how Tanaka managed to bend the system to suit his purposes, see Inoki, pp. 245–50.

The most complete and authoritative work on the Lockheed scandal remains Tachibana's four-volume *Rokuiido Saiban Buchoki*, which was published in paperback in 1994.

CITIZEN NICK

Material on Koreagate was obtained from the U.S. Congressional Report, *Hearings Before the Subcommittee on International Organizations on International Relations*, "Activities of the KCIA in the US," March 17, 1976; also *Japan Times*, June 4, 1977.

In the Fujita case, the author relied on interviews with Zappetti, Vince Iizumi, Akio Nomura, and Yutaka Mogami, who were closely involved. Fujita is now dead. Said Nomura, a close friend of Fujita's, "What Fujita did was wrong. But I understand why he did it—Nick treated him too badly."

The Grolier editorial incident came from interviews with Grolier executives Richard Walker, Hiroo Nakao, and Phil Yanagi, who were caught in the middle of the conflict.

DEA CULTURAL WALL

Sessions and Mueller gave their testimonies before the U.S. Senate in November 1991. See U.S. Senate Report on "The New International Criminal and Organized Crime," 1993.

In addition to the aforementioned fifty-nine page Senate report, the material on the DEA in Japan is from a three-part series entitled "Japan's *La Cosa Nostra*" by Hiroaki Furano of the Kyodo News Agency, released in February 1984, as well as from interviews with a U.S. crime investigator who wishes to remain anonymous and Steve Weissman, who was with the Tokyo Bureau of the New York *Times* in the early 1990s and was covering the subject. Also see "*Roppongi Konnekushon*" (Roppongi Connection) in the *Shukan Asahi* of June 7, 1991, pps. 20–23, for material on the underground drug scene in Roppongi and the arrest of Shintaro Katsu, and the feature article "*Yakuza No Keizai Gaku*" (Gangster Economics) by Atsushi Mizoguchi in the now defunct monthly magazine *Marco Polo*, November 1991, pps. 60–69.

7. THE GREAT TRANSFER OF WEALTH

A NOTE ABOUT EXCHANGE RATES

The dollar was fixed at 360 yen to the dollar in 1949 and stayed there until 1971, when it was taken off the gold standard by then U.S. President Richard M. Nixon and allowed to float against other currencies. The move was designed in part to alleviate the $3 billion trade imbalance with Japan. It slipped to 300 yen in a matter of months, then to 240 (and to 190 by the end of the decade), before being revived in the Reagan administration, when it rose to a plateau of 263 in February 1985.

The move off the gold standard was one of the year's two "Nixon shocks," as the Japanese referred to them. The other was the surprise announcement by Nixon that Henry Kissinger had been carrying out secret negotiations with the Chinese government to establish diplomatic relations without consulting with or even notifying the Japanese government, which the latter saw as a humiliation.

However, the *doru shokku*, as it was known, gave the Japanese unprecedented spending power and provided further impetus to Japan's growth.

For a description of the G-7 Plaza Summit of 1985, see James Fallows, *Looking at the Sun*. Trade and financial statistics on Japan for the period are from *Japan Almanac* data provided by MITI, MOF, and other government agencies. The bar and nightclub count comes courtesy of Azabu Ward Office. Educational statistics are from *World Almanac*.

"The Greatest Transfer..." quote came from Tokyo-Kenneth Courtis, an economist with Deutsche Bank, Tokyo.

The "... essentially racists..." quote is from John Roberts.

Additional U.S. Japan trade data and information provided by ACCJ and the Boston Consulting Group.

Construction data came from the *Japan Almanac* (courtesy of the Ministry of Construction), which pointed out that Japan in the 1990s had twice as many cars as in the 1970s but only one-tenth more road space, thereby justifying the increased construction of highways. See Patrick Smith, *Japan: A Reinterpretation*, pp. 180–82, for an excellent essay on the construction state; and Schlesinger, *Shadow Shoguns*, pp. 240–41.

The pig farming saga was related by Zappetti, Aksenoff, and Vince Iizumi. Hog farming data are from *Japan Almanac* (Ministry of Agriculture, Forestry and Fisheries).

KEIZAI YAKUZA

"Tani" is a pseudonym for a Roppongi gangster.

Miyashiro's U.S. arrest record appears in Kaplan and Dubro, *Yakuza*, p. 248. Miyashiro was also profiled and interviewed in the *Shukon Taisho* weekly magazine article *"Kore Ga Daigaku No Oyabun Da"* [These are the College Gang Bosses], January 29, 1990, pp. 38–47. He was also interviewed in Mark Schilling's "After Dark" column, *Japan Times Weekly*, August 3 and 10, 1991.

Kobayshi's role in the election of Nakasone is described in part 1 of a twelve-part series, "Politicians and Gangsters—The Unholy Alliance," appearing in the *Mainichi Daily News*, beginning on May 4, 1991, p.1. (During the 1982 campaign for LDP president, Nakasone had been harangued by right-wingers from Kobayashi's Nihon Seinensha, protesting his ties to LDP kingmaker Kakuei Tanaka, who was being tried for bribery in the Lockheed affair. Nakasone's associates made a request through certain channels and the harassment suddenly stopped.

The 1985 police investigation that uncovered over 100 instances of extortion by the Roppongi office of the Kobayashi-kai was reported in the October 15, 1985, issue of the *Asahi Shimbun* (*Yukan*, or evening edition), p. 11. Other data on the Kobayashi-kai came from Yomiuri Shimbun, June 20, 1993.

Katsushi Murata's life and exploits were described in *"Jiken No Ato"* [After the Scandal], *Shukan Sankei*, December 2, 1982; in the *Sunday Mainichi*, April 9, 1989, pp. 220–21; in *"Hanin Ga Kataru"* [The Criminal Talks], *Shukan Shincho*, December 2, 1989, pp. 129–31; and Oshita Eiji, *Eikyu No Rikidozan*.

A NOTE ABOUT THE END OF THE OLD YAKUZA ERA
AS REPRESENTED BY KATSUSHI MURATA

During a period of several years, beginning in the 1980s, there was a public revival of interest in yakuza, ignited by a best-selling novel about gang and prison life, *Hei No Naka No Korenai Men Men* [Those Behind Walls Who Don't Learn Lessons], penned by a retired gangster named Joji Abe, which made him wealthier than he had ever been in his previous life. Abe's success inspired other such works: a best-selling novel about yakuza wives, *Gokudo No Onnatachi* [Gang Women], which became a hit movie and was followed by several book and film sequels. Among them were *The Lonely Hitman,* a book based on a real-life antique dealer in Osaka who rubbed people out in his free time, which sold 180,000 copies and was also turned into a film; and a popular nonfiction book and movie, *Kizu* (Scar), depicting the life of a famous Shibuya gangster, Kei Hanagata. Abe even had his own talk show on Asahi TV.

Sociologists explaining the phenomenon said that the Japanese were drawn to the world of the *gokudo* (villain) and its strict moral code of honor and obligation because those traditional values were disappearing from modern Japanese society. And Abe was the first to agree, for he believed that the real *gokudo,* as he knew them, were fading way as well—which was somewhat ironic, given the suspicions that the old *bakuto* and *tekiya* had once held for members of Abe's generation.

"For many years, up until the time of the Olympics," he said in an interview, "being a yakuza meant living by a certain spirit and code—being unafraid, sacrificing yourself for others. The yakuza I knew put value on *giri* and *jingi*—duty and loyalty. It all began to change as Japan began to accumulate vast wealth. A new breed of gangsters appeared whose sole interest was money."

No better example of the dying breed of mobster existed, said Abe, then his prison cellmate, Katsushi Murata, famous all over Japan as the man who killed Rikidozan.

Murata was given grudging respect, even by the authorities. Gushed an admiring police investigator, a man who had once arrested Murata on suspicion of gambling, "The man has ability and talent. He has a way of running his gambling sessions that one can't easily detect. What's more, Murata has a strong character. If you don't have something special, you don't rise to the top rank in a gang the way he did."

Murata made the national headlines once more in 1989, but in a way that none of his admirers had ever imagined, when suddenly, he was in jail again— arrested on suspicion of aiding and abetting his wife in a case of assault and extortion. According to police reports and press accounts, the trouble stemmed from an unpaid loan in the sum of 1,200,000 yen that Murata's wife, Megumi, had guaranteed on behalf of one of her hostesses. The hostess, a nineteen-year-old minor identified only as "A" by police, had been paying the money back in monthly installments and had whittled the debt down to 700,000 yen when medical expenses for a sudden illness caused her to halt payment. Late one frigid night in February, Megumi and her husband broke into "A"'s suburban Tokyo apartment and, according to police reports, began punching and kicking the teenaged hostess. When "A" sought refuge in the toilet, Megumi pulled her out by the hair and continued the assault. Unable to locate any cash, "A"'s assailants left, but the next evening, Megumi returned with a truck and three of her employees, who hauled away some of "A"'s belongings, including a laser disc, a stereo, a washing machine, and an electric gas range, worth an estimated 1.2 million yen. The police issued several arrest warrants. Murata, who checked his various pets into a neighborhood pet clinic prior to turning himself in, told police that he had only stood by and watched. The investigator on the case, noting how worn and flabby his suspect appeared, said he believed it. "With his diabetes," he told reporters, "he doesn't look like he has the energy to hit anyone." See *Yukan Fuji*, March 25, 1989; *Sankei Shimbun*, March 25, 1989; "*Hakaba No Kage De Rikidozan Mo Naiteiru?*" [Is Rikidozan Crying in the Shadow of His Grave?], *Sunday Mainichi*, August 19, 1989. The charges against Murato were dropped and his wife settled out of court.

An excellent article on the old and new versions of the yakuza was "The Honourable Mob," *The Economist*, January 27, 1990, pp. 21–24.

An excellent survey of the *keizai yakuza* was the cover story of the November 21, 1991, edition of the *Far Eastern Economic Review*, pp. 28–35, entitled "Power to the Yakuza."

"Total annual revenue . . . exceeded that of . . . drug trafficking" and "lender bank in the Pebble Beach transaction—mob connected," from "A Japanese Laundry Worth $1 Billion?" *Business Week*, May 24, 1993, p. 30.

Also informative was "The New International Criminal and Asian Organized Crime Report," prepared by the U.S. Senate in 1993, after extensive hearings. It focuses on money laundering, Ken Mizuno, and Minoru Isutani, among other subjects.

Ken Mizuno descriptions and currency law violations charges also appear above, and in "Fraud Suspect Amassed Huge Gambling Debts," *Japan Times*, March 29, 1992, p. 2; the *Mainichi Daily News*, issues of April 29, 1992, "Golf Club Developer Declared Bankrupt"; May 14, 1992, "Four Charged with Tax Evasion in Golf Club Membership Sales," and June 14, 1992, "Mizuno Illegally Funneled over 32 Billion Yen to U.S." Also see "Ken International Ordered to Pay 13.4 Billion Yen in Back Penalty Taxes," *Asahi Evening News*, June 12, 1992, p. 4; "U.S. Agents Seize Ken Mizuno Resort," *Mainichi Daily News*, August 20, 1992, p. 4; and "Mizuno Group Pleads Guilty in Golf Membership Scam," *Mainichi Daily News*, October 16, 1992, p. 12.

Also see "Agents Seize Palm Springs Resort of Japanese Tycoon," *Los Angeles Times*, August 19, 1992, p.D-2. "High Roller's Past, Fortunes Fueled Probes," by Karl Schoenberger, *Los Angeles Times*, March 16, 1992, p.A-1. "Mizuno's Former Company Agrees to $65 Million Forefeiture," U.P.I. October 5, 1993. "Japanese Firm Agrees To Forfeiture," by Karl Schoenberger, *Los Angeles Times*, October 5, 1993, p.D-3. Also "*Gorufu Gyokai No Mondai Oni, Mizuno Ken to iu Otoko*" [The Problem Ogre of the Golf World: A Man Called Ken Mizuno], *Shukan Bunshun*, September 12, 1991, pp. 194–97," and "*Mizuno Ken Moto Scacho, 11 Nen Choeki*" [Former President Ken Mizuno Sentenced to 11 Years"], *Asahi Shimbun*, Yukan, March 25, 1997, p. 14.

BANKS, BOB HOPE, AND PRESCOTT BUSH

The mob-backed Hope Golf Club scam episode was related by American Richard Roa, who was the Tokyo sales manager for the organization and was caught in the middle of the scam. Certain details were confirmed by Hope's lawyer at the time, Ed Burner. Desmond Muirhead, a golf architect involved with Hamada and Nicklaus, confirmed other details of that particular venture, as did Takeaki Kaneda, a former national golfing champion in Japan and a *Sports Illustrated* representative in Tokyo who unsuccessfully tried to warn Nicklaus away from the deal. Kaneda said that Nicklaus told him years later he wished he had listened to Kaneda's advice.

A NOTE ABOUT MOB TAKEOVERS

Yakuza moneylenders have used their loan operations as a very effective takeover wedge, which gives the lie to MOF claims that the Japanese system of managed capitalism was somehow better than that of the United States because it prevented leveraged buyouts.

One very good example of such a takeover involved the Arabian Nights restaurant, which opened in 1985 on a Roppongi back street. Owned and operated by an Iraqi businessman, it was one of the most beautiful restaurants in the city. All the decor, including the gold-plated fixtures, was imported from the Middle East, as was a chef who specialized in Arabic food.

It cost the Iraqi $2–3 million to get the operation off the ground, plus an extra $2 million he borrowed from a Japanese bank to get the lease. But business was slow and costs were surprisingly higher than usual. Unbeknownst to the owner at the time, the meat, the vegetable, and the *oshibori* (hot towels) vendors were all friends of the Japanese floor manager and were charging double the going price for their wares.

Soon, the Iraqi found himself in need of 30 million yen to pay his staff, make bank payments, and meet other obligations. Confident that a payment would soon be coming from an associate in the Middle East, he went, through an intermediary, to a Tokyo loan shark, a young Korean man who drove a fancy sports car and who offered to loan the Iraqi the 30 million yen for thirty days if the restaurant was put up as security.

The Iraqi agreed and signed the necessary documents, and the loan shark brought out a suitcase of money, putting 30 stacks of 100 crisp new 10,000-yen notes on the table, neatly lined up. He promptly took out 13 million yen as his "commission." Then handed over another 3 million yen to the intermediary as *his* commission. That left the Iraqi with 24 million, and the ink on the loan document hadn't even dried yet.

The Iraqi restaurateur paid his bills, and at the end of the thirty days, the 30 million being late arriving from the Middle East, found himself physically barred from his restaurant by several yakuza, under the direction of the moneylender, who became the new owner.

There is a veritable mountain of published data in Japanese and English on Kanemaru and the illegal contributions he received. The March 9, 1995, edition of the *Asahi Shimbun* contains an excellent full-page graph of how the illicit funds were distributed.

The Political Spectrum column of the *Asahi Evening News,* August 15, 1991, and the Kyodo News Report "Black Current" contain good summaries of the activities of gang boss Susumu Ishii, the brokerage houses, and the LDP.

The open court testimony by the Inagawa-kai associate in regard to the relationship between the Liberal Democratic Party and the yakuza was reported in "Black Current."

The *Far Eastern Economic Review* cover story of November 21, 1991, quoted Jiro Ode, president of a finance company in Osaka with extensive contacts in the underworld, who said, "the Yakuza are part of the LDP. It is a relationship of mutual help, friendship, cooperation, and support. There are no straight lines, nothing dividing them. Everyone is gray."

Shin Kanemaru, in announcing his resignation as vice-premier on August 27, 1992, admitted that he received 500 million yen in illicit contributions from Sagawa Kyubin. This stunning admission was reported on page 1 of the *Asahi Shimbun,* morning edition, August 28, 1992, and in every other Japanese daily.

On November 27, 1992, Kanemaru testified under oath to legislators from a hospital bed that Susumu Ishii, the head of the Inagawa-kai gang syndicate, had indeed helped stop a rightist group from harassing former Prime Minister Noboru Takeshita in 1987, when Takeshita was running for the LDP presidency. This admission was also splashed across the front pages of all of the Japanese dailies the next morning.

The head of Tokyo Sagawa Kyubin, Hiroyasu Watanabe, had earlier testified in a pretrial deposition that Kanemaru had sought his help to stop the rightist group from harassing Takeshita, fearing the smear campaign would hurt Takeshita's bid for the LDP presidency, and that he in turn had sought the help of Inagawa-chief Ishii. See "Kanemaru's Reliance on Gangs Comes Out," *Asahi Evening News,* September 24, 1992, p. 4.

Kanemaru was arrested on March 6, 1996, and made a full confession in regard to illegal donations he had accepted, mostly from construction-related firms. His lengthy confession was excerpted in English in the July 28, 1993, edition of the *Mainichi Shimbun,* for those who may be interested.

"Obituary, Shin Kanemaru," *Economist,* April 6, 1996, p. 108, offered a concise but detailed history of his colorful career.

A good overview of the machinations of Susumu Ishii, Sagawa Kyubin, and the brokerage houses appears in the October, November, and December 1992 issues of *Tokyo Insideline,* an informed if somewhat irreverent monthly newsletter on Japanese politics, published and edited by Takao Toshikawa, which became part of *The Oriental Economist* in 1997. A summary of the ramping of the Tokyu stock appeared in the *Asahi Evening News,* August 24, 1991.

For material on the Tokyu stock crash, the Nomura scandal, and the Sagawa-

Kyubin scandal, the author relied on the very heavy reportage in the Japanese media of the scandal in the early 1990s, among them: "*Beikoku nara, Okurasho Kambu Mo Kemusho Iki*" [If This Were America, the Head of the Finance Ministry Would Go to Prison Too], *Shukan Asahi*, July 26, 1991; "*Tabuchi Kaicho No Jinin de Sumu no Ka?*" [You Think This Will End with the Resignation of Chairman Tabuchi?] and "*Yakuza to Sejika Ni Kuwareta Ni-sen Oku Yen*" [2 Trillion Yen Eaten by the Politicians and the Yakuza], both in *Shukan Asahi*, August 2, 1991. Also useful was an exclusive interview with Susumu Ishii, which appeared in an article entitled *Yakuza No Kigyo Ka Wa Koko Made Susundeiru* [Gangster Business Has Come This Far], in the *Shukan Posuto*, August 2, 1991, pp. 36–40, and "*Nomura Shoken Kambu wa 'Soba Soju' wo Mitomeita*" [The Management of Nomura Securities Admits Manipulating the Market], *Shukan Asahi*, September 6, 1991.

The aforementioned "Black Current" article by Kyodo, April 2, 1992, was also informative, as was the article in the respected weekly *Shukan Asahi*, "*Hachi Nin No Shisha Tachi No Sagawa Jiken*" [The 8 Deaths of the Sagawa Incident], December 18, 1992, pp. 27–29, which describes, among other things, the suicide of Hiroshi Aoki, former chief secretary to former PM Noboru Takeshita, found hanging from a rope in his Tokyo apartment, with his wrists and ankles slashed for good measure, on April 26, 1989, the morning after Takeshita announced his resignation. (The resignation and the suicide followed the disclosure that Aoki had obtained 50 million yen from an employment firm called Recruit Cosmos in a shares-for-favors scandal in 1989. However, it was widely rumored that there were other factors that had driven Aoki to kill himself, and the authorities regarded his death as an impediment to the Sagawa investigation.) The article also discusses the demise of Yasutoshi Kuwabara, chief secretary to Takeshita in his home province of Shimane, who also hanged himself in June 1991. Kuwabara thus became the twenty-fifth political aide to have committed suicide to atone for scandal in the postwar era. In addition, there was the former Diet member connected to the case who died unexpectedly from "water on his lungs" in 1991, while resting in a Tokyo hospital to "stay away from the media."

Takeshita was the fourth postwar prime minister to resign because of scandals. His successor lasted three months before being ousted in a sex scandal and was followed by two more prime ministers in the next four years.

The sequence of events describing West Tsusho, its activities in the United States, its relationship with Prescott Bush, and the revelation the company was a gang front were made in documents obtained from the U.S. Securities and Exchange Commission by the Japanese Kyodo News Service and published on June 8, 1991, in the *Asahi Shimbun, Nikkan Sports, Nihon Keizai Shimbun, Asahi Evening News*, and *Japan Times* of the same day.

The author also relied on "Web of Intrigue," *Far Eastern Economic Review*, March 19, 1992; Robert I. McCartney, "*The President's Brother Is Sued*," Washington Post Service, June 17, 1992; and the follow-up story, "Sagawa Tied to Yakuza over Golf Course in New York," *Mainichi Daily News*, February 18, 1992.

CRAZY WONG AND THE GOLD SCAM

The gold scam story was related by Nick Zappetti, longtime Tokyo jeweler Ome Asakura, better known as "Crazy Wong," and Yutaka Mogami, who translated some court documents in relation to Wong's suit. Franco and Roberto have fled to parts unknown.

The first quote by the Akasaka boss was confirmed by Nomura and Zappetti's wife Yae.

There are minor discrepancies in the different accounts. Wong says he may have had a receipt for $40,000, as described by Zappetti, but that he can't remember for sure. He did say that he had obtained a receipt for the *entire* amount, however, which he procured some days after his purchase of the fake gold, something which Zappetti did not mention. Zappetti said that he thought Crazy Wong, being the professional that he was, had been able to tell whether the rest of the gold was real or not. Wong said he only went along with the deal without unwrapping every piece because he had trusted Nick—his "friend" of thirty years.

Crazy Wong was convinced that Zappetti set him up because Zappetti's business was starting to fail and he needed the money.

"If Nick was really a victim," said Wong, "then he should have apologized to me. The incident was his responsibility. But he never did. When I went to talk to his wife, Yae, about the matter, she said it wasn't any of her concern. She said, 'Why don't you sue my husband and send him to jail?'"

Wong denied any ties to the Japanese underworld and said he was an honest jeweler. If gangsters sometimes came to his shop to buy and sell, he said he couldn't help it. He also said he was not aware the gold Franco and Roberto had had been smuggled.

After Zappetti died, in 1992, Wong tried unsuccessfully to pursue the suit with Zappetti's widow. No one ever heard from Franco or Roberto again (or Zack). Zappetti put in a request to Interpol to track them down, but they were never found. Zappetti went to his grave trying to figure the scam out. Twice during the succeeding five years Wong was robbed by Chinese gangs infiltrating the city to the tune of several hundred thousand dollars worth of cash and merchandise.

8. BLACK RIDER

Material in this section came from interviews with Zappetti, Frank Nomura, Vince Iizumi, Yae Koizumi, Leron Lee, Barry Nemcoff, Yutaka Mogami, and Tokyo attorney Kuzo Tanaka, who represented Zappetti in the Nihan Kotsu appeal, as chief counsel. It is Vince Iizumi's conviction that his father would never have won the appeal, as was Tanaka's. Said the lawyer, "Mr. Zappetti did not properly understand his situation. If I had not acted he would not have received *any* money. No other lawyer could have pulled that off. But still they criticized me. Neither he nor anyone in the family ever thanked me. It was only after he had recovered that he changed his mind and said he deserved more. Some of the things he says are bullshit."

Zappetti, of course, went to his grave believing just the opposite was true, that he had been denied his chance for legal victory and, like so many other *gaijin*, victimized by his adopted country.

Zappetti complained about his sexual impotence to anyone who would listen. However, when a sympathetic listener, U.S. Embassy official Barry Nemcoff, told him about a new prosthetic penile device on the market in the United States, Zappetti's interest immediately turned to business. He wanted to find a way to import and market the devices in bulk in Japan for Japanese men, because, as he put it, they had such small genitalia they were bound to want to own the much larger U.S. product.

Zappetti showed the note from his attorney to the author. The nighttime visit to the lawyer's office was related by Zappetti, with great relish.

RIO BRAVO

The "Lazy and illiterate" remark was made by Yoshio Sakurauchi, the speaker of the Lower House of Parliament in Japan, in January 1992. His exact words were, "American workers want to get high salaries without working. They cannot take orders because 30 percent of them are illiterate."

Nakasone's remark was, "The level of knowledge in the United States is lower than in Japan due to the considerable number of blacks, Puerto Ricans, and Mexicans." He made it in 1986. See Terry McCarthy, "Why Japanese Are Rude about Foreigners," *Independent,* reprinted in *Singapore Straits Times,* January 31, 1992.

A NOTE ABOUT JAPAN BASHING

America's neurosis in regard to Japan was tempered by a comparative lack of interest in its most important ally and a corresponding lack of knowledge that was at times stunning. In 1991, when asked by a touring Japanese news crew what "Japan bashing" (perhaps the most widely understood English phrase in Japan after "okay" and "sex") meant, a Houston official replied, in all seriousness, that it was an activity whereby "Japanese walk down the street and hit other Japanese over the head with a pole." Sometime earlier, a D.C. lawmaker quizzed a visitor from Tokyo University as to when North Japan and South Japan were going to reunite. A 1993 survey revealed that two out of every five Americans were unaware the United States even had a trade problem with Japan.

A NOTE ABOUT FREE TRADE

A clear-cut reflection of the differences between the concept of Japanese capitalism and American capitalism was the exercise in the early 1990s involving NTT, the giant semi-state-owned corporation, when it concluded the price of the pagers they were purchasing was out of line with the global norm and as a result they demanded the major pager manufacturers lower their prices by nearly 50 percent. Only Motorola, the lone foreign maker in the group, was able to comply with such a dramatic drop. Within a month, however, Motorola was asked to raise its unit price back up to correspond with what the Japanese makers could meet. In the United States, the business most likely would have all shifted to the cheapest supplier. (From an interview with Dr. Robert M. Orr.)

Another reason son Vince did not want to remain in his father's business was a conflict over strategy. Vince's main complaint was about his father's and Yae's insistence on keeping the Roppongi branch going, purely out of "pride." "They should have sold the Roppongi place and gone with Yokota, which was raking in the money," he said, "but they didn't want to give up the prestige of having a place in Roppongi."

The psychiatrist Shu Kishida was the author of *Monogusa Seishin Bunseki* (Tokyo Seishi, 1978). (His philosophy made an interesting contrast to that of another Japanese psychiatrist, Misao Miyamoto, trained and educated in the States, who said Japan was suffering from a neurosis he called "narcissistic infantilism.")

The comment in regard to *Rising Sun*, by Michael Crichton, was made by *Bungei Shunju* editor Hidesuke Matsuo. The Japan expert was Kent Calder.

Zappetti related all the details of domestic strife with his wife Yae Koizumi in an interview with me—and indeed to anyone else who would listen. She, however, did not want to submit to a formal interview on the subject. Still, I, along with many others, witnessed them arguing many times in the restaurant. The headwaiter's remark about their relationship was, "They love each other ... but they also hate each other." The estimate of Yae's wealth was made by Zappetti. I personally witnessed the battle of the lights and music.

A New Jersey-based sister-in-law of Zappetti's who saw the couple together said she was impressed at Yae's devotion. "The beauty queen seemed to be more interested in Nick's money," Mary Zappetti recalled in a 1998 interview, "but Yae, she really cared for Nick. I could tell."

The "transistor salesman" remark was originally made by then French President Charles De Gaulle, when then Japanese Prime Minister Hayato Ikeda visited France. Said DeGaulle, "I expected a statesman and I got a transistor salesman." Others quickly picked up on it.

President Reagan was invited to Japan by the Fuji-Sankei communications group. (Said Zappetti, "It was his reward for letting the Japanese win at trade.")

For material on Trump and Yokoi, see "Trump's Tower," *Vanity Fair*, May 1995.

Zappetti also wrote a letter to American financial operator T. Boone Pickens, offering his help in "any way possible." In the late 1980s, T. Boone Pickens had bought a "controlling interest" of 26 percent in Koito Manufacturing Company, a parts supplier for the automotive giant Toyota Motors, and found he could not even get himself appointed to the board, so entrenched was the almost feudal system of subcontractors and suppliers. (Toyota, which owned 19 percent of

Koito's stock but was Koito's largest customer, held three board seats.) Pickens complained loud and long about Japanese monopolistic practices, but government officials were totally indifferent. Toyota was a corporate community, they said, not a toy for leveraged buyout artists from abroad. Pickens did not respond to Zappetti's missive. Eventually he gave up and sold his shares.

THE FALL

The stock compensation scandals were widely reported during the early 1990s. Interestingly enough, the minister of finance at the time was Ryutaro Hashimoto, who, having vowed to clean house, then proceeded to preside over a series of other financial scandals as prime minister throughout the rest of the decade, before being forced to resign in 1990.

The material about Susumu Ishii is from the interview in *Shukan Posuto*, August 2, 1991, pp. 36–40.

For material on the Tokyo stock crash, the Nomura scandal, and the fallout from the Sagawa-Kyubin, the author relied on the newspaper accounts and other reports in the Japanese media during the scandals in the early 1990s, among them the interview with Shin Kanemaru, *Shukan Asahi*, May 31, 1991, pp. 20–24; "*Beikoku nara, Okurasho Kambu Mo Kemusho Iki*" [If This Were America, the Head of the Finance Ministry Would Go to Prison Too], *Shukan Asahi*, July 26, 1991; "*Tabuchi Kaicho No Jinin de Sumu no Ka?*" [You Think This Will End with the Resignation of Chairman Tabuchi?] and "*Yakuza to Sejika Ni Kuwareta Nisen Oku Yen*" [2 Trillion Yen Eaten by the Politicians and the Yakuza], both in *Shukan Asahi*, August 2, 1991. Also referenced were the interview with Susumu Ishii in *Shukan Posuto*, August 2, 1991; "*Nomura Shoken Kambu was 'Soba Soju' wo Mitomeita*" [The Management of Nomura Securities Admits Manipulating the Market], *Shukan Asahi*, September 6, 1991; "Black Current"; and "*8 Nin No Shisha Tachi No Sagawa Jiken*" [The 8 Deaths of the Sagawa Incident], *Shukan Asahi*, December 18, 1992, pp. 27–29.

The Inagawa family insolvency was reported in "Late Inagawa-kai Boss Left Billions in Debts: Family," *Asahi Evening News*, June 5, 1992.

Senator Hollings's callous, xenophobic remarks were the subject of an acerbic editorial, in the "Hollings' Stupid Remarks," *Mainichi Daily News*, March 7, 1992. The remarks were made by Ernest Hollings, a senator from South Carolina, on March 2, 1992, at a speech at a factory in his home state. Hollings later issued a statement denying he was engaging in Japan bashing, explaining that the mushroom reference was intended as a joke. Hollings exact quote was, "You could draw a mushroom cloud and put beneath it, 'made in America by lazy and illiterate Americans and tested in Japan.'" Hollings's remarks were in response to the widely quoted remarks made earlier by House of Representatives Speaker Yoshio Sakurauchi, in January 1992, to the effect that American workers were lazy and illiterate.

The final visit to Hokkaido was described by Zappetti, as was his plot to wreak revenge on enemies.

EPILOGUE

When Kanemaru was arrested on March 6, 1993, on charges of tax evasion, a flood of newspaper and magazine articles on the Sagawa Kyubin scandal and his connection to the mob followed. See "Goldfinger," *Asiaweek*, July 14, 1993. Kanemaru's confession of March 6 was printed in full in the *Mainichi Shimbun*, July 26, 1993, which described how he received illegal secret donations from the construction industry and also the transportation industry and corporations in the cement industry. Also see Chalmers Johnson, "The Tremor: Japan's Post Cold War Destiny," *The New Republic*, July 1993; Shin Kanemaru obituary, *Economist*, April 6, 1996, p. 108; and Schlesinger, *Shadow Shoguns*, pp. 245–46.

"Foreigners Beware" was translated by *Tokyo Insideline*, May 31, 1992.

A NOTE ABOUT THE PLAZA SUMMIT OF 1985

Blaming the Plaza accord was a familiar mantra heard throughout the 1990s among Japanese political and economic commentators. However, it begs the question of why so much borrowing on such shaky collateral (skyrocketing land and stock prices that were destined eventually to come down) was allowed by the banks and other lending institutions during the bubble era. When the bubble burst, as stock fell, banks were left with yakuza borrowers who refused to repay their loans and relinquish their assets.

In regard to *jusen* loans, there was a wealth of material in the daily newspapers and weekly magazines in the mid-1990s. In Japanese, especially useful was an article by Raisuke Miyawaki, *"Furyo Shakin Jitsu Wa Boryokudan Kinyu"* [Bad Loans Are Really Mob Money], *Shukan Bunshun*, December 7, 1995, pp. 38–41. Of particular interest in English was the *BusinessWeek* International Edition cover story, "The Yakuza and the Banks," January 29, 1996.

A NOTE ABOUT THE JAPANESE STOCK MARKET

The percentage of individual investment sank from 60 percent in 1950 to 22.4 percent in 1997. Of Japan's publicly held shares, 50–70 percent remain effectively untraded because of *keiretsu*, cross-holding shares. Mitsubishi Motors, Mitsubishi Real Estate, Mitsubishi Heavy Industries, Mitsubishi Banks, and Mitsubishi Shoji all own each other's stock.

The shooting of the Sumitomo bank executive was discussed in *"Shiten-cho Naze Korosareta No ka?"* [Why Was the Branch Manager Killed?], *Sunday Mainichi*, October 2, 1994, pps. 26–30.

The *Shukan Gendai* article naming Ryutaro Hashimoto and others was published in *Shukan Gendai*, May 21, 1997, and referenced by Velisarious Kattoulas, in the *International Herald Tribune*, May 21, 1997, p.13.

The name of the LDP politician who made the bold statement about gangster connections in 1997 was Eitaro Itoyama. His article appeared in the *Gekan Hoseki* in October 1997, pp. 66–78, entitled "*Seijika to Boryokudan*" (Politicians and Gangsters). It was the subject of an article by Professor Gregory Clark, "Japan and Its Economy Have a Crime Problem," *International Herald Tribune,* October 8, 1997.

U.S.-Japan cooperation in regard to Ken Mizuno is described in "Movie Mansion Sold for $1.8 Million," U.P.I., October 5, 1995.

David E. Kaplan, "Yakuza Inc.," *U.S. News & World Report,* April 13, 1998, pp. 40–45, offers an introduction to the dangers facing American investors in Japan in the late 1990s. Also see "*Hashimoto Ryutaro 'Baikoku Seiken' Nihon wo Beikoku no Shokuminchi ni shita*" [Hashimoto's "National Sale Regime" Has Made Japan an American Colony], *Shukan Posuto,* May 8–15, 1998. The *Rokka-Kan Bunko Joho Senta* provided information about the CIA and the FBI in Japan, investigating crime—as did the weekly magazine *Shukan Jitsuwa,* June 25, 1998.

A NOTE ABOUT CONTINUED CORRUPTION

The year 1998 saw the suicide of a Dietman on the verge of being arrested for corruption and bribery in affairs with a top brokerage house, as well as the arrest of several securities company executives and a slew of *sokaiya* busts. It was business as usual, in a sense. What was surprising was the number of cases involving the vaunted bureaucracy: the arrest of several Finance Ministry officials on bribery charges; the suicide of an MOF bureaucrat; and the resignation of two others in key positions, including the minister of finance. This was followed by the resignation of the head of the Bank of Japan over allegations that bankers had received market tips and other insider information in exchange for lavish wining and dining and the unprecedented arrest of a senior official at the Bank of Japan on suspicion of corruption.

Whether this was just the result of a sudden burst of righteous activity by a procurator's office embarrassed by its continuing inability to control corruption—highlighted by the fall of Yamaichi, Japan's oldest securities company, because of devious accounting and outright bribery—or whether it signified yet an increase in the level of dishonesty and/or incompetence of those in the civil service was hard to say. Some observers believe there was more than the usual level of concern among career bureaucrats, nearing the retirement age of fifty-five, about their chances of successfully following the traditional path of graduating to comfortable, high-paying board jobs in the businesses they had been regulating over the years, given the seemingly unending recession and the advent of Tokyo's own "Big Bang," when deregulation would finally mean honest competition in the financial sector.

Despite the prosecutorial blitz, some basic facts remained unchanged. Japanese voters still expected their politicians to be "favor givers"—more perhaps than those in the West. Officially, politicians continued to distribute amounts equal to four to five times their income and unofficially twice that much, the money going to extra staff, providing trips for rural constituents, offering wedding gifts to organizing local functions, and so on. LDP politicians with hefty ambitions continued to enrich themselves in ordered to be able to disburse funds to build power bases within their party factions. Moreover, with media advertising in election campaings severely limited, and door-to-door canvassing prohibited by law, the ways in which candidates could reach out to the voters were not as abundant as in the United States and other countries. Thus was money politics an incontrovertible, accepted part of the system, resisting all attempts at reform, the seemingly endless scandals met, generally speaking, with a resounding thud of public indifference.

The unholy triangle of business, politics, and the underworld continued on its merry way.

Richard Mitchell, in his excellent book *Political Bribery in Japan,* while acknowledging that there is just as much corruption in the United States as in Japan, noted one basic difference in his summation:

> Throughout American history, even in times of low enforcement of bribery laws, the idea that bribery was morally wrong remained widespread and deep rooted. The strong anti-bribery ethic provided a kind of punishment in lieu of criminal sanctions; public humiliation faced those who offered or took bribes. In the Japanese case, in contrast, the cultural context in which political bribery takes place results in a different outcome: a politician caught taking a bribe may feel shame at public exposure but may not feel a sense of moral guilt. Moreover, political careers flourish despite convictions for bribery.

Mitchell noted that penal codes and enforcement patterns are similar, but added,

> Prosecution in Japan, however, is more difficult, because in the United States payment to an official is considered bribery: the prosecutor need not prove that the one offering the bribe received a favor from the official accepting it. This is not the case in Japan, where the procurator must prove that the official received the money, did a favor in return, and understood that the money was meant as a bribe (p. 155).

He added, "Political bribery will continue to flourish (in Japan) because electing new political leaders and enacting election reform laws will not alter the basic culture" (p. 157).

He seemed to be saying, in other words, that the system of governance in Japan is intrinsically corrupt and that money politics is too deeply entrenched.

The Seidenstecker quote appeared in *Tokyo Rising,* pp. 242–43.

The LAPD OCID representative's name is Ken Beno (retired). His quote in regard to Machii-Ross mob money laundering appeared in the *Mainichi Daily News,* March 3, 1992, with the headline, "With New Law, More Yakuza Going Overseas." (The Ross half of the partnership belongs to one Kenneth Ross, an ex-California state congressman, who has strongly denied any wrongdoing or having more than a passing knowledge of his partner's former life.)

Tashiro's attack on the newspaper building was reported in the daily papers: "Gangster Arrested in Shooting at Mainichi," *Yomiuri Shimbun,* September 25, 1994; "Gang Boss Arrested in Mainichi Shooting," *Mainichi Daily News,* October 13, 1994; "Mainichi Attacker Given 6 Yrs. in Prison," *Mainichi Daily News,* February 25, 1995.

Also see "Sunday Headline," *Sunday Mainichi,* October 2, 1994, p. 21.

Inoki's visit to Pyonyang in 1995 was described by eyewitness Greg Davis, a *Time* photographer.

A NOTE ABOUT KOREANS IN JAPAN
Statistics in 1993 showed that about 80 percent of Korean youth living in Japan used Japanese names. As the *Asahi Shimbun* commented in an editorial about this phenomenon, this demonstrated a "suffocating atmosphere in which they [Koreans] would be viewed as being different and placed at a disadvantage if they did otherwise." *Asahi Shimbun,* May 5, 1995.

A NOTE ABOUT THE JAPANESE ECONOMY
Perhaps the most interesting fact about Japan's long recession was that as of mid-1998, according to a variety of sources, the Japanese controlled approximately one-third of all the savings in the world, some ten trillion dollars, or an average of $85,000 per person and $250,000 per family. The Japanese also owned $800 billion in overseas assets even when the yen had dropped in value to ¥140 to one U.S. dollar. That, combined with one of the world's great manufacturing bases and a disciplined workforce, kept Japan the world's second-largest economy—despite the pervasive economic gloom over stagnant growth and $1 trillion bad debt. Japan also owned $200 billion worth of U.S. T-Bonds as this book went to press, the liquidation of which had the potential to radically affect interest rates in America and cause great "confusion" in markets worldwide.

INTERVIEWEES
Kagari Ando, Kozo Abe, editor *Yukan Fuji;* Joji Abe, author and Ando gang member (ret.); James L. Adachi of Adachi, Henderson, Miyatake and Fujita; Kyoko Ai; Eugene Aksenoff, M.D. and director of the International Clinic in Tokyo; Millard "Corky" Alexander, editor in chief *Tokyo Weekender;* Robert Acquilina, U.S. Marine History Office, Washington, D.C.; Shin Asahina, Bushell and Asahina Law Office; Ome "Crazy Wong" Asakura, jeweler; Kosuke Asakura, James Bailey, journalist; Ed Barner, attorney-at-law, Burbank; Joseph Bernard,

attorney-at-law, Washington, D.C.; Leith Bernard, Richard Berry, *Time;* Mona Beyer; Richard "The (Masked Man) Destroyer" Beyer, professional wrestler; Thomas L. Blakemore, Blakemore & Mitsuki; Frances Blakemore, Jim Blessin, manager Sanno Hotel Tokyo (ret.); Alan Booth, author; Mark Brazeal, attorney-at-law, San Francisco; Rosser Brockman, attorney-at-law, San Francisco; Yin Wa Mah Brockman, leading social light of San Francisco.

B.J. "Jug" Burkett, war author; Raymond Bushell, Bushell and Asahina; Frances Bushell; John Carroll, journalist; Ryu Chang, Akasaka hostess; Ann Christensen, Glen Christensen, Toshi Cooper, Glen Davis, author; Greg Davis, *Time* photographer; Jack Dinken, longtime Tokyo businessman; Bill Dorman, CNN; Hal Drake, *Stars and Stripes* (ret.); Kazuko Drake, Clark Frogley, FBI Bureau, U.S. Embassy, Tokyo; John Fuji, AP; "Shig" Fujita, *Asahi Shimbun;* Frank Gibney, director, Pacific Rim Institute; Frank Gibney, Sr., *Time;* Carl Goch, professional wrestler; Harry Godfrey, Kroll Associates, Tokyo; Ward Grant, publicist, Bob Hope Enterprises; Clyde Haberman, New York *Times* columnist; David Halberstam, author; Yuji Hanabusa, Etsuko Hayano, Fusakazu Hayano, Asahi Chemical; Hiroshi Hirano, TSK; William Horsley, BBC; Andrew Horvat, author; David Howell, instructor; Meiji Gakuen; Mariko Imagawa, Asahi TV; Atsushi Imamura, Bungei Shunju; Naoki Inose, author, TBS news commentator; Shintaro Ishihara, novelist; Hiroshi Ishikawa, Vince Iizumi, H. Ikeda; Reid Irvine, "Accuracy in Media"; Koji Itakura, Asahi TV; Takeaki Kaneda, golf consultant; David Kaplan, author, senior writer, *U.S. News & World Report;* Koichi Kawamura, artist; Machiko Kawamura, designer; Reimi Kawamura, NHK; Jiro Kawamura, editor, *Asahi Shimbun, Shukan Asahi.*

Eugene Kim, Ginza hostess; Noriko Kobayashi, translator; Machiko Kondo, UNCHR Tokyo; Mike Knapp, Everett Knapp, Jesse Kualahula, sumo stable master; John Lagant, Leron Lee, Vicquie Lee, J. Anthony Lukas, author; Elmer Luke, editor; Katsuji "Ma-Chan" Maezono, manager "3-2-8," Azabu; Kiyondo Matsui, editor in chief *Shukan Bunshun;* Midori Matsui, translator; M. Matsui, Machii-Ross in Santa Monica; Hideyusuke Matsuo, *Bungei Shunju;* William Miller, literary agent, Tokyo; Dr. Masao Miyamoto, psychiatrist; Yutaka Mogami, MPD (ret.); Desmond Muirhead, golf architect; Leslie Nakashima, UPI; Mayumi Nakazawa, author; Hiro Nakao, President Grolier Japan (ret.); Chris Nelson, Barry Nemcoff, USIS (ret.); John Neuffer; Akio "Frank" Nomura, waiter, bartender, club manager; Katsuya Nomura, manager; Yakult Swallows; Don Nomura, agent; Jiro Numata, *Sumiyoshi Rengo-kai;* Professor Kan Ori, Sophia University; Miko Orr, Robert Orr, vice president, Motorola Japan; Ned Oshiro, Tokyo Disneyland; Doug Palmer, attorney-at-law, Seattle; Noriko Palmer, Jim Phillips, aircraft consultant.

Tim Porter, photographer; Richard G. Roa, business consultant, Tokyo; John Roberts, author; Richard Roa, publicist; Masako Sakata, president, Imperial Press; William Salter, CPA, Tokyo; Eduardo Sanchez, advertising executive; Hiroshi Sasaki, journalist; Kenichiro Sasae, Foreign Ministry of Japan; Nobuko Sasae, simultaneous interpreter; Keiko Sato, Tetsuo Sato, attorney-at-law, Tokyo;

Professor Bruce Scott, Harvard University; Mark Schrieber, author; Tom Scully, editor; Professor Robert Seward, Meiji; David Shapiro, author, playwright; Hitomi Shapiro, actress; Derek Shearer, director public policy, Occidental College; Takashi Shimada, Richard Siracusa, attorney-at-law, New York City; Dwight Spenser, Robert Spenser, Ernie Solomon, Albert Stamp, Martin P. Steinberg, Albert Stovall, Roger Suddith, Reikichi Sumiya, editor *Asahi Geinno*, Toshiro Suzuki, general manager, Encyclopaedia Britannica, Japan (ret).

Yoshiko Takaishi, Kenichi Takemura, author, TV commentator; Masayuki Tamaki, author; Kozo Tanaka, Tanaka Kozo law office, Tokyo; Masahiro Tani, *Sumiyoshi Rengokai*, Hide Tanaka, *Asahi Shimbun*, Takao Toshikawa, *Tokyo Oriental Economist;* The Honorable Judge Edwin Torres, New York City; William Triplett, U.S. Senate Foreign Relations Committee; Ichiro Tsuge, *Shukan Asahi;* Douglas Victoria, Professor Ezra Vogel, Harvard University; Larry Wallace, Drug Enforcement Agency (killed in action); Richard Walker, vice president, Grolier (ret.); John Wheeler, Japan Society, New York; Steven Weissman, New York *Times;* Juan Williams, *Washington Post;* Phil Yanagi, Junji Yamagiwa, author, NHK commentator, Atsushi Yoneyama, Nick Zappetti, Mary Zappetti, Patricia Zappetti, Rose Zappetti.

Among those who refused one-on-one interviews were Hisayuki Machii (due to poor health) and Joseph Nicola. Yae Koizumi, Zappetti's second and fourth wife, participated in some of the taped discussions I had with her husband, but declined to be interviewed one-on-one. I interviewed three organized crime figures in Tokyo, one member of the Tokyo Metropolitan Police Department, and one individual associated with the Los Angeles Police Department, all of whom wished to remain anonymous.

Ray Dunston, Mike Sullivan, and Miyoko, Tani, and Zack are pseudonyms for people who did not want to be interviewed or identified.

BIBLIOGRAPHY

BOOKS IN ENGLISH

Abramson, Ann. "The Rockefellers in Japan (The Role of American Big Business in the Reshaping of Postwar Japan)." Unpublished ms., Department of History, University of Wisconsin, 1975.

Asahi Shimbun. *Japan Almanac*. Published annually by Asahi Shimbun, Tokyo (in English and Japanese).

Axelbank, Alex. trans. *Black Star over Japan*. New York: Hill & Wang, 1972.

Blakemore, Thomas L., *The Criminal Code of Japan (1947)*. Tokyo: Nippon Hyoronsha, 1950.

Brines, Russell. *MacArthur's Japan*. New York: Lippincott, 1948.

Buruma, Ian. *Behind the Mask*. New York: Pantheon, 1984.

Chapman, William. *Inventing Japan*. New York: Prentice Hall, 1991.

Cohen, Theodore. *Remaking Japan: The American Occupation as New Deal*. New York: Free Press, 1987.

Collier, Peter, and D. Horowitz. *The Rockefellers*. New York: Holt, Rinehart and Winston, 1976.

Crichton, Michael. *Rising Sun*. New York: Ballantine, 1993.

Curtis, Gerald L. *The Japanese Way of Politics*. New York: Columbia University Press, 1988.

Davis, Glen, and John Roberts. *An Occupation without Troops*. Tokyo: Yen Books, 1996.

De Vos, George and Chang Soo Lee. *Koreans in Japan*. Berkeley: University of California Press, 1981.

Dower, John. *Empire and Aftermath*. Cambridge: Harvard University Press, 1979.

Emerson, John K. *The Japanese Thread*. New York: Holt, Rinehart and Winston, 1978.

Fallows, James. *Looking at the Sun*. New York: Pantheon, 1994.

Field, Norma. *In the Realm of a Dying Emperor*. New York: Pantheon, 1991.

Fields, George. *From Bonsai to Levis*. New York: Mentor, 1985.

Finn, Richard B. *Winners in Peace: MacArthur, Yoshida and Postwar Japan*. Berkeley: University of California Press, 1992.

Gayn, Mark. *Japan Diary*. Tokyo: Tuttle, 1981.

Gibney, Frank. *Japan: The Fragile Superpower*. New York: Norton, 1975.

Gunther, John. *Inside Asia*. New York: Harper, 1938.

Halberstam, David. *The Fifties*. New York: Villard, 1993.

————. *The Reckoning*. New York: Morrow, 1986.

Halloran, Richard. *Japan—Images and Realities*. Tokyo: Tuttle, 1970.

Hartcher, Peter. *The Ministry: How Japan's Most Powerful Institution Endangers World Markets*. Boston: Harvard Business School Press, 1998.

Holstein, William J. *The Japanese Power Game*. New York: Scribners, 1990.

Horsley, William, and Roger Buckley. *Nippon New Superpower: Japan since 1945*. London: BBC Books, 1990.

Huddleston, Jack. *Gaijin Kaisha*. Tokyo: Tuttle, 1991.

Ishihara, Shintaro. *The Japan That Can Say No*. New York: Simon & Schuster, 1991.

Johnson, Chalmers. *Conspiracy at Matsukawa*. Berkeley: University of California Press, 1972.

————. *MITI and the Japanese Miracle*. Stanford: Stanford University Press, 1982; Tokyo: Tuttle, 1986.

Kahn, Herman. *The Emerging Japanese Superstate*. New York: Prentice Hall, 1969.

Kaplan, David E., and Alec Dubro. *Yakuza*. Reading, Mass.: Addison-Wesley, 1986.

Kennedy, Paul. *The Rise and Fall of the Great Powers*. New York: Random House, 1987.

Kodama, Yoshio. *I Was Defeated*. Tokyo: Robert Booth and Taro Fukuda, 1951.

————. *Sugamo Diary*. Tokyo: Taro Fukuda, 1960.

Livingstone, Jon, Moore, Joe, and Oldfather, Felicia. *Postwar Japan: 1945 to the Present*. New York: Random House, 1973.

Manchester, William. *American Caesar*. Boston: Little, Brown, 1978.

McGill, Peter. *Tokyo*. American Express Travel Guides. London: Mitchell Beazley, 1993.

Mitchell, Richard H. *The Korean Minority in Japan*. Berkeley: University of California Press, 1967.

————. *Political Bribery in Japan*. Honolulu: University of Hawaii Press, 1996.

Morris, Ivan. *Nationalism and the Right Wing in Japan*. New York: Oxford University Press, 1960.

National Police Agency. *White Paper on Police*. Published annually by the Government of Japan.

Owen, John. *Authority without Power: Law and the Japanese Paradox*. New York: Oxford University Press, 1992.

Prestowitz, Clyde V., Jr. *Trading Places: How America Allowed Japan to Take the Lead*. New York: Basic Books, 1988.

Roberts, John. *Mitsui: Three Centuries of Japanese Business*. Tokyo: Weatherhill, 1973.

Rome, Florence. *The Tattooed Men*. New York: Delacorte Press, 1975.

Saga, Junichi. *The Gambler's Tale: A Life in Japan's Underworld*. Translated by John Bester. Tokyo: Kodansha International, 1991.

Sampson, Anthony. *The Arms Bazaar: From Lebanon to Lockheed*. New York: Viking, 1977.

Schlesinger, Jacob M. *Shadow Shoguns*. New York: Simon & Schuster, 1997.

Sedensky, Eric C. *Winning Pachinko: The Game of Japanese Pinball*. Tokyo: Yen Books, 1991.

Seidensticker, Edward. *Tokyo Rising: The Great City since the Great Earthquake*. New York: Knopf, 1990.

Singer, Kurt. *Mirror, Jewel and Sword: A Study of Japanese Characteristics*. New York: George Braziller, 1973.

Smith, Patrick. *Japan: A Reinterpretation*. New York: Pantheon, 1997.

Sweeny, Charles, W. Maj. Gen. *War's End*. New York: Avon. 1997.

Thayer, Nathaniel B. *How the Conservatives Rule Japan*. Princeton: Princeton University Press. 1969.

Van Wolferen, Karel. *The Enigma of Japanese Power*. London: Macmillan, 1989.

Vogel, Ezra F. *Japan as Number One*. Tokyo: Tuttle, 1980.

Waley, Paul. *Tokyo: City of Stories*. Tokyo: Weatherhill, 1991.

Wildes, Harry Emerson. *Typhoon in Tokyo: The Occupation and Its Aftermath*. New York: Macmillan, 1954.

Woodall, Brian. *Japan Under Construction: Corruption, Politics and Public Works*. Berkeley: University of California Press, 1996.

Yanaga, Chitoshi. *Big Business in Japanese Politics*. New Haven: Yale University Press, 1968.

———. *SCAPINS*. Tokyo General Headquarters Supreme Commander for the Allied Powers, 1952.

———. *Japan's Subtle Apartheid: The Korean Minority Now*. Pamphlet published by Research/Action Institute for Koreans in Japan. March 1990.

BOOKS IN JAPANESE

Abe, Joji. *Hei No Naka No Korenai Menmen* [Those Behind Walls Who Don't Learn Lessons]. Tokyo: Bungei Shunju, 1986.

Ando, Noboru. *Yakuza To Koso (1)* [Gangsters in Conflict]. Tokyo: Tokuma Shoten, 1972.

———. *Yakuza to Koso (2)* [Gangsters in Conflict]. Tokyo: Tokuma Shoten, 1972.

————. *Yakuza to Koso (3)* [Gangsters in Conflict]. Tokyo: Tokuma Shoten, 1972.

Arahara, Bokusui. *Dai Uyuoku Shi* [The Great History of the Right Wing]. Tokyo: Dai Nippon Kokumin To, 1966.

Asahi Shimbun. *Tokyo Kono 30 Nen* [Tokyo in These 30 Years]. Tokyo: Asahi Shimbun Sha, 1984.

Baba, "Giant." *Kosei Yutaka Riingu Gaitachi* [Individualistic Guys of the Ring]. Tokyo: Baseball Magazine-sha, 1987.

Berrigan, Daniel. *Yakuza No Sekai: Nihon No Uchimaku* [Yakuza Society: Behind the Japanese Curtain]. Tokyo: Kindai Shisosha, 1948.

Baseball Magazine Co. Editorial Staff. *Nihon Puro-Resu Zen-Shi* [The Complete History of Pro Wrestling]. Tokyo: Besuboru Magajinsha, 1995.

Fujita, Goro, ed. *Koan Daiyoran* [Great Directory of Public Security]. Tokyo: Kasakura Shuppan, 1983.

————. *Koan Hyakunenshi* [100 Year History of Public Security]. Tokyo: Koan Mondai Kenkyu Kyokai, 1979.

————. *Ninkyo Daihyakka* [The Great Encyclopaedia of Chivalry]. Tokyo: Ninkyo Kenkyu Kai, 1986.

————. *Ninkyo Daihyakka Bessatsu* [The Great Encyclopaedia of Chivalry; Supplement]. Tokyo: Ninkyo Kenkyu Kai, 1987.

Honda, Yasuharu. *Kizu: Hanagata Kei to Sono Jidai* [Scar: Kei Hanagata and His Era]. Tokyo: Bungei Shunju, 1983.

Ino Kenji. *Kodama Yoshio no Kyozo to Jitsuzo* [The Image and Reality of Yoshio Kodama]. Tokyo: Sokon Shuppan, 1970.

————. *Yakuza to Nihonjin* [Gangsters and the Japanese]. Tokyo: Mikasa Shoto, 1974.

Inoki, Antonio. *Tatta Hitori No Toso* [One Man's Battle]. Tokyo: Shueisha, 1990.

Inose, Naoki. *Shisha Tachi No Rokkuiido Jiken* [The Lockheed Dead] Tokyo: Bunshun Bunko, 1987.

————. *Yobo No Medeia* [Ambitious Media]. Tokyo: Shogakkan, 1990.

Ishihara, Shintaro, and Akio Morita. *No To Ieru Nihonjin*. Tokyo: Kobunsha, 1989. Translated as *The Japan That Can Say No*. New York: Simon & Schuster, 1991, with Ishihara as the sole author.

Itagaki, Shinsuke. *Kono Jiyuto: Maboroshi No Chika Tekikoku.* [This Liberal Party: The Phantom Underground Empire]. 2 vols. Tokyo: Banseisha, 1976.

Kishida, Shu. *Monogusa Seishin Bunseki* [Lazy Psychoanalysis]. Tokyo: Seishisha, 1978.

Keisatsu Cho Hen. *Keisatsu Hakusho* [Police White Paper]. Tokyo: Okura-sho Insatsu Kyoku. Published annually.

Kodama, Yoshio. *Akusei, Jusei, Ransei* [Maladministration, Gunfire, Chaotic Times]. Tokyo: Kobundo, 1961.

Kotchian, Carl. *Rokkiido Urikomi Sakusen Tokyo No 70 Nichi-Kan* [Lockheed Sales Mission: 70 Days in Tokyo]. Tokyo: Asahi Shimbun. 1976.

Kurita, Noboru. *Rikidozan.* 2 vols. Tokyo: Buronzu Sha. 1981.

Misuta X. *Puro-resu Gekido 40 Nen Shi No Yomikata* [How to Read 40 Years of Exciting Pro Wrestling]. Tokyo: Pokettobukku sha, 1995.

Muroboshi, Tetsuro. *Jitsuryoku Nihon Oshoku Shi* [A History of Japanese Corruption: An Authentic Account]. Tokyo: Chikuma Bunko, 1988.

Onaruto. *Yaocho* [Fix]. Tokyo: Rokusaisha, 1996.

Oshita Eiji. *Eikyu No Rikidozan* [Rikidozan Forever]. Tokyo: Tokuma Shoten, 1991.

Tachibana, Takashi. *Kyoaku vs. Genron: Tanaka Rokkiido Kara Jiminto Bunretsu Made* [Evil versus Free Speech: From Tanaka Lockheed to the Split of the LDP]. Tokyo: Bungei Shunju, 1993.

————. *Rokuiido Saiban Bochoki* (A Record of the Lockheed Trials). Tokyo: Asahi Shimbunsha, 1981 (vol.1); 1982 (vol. 2); 1983 (vol. 3); 1985 (vol. 4). (Special paperback edition of all four volumes published in 1994 by Asahi Shimbunsha Bunkobun.)

Takahashi Kunio. *Tokyo Jidai* [Tokyo Era]. Tokyo: Asahi Shimbun, 1984.

Takashina Shuji and Haga Toru. *Sekai Toshi No Joken* [Conditions of World Capitals]. Tokyo: Chikuma Shobo, 1992.

Taoka, Kazuo. *Yamaguchi Gumi Sandaime: Taoka Kazuo Jiden* [The Autobiography of Kazuo Taoka, Third Generation Yamaguchi Gang]. 3 vols. Tokyo: Tokuma Shoten, 1974.

Tokyo-to. Minato-Kuyakusho. *Minato-ku shi* [A History of Minato Ward]. Minato Ward Office of Tokyo, 1960, 1979.

Tokyo-to. Shibuya Kuyakusho. *Shibuya-ku Shi* [A History of Shibuya Ward]. Shibuya Ward Office of Tokyo, 1966.

Ushijima Hidehiko. *Mo Hitosu No Showa Shi (1): Shinso Kairyu No Otoko: Rikidozan.* [One More Showa History [1]: Rikidozan, Man of Deep Currents]. Tokyo: Mainichi Shimbunsha, 1978.

Ushijima, Hidehiko. *Rikidozan. Osumo, Puro-Resu Ura Shakai* [Rikidozan: The Hidden World of Sumo and Professional Wrestling]. Tokyo: Daisan Shokan, 1995.

————. *Uyoku Jiten* [Right-Wing Dictionary]. Tokyo: Shakai Mondai Kenkyu-kai, 1970.

Yamanouchi, Yukio. *Sabishigariya Hittoman* [The Lonely Hitman]. Tokyo: 1989.

Za Desutoroiya (The Destroyer). *Yottsu no ji no Hitori Goto* [Tale of the Figure-Four Leglock]. Tokyo: Besuboru Magajin Sha, 1984.

FILMS AND VIDEOS IN JAPANESE

Rikidozan to Sono Jidai [Rikidozan and His Era]. 60 minutes. Beungei Shunju, 1995.

Rikidozan. 61 minutes. Pony, Canyon, 1978.

Chi To Okite [Blood and Law]. Shochiku Film Studios, 1966. Video: *Nikkatsu Meisaku Eigakan.* 1994.

Chi No Sakazuki [Blood Toast]. Shochiku film Studios, 1969. Video: *Nikkatsu Meisaku Eigakan.* 1994.

KEY MAGAZINE ARTICLES IN JAPANESE

"*Kodama No kage De odoru Aru Fuikusa*" [The Fixer Who Danced in Kodama's Shadow]. *Asahi Journal,* October 1, 1976, pp. 12–16, and October 8, 1976, pp. 14–19.

"*Kodama Yoshio To Wa Nanika?*" [What Is Yoshio Kodama?]. *Bungei Shunju,* May 1976, pp. 94–130.

DOCUMENTS

Multinational Corporations and United States Foreign Policy. Hearings Before the Subcommittee on Multinational Corporations of the Committee on Foreign Relations, United States Senate. Ninety-Fourth Congress Second Session on Lockheed Aircraft Corporation Part 14 February 4 and 6 and May 4, 1976. Printed by the Committee on Foreign Relations. U.S. Government Printing Office, Washington, D.C., 1976. 70-4670

The New International Criminal and Asian Organized Crime Report. Prepared by the Permanent Subcommittee Investigation of the Committee on Governmental Affairs. U.S. Senate. 102nd Congress, 2nd Session, December 1922. U.S. Government Printing Office, Washington, D.C., 1993. 102-29.

INDEX

ABOUT THE AUTHOR

Robert Whiting is the author of *You Gotta Have Wa* and one of the very few Westerners to write a weekly column in the Japanese press. He has appeared as a commentator in documentaries about Japan and on such shows as *Larry King Live* and *The MacNeil-Lehrer Newshour*. He has also written for *The New York Times, Sports Illustrated, Smithsonian, Newsweek International, U.S. News and World Report,* and *Time,* among other publications. He lives in Japan.